Making Waves

This study investigates the three main waves of political regime contention in Europe and Latin America. Surprisingly, protest against authoritarian rule spread across countries more quickly in the nineteenth century, yet achieved greater success in bringing democracy in the twentieth. To explain these divergent trends, the book draws on cognitive-psychological insights about the inferential heuristics that people commonly apply; these shortcuts shape learning from foreign precedents such as an autocrat's overthrow elsewhere. But these shortcuts had different force, depending on the political-organizational context. In the inchoate societies of the nineteenth century, common people were easily swayed by these heuristics: Jumping to the conclusion that they could replicate such a foreign precedent in their own countries, they precipitously challenged powerful rulers, yet often at inopportune moments – and with low success. By the twentieth century, however, political organizations had formed. Their leaders had better capacities for information processing, were less strongly affected by cognitive shortcuts, and therefore waited for propitious opportunities before initiating contention. As organizational ties loosened the bounds of rationality, contentious waves came to spread less rapidly, but with greater success.

Kurt Weyland is the Lozano Long Professor of Latin American Politics and professor of government at The University of Texas at Austin. He received his PhD in political science at Stanford University in 1991. Based on intensive field research in Argentina, Bolivia, Brazil, Chile, Costa Rica, Peru, and Venezuela, he has written three books and numerous journal articles on democracy, economic and social policy, populism, and diffusion processes in Latin America. Many of his articles and books have drawn on cognitive-psychological insights about bounded rationality to shed new light on puzzling political phenomena, such as the adoption of risky reforms in fragile democracies and the rash, ill-considered emulation of foreign precedents and models in a wide range of countries.

Making Waves

Democratic Contention in Europe and Latin America since the Revolutions of 1848

KURT WEYLAND

University of Texas at Austin

CAMBRIDGE
UNIVERSITY PRESS

CAMBRIDGE
UNIVERSITY PRESS

32 Avenue of the Americas, New York NY 10013-2473, USA

Cambridge University Press is part of the University of Cambridge.

It furthers the University's mission by disseminating knowledge in the pursuit of education, learning, and research at the highest international levels of excellence.

www.cambridge.org
Information on this title: www.cambridge.org/9781107622784

First published 2014

Printed in the United States of America

A catalog record for this publication is available from the British Library.

Library of Congress Cataloging in Publication data
Weyland, Kurt Gerhard.
Making waves : democratic contention in Europe and Latin America since the revolutions of 1848 / Kurt Weyland.
   pages   cm
Includes bibliographical references and index.
ISBN 978-1-107-04474-6 (hardback) – ISBN 978-1-107-62278-4 (paperback)
1. Government, Resistance to – Europe – History – 19th century.   2. Government, Resistance to – Europe – History – 20th century.   3. Government, Resistance to – Latin America – History – 20th century.   4. Regime change – Europe – History – 19th century.   5. Regime change – Europe – History – 20th century.   6. Regime change – Latin America – History – 20th century.   7. Democracy – Europe – History – 20th century.   8. Democracy – Latin America – History – 20th century.   9. Europe – Politics and government – 19th century.   10. Europe – Politics and government – 20th century.   11. Latin America – Politics and government – 20th century.   I. Title.
JN10.W48   2014
321.09'094–dc23   2013044142

ISBN 978-1-107-04474-6 Hardback
ISBN 978-1-107-62278-4 Paperback

Cambridge University Press has no responsibility for the persistence or accuracy of URLs for external or third-party Internet Web sites referred to in this publication and does not guarantee that any content on such Web sites is, or will remain, accurate or appropriate.

Contents

Acknowledgments

Books result from years of systematic, painstaking research and patient, sometimes painful, writing and revising. But their origin can be unplanned and serendipitous. This happened with the present book. After completing *Bounded Rationality and Policy Diffusion: Social Sector Reform in Latin America*, I was groping around for a promising new topic, but without much success. Then, in late 2006, I received an invitation from Kirk Hawkins to present my "work in progress" at Brigham Young University. But I had little work to present, and certainly no progress! Hurriedly I wrote up some notes that applied the cognitive-psychological ideas of my diffusion book to the analysis of political regime contention: I conjectured that inferential shortcuts help explain why challenges to authoritarian regimes often spread in dramatic waves, as occurred recently during the "Arab Spring." Given the unconventional nature of this claim, I left for Provo with trepidation. But unexpectedly, my hosts there found these ideas exciting and urged me with great enthusiasm to go ahead with the project.

I am glad I followed their advice. This study has been an exciting project from beginning to end. The main reason is its empirical and theoretical sweep. As regards the subject matter, it made sense to go back to the single most dramatic wave of political regime contention in recorded history, namely the revolutions of 1848. Yet this tsunami, which affected large parts of a whole continent within one month, contrasted starkly with the slower diffusion processes unfolding in Europe in 1917–19 and in South America from the late 1970s to the late 1980s. This observation of striking differences gave rise to the puzzle that the present volume seeks to explain. To compare three momentous waves that happened in two centuries, I had to research a vast range of historical developments in a variety of countries. How much I have learned! For the twenty-five preceding years, I had concentrated mostly on Latin America, a tremendously interesting continent. But after a quarter-century, the intellectual payoff of reading another book on that region was often limited. Not so with the new project: Every book, every article taught me about institutions, structures, developments, people, and events about which I had known little.

In theoretical terms, this project led me on an interesting journey as well. I started out by applying the ideas advanced in my last book, arguing that the rash inferences suggested by cognitive shortcuts can account for the rapid but largely unsuccessful diffusion of revolution in 1848 (Weyland 2009). But then how to explain the slowdown of diffusion in 1917–19 and especially during the "third wave of democratization" in Latin America? To elucidate the repercussions of the Russian Revolutions, I developed an organizational macro-argument to complement the cognitive-psychological micro-foundation proposed in the preceding book (Weyland 2012b). And to explain the distinctive characteristics of the third wave, I extended this organizational line of reasoning to the input side of diffusion by analyzing the historical transformation of contentious precedents. In these ways, I gradually constructed a complex edifice that, in the stratosphere of theory, resembled the fantastic towers, buildings, and bridges that my sons Andi and Niko used to erect with their wooden building blocks; and it was similar fun to "see" this structure take shape!

This book has particular personal significance. Given my training and trajectory as a Latin America specialist, a good part of this study examines the southern subcontinent. But the other half examines Europe, and as the reader will quickly discover, those chapters focus primarily on Germany, my home country. Analyzing German history is, for obvious reasons, a difficult task – and I am not even analyzing the worst period. I avoided the whole topic for decades, even left Germany to settle in the United States, a (comparatively) uncomplicated country. But like other people who reach advanced middle age, I felt a longing to "go home" in my academic endeavors. And with the ideas about contentious diffusion, maybe I finally had something to say about major events in German history, such as the revolutions of 1848, which in one of their last tragic episodes played out in my provincial hometown, Kaiserslautern (Schneider and Keddigkeit 1999).

The cover photo with its tumbling dominoes, a common metaphor of diffusion, captures the interwoven themes of this book. For the twentieth anniversary of the fall of the Berlin Wall, a thousand colorfully painted foam dominoes were placed on the former East-West divide and then toppled in celebration of this high-profile episode of democratic contention. The collapse of communism constituted the most stunning surge in the third wave of democratization, which my study examines in its advance through South America in Chapters 6 and 7 and in its other regional manifestations in Chapter 8. Moreover, the setting of the joyous ceremony evokes the two earlier diffusion waves analyzed in this book, especially in Chapters 4 and 5. The plaza in front of the Brandenburg Gate, right where the dominoes are falling, is named after March 18, the traumatic day that brought the most violent street fighting of the 1848 revolution in Berlin. The same area also saw many of the crucial events of the November

Revolution of 1918, for instance, the proclamation of the German republic from the Reichstag building next door. What picture could better encapsulate the multiple topics of my research?

While I am responsible for the unusual scope and complex argument of this book, numerous other people have helped me conduct this investigation, build the theory, and push me forward with the whole project. First and foremost, I thank Joe and Teresa Lozano Long for the generous resources that they have made available. Moreover, I am very grateful to Gary Freeman, the Government Department, and the College of Liberal Arts, all at the University of Texas, who over the years supported this project in important ways. Thank you also to the hardworking research assistants who collected and processed vast amounts of material over the years: Michelle Silva, Brian Smiley, Randy Uang, and especially Riitta Koivumäki and Fernando Rosenblatt. Andrew Stein helped with a steady stream of great documents, and Francisco Bulnes of CIDOC, Universidad Finis Terrae, in Santiago de Chile gave me access to a wealth of oral history transcripts. Eduardo Dargent was very helpful in setting up crucial interviews for me in Lima.

Over the years, I received a wealth of suggestions, comments, and ideas from Zoltan Barany, Jonathan Brown, Jason Brownlee, Tulia Faletti, Robert Fishman, Gary Freeman, John Higley, Scott Mainwaring, Pat McDonald, Ami Pedahzur, Dora Piroska, Kenneth Roberts, Nivien Saleh, David Samuels, Hillel Soifer, Sidney Tarrow, and Mark Traugott, all of whom were kind enough to read papers or draft chapters that I folded into this book. For their excellent comments at organized conference and workshop presentations I thank Kevin Arceneaux, Mark Beissinger, Graeme Boushey, Valerie Bunce, Ruth Collier, Gorana Draguljic, Frances Hagopian, Jonathan Hartlyn, Evelyne Huber, Scott Mainwaring, John Markoff, Covadonga Meseguer, Anne Nguyen, Philippe Schmitter, Charles Shipan, and John Stephens. Workshops at Temple University, Universidad Diego Portales (Santiago de Chile), University of Michigan, University of Pennsylvania, University of Pittsburgh, University of Zürich, and Yale University proved highly stimulating and productive. I am very grateful to Doug Biow of UT's Center for European Studies for providing the resources and administrative support for a workshop on "Spontaneity and Organization in European Democratic Contention" (February 2011), at which Kathleen Canning, Zach Elkins, David Shafer, and Jonathan Sperber offered stimulating feedback on a crucial part of this project.

As for all my work over the last decade, the Latin America Faculty Working Group at UT (Dan Brinks, Henry Dietz, Zach Elkins, Ken Greene, Wendy Hunter, and Raúl Madrid) proved essential with its outstanding feedback and advice on this evolving project. What a privilege to have such a talented group of colleagues! Other crucial contributions to this study arose from the day-long book workshop held at UT in December 2011. My departmental colleagues and PhD students, especially Joe Amick, Steven Brooke, Matt Buehler, John Higley, Matt Johnson, Riitta Koivumäki, Stuart Tendler, Jeffrey Tulis, and Kristin Wylie (in addition to the colleagues named earlier), provided an abundance of comments, suggestions, and criticisms; and Josh Mishrikey faithfully recorded the many hours of discussion. Truly unique was the input of the two invited discussants, Ruth Collier and Frances Hagopian, who offered a total of fifty (!) pages of written comments and then followed up with further suggestions throughout the day.

Bits and pieces of my theory and case studies have appeared in earlier publications. Chapters 2 and 4 draw on my article, "The Diffusion of Revolution: '1848' in Europe and Latin America," published in *International Organization* 63:3 (July 2009), pp. 391–423. Chapters 2, 4, and 5 include material from my piece on "Diffusion Waves in European Democratization: The Impact of Organizational Development," which appeared in *Comparative Politics* 45:1 (October 2012), pp. 25–45. Chapter 8 relies in one section on my essay entitled "The Arab Spring: Why the Surprising Similarities with the Revolutions of 1848?" in *Perspectives on Politics* 10:4 (December 2012), pp. 917–34. I thank these journals and their publisher, Cambridge University Press, for giving me permission to use this material.

This project could have been overwhelming and all-consuming. But my sons, Andi and Niko, guaranteed proper balance in my life, with exuberant Lego structures, wild soccer playing and noisy soccer watching, plentiful Latin homework, insane jokes, and a great deal of horsing around. Words cannot convey what I owe Wendy Hunter; I tried in my earlier books, but without full success. Constituting a bit of an academic homecoming, this book is dedicated to two old *Lautrer*, my parents Else and Dr. Helmut Weyland.

Introduction: Puzzling Trends in Waves of Contention

Political regime changes and conflicts over such transitions often occur in clusters and advance like waves. As one country transforms its constitutional framework, discontented actors in other countries take inspiration from this precedent and start to undertake similar efforts. The frontrunner's success encourages them to challenge their own rulers and push for transforming the way in which political authority is exercised. As a result of such demonstration effects, regime contention frequently snowballs and sometimes triggers avalanches (Markoff 1996; Berg-Schlosser 2009; Hale 2013). For instance, the French revolutions of 1830 and especially 1848 set in motion dramatic diffusion processes; within one month of "Citizen King" Louis Philippe's overthrow in February 1848, half of Europe stood aflame, engulfed by protests and rebellions against autocratic princes (Sperber 1994; Dowe et al. 2001). The Russian revolutions of 1917 also spurred contention and regime change throughout Central and Eastern Europe from 1917 to 1919, and the "third wave of democratization" that started in Southern Europe in 1974 rippled across the world during the subsequent two decades (Huntington 1991; Kurzman 1998; Markoff 2009; Lehoucq 2011; Mainwaring and Pérez-Liñán forthcoming).

These waves of regime contention have had divergent characteristics, however. The differences in timing are particularly striking. Regime conflict during the third wave unfolded over the course of two decades (1974 to early 1990s), whereas the 1848 revolution spread explosively within days (Traugott 2010: 131–42): Louis Philippe's downfall on February 24 triggered mobilization and protests in Baden on February 27 (Real 1983: 47–50), Stuttgart on March 3, Munich on March 6–7, Vienna on March 13–15, Berlin on March 18–19, and Copenhagen on March 20–21. Beginning in April, it also had repercussions in faraway Brazil (Quintas 2004: 67–95), Colombia (Posada-Carbó 2002: 224–40), Chile (Collier 2003: 79, 84–92; Wood 2011: 158–64, 193–202), and even the United States, where it helped set the context for the July 1848 Seneca

Falls Convention for women's rights (Howe 2007: 846–47; broad overviews in Dowe et al. 2001 and Thomson 2002; see also Hobsbawm 1996a: 10–11). Thus, contention spread almost as fast as news of the Paris events traveled before television and cell phones. Rebellion also proved quickly contagious in 1830, when the French king's overthrow in July triggered protests and uprisings in Belgium, the Prussian Rhineland, Brunswick, and Southern England in August, Berlin and some German middle states such as Saxony in September, Switzerland in October, and Poland in November (Church 1983). In November, the Parisian July Revolution also gave an impulse to the English movement for electoral reform, contributing to the suffrage extension of 1832 (Ertman 2010: 1007, 1009).

In the twentieth century, by contrast, regime contention in Europe and Latin America spread much more slowly. The wave of rebellions inspired by the Russian revolutions of 1917 got under way only in late 1918 and early 1919, more than a year after the triggering events. The third wave of democratization advanced at an even more leisurely pace. In South America, for instance, regime contention erupted two to three years after the Mediterranean precedents in Peru in 1977, then in Bolivia in 1978 and again in 1982, in Argentina in 1982, in Brazil and Chile in 1983, and in Uruguay in 1984. Actual transitions happened in Ecuador in 1979, Peru in 1980, Bolivia in 1982, Argentina in 1983, Uruguay in 1984, Brazil in 1985, Paraguay in 1989, and finally Chile in 1990. Thus, the third wave took more than a decade to unfold in Latin America (Markoff 2009: 58), whereas the 1848 revolutions swept across Europe in less than one month. The data in Tables 1.1–1.4 demonstrate these stark differences in diffusion's speed.[1]

That efforts at regime change in Europe and Latin America diffused more quickly during the nineteenth century than the twentieth is puzzling.[2] Given tremendous advances in communication and transportation, one would expect acceleration. But the fastest diffusion process in the history of democratization occurred early, in 1848.[3]

Speed does not equal success, however. On the contrary, there is an inverse relation between diffusion's speed and its success – defined here as significant, non-fleeting steps toward political liberalism and democracy (specified in greater detail in the concept section in this chapter). In the most dramatic wave, 1848, challenges against rulers spread immediately, but rarely led to significant effective transformations; the only substantial advance toward liberal

---

[1] These measurements rely on Polity IV because it is the only comprehensive data set that covers the nineteenth century. Certainly, however, Polity IV – like all these kinds of datasets – has serious problems (Munck and Verkuilen 2002; Bowman, Lehoucq, and Mahoney 2005).

[2] An obvious exception is the collapse of communism in Eastern Europe in 1989, which the concluding chapter discusses in some depth.

[3] Even the wave of regime contention that started to sweep across the Arab world in early 2011 (which is also examined in the Conclusion) did not unfold as rapidly as the day-by-day progression of the tsunami of 1848.

TABLE 1.1 *Speed of Emulative Regime Contention and Change in Polity Scores in Europe, 1847–50*

	Speed in Years	Democracy	Autocracy	Δ Polity Score	Comment
Britain	.1	6–6	3–3	0	
Belgium	.1	2–2	6–6	0	
Netherlands	.1	0–3	7–6	+ 4	
Denmark	.08	0–5	9–3	+ 11	
Norway	.1	0–0	7–7	0	
Sweden	.1	0–0	7–7	0	
Russia	.2	0–0	10–10	0	
Baden	.02	1–0	5–7	−3	
Württemberg	.03	2–2	6–6	0	
Bavaria	.04	0–0	8–7	+1	
Saxony	.05	0–0	9–7	+2	
Prussia	.06	0–0	9–8	+1	
Austria[a]	.05	0–1	10–7	+4	Big overestimation
Hungary[b]	.03	–	–	–	Worsening oppression
Moldavia[b]	.15	–	–	–	No change
Walachia[b]	.15	–	–	–	No change
Papal States	.1	0–0	9–9	0	
Piedmont	.1	0–0	10–7	+3	
Modena	.1	0–0	10–10	0	
Parma	.1	0–0	10–10	0	
Tuscany	.1	0–0	10–10	0	
Average	~ .1			1–1.2	

[a] Progress in Austria is strikingly overrated, e.g., by comparison to Prussia, which kept and applied its royally decreed constitution, whereas Austria never put it in operation and abrogated it quickly.

[b] Not being independent states, Hungary, Moldavia, and Walachia are not covered by Polity IV. But they were important sites of contention in 1848 and are therefore included here based on scholarly analyses, especially Dowe et al. (2001) and Sperber (1994).

democracy resulted from preemptive reforms in Denmark, Piedmont, and – to a lesser extent – the Netherlands. By contrast, twentieth-century challenges spread more slowly, but had a higher rate of success, as evident in Germany's and Austria's democratization and British, Italian, and Swedish suffrage reforms in 1918–19.[4] In Hungary, however, an incipient communist revolution was violently suppressed, ushering in authoritarian rule. There were even more successful regime transitions during the third wave; in South America, democracy prevailed sooner or later, even where authoritarian incumbents

[4] The substantial democratic advances of 1918–19 appear clearly in the statistical analysis of Freeman and Snidal (1982: 320–21, 323, 325) and the comparative-historical investigation of Collier (1999: 35, 77–79).

TABLE 1.2 *Speed of Emulative Regime Contention and Change in Polity Scores in Europe, 1916–19*

	Speed in Years	Democracy	Autocracy	Δ Polity Score	Comment
Belgium[a]	1	8–9	1–0	+2	
Netherlands	~ 1	4–10	6–0	+12	
Sweden[a]	1	9–10	1–0	+2	
Germany[b]	1 – 1.5	5–6	3–0	+4	Big underestimation
Austria	1 – 1.5	1–8	5–0	+12	
Hungary	1	1–1	5–2	+3	Too positive
Britain[a]	1	8–8	0–0	0	Underestimation
Italy	2	3–3	4–4	0	
France[a]	1.5	8–9	0–0	+1	
Average	~ 1.3			+ 4	

[a] Progress in Belgium, Sweden, Britain, and France started from an already high level of "democracy" and low level of "autocracy"; therefore, it was inevitably limited by this ceiling effect, which was not at play in 1848.
[b] Progress in Germany is underestimated greatly. The country instituted a competitive democracy in 1919, so by any reasonable assessment, the change on the democracy score should be much higher than +1.

TABLE 1.3 *Speed of Emulative Regime Contention and Change in Polity Scores in South America, 1974–90*

	Years of Contention	Speed in Years	Democracy	Autocracy	Δ Polity Score	Comment
Argentina	1982–83	6	0–8	8–0	+16	
Bolivia	1977–80	2–4	0–0	7–7	0	First effort
Bolivia	1981–82	5–6	0–8	7–0	+15	Second effort
Brazil	1983–85	8/1 Arg	2–7	5–0	+10	
Chile	1983–85	8/1 Arg	0–0	7–6	+1	First effort
Chile	1986–89	10–13	0–8	6–0	+14	Second effort
Ecuador	1978–79	2–3	0–9	5–0	+14	
Peru	1977–80	1–4	0–7	7–0	+14	
Uruguay	1983–85	8/1 Arg	0–9	7–0	+16	
Average		~ 5			+11	

Note: The average includes both the initial failures and the eventual successes in Bolivia and Chile. "1 Arg" in Speed column means one year after the Argentine protests erupting in 1982.

offered stubborn resistance (as in Chile) or where fleeting new dictatorships temporarily interrupted a transition (as in Bolivia).

Thus, as the diffusion of regime contention has diminished in speed, its success rate has increased over the last 200 years in the Western world. In 1848,

TABLE 1.4 *Speed of Emulative Regime Contention and Change in Polity Scores in Europe, 1830–31*

	Speed in Years	Democracy	Autocracy	Δ Polity Score	Comment
Belgium[a]	.1	1–2	7–6	+2	Underestimation
Britain	.2	4–4	6–6	0	Yet 1832 reform
Switzerland[b]	.3	–	–	–	Progress in several cantons
Spain	.6	1–1	7–7	0	
Poland (Russia)	.3	0–0	10–10	0	Worsening oppression
Saxony	.2	0–0	10–7	+3	
Prussia	.2	0–0	10–10	0	
Austria	.2	0–0	10–10	0	
Papal States	.5	0–0	9–9	0	
Piedmont	.5	0–0	10–10	0	
Modena	.5	0–0	10–10	0	
Parma	.5	0–0	10–10	0	
Tuscany	.5	0–0	10–10	0	
Average	~ .4			~ .4	

[a] Progress is underestimated in Belgium, which adopted a liberal constitution that turned into a model for Continental Europe.
[b] Because of its decentralized structure, Switzerland in 1830 is not covered by Polity IV.

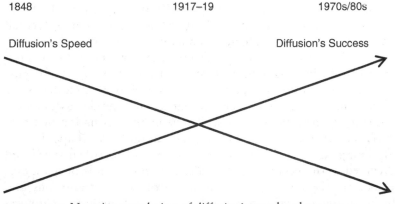

FIGURE 1.1 Negative correlation of diffusion's speed and success.

many dominoes quickly trembled but few were knocked down; in the twentieth century, they did not shake immediately, but then many did fall. The inverse relation between the speed of diffusion and the degree of regime change that it managed to prompt is clear. Figure 1.1 depicts this inverse relationship.

What accounts for these two trends and their negative correlation? My study seeks to answer this puzzling question by comparing the mechanisms that propelled the spread of regime conflict in 1848, 1917 to 1919, and the late 1970s to 1980s in Latin America. Based on a wealth of contemporaneous documents, eyewitness reports, and personal interviews with leading participants in three third-wave cases, the book reconstructs the perceptions, thoughts, and decision making of the protagonists. In this way, it elucidates how and why they took inspiration from foreign precedents; why some actors sought to emulate the triggering event immediately whereas others preferred to wait; and why some succeeded in advancing much farther toward their goals than did others.

With this analysis, the book sheds new light on political processes that have attracted tremendous scholarly attention. Starting in the late 1970s, democratization has arguably been *the* single most-studied topic in comparative politics; thousands of articles and hundreds of books, many written by the leading lights in the field, have investigated all aspects of regime transition and consolidation. Most of these studies have focused on domestic factors, however, following the guidance of seminal early contributions, especially O'Donnell and Schmitter (1986: 18–19). Only during the last decade have scholars picked up on some early conceptual and theoretical discussions (see especially Huntington 1991: 31–34, 100–06; Kurzman 1998; Whitehead 1986) and conducted systematic empirical studies of external impulses and democratic diffusion. These efforts to capture the wave-like character of regime change have mostly applied statistical techniques to establish that "diffusion is no illusion" (Brinks and Coppedge 2006; see also Wejnert 2005; Gleditsch and Ward 2006; Teorell 2010: 80–89, 99; Torfason and Ingram 2010). Yet whereas these analyses convincingly document powerful demonstration and contagion effects, they do much less to unearth the causal mechanisms that produce these horizontal impulses (Teorell 2010: 11, 15, 99, 155; see also Graham, Shipan, and Volden 2013: 690–96).

The present book attempts to push the democratization and diffusion literature a step forward by investigating the forces that drive the spread of regime contention. What are diffusion's underlying causes and driving mechanisms? Why do political impulses cross borders? In particular, why do discontented sectors in one country infer from a regime change in another nation that they can accomplish the same feat? And how do these causal forces shape the patterns of diffusion, giving rise to the negative correlation between speed and success highlighted in the beginning? By addressing these kinds of questions, the book elaborates the international dimension of regime transitions and helps rectify the imbalance arising from the long-standing emphasis on domestic factors.

This analysis contributes new insights not only to the vast literature on democratization but to the study of modernization and globalization as well. The striking slowdown of diffusion in Europe and Latin America challenges the conventional wisdom, which predicts acceleration, given tremendous advances in communication and transportation and an increasingly dense web of transnational contacts, links, and networks (e.g., Huntington 1991: 101–02). But contrary to these views, the swiftest diffusion processes occurred early in the history of Western democratization. In fact, as Chapters 3, 4, 6, and 7 show, foreign precedents had a more direct and powerful impact in 1848 than during the third wave.

These counterintuitive findings suggest the need to rethink modernization and globalization and their effects on political change. The conventional image depicts these processes like a stream – a fairly uniform process by which international factors steadily advance, gain greater force, and increasingly reshape domestic structures and processes. But maybe modernization and globalization are more like a tangle of currents and eddies – an ever more complicated intermingling of multiple processes that may flow together, but also interfere with each other (cf. Rosenau 2003: ch. 9)? This growing complexity may blunt globalization's impact and give domestic actors room of maneuver to pick and choose which impulses to act on and which ones to deflect. Rather than overwhelming domestic forces and homogenizing internal structures and processes, modernization and globalization may paradoxically augment the menu of choice and produce growing variety and diversity.

In sum, by shedding new light on the much-discussed processes of democratization, modernization, and globalization, this book holds considerable theoretical and substantive relevance.

THE MAIN ARGUMENT

What explains the surprising slowdown in the spread of political regime contention and the simultaneous increase in its success? This book advances a novel theory that invokes mechanisms of bounded rationality and that – as its main explanatory factor – highlights organizational developments, especially the emergence and spread of mass parties and broad-based interest associations.

Why do people emulate a foreign precedent, such as an autocrat's downfall in a neighboring country, and engage in regime contention in their own polity? My research suggests that this decision is not based on careful, rational cost/benefit calculations that thoroughly process the relevant evidence. Instead, people regularly resort to cognitive shortcuts that draw disproportionate attention to striking, dramatic events, such as the unexpected overthrow of a seemingly powerful prince, and that inspire rash, exaggerated hopes in the replicability of this successful transformation. Specifically, two cognitive shortcuts that people commonly use to cope with complex, uncertain information – the heuristics of availability and representativeness – propel the diffusion of regime contention.

The availability heuristic makes people attach a rationally unjustified degree of significance to particularly vivid, striking, easily accessible events, such as a regime collapse across the border. This inferential shortcut gives a foreign precedent disproportionate weight and impact on their judgments.

The representativeness heuristic, which overrates similarity as a base of judgment and therefore draws excessively firm conclusions from small samples, induces people to conclude from this single case of a regime change in another country that they can accomplish the same feat in their own polity. People thus overestimate the evidentiary value of this foreign success and jump to the conclusion that a challenge to their own government is feasible and promising as well. These facile inferences provide the underlying impetus for regime contention to spread and thus propel waves of democratization.

The heuristics of availability and representativeness are crucial for explaining dramatic yet largely unsuccessful tsunamis of regime contention, as in 1848 (Weyland 2009; see also Weyland 2012a). Applying these cognitive shortcuts, critical masses of people rashly inferred from the overthrow of the French king that they could accomplish a regime change in their own country as well. Therefore, they quickly poured into the streets and started to protest. But their beliefs soon proved wrong and their high hopes turned to frustration. The established authorities in Central and Eastern Europe stood on much firmer ground than did their colleagues in Paris. In particular, they retained command over the forces of organized coercion, which they used to renege on initial concessions, suppress mass mobilization, and tighten the reins of autocratic rule again. In sum, people's heavy reliance on cognitive shortcuts produced quick but unsuccessful diffusion: Haste made waste.

My theory argues that organizational developments account for the subsequent slowdown and increased success of diffusion. Before the secular growth of mass parties and labor unions beginning in the second half of the nineteenth century, decisions on whether to challenge established rulers were made by individuals or small, often informal groupings (cf. Rudé 2005: 245–46, 259–68). These people commonly had sparse information, limited processing capacity, and little experience in making political decisions. Therefore, the cognitive heuristics of availability and representativeness held particular sway, triggering a quick, rash spread of contention; yet these ill-conceived challenges frequently failed.

After the emergence of mass organizations, by contrast, common people tended to follow cues from their representative leaders, whose institutional position gave them much better access to information, greater processing capacity, and considerable experience in politics. Leaders were therefore less subject to cognitive heuristics. While also imperfect and distorted by inferential shortcuts, their rationality was less bounded than that of common individuals was. Consequently, leaders did not as easily throw caution to the wind and get carried away by foreign precedents. Instead, they assessed the prevailing opportunities and risks more carefully and led their followers into challenges only where the chances of success seemed reasonable (cf. Tilly, Tilly, and Tilly 1975: 192–97, 212, 227, 237, 254). As a result, regime contention spread more slowly, but was more successful. Because organizational ties extended the bounds of rationality, regime challenges diffused in a less indiscriminate and more realistic way (Weyland 2012b).

As Chapter 5 shows, representative leadership made a crucial difference in the democratization wave that followed upon the emergence of mass organizations and that was triggered by the Russian revolutions of 1917. Interestingly, both the tsar's overthrow in February and the Bolshevist power grab in October stimulated – in line with the heuristics of availability and representativeness – some immediate unrest at the mass level. But party and union leaders, less susceptible to the rash inferences suggested by cognitive shortcuts, did not believe the time was ripe for regime contention in the midst of total war. Therefore, they undertook strenuous efforts to tame this spontaneous unrest. Instead, they proceeded to push for democratization when Austria's and Germany's defeat in World War I opened up a golden opportunity for achieving constitutional change, and these efforts were crowned with success. The experiences of 1917–19 thus show that the emergence of organizational leadership had expanded the bounds of rationality. As a consequence, regime contention spread more slowly than it did in 1848, but attained significantly greater success.

What then explains the further slowdown and even greater success of contention's diffusion during the cluster of Latin American transitions in the 1970s and 1980s? Whereas my theory points to changes on the reception side of diffusion to account for the differences between the first two waves investigated in this book, it highlights the transformation of the stimulus side to explain the distinctive features of the third wave of democratization in Latin America. The precedent that exerted the greatest effect in stimulating emulation efforts was not revolution à la France (1848) and Russia (1917), but rather Spain's negotiated regime change. This pacted transition turned into the main foreign model that Latin American opposition forces sought to imitate. The change in the principal impulse of contagion and demonstration effects, which resulted from the further advance of organizational development, entailed an additional reduction in diffusion's speed, and an even higher rate of actual transitions to democracy.

How did the emergence and proliferation of broad-based organizations reshape the external stimuli that set in motion diffusion processes? Before the rise of mass parties, challengers lacked the capacity to sustain collective action. To effect regime change, they had to rely on crowd protests and "revolutionary" efforts to overwhelm reigning autocrats quickly. This all-or-nothing strategy was highly risky, but when it did achieve success, it served as a dramatic, powerful signal that stimulated a rash of emulation efforts elsewhere. The resulting diffusion waves spread quickly, but brought many failures.

By contrast, after political parties arose and achieved institutional consolidation, opposition forces could apply pressure over the medium and long run. Therefore, they backed away from dangerous crowd assaults and moved instead toward reformist strategies. Once well-organized parties, which had emerged first on the left, spread across the ideological spectrum during the twentieth century, most relevant societal forces acquired political representation. Therefore, they could work out disagreements and conflicts, including the question of regime change, via negotiation and compromise with the established authorities. Because of their lower costs and risks (compared to "revolutionary" challenges), pacted transitions therefore came to prevail, especially during the third wave of democratization in Europe and Latin America. While more likely to bring success, however, these prudent efforts were sober and unexciting. Therefore, they did not turn into dramatic signals that would have elicited mass enthusiasm and triggered a rash of imitation attempts. But organizational leaders in other polities learned from pacted transitions and looked for the right moment to proceed in similar ways. For these reasons, the impact of advanced organizational development on the stimulus side of diffusion contributed to the deceleration of contentious waves as well as their increasing success.

While the transformation of the reception side of diffusion and the subsequent change on the stimulus side most clearly explain the different features of the three democratization waves under investigation, additional consequences of organizational development contributed to the inverse correlation between the speed and success of contention's diffusion. In this vein, the formation of mass organizations and their spread from the left to the center and right of the political spectrum entailed the crystallization and differentiation of ideological positions. The new parties and unions defined and announced their goals and programs and established relations to foreign organizations of similar orientation. Accordingly, different political forces gravitated toward different foreign precedents and took inspiration from diverse sources. Whereas in 1848 all eyes were directed toward Paris, during the third wave there were various foreign models that appealed to different parties and groupings.

This variety of foreign models helped slow down the eruption and advance of regime contention, because there was no consensus on which path to take. But this diversity also stimulated a process of learning. Opposition forces experimented with a menu of options and – sometimes after considerable trial and error – figured out which strategy held the greatest promise. Whereas in 1848 challengers put all their bets on emulating the Parisian rebellion, opposition forces in the third wave had various irons in the fire. Therefore, they had a higher chance of ending up with the right weapon for dealing authoritarian rule the decisive blow. While it took a while to weed out unpromising alternatives and settle on a predominant strategy, this variety of options increased the likelihood of eventual success.

The emergence of organizations also shifted the balance of political attention from foreign to domestic developments, which helped give the diffusion of political regime contention lower speed but greater success over the course of European and Latin American history. The appearance of mass organizations clarified the political landscape and gave people a much better sense of the domestic constellation of power. Before the rise of political parties and unions, the distribution of political preferences and effective power capabilities was shrouded in fog. In an amorphous polity, it was virtually impossible to know how widespread and intense oppositional sentiment against incumbent autocrats was. Because the domestic political situation was difficult to ascertain, people attributed particular evidentiary value to foreign precedents. These observable events offered some base for drawing inferences about the strength and determination of government versus opposition. Lacking strong domestic yardsticks, people were eager to grasp at foreign straws – like the drunkard looking for his key under the lamppost, because that is where the light is!

With the secular advance of organization, however, domestic politics coagulated and observable entities emerged from the primeval soup. Collective actors arose that followed pretty steady trajectories and were fairly predictable in their courses of action. As the constellation of power became clearer and the domestic fog lifted, oppositionists had more reason to look internally and attribute less importance to external precedents. Therefore, attention shifted toward the internal opportunity structure. Whereas in 1848 all eyes were directed toward Paris and the French events quickly triggered emulation efforts, external precedents had a more limited impact in later waves; they did not sweep domestic challengers off their feet and induce them to immediate action. Instead, in organizationally denser polities external impulses prompted regime contention only when the domestic situation looked promising. This is a final way in which the rise of collective organizations slowed down the diffusion of democratization efforts while bringing greater success.

By highlighting these aspects and stages of the secular development of political organizations and by elucidating their complex repercussions, my theory offers a comprehensive explanation of the inverse trends in diffusion features.

THEORETICAL CONTRIBUTIONS

By demonstrating how changes in organizational settings reshape the operation of cognitive shortcuts and thus transform the diffusion of regime contention, the book contributes to broader theory building in political science. The most important issue it addresses concerns the role of rationality in politics. Starting from the well-established finding that political rationality is distinctly bounded (e.g., McDermott 2004; Jones and Baumgartner 2005; Weyland 2007), the study embeds this cognitive-psychological micro-foundation in organizational macro-factors. Above all, it shows how the development of organizations alters the bounds of political rationality. These constraints loosen as mass parties and broad-based interest associations emerge and proliferate.

In the 1990s and early 2000s, a lively, often controversial debate raged about the proper approach to social science. Advocates of rational choice criticized long-dominant structuralist and culturalist frameworks that highlighted supra-individual factors; they insisted that theories about social and political macro-phenomena had to rest on micro-foundations, which they identified with individual, self-interested rationality (Lichbach 2003). Rational choice achieved a partial victory in this debate. Many scholars have acknowledged the need for micro-foundations; macro-approaches have lost support or have felt compelled to construct some model of individual decision making on which to base their own arguments.

At the same time, however, a wealth of laboratory experiments and field studies has proven that the notion of rationality postulated by rational choice, which assumes systematic information processing and undistorted, balanced logical calculations, is unrealistic. Because normal mortals regularly deviate from rational standards, social science needs to build its theoretical edifices on well-corroborated insights about people's actual patterns of decision making, which embody a clearly bounded version of rationality (Kahneman and Tversky 2000; Gilovich, Griffin, and Kahneman 2002; Hastie and Dawes 2010: espec. ch. 4–7; Kahneman 2011).[5] Interestingly, economics has been revolutionized by absorbing the lessons of cognitive psychology (Camerer, Loewenstein, and Rabin 2004), and some political scientists have charted the same course (Gowda and Fox 2002; McDermott 2004; Jones and Baumgartner 2005; Weyland 2002, 2007). Even some advocates of rational choice now recognize the need to consider people's "cognitive limitations" (Levi 2009: 117–18, 127, 131) – which may well lead them beyond rational choice!

Political scientists who draw on cognitive psychology have so far focused on the micro-foundational level, demonstrating that the individual judgments and political decisions of citizens and presidents diverge significantly from rational-choice predictions (see the trailblazing books by McDermott 1998, 2004). These studies were essential in establishing the need to start from insights about bounded rationality. Now the task turns to building political-science theories that go beyond individual-level inferences and choices and that capture collective action and its institutional repercussions, which are decisive for politics.[6] The present book contributes to this crucial next step in theory construction by explaining how organizational developments mediate the bounds of rationality. According to my central argument, these bounds were especially tight before the emergence of organizational ties. They loosened as organizational ties tightened and representative party and union leaders emerged, whose guidance many citizens came to follow.

With this theory, the book integrates individual-level insights from cognitive psychology with organizational arguments from political science and historical sociology. My argument is not merely additive; it does not just place a collective institutional layer on top of a cognitive-psychological micro-foundation. Instead, I demonstrate how organizational developments shape the very bounds of rationality, which are narrower in inchoate societies than in organizationally

---

[5] Theories of cognitive heuristics that highlight their benefits as "adaptive tools" (Gigerenzer and Selten 2001) base their claims on rather stable task environments – a very different setting from the times of turmoil and flux investigated in this book.

[6] Organization theorists, such as Hodgkinson and Starbuck (2008a: 9) in their major overview, highlight the need to fill the same kind of gap in that literature.

denser polities. Above all, their institutional position gives representative organizational leaders information access, calculating capacity, and political experience and thus makes them less susceptible to the inferential shortcuts documented by cognitive psychology. Thus, leaders' organizational role extends their bounds of rationality while giving them the influence to inform and direct their followers.

Bounded rationality is not singular or uniform (Bendor 2010: 39–44), especially in shaping collective decision-making and organizational behavior (Simon 1976: 240–41). Besides individual-level differences found by cognitive psychologists, the procedures and institutions that structure political decision-making exert a substantial effect on decision quality. For instance, conformity, cliquishness, and hermeticism can give rise to groupthink that reinforces distortions and biases (overview in McDermott 2004: 249–55), as in communist and fascist organizations. By contrast, more pluralistic, democratic mechanisms that facilitate wide-ranging information-processing, allow for diversity and debate, and produce conclusions via persuasion or compromise rather than intimidation and imposition, can reduce deviations from full rationality. Although representative organizational leaders are also subject to bounded rationality, as Chapters 5 through 7 demonstrate, their judgments and actions are less at risk of suffering distortion than those of common citizens who on their own seek to make sense of complex, fluid, and uncertain political phenomena.

By developing this line of reasoning, my study integrates boundedly rational micro-foundations with organizational macro-factors more organically than has been done so far. By elucidating the profound interaction between these two levels, the book begins to build a theory of politics that stands on the solid empirical base provided by cognitive psychology and applies these insights to explain the changing patterns of collective political action and their regime outcomes.

My arguments also speak to several specific literatures, such as the study of collective action, which plays a crucial role in conflicts over political regime change. After the earth-shattering impact of Mancur Olson's *Logic of Collective Action* (1965), many analysts of political participation and social movements embraced rationalist premises, emphasizing the crucial role of organization and leadership for making activism possible; spontaneity was theoretically ruled out. But the Olsonian approach clearly under-predicts citizen cooperation and political action; as numerous field studies and experiments demonstrate, there is much more political participation and social movement activity than individual-level calculation and organizational guidance can account for. More and more social movement theorists have therefore diverged from the strict rationalist framework by highlighting solidaristic incentives, symbolic motivations, or even emotions as driving forces of political activism (see e.g. Goodwin, Jasper, and Polletta 2001; broad overview in Tarrow 2011).

The present study complements this burgeoning literature by demonstrating that in organizationally inchoate polities, striking external precedents interpreted via cognitive shortcuts can prompt rather spontaneous outbursts of political contention. These foreign events lead people to overestimate the chances of challenging their own rulers successfully. As these rash inferences skew their cost/benefit calculations, they prompt collective action under conditions that strictly rational assessments regard as unpropitious. The dramatic impact of foreign precedents thus brings forth much more collective action than Olsonian approaches expect. Overestimating the replicability of a foreign success, amorphous masses of people who are not guided by organizational leaders pour into the streets and defy autocratic rulers. The rash belief in the feasibility of these challenges also gives rise to the sense of liberation and enthusiasm that theorists of emotions highlight; and the suddenly rebellious crowds draw on their informal bonds of solidarity, especially family or friendship networks, and invoke culturally available symbols to give their contentious efforts greater strength. Thus, my theory can account for outbursts of spontaneous, unorganized collective action; and by documenting the short-circuited inferences that inspire such action, my theory specifies the root cause that sets in motion the other mechanisms documented by recent social movement scholars.

In particular, this study puts threshold models and cascade theories of political activism on a stronger footing by documenting the crucial role of cognitive heuristics for triggering leaderless crowd contention. According to Marwell and Oliver (1993), collective action often does not require widespread participation; a critical mass of people suffices for providing public goods. Whenever some citizens hold particularly intense preferences, such a core group of committed activists can form. But as Lohmann (1994, 2000) and Kuran (1995) highlight, oppositionists who would like to challenge the status quo have incentive to hide their true intentions out of fear of disapproval or repression. This prudent "preference falsification" (Kuran 1995) is overcome only when a sudden indication of regime weakness suggests that a good opportunity for initiating a challenge has arrived. Once the most discontented people defy an autocratic ruler in public, this courageous step may induce other strong oppositionists to join, which can then induce even less fervent opponents to pour into the streets. Thus, as ever wider circles reveal their true preferences, protest quickly mushrooms.

My book demonstrates how striking foreign events can spark such cascades of contention – but not in conventionally rational ways. Instead, critical masses of people overestimate the significance of the external precedent and jump to conclusions about its replicability. Thus, I corroborate cascade theories that invoke cognitive heuristics (Kuran 1995: 74, 158–66, 180, 258; Kuran and Sunstein 1999). By contrast, the informational assumptions underlying claims of full rationality are unrealistic. Lohmann's model (2000: 663, 668–69), for instance,[7]

---

[7] Buenrostro, Dhillon, and Wooders (2007) also design a rationalist model of protest spreading across countries. But their failure to take repression into account – that is, to consider the tremendous risks facing protesters – makes this model inapplicable to the contentious waves examined in this study.

assumes that regular citizens know the distribution of preferences among the population, that is, the proportion of extremists, moderates, and status-quo supporters. But this premise is implausible, especially at times of tremendous political fluidity and fundamental "confusion" (Kurzman 2004; Goodwin 2011); even leading advocates of rational choice admit that under such conditions rational cost/benefit calculations are infeasible (Tsebelis 1990: 32–38). The present study, with its emphasis on cognitive shortcuts, captures the dynamics of these cascades, in which common people face enormous uncertainty, can fall prey to wild rumors, and draw rash inferences and distorted conclusions, much better than purely rationalist models.

My book also contributes to the burgeoning literature on political contention (McAdam, Tarrow, and Tilly 2001), which is widely criticized for merely offering a toolbox of causal mechanisms, without specifying the conditions and consequences of their usage. The analysis below shows, by contrast, how basic microfoundational mechanisms propel the spread of political contention and condition its outcomes. Even more importantly, I demonstrate that macro-organizational developments profoundly affect these micro-processes; in fact, they transform the whole landscape of political contention by reshaping its predominant modes. Over the last 200 years, as crowd protests have become more and more tamed by representative leaders, channeled into symbolic demonstrations of discontent, and used for efforts to negotiate regime transitions, opposition strategy has changed fundamentally: In Europe and Latin America, there has been a gradual albeit halting and still-incomplete shift from "transgressive" to "contained" contention (McAdam, Tarrow, and Tilly 2001: 7–8). This argument complements the claims that the "repertoire of contention" – its prevailing tactics – evolved in the late eighteenth or early nineteenth century (Tilly 1995; Tilly 2003: 30–33; Tilly 2008: 41–45, 59; Tarrow 2011: 39–51). This replacement of reactive protests in dispersed locales by more proactive challenges against the central power holders was certainly significant; but it was only a stepping stone toward a more important later transformation that adapted contention to the opportunities and limitations prevailing in organized modern polities.

Furthermore, this study offers a new perspective on democratization and weaves together different strands in this ample, rich literature. These writings are often shaped by the time period and regional experiences on which they focus. For instance, O'Donnell and Schmitter (1986) and Huntington (1991), with their emphasis on elite negotiations and moderate transitions, reflect Southern Europe and South America of the late 1970s and early 1980s; in contrast, Rueschemeyer, Stephens, and Stephens (1992) draw their theoretical emphasis on bottom-up pressure spearheaded by the working class from the European struggles of the nineteenth and early twentieth centuries (similar Markoff 1996 with his stress on social movements).[8] Whereas Collier (1999)

---

[8] The authors apply their argument to the third wave in Latin America as well, but admit that the working class in that region did not play the role of protagonist attributed to it in the central theory.

seeks a compromise between these two approaches by stressing underlying similarities in workers' role in both time periods and regions, my book highlights profound historical change, especially the slow and halting replacement of spontaneous crowd protests by organized bottom-up challenges and eventually by elite-negotiated transitions. What Rueschemeyer, Stephens, and Stephens (1992) and O'Donnell and Schmitter (1986) highlight were different stages in this glacial process. Moreover, by showing that the historical starting point was unorganized mass contention, this study complements the heavy emphasis on elite negotiations in Higley and Gunther (1992), Higley and Burton (2006), and Congleton (2011), who downplay the significance of "revolutionary" challenges from below. In sum, this study takes a step back from the democratization literature. In its sweeping historical perspective, it explains the change in the predominant modes of democratic opposition and transition. By contrast, the writings that focused on specific areas and epochs simply highlight either transgressive or contained contention but do not explain the shift from one mode to the other.

Moreover, my study systematically accounts for the changing mix of external stimuli and domestic factors in democratization efforts (for a recent account focused on "competitive authoritarianism," see Levitsky and Way 2010). Though they wrote during the most massive and wide-ranging wave of regime transitions, O'Donnell and Schmitter (1986: 17–21) did not attribute much importance to foreign influences.[9] Huntington (1991: 31–33, 85–106) called attention to the diffusion aspect and developed interesting ideas about various mechanisms propelling the cross-national spread of democratization, but he offered only suggestive evidence and plausible explanations. This book develops a full-fledged theory and offers an in-depth analysis of changes in diffusion patterns. Above all, external precedents had more force in triggering regime contention in inchoate polities, but shaped regime outcomes to a lesser extent. The emergence of mass organizations then led to the ever more thorough filtering of foreign influences, but also gave those impulses that domestic leaders pursued at propitious moments more effect in producing advances toward democracy. Thus, precisely because external stimuli came to have less direct, immediate force in stimulating regime contention, they ended up making a greater difference in terms of institutional reform.

Last but not least, this book advances diffusion studies, a flourishing field in contemporary social science (e.g., Markoff 1996; Simmons, Dobbin, and Garrett 2008; Meseguer 2009; Givan, Roberts, and Soule 2010; Graham, Shipan, and Volden 2013). This literature has made great progress in establishing the importance of demonstration and contagion effects empirically, especially

[9] One of the three coordinators of the "transitions" project had a chapter on "international aspects of democratization" in the original collection, but even there he emphasized the "primary importance" of internal forces (Whitehead 1986b: 4). Later, however, he edited a whole volume examining the "international dimensions of democratization" (Whitehead 2001).

via ever more sophisticated statistical methods (see, e.g., Brinks and Coppedge 2006; Gleditsch and Ward 2006; Torfason and Ingram 2010). Based on this achievement, in recent years attention has shifted to investigating the causal mechanisms that drive diffusion processes. This emerging debate has essentially pitted advocates of more objectivist approaches, who invoke coercion, competition, or rationalist self-interest calculation, against more subjectivist frameworks that highlight normative or symbolic motivations or social peer pressures. The present book extends my earlier efforts (e.g., Weyland 2007) to introduce an alternative based on cognitive psychology that – as Chapter 2 explains – mediates between those two poles; in particular, I develop this core claim into a more full-fledged theory of political diffusion by explaining and documenting how changing organizational settings affect the bounds of rationality.

In conclusion, this study speaks to several important bodies of literature in our discipline and the social sciences in general.

RESEARCH DESIGN

To substantiate my theory about the diffusion of democratization, the book examines the only three clusters of regime contention that consistently qualify as "waves of democratization" (Kurzman 1998: 45–56), namely the revolutions of 1848 and of 1917/19 and the "third wave" of democratization, which unfolded in Southern Europe and Latin America from the mid-1970s to the late 1980s.

As the term "wave" implies, these three diffusion processes constitute compact temporal clusters of connected events that stand out from the ongoing historical trend. There was a distinct bunching of horizontally linked episodes of regime contention – a clear upsurge followed soon by a downswing. A pebble tossed into a pond causes a crisp wave that spreads across the tranquil surface; then the ripples fade, and calm returns. A wave thus brings a temporary increase in certain linked phenomena or events – a noteworthy boost, which then tapers off and recedes toward the preexisting trend. Spreading in this wavelike fashion, diffusion follows the S-shaped curve of cumulative frequency highlighted in the literature (Rogers 2003: 23). Observers can recognize and delimit waves by noting a departure from, and then, an eventual return to the historical trend. The inflection stemming from the initial trigger is usually clear; because undulations die down more slowly, the exact end point of a wave may be harder to determine. In regard to the topic of the present book, the outbreak of political contention quickly places the regime issue at the top of the agenda, but how this controversial question is resolved can take considerable time.

Kurzman (1998; see also Mainwaring and Pérez-Liñán forthcoming: ch. 3) argues that "waves of democratization" can be defined in different ways, namely as time periods during which the level of democracy increases in the world, during which transitions to democracy outnumber breakdowns, or during which there are significant linkages between different transitions (especially where these linkages are predominantly horizontal and do not result from vertical imposition by a great power). According to his statistical and qualitative analysis, only three bunched processes qualify under all of these definitions, namely the clusters of regime contention that took place in 1848, in 1917–19, and during the 1970s to late 1980s. These three clusters also display the temporal compactness emphasized above (especially if the third wave of democratization is examined in its regional manifestations, as this book does for Latin America). Given that the concept of wave is by nature somewhat fluid, it is best to focus on event clusters that fulfill all of these criteria and thus qualify most clearly and incontrovertibly. To put case selection on a robust foundation, the book therefore investigates those three waves.

These three clusters of regime contention constituted watersheds in the political development of many countries; even the tsunami of 1848 with its low rate of success had crucial lasting consequences, as has often been emphasized in the German case, for instance. As "critical junctures," these three waves thus deserve analysis in their own right. By drawing virtually all political forces into high-stakes interaction and conflict, these momentous episodes also throw light on the underlying distribution of political preferences and constellation of power. A focus on these three waves thus serves as lenses and elucidates the historical processes that gave rise to these political configurations, in line with my developmental macro-organizational argument.

My comparatively strict, multiattribute conceptualization excludes some series of political changes that other authors call waves. In particular, Huntington's first wave of democratization founders according to Kurzman (1998: 50–54) on the linkage concept, which is of special significance for the present analysis of diffusion. The initial case of this supposed wave, for instance, the emergence of Jacksonian democracy in the United States (Huntington 1991: 16), had no observable impact on other countries and did not stimulate emulation efforts (Weyland 2009: 411–12). Moreover, Huntington's first wave unfolded over nearly a century;[10] therefore, it does not feature tight clustering, nor does it stand out from the historical background trend. Even the suffrage extensions that became ever more frequent in the late nineteenth and early twentieth centuries (Freeman and Snidal 1982) do not show sufficient interconnection or temporal clumping to qualify as a clear-cut wave. Similarly, the "democratic revolution" of the late eighteenth century (Palmer 1959; Bayly 2004: ch. 3; Winik 2007; Osterhammel 2009: 747–56; Sperber 2011) took more than a decade (1776–89) to get under way and affected such a small number of countries (emulators France, the Netherlands 1780–87, and Poland 1788–95) that it does not constitute a distinct wave, despite its great world-historical significance (Markoff 1996: 2–3, 49–51). Thus, by the fairly

---

[10] Berg-Schlosser (2009: 44–46) goes even farther by including almost 150 years in his "first long wave, 1776–1914."

precise definition applied in this book, waves of democratization are rare; the "revolutions" of 1848 and 1917–19 and the third wave of democratization really stand out.

Obviously, these high-stakes processes occurred in very different time periods. How can one analytically bridge this historical distance? Do fundamental differences in sociopolitical and ideational context, the advance of world-historical developments, or learning from wave to wave not preclude valid inferences? For instance, 1848 and 1917–19 are commonly labeled as (political) revolutions, whereas the third wave in southern Europe and Latin America constituted a cluster of nonrevolutionary regime transitions. Also, the stages and tasks of democratization in the first half of the nineteenth century and the second half of the twentieth century differed: Most revolutionaries in 1848 sought liberalization, not full democratization; but the delegitimation of intermediate constitutional frameworks effectively put only full democracy on the agenda during the third wave,[11] at least in the two regions under investigation. These difficult issues arise fundamentally from conceptual questions, namely how democratization should be defined and whether democratization and political revolution are best seen as distinct processes or as variants of a broader, more abstract category of transformative political change. Therefore, these topics will be addressed in the following section on conceptual issues.

The main point to clarify in the present section on research design is the very logic of comparing three distinct and historically distant waves of conflicts over political regime type. This book avoids some tricky inferential issues, which have spurred controversies between historically oriented scholars and social scientists (Sewell 2005; Malia 2006), by not assuming uniformity across these three diffusion processes. Accordingly, I do not propose an explanation that pretends to apply equally to all three waves. Studies that advance such general arguments must claim causal homogeneity and assume that all factors operate in the same way and exert the same effect despite different settings; such studies thus deny the importance of contextual variation and world-historical change. As Sewell (2005: ch. 3) and Malia (2006: appendix II) highlight, these assumptions are questionable; they can induce analysts to "see" homogeneity artificially through their analytical lenses. Contextual settings are so complex and historical changes so multifaceted that it is implausible that these processes arise from the same mix of variables. Efforts to uncover homogeneous causal

---

[11] Certainly, Latin American military regimes that felt compelled to move away from open authoritarian rule sought to institute "relative democracy" or "strong democracy," in the terms of Brazil's military president Ernesto Geisel (1974–79; see Alves 1985: 142). But these limited, stunted versions of democratic rule did not have a chance of being instituted because in Latin America, exposed to the influence of Western democracies, formal abridgments of democracy were no longer legitimate. Moreover, democratic competition induced civilian political forces to chip away at initial military tutelage and eliminate all remnants of authoritarian rule (Hunter 1997), even in countries where the armed forces relinquished power from a position of strength, as in Brazil and Chile.

patterns in different time periods and regions therefore face considerable inferential problems.

The present comparison of three democratization waves from two centuries avoids the core of these problems by advancing a developmental argument. The same individual-level mechanisms, especially cognitive heuristics, that seem basic to the human mind (Kahneman 2011), played out differently and had variegated effects, depending on changing political-organizational settings. By demonstrating that the bounds of rationality loosened with the strengthening and proliferation of organizational ties, the book elucidates the profound inter-action of micro-foundations and evolving macro-structures; it thus emphasizes causal heterogeneity across history. The same causal micro-mechanisms oper-ated differently and had diverse effects due to contextual transformations. The three-wave comparison is designed not to unearth uniform, unchanging pat-terns, but to highlight substantial differences across these processes.

By developing and assessing this interactive argument, the book seeks to meld the analytical approaches of political science and history. It pursues the social-scientific quest for uncovering constant mechanisms that drive many specific events and therefore abstracts from particularity quite boldly. But it also recognizes changes in the operation and the effect of these mecha-nisms across world-historical time and regional context and explains them with fundamental developments, especially organizational advances. In these ways, my study seeks to capture the unfolding and transformation of polit-ical patterns through history: Diffusion processes become more complex as new layers of actors appear and then enter into multiple interactions. Traces of earlier stages persist, as in the spontaneous mass mobilization sparked in part by the Russian revolutions in April 1917 and January 1918; but as orga-nizational leaders' domestication of these contentious impulses shows, new developments come into play, deflect bottom-up pressures, and produce out-comes that are qualitatively different. Then, as organization spreads across the ideological spectrum and reshapes the stimulus side of diffusion as well, exter-nal influences on regime contention multiply and cognitive shortcuts operate in particularly complex ways. Due to these interaction effects, especially the mutual influence of cognitive micro-foundations and changing organizational macro-structures, causality is heterogeneous. And given that organizational developments tend to have a certain directionality, world-historical time plays a significant role.

Thus, the book draws together history and political science and seeks to enrich both disciplines. History uncovers and digests a tremendous wealth and diversity of political experiences, but it can be too enamored with particularity (Wehler 1977: 25) to draw broader conclusions and thus risks losing relevance and interest. If the past is truly unique and incomparable to the present, how much analytical importance does it hold? Political science, in turn, seeks gener-alization to unearth broadly applicable patterns, but this quest can lead to such high levels of abstraction and interpretive flexibility ("self-interest," "utility") that its findings become too generic to yield real insight. Moreover, the drive to become more scientific and base inferences on hard data has brought a focus on recent events and leaves out vast stretches of political experience that occurred in earlier times when statistical data was spotty and representative surveys nonexistent. Should a generalizing discipline not examine this rich treasure of occurrences as well, despite methodological limitations?

Last not least, the nomothetic effort to abstract from contextual specificity has led to a pointillistic approach based on the hope that the findings of innumerable tightly focused studies will add up to a beautiful canvas à la Georges Seurat. But what if the underlying ceteris paribus assumption does not hold, and the little dots contributed by countless hypothesis-testing articles do not align in clear patterns, but end up creating white noise? What if the results of specific scientific investigations are so variegated and disparate that researchers cannot make sense of broader developments to arrive at a bigger picture?

To avoid these issues, scholars need to take contextual settings seriously, consider developmental trends, and pay attention to the long sweep of history (Abbott 2001: ch. 2; see also Hall 2003).[12] At the same time, they need to avoid drowning in particularity and apply a comparative perspective that uses the analysis of similarity and difference to uncover change over time as well as fundamental continuities. By drawing on micro-foundational insights from cognitive psychology that claim universal validity while demonstrating how organizational developments shape the operation of these cognitive mechanisms and affect their political impact, my book seeks to combine the concerns of history and social science and offer a deeper and richer understanding of crucial events and developments than each discipline alone tends to provide.

METHODOLOGICAL PROCEDURES

The melding of social science and history, especially the reliance on cognitive psychology to elucidate political processes that occurred decades or centuries ago, raises important methodological challenges. How can researchers document cognitive inferences from distant historical time periods? In general, how can they reconstruct the ways in which participants perceived and thought about foreign precedents, drew lessons from them, and decided whether and how to emulate them? Whereas most of the diffusion literature applies statistical techniques, the present focus on people's information-processing, inferences, and choices calls for a qualitative and interpretive approach.

Fortunately, participants, eyewitnesses, and other contemporaneous observers produced a wealth of materials in which they preserved their perceptions, experiences, thoughts, calculations, and actions for later generations. The contentious waves investigated in this book constituted such watersheds in

---

[12] For a strikingly negative evaluation of comparative historical analysis, derived from the questionable quest for the "testing" of generalizations, see Coppedge (2012: 140–50).

the personal and political lives of people from various sectors of society and different political persuasion (see, e.g., Bismarck 1898; Fontane 1920; Schurz 1988: 99–101) that many authors picked up the pen and recorded their impressions and thinking for posterity. Many people wrote right at the time in letters and diaries, others years or decades later in their memoirs; some of these eyewitness accounts were published only posthumously. This urge to preserve one's observations prevailed even for the earliest wave examined in this volume, that of 1848 (among others, Wolff 1898; Streckfuss 1948; Jessen 1968; Lewald 1969; Frank-Döfering 1988; Fenske 1996; Temme 1996). While some reports merely describe observable political behavior and contentious events (e.g., *Berliner März-Revolution* 1848), many others, especially diaries, letters, and memoirs, offer an abundance of fascinating insights into people's mental operations – both their own and those of actors close to them.

Liberal aristocrat Karl Varnhagen von Ense (1862), for instance, not only chronicled in his extensive diaries and autobiographical studies the evolution of his own thinking about the unfolding 1848 revolution, but also provided many frank and unflattering reports about the sentiments prevailing among Prussian elites, especially at the court of indecisive King Friedrich Wilhelm IV. In a similar vein, students who turned revolutionary, such as Paul Boerner (1920) and Carl Schurz (1988), describe the inferences that they quickly drew from the Parisian news and the resulting surge of contentious enthusiasm. Even the stolid military commander of Berlin wrote a massive account of the protests that indicates his thoughts and calculations (Prittwitz 1985). The posthumously published letters and confidential memos of Clemens Metternich (1883) – for decades the mainstay of reaction in Europe – and the epistolary exchanges of Prussian king Friedrich Wilhelm IV with many other European princes (Haenchen 1930) offer particularly direct, intimate access to their thinking. Thus, there is a considerable amount of primary source material on the tsunami of 1848 (even some from Latin America, e.g. Vicuña Mackenna 2003), which allows for a reconstruction of actors' perceptions and thoughts.

Of course, there is even more such evidence on the wave of 1917–19 and especially on the democratization efforts of the 1970s and 1980s. For the diffusion process of the early twentieth century, this book relies on a wealth of materials, especially from Germany. Particularly instructive were the published speeches, letters, or memoirs of six of the eight members of the provisional revolutionary governments of 1918–19 (Barth 1919; Noske 1920; Scheidemann 1921, 1929; Ebert 1926; Haase 1929; Dittmann 1995), their leading radical critics (Ledebour 1954; Luxemburg 1970; Liebknecht 1974), and many other important participants of various political persuasions (Runkel 1919; Bauer 1923; Müller 1924, 1925, 1926; Baden 1927; Müller-Franken 1928; Keil 1947; Stumpf 1967; Leviné-Meyer 1973; Retzlaw 1976; Bernstein 1998; Toller 2009).

For the third wave of democratization, my research complemented the even greater wealth of written documents through interviews with leading decision-makers, especially from Chile. Because this country underwent the last South American transition, many participants were still alive during my research trip in 2007. I managed to converse at length with approximately twenty of them, from both the opposition and the authoritarian regime. My interlocutors – many well into their 80s in 2007 and two by now dead – included democratic former presidents Patricio Aylwin and Ricardo Lagos; President Pinochet's former ministers Sergio Onofre Jarpa, Sergio Fernández, Carlos Cáceres, and Hernán Felipe Errázuriz; his legal counsel Ambrosio Rodríguez; and a wide range of leading politicians from various parties, including Genaro Arriagada, Edgardo Boeninger, Alberto Cardemil, Germán Correa, Gutenberg Martínez, Sergio Molina, Ricardo Núñez, Enrique Silva Cimma, and Andrés Zaldívar. Given the more distant time period of their democratization, my interviews were sparser in Brazil and Peru, but I succeeded in speaking with some crucial actors, such as Peru's former military president Francisco Morales Bermúdez, and leading politicians, including Javier Diez Canseco, Javier Valle-Riestra, Javier Alva Orlandini, Javier Silva Ruete, Roberto Saturnino Braga, Wellington Moreira Franco, and – via e-mail – José Dirceu.

Certainly, all of these sources can suffer from distortions and biases. Actors commonly overestimate their own importance and exaggerate their originality, which can induce them to downplay foreign influences.[13] Probably due to fading memories, my interviews in fact yielded fewer references to external inspirations than my interlocutors had mentioned in their own earlier writings. But the variety of primary documentation allows for cross-checking different sources and for reconstructing actors' perceptions, inferences, and calculations with reasonable reliability. It is especially telling that participants of different political persuasion often seemed to rely on similar cognitive inferences. Accordingly, a striking foreign precedent of successful regime contention induced both oppositionists and conservative sectors to see their own government as precarious and to overestimate the ease of toppling it. This convergence in conclusions among political adversaries and ideological opposites cannot be due to wishful thinking. Instead, it reflects common cognitive shortcuts, which people of different persuasions apply. Thus, these shared inferences increase confidence in the findings of this book.

Pragmatic considerations and theoretical reasons led me to draw a disproportionate part of the evidence for this book from Germany and Chile. My research on the third wave ended up yielding a much greater wealth of materials in Chile than in Brazil and Peru (not to speak of the likely results in other countries I considered studying, such as Bolivia). For the two preceding waves, language competence counseled a focus on my home country, Germany.

More importantly, these two countries deserve special attention from a theoretical perspective as well. My book designs a new, complex argument; it

---

[13] Interestingly, however, the research for my book on the spread of Chilean-style pension privatization uncovered many frank admissions of large-scale copying (Weyland 2007: 117–19).

embarks on theory development, not hypothesis-testing. Accordingly, the empirical sections are meant primarily as plausibility probes. It therefore makes sense to concentrate on cases that exemplify the arguments most clearly and show the underlying historical developments in stark relief. In methodological terms, the most instructive cases are those that have the clearest scores on the main independent variables. Since the first step in my macro-structural theory highlights the move from amorphous, inchoate societies to polities featuring consolidated broad-based organizations, no case could exemplify this process and its political ramifications more clearly than Germany, where the Social Democratic Party built the strongest, most comprehensive mass organization in all of Europe. Further steps in my theory involve the political-ideological differentiation of mass organization. In Latin America (perhaps the Third World overall), the clearest example is Chile with its well-developed party system, which has for decades spanned the full range of the ideological spectrum. Because these two countries feature the most distinctive scores of my main causal factors, they are of particular interest for observing the causal mechanisms postulated in my theory and for assessing whether they bring forth their supposed outcomes.

CENTRAL CONCEPTS

A study that compares high-profile, controversial political transformations across two centuries has a particular obligation to clarify its central concepts. Given obvious differences in regional and world-historical context, it is important to establish the analytical equivalence of the phenomena under investigation, as mentioned in the preceding section. Moreover, the wide-ranging comparisons conducted in this volume require concepts at a fairly high level of abstraction; their boundaries therefore need explicit delimitation.

Political Regime Contention

The book examines conflicts over political regime change and their success in producing actual steps toward democracy. Since over the course of history, these conflicts have differed in tactics, strategy, and character, I borrow from McAdam, Tarrow, and Tilly (2001: 4–9; quotation on p. 5) the broad and admittedly vague concept of political contention, which denotes "collective political struggle" – "episodic, public, collective interaction" about significant, salient claims that involves a government and "affect[s] the interests of at least one of the claimants" (similar Tilly and Tarrow 2007: 4–11 and recently Tarrow 2012: 3). When directed at the government, contention consists of collective challenges to established authorities, institutions, or policy programs, coming from sectors that seek greater political influence, civic or social rights, symbolic recognition, or material benefits. Because these challenges make important claims and involve collective mobilization, there is a good chance that they may spiral beyond official institutional arenas, draw in additional sectors, either as supporters or opponents of these challenges (cf. Schattschneider 1975: 2–11), and escalate beyond the original intentions of their initiators. Contention can thus bend or break established formal or informal procedures of demand and decision making and push beyond the status quo by pursuing lasting change in political institutions or outputs.

Because this book focuses on conflicts that erupted during the long struggle for democratization, it coins the concept of political regime contention. This notion is defined as forceful challenges to political incumbents, even with extralegal means, that seek to redesign the formal and informal rules governing the exercise of political authority. In other words, these efforts at profound political change seek to transform established institutional rules, mechanisms, and patterns. The conflicts that often result can spill into the streets, mobilize new types of participants, and make the final outcome dependent on power capabilities that are not officially recognized by the current regime. In particular, political regime contention draws in mass actors, invokes the majoritarian logic derived from the principle of popular sovereignty, and directs this pressure, which can include the threat or actual use of violence, toward reshaping the existing institutional framework. This idea was expressed in the famous slogan used by the East German mass movement against communism in 1989: "We are the people!" Even a repressive post-totalitarian regime felt compelled to cede to this extraordinary challenge, especially after losing Soviet protection.

Due to its conflictual nature and expansive dynamic, political regime contention often has transgressive elements or tendencies; as the theory developed in Chapter 2 argues, transgression prevailed especially during many early episodes in the struggle for political liberalism and democratization. According to McAdam, Tarrow, and Tilly (2001: 7–8), the distinctive feature of transgressive contention is that it involves "newly self-identified political actors, and/ or ... innovative [types of] collective action"; it "adopts means that are either unprecedented or forbidden within the regime in question" and thus deviates clearly and often starkly from the formal rules and officially accepted procedures for effecting political change.

Yet while potentially transgressing the established constitutional framework and seeking to overhaul it substantially, regime contention always resorts to the logic of politics to accomplish challengers' goals; it does not rely primarily on naked violence. The occasional use of violence is designed more to convey the intensity of political preferences and force concessions, not to destroy the adversary with sheer force. Therefore, political regime contention in my definition excludes organized, militarized force such as guerrilla campaigns or terrorism. It does, however, encompass the political demonstration of power capabilities via mass rallies, protests, and uprisings, which often spearheaded pressures for liberalization and democratization in the nineteenth and early twentieth centuries and played a crucial role in the third wave of democratization as well (O'Donnell and Schmitter 1986: 53–56).

In the course of democratization history, however, the representative leaders of the emerging broad-based organizations sought to domesticate mass contention and then channel it into efforts to effect regime change via elite-level negotiations. Instead of trying to force out authoritarian rulers through confrontation, such bargaining strives for compromise and hopes to accomplish regime transitions in ways that incumbents can accept, however begrudgingly. As Chapter 3 analyzes in depth, the taming of bottom-up pressures thus brought a slow and halting shift from transgressive to "contained contention," in which "all parties [to the collective political struggle] are previously established actors employing well established means of claim making" (McAdam, Tarrow, and Tilly 2001: 7; see also Tarrow 2011: 111–15).

Because it includes both transgressive and contained variants, political regime contention is an amorphous concept that comprises a wide variety of political behaviors, tactics, and strategies. In line with classical approaches to conceptualization (Sartori 1984), the transitions literature of the 1980s and 1990s preferred more narrowly confined, internally homogeneous notions and therefore distinguished different processes of political change. The seminal contribution of O'Donnell and Schmitter (1986: 11, 14) deliberately separated democratic transition from revolution. This strict conceptual boundary reflected the empirical finding that radical efforts to effect profound transformations of state and society can hinder the revamping of the political regime: Raising the stakes of change can impede change.

The definitional clarity pursued by classical conceptualization has important scholarly advantages and is preferable for many purposes, such as examinations of the outcomes of political change. But for the present investigation of processes of change, the imposition of clear borderlines may be unrealistic and hinder more than help understanding. In the judgments and calculations of many participants, on which my research concentrates, it was often unclear what type of political change was underway: Would challenges to autocratic governments turn into a full-scale revolution that could overturn the foundations of state and society, or would they affect only the political authority structures, that is, the regime? In fact, the target and depth of change were among the main bones of contention. For instance, would the Chilean transition of the 1980s remain confined to redemocratization, or would it unleash radicalism and revive the revolutionary projects pursued before the 1973 military coup, as far-left groupings hoped and the authoritarian right feared? Similarly, would the German revolution of November 1918 usher in a Soviet-style system run by worker and soldier councils – or their self-appointed vanguard – or would it bring the last step toward full democracy via the election of a constituent assembly?

As these examples show, the contentious episodes under investigation were so mercurial, fluid, and open-ended that their direction and nature were unclear to most participants. From the perspective of the actors, on whose perceptions, inferences, and calculations this book concentrates, it is therefore problematic to insist on clear-cut distinctions derived from the subsequent unfolding and eventual outcomes of these complicated, multifaceted processes. In fact, participants' lack of clarity about the nature and ramifications of the conflicts in which they were involved contributed to the uncertainty and "confusion" (Kurzman 2004) that enveloped actors of all stripes. The broad, open concept of political regime contention does more justice to these shifty conjunctures than tighter notions that presuppose the endpoint of change. My concept highlights the principal target of contention at the initiation of the conflict but leaves open the possibility that change could deepen and come to affect more fundamental layers of state and society.

The three waves examined in the present book fit this broad definition. The primary goal of most revolutionaries in 1848 was political regime change, such as a transition from absolutist to constitutional monarchy or the declaration of a republic. Many protesters in Central Europe also demanded the creation of nation states, whereas advocacy for various socioeconomic changes was more mixed. In 1918–19, democratization was the top priority for most challengers, whereas a revamping of the socioeconomic order, on which these groupings disagreed markedly, would come later. And during the third wave of democratization, the restoration of political liberty and civilian rule was at the forefront of contentious efforts. As mentioned, actors on both extremes of the ideological spectrum saw a chance that these conflicts would escalate to challenges to the "capitalist system," but this issue never occupied the top of the political agenda. Given the central focus on constitutional issues, yet the possibility of further repercussions, the three waves of challenges qualify as political regime contention.

My central concept, which encompasses various types of political change and goes beyond strict distinctions between democratization and revolution, is also in line with recent trends in the comparative literature. The scholarly community drew a clear borderline between democratization and revolution for a limited time period only, which lasted from Skocpol's (1979: 4–5) restrictive conceptualization of social revolution to the softening of the definition of "revolution" (Goldstone 2003: 53–55) and the fading of the transitions literature in the 1990s. Both before and after, a number of authors examined "democratic revolutions;"[14] this notion appears in the postcommunist "color revolutions" as well. Thus, studying processes of change that do not fit neatly into the conceptual compartments of democratization versus revolution is not an idiosyncrasy of this book. Scholars commonly analyze and compare challenges

[14] See, e.g., Palmer (1959), McFaul (2002: 221–23), and Thompson (2004); see also Goldstone, Gurr, and Moshiri (1991), which includes cases of democratization such as the Philippines (1986) in its study of revolution. From the perspective of the theory developed in Chapter 2, and as explained especially in Chapter 3, scholars contrasted democratic transition and revolution when attention focused on Southern Europe and Latin America, where – as a result of polities' relatively high level of organizational density – democratization advanced predominantly via negotiations, not mass uprisings. As the third wave reached other areas of the globe where mass organization was more incipient, street protests became more central for the advance of democratization, and specialists on these cases therefore disregarded the conceptual distinction that early transitologists had drawn.

that are amorphous in nature and open in outcome, but that aim first and foremost at regime change.

Last but not least, this book not only encompasses different types of political regime contention, but also accounts for the protracted shift from transgressive to contained modes of contention; specifically, it explains why abrupt revolutionary uprisings predominated in 1848 and played a great role in 1918–19, whereas more gradual, less confrontational transitions prevailed in Europe and Latin America during the 1970s and 1980s. Chapter 3 demonstrates that in the largely unorganized polities of the mid-nineteenth century, revolutionary assaults on the established authorities were the principal option for effecting regime change that was available to challengers. By contrast, the emergence of political mass organizations and their slow spread across the ideological spectrum allowed for less risky reformist approaches, which played a substantial role in 1918–19 and then congealed to the model of negotiated regime transitions prevailing during the third wave. By explaining the shift from democratic revolutions to more peaceful modes of regime change, my book endogenizes the transformation of the main stimuli of contentious waves and incorporates the changing characteristics of political regime contention into its developmental macro-argument. Rather than constituting a conceptual problem, the move from "revolution" to transition in the history of European and Latin American democratization constitutes a crucial part of the fundamental change that this volume accounts for. In metaphorical terms, this book does not conduct invalid comparisons by equating tigers with house cats, but it explains how wild bulls were tamed into manageable plow animals and how that domestication, in turn, affected the fate of china shops – that is, the delicate processes of emulative regime change.

Democratization

In its focus on political regime change, this book conceptualizes democratization as a process that can unfold with highly differential speed, ranging from a sequence of stepwise advances to an abrupt full transition. This point is crucial to a study with a long historical time frame. But it is not always highlighted in the literature (yet see recently Capoccia and Ziblatt 2010: 940), for a simple reason: Because the global spread of democratic values and norms during the twentieth century delegitimated long-standing expedients such as suffrage restrictions and in this way eliminated the formal, official versions of hybrid regime types,[15] the available options in institutionalized polities have

---

[15] O'Donnell and Schmitter (1986: 42, 44). The recent literature on hybrid regime types such as "competitive authoritarianism" (Levitsky and Way 2010; see also Schedler 2006) highlights informal deviations from formal rules of democratic competitiveness, such as unfair incumbency advantages, manipulation of the mass media, and harassment of the opposition. These subterfuges differ from the formal restrictions on suffrage or the power of elected authorities that were commonplace in the nineteenth century.

crystallized ever more clearly into a binary choice between strict authoritarian rule and full democracy. This bifurcation has ruled out gradual advances; transitions have come to mean a quick and complete move from authoritarian rule to democracy (Collier 1999: 13).

In earlier time periods, by contrast, regime change was often very gradual and slow, as exemplified by the suffrage reforms adopted in Britain over the course of almost a century (1832–1928); many other European countries also instituted democracy step by step – or two steps forward, one step back (cf. Markoff 1999; Keane 2009: part 2, ch. 4; Przeworski 2010: ch. 3). Historically oriented political scientists therefore emphasize the need to investigate democratization as a set of episodes (Capoccia and Ziblatt 2010: 940–45), rather than focusing only on the last step, the final crossing of the threshold to full democracy (as Rueschemeyer, Stephens, and Stephens 1992 and, in terms of "special emphasis," Collier 1999: 23, do). In fact, where politics is less institutionalized and rule-bound than in Europe and where informal governmental manipulation can therefore defang formally democratic mechanisms (e.g., where fraud can distort elections), there have been drawn-out, piecemeal transitions even in recent decades, as in Mexico during the 1980s and 1990s; the new literature on competitive authoritarianism and similar hybrid regime types (see especially Levitsky and Way 2010) also suggests that democratization can proceed via a sequence of steps as informal restrictions on open, fair competition are slowly removed.

Because political regime change often advanced gradually in previous centuries, this book investigates waves of contention that affected various steps in the transition process. In 1848 in Central Europe, few participants pushed for full democracy. Most reformists tried to institute liberal, constitutional monarchies; they did not seek a total transformation of the existing, absolute autocracies, but confined themselves to promoting limited, partial change. When the present study assesses the success of these contentious efforts, it deliberately takes as its measuring rod the main participants' goals. This context-dependent assessment is more realistic and analytically useful than measuring the degree of progress toward full democracy. Since most actors did not even intend to go that far, it would be unfair to hold them to such an absolute standard; it would also make little analytical sense because their efforts would a priori be disqualified as failures.

The context-dependent measurement of democratizing success makes the second observation that motivates this book, concerning the greater achievements of later waves of political regime contention, particularly striking. In objective terms, the protagonists of these more recent conflicts set themselves a particularly ambitious goal by trying to effect a full transition from authoritarian rule to democracy. Given the big step that they sought to take, it is noteworthy that they attained a significantly higher rate of success than their forebears, who "merely" attempted to push liberalization or democratization one of several steps forward.[16] In this broader perspective, my approach to measuring the success of political regime contention has the analytical advantage of biasing assessments against one of the study's main findings – which is therefore especially significant.

This measurement procedure also provides an analytical cushion against modernization theory claims that advances in socioeconomic development facilitated the establishment and maintenance of democracy over the course of history. These arguments, which continue to be the subject of considerable debate (e.g., Przeworski et al. 2000; Doorenspleet 2004; and Teorell 2010: 57–58 versus Boix and Stokes 2003 and Epstein et al. 2006; see also Mainwaring and Pérez-Liñán forthcoming: ch. 4 and Lehoucq 2012: 67, 70–71), postulate a secular increase in the chances of democratization. My context-dependent approach to evaluating the success of emulation efforts can accommodate this change in structural conditions, which coincided with the more ambitious goals of the main initiators of democratic contention. Because oppositionists' task became more demanding with the discrediting of intermediate regime types (such as limited suffrage), my assessment of their accomplishments does not yield an artificially high rate of success even if modernization theory is correct and democratization has, indeed, become easier than in the nineteenth century.

Specifically, democratic contention is counted as successful if collective challenges to authoritarian incumbents achieve significant, non-fleeting steps toward political liberalism or democracy. The crucial indicator is that such an advance is accomplished in the short run and sustained over the medium run, even if it ends up being abolished in the long run, as during the "reverse wave" of the interwar years (Huntington 1991: 17–18). Accordingly, this study defines success in terms of regime transition, not consolidation,[17] as distinguished by the democratization literature of the 1980s and 1990s. Of course, this definition implies a significant change on the regime dimension; an autocrat's displacement is not sufficient as such because another authoritarian ruler may quickly take control. Instead, only where regime contention achieves significant progress toward political liberty or competitive popular rule and where this advance is maintained for at least three years has there been success in the terms of this book.[18]

My focus on transitions to political liberalism and democracy, rather than the new regime's consolidation, constitutes another reason why frequently

---

[16] Of course, any challenge to an absolute ruler who claimed the divine right of kings meant dramatic defiance, drew the wrath of the established authorities, and exposed the challengers to repression. In the twentieth century, by contrast, authoritarian rule stood on more precarious bases of legitimacy, and democracy had turned into a common regime form, losing its radical nature. Considering the context, the magnitude of defiance in all of these contentious episodes was comparable.

[17] Higley and Gunther (1992), by contrast, seek to explain democratic consolidation.

[18] Accordingly, Germany's democratization in 1919 counts as a success, as in Collier (1999: 26) – despite the later catastrophe.

proposed modernization arguments cannot easily account for the increasing success of democratic diffusion that this book highlights. Such claims offer more convincing explanations of democratic consolidation than transition (Przeworski et al. 2000; Teorell 2010: 57–58; Mainwaring and Pérez-Liñán forthcoming). As the literature of the 1980s and 1990s amply documented (O'Donnell and Schmitter 1986: 18–20; Karl 1990: 2–5), transitions that bring effective regime change (even if the fledgling democracy may later succumb to authoritarian regression) have occurred in a striking variety of countries, with diverse socioeconomic (and political-institutional) characteristics. Accordingly, the increase in democratic success that this study highlights is not determined by changes in structural preconditions. Instead, central elements of political agency, especially the inferences and calculations foregrounded by my cognitive-psychological approach, matter a great deal.

Diffusion

Diffusion is usually defined in a straightforward way as the process by which influences from outside reasonably autonomous decision-making units significantly increase the likelihood that these polities will emulate an institutional or policy innovation developed elsewhere (adapted from Weyland 2007: 16–17). In the prototypical case of horizontal diffusion, one unit's initial adoption decision triggers replication by other units, as in the spread of the Bismarckian social security system or of Chilean pension privatization. By identifying diffusion with replication, this conceptualization foresees a trend toward convergence: The followers imitate the frontrunner; therefore, similarity spreads amid diversity. This simple conceptualization is useful for the analysis of policy diffusion, which examines the spread of an ideational principle or institutional blueprint; policy decisions tend to boil down to a choice between adoption (perhaps with adaptations or modifications) versus non-adoption.

Conflicts over political regime change are much more controversial and complex, however, because they call into question the political survival of the established authorities, which policy decisions affect at most indirectly. Governments' responses to foreign contentious impulses are therefore not confined to adoption versus non-adoption, that is, capitulation versus resistance; instead, incumbents often use proactive expedients to avoid getting caught up in a wave of regime conflict. If they recognize their weakness, they can enact preemptive reforms that meet the challengers part of the way and thereby seek to take the wind out of their sails, forestalling full replication. If the established authorities command great strength, by contrast, they block replication by cracking down on any opposition and thus making the imitation of a foreign precedent much less likely. This outcome *lowers* the chances of replication and entails increasing *divergence*. Yet these countermeasures also resulted from an external impulse; after all, it was the approaching wave of regime contention that prompted this repressive response. Thus, external impulses toward regime change can have a cleaving effect, triggering emulation in some cases and moves in the opposite direction in others (Weyland 2010; Gunitsky 2013: 51–56).

Because these contrasting reactions and the resulting diversity of outcomes are products of spreading impulses for change, it makes sense to define the diffusion of political regime contention more broadly than via increases in the likelihood of replication, that is, repetition of the triggering event. Instead, this type of diffusion is better conceptualized as the spread of external impulses for a political transformation that significantly alter the likelihood of a substantial move away from the status quo, in either direction – toward the originating experience or away from it. This definition depicts diffusion as a wave of stimuli that propels change, but that does not necessarily produce a uniform outcome.[19] Instead, depending on factors such as the responses of the challenged governments, diffusion can have a polarizing impact, prompting advances toward democratization in some polities yet serious setbacks elsewhere.

Since external stimuli do not always lead to successful emulation, diffusion should not be defined via increased chances of replication. Besides replication or preemptive reform, which constitutes full or partial success from the challengers' perspective, blocked change or backlash is possible as well. Moreover, mixed strategies, such as early governmental concessions followed by subsequent repeal and tightened repression, can bring varying degrees of success and failure, depending on the shifting balance of power among contending political forces. Since all of these outcomes can result from external impulses, the diffusion of regime contention is often a complex, multifaceted, fragmented process. It does not necessarily advance in a uniform wave, but in a jumble of riptides, crosscurrents, and undertows (Weyland 2010).

The broader definition of political regime diffusion applied in this book is well-suited to analyzing complex and highly contested historical events and processes. It also has the analytical advantage of biasing the investigation against my central argument. Some of the few successes of early waves of democratization were not the products of full replication, but of preemptive reform. In particular, the biggest advance toward liberalism and democracy in 1848 occurred when the Danish king sought to avoid the approaching tsunami of protest and rebellion by renouncing absolutism and promising a constitutional reform that ended up instituting universal suffrage. Similarly, crucial steps toward Germany's democratization resulted from changes enacted by the kaiser's last government in October 1918 to forestall rapidly rising bottom-up demands inspired in part by the Russian revolutions (and to obtain

---

[19] Elkins and Simmons (2005: 36–38) also delink the concept of diffusion from the outcome of replication. But I wonder whether one can confine diffusion to a mere process without stipulating that this process affects the probability of a change in the status quo. Many concepts that Elkins and Simmons (2005: 37) subsume under their definition of diffusion-as-process, such as contagion, imitation, or policy transfer, actually imply the likelihood of affecting outcomes.

better armistice conditions from the Western democracies). A strict definition of diffusion via the increased likelihood of replication may miss these democratizing achievements, which resulted from incumbent attempts to avoid a repeat of the triggering experiences. Therefore, it would score these waves even lower on the success dimension, suggesting a stronger negative correlation between diffusion's speed and success than the present analysis finds.

ORGANIZATION OF THE VOLUME

To elucidate three waves of political regime contention, this book develops a complex, developmental theory and substantiates it layer by layer by examining these diffusion processes sequentially. After discussing a number of alternative frameworks (theories of modernization and globalization, arguments about nationalism, world system theory and constructivism, and rational choice), Chapter 2 develops the central theoretical arguments, which were introduced in this chapter, in greater depth. My explanation rests on a cognitive-psychological micro-foundation, which brings forth different types of emulation decisions and diffusion processes depending on changing macro-contexts. Specifically, the chapter details how the emergence and spread of broad-based organizations led to the ever more complex processing of external stimuli of regime contention and how it produced a greater variety of such stimuli as well.

Chapter 3 traces the latter development in depth, demonstrating how external precedents for contentious waves – that is, the triggers of diffusion processes – changed through history. Whereas the waves of 1848 and 1917–19 were set in motion by the revolutionary overthrow of autocrats in Paris and St. Petersburg, respectively, the third wave of democratization flowed from various precedents, most of which were not revolutionary. The case that served as the main model for Latin America, Spain's negotiated path toward democratization, was feasible only in polities with a good deal of organizational density. Thus, the rise and proliferation of broad-based organizations, the macro-structural development highlighted in this study, underlay this transformation of the stimulus side of diffusion.

The subsequent four chapters substantiate my theory step by step by analyzing the waves of 1848–49, 1917–19, and the 1970s and 1980s sequentially; given the complexity of the third wave, an overview chapter is followed by a case study of Chile's experiences. Chapter 4 focuses on the micro-foundations of my explanation by documenting the operation of cognitive shortcuts in settings in which they held particular sway and were therefore clearly visible, namely the organizationally inchoate polities of the mid-nineteenth century. Chapter 5 shows how these inferential heuristics were contained after the emergence of organizational leadership, the central macro-level development highlighted by my theory. In the early twentieth century, cognitive shortcuts still captivated mass actors, but representative leaders sought to tame their political effects because they had the institutional capacity to cross-check rash inferences and therefore advocated greater prudence.

Whereas these chapters analyze the reception side of diffusion, Chapter 6 turns to the input side to do justice to the heterogeneous, fragmented nature of the third wave of democratization. It documents another layer of my framework by emphasizing the rise of the pacted transition model, which provided the major inspiration for this diffusion process. Democratic challengers in Latin America during the 1970s and 1980s faced a broader menu of options, which prompted disagreements and conflicts and thus slowed down emulative regime contention; but it also allowed for learning and in that way increased success. Chapter 7 examines the corresponding complexity on the reception side of diffusion. It analyzes how the ideological crystallization of different political organizations in Chile induced them to gravitate toward divergent external models. Therefore, various diffusion efforts proceeded simultaneously and interfered with each other. But political learning eventually induced the democratic opposition to discard unpromising options and settle on a realistic strategy that ended up bringing success.

Chapter 8 concludes by summarizing the empirical findings and theoretical insights of this book. Then it assesses the applicability of my theory to other diffusion processes, such as the revolutions of 1830; the third wave of democratization in Africa; the fall of communism; the color revolutions in the postcommunist world; and the Arab Spring. Finally, I draw out the broader theoretical implications of my theory by discussing the broad topic of globalization and by offering some building blocks for bounded-rationality theories of politics.

2

A New Theory of Political Diffusion: Cognitive Heuristics and Organizational Development

What explains the surprising trends highlighted in this volume, namely the historical slowdown in the diffusion of political regime contention and its increasing success? What underlies the negative correlation between these two developments? This chapter first demonstrates the insufficiency of explanations derived from various extant approaches. Then it develops a new argument that, resting on cognitive-psychological micro-foundations, highlights political-organizational macro-developments.

The first section shows that neither hypotheses about shrinking distances among countries nor about deepening gulfs between them can account for the observed changes in diffusion patterns. The former, derived from modernization and network theories, predict acceleration, not deceleration; and the latter, based on theories of nationalism, expect diminishing rather than increasing success. Specifically, modernization and globalization have produced a much "smaller" world where information circulates amply and instantaneously. How do these trends square with the slowdown of diffusion? Alternatively, as nations stress their unique identity, they should become more immune to external inspirations that are increasingly perceived as foreign and therefore inapplicable.

By contrast to these arguments about uniform trends in the international arena, other theories depict diffusion as a product of inequalities in the global system. These theories stress either push or pull factors; accordingly, they emphasize the "overwhelming" impact of innovative experiences and precedents on potential followers, or the autonomous initiative of the importers of these new models. As regards push factors, world system theory and constructivism suggest that forceful influence or normative and symbolic appeals promote external models and induce weaker, more backward countries to adopt them. By contrast, rational choice stresses pull factors, namely the recipient countries' self-interested, autonomous learning from the successes of more advanced countries.

But these approaches do not offer a persuasive explanation either. World system theory and constructivism predict a speed-up of diffusion: With the gradual advance of liberalism and democracy over the last two centuries, political regime contention moved downward in the global hierarchy to countries that were much more subject to external pressures and influences than the nations of the North Atlantic area that were the main battleground during the nineteenth and early twentieth centuries. For instance, the "hegemonic" United States should have been able to push its preference for democracy much more quickly on Latin America during the 1970s and 1980s than France, which was only one of five European great powers at the time, could in 1830 and 1848. Regarding rational learning, the distinctly mixed success of earlier waves of political regime contention should have counseled caution in 1848 – but instead, people across Europe immediately jumped on the bandwagon and unleashed a tsunami. Moreover, my research conclusively shows that people's decision-making process about joining in externally inspired protests and challenges differed starkly from the systematic, thorough, and balanced procedures of full rationality. People eagerly and rashly jumped to conclusions, rather than assessing the promise and applicability of foreign precedents carefully.

Because the conjectures derived from major extant approaches cannot convincingly account for the changing features of diffusion, the second part of this chapter develops a novel theory. And because rational choice does not provide a realistic micro-foundation, I draw on an alternative that has found robust empirical corroboration, namely cognitive-psychological insights on bounded rationality. Laboratory experiments and field studies document that people deviate in their inferences and judgments from the ideal-typical maxims of comprehensive rationality. Normal mortals do not process ample information systematically; they commonly engage in selective perception and apply cognitive shortcuts that produce inferences efficiently and thus allow them to make pressing decisions – but at the risk of distortions and biases. The use of cognitive heuristics, rather than strict rules of logic, is especially pronounced in situations of profound uncertainty, as it prevails when challenges to established authorities gather steam.

As explained in depth below, cognitive heuristics draw disproportionate attention to striking experiences, such as a regime collapse in another country, and lead people to infer rashly that they can attain a similar success. These mechanisms of bounded rationality propel the rapid spread of political regime contention. Yet because the underlying inferences are ill-considered and problematic, these efforts result in frequent failure. These tendencies – quick diffusion with limited success – prevailed in the first half of the nineteenth century, when cognitive heuristics held full sway because common people, not leaders, decided whether to emulate foreign precedents and engage in political regime contention. In 1830 and 1848, there were no large-scale political organizations with representative leaders who could have guided people's choices and actions. Instead, politically inexperienced individuals who had tenuous access to information had to decide on their own whether to join protests, and they drew heavily on cognitive heuristics to make up their minds. Thus, before the rise of mass-based political parties and interest associations, rationality was tightly bounded, triggering rash challenges under unpropitious conditions. The prevalence of cognitive heuristics in organizationally inchoate polities explains the high speed yet limited success of the waves of 1830 and 1848 – that is, one pole of the negative correlation between diffusion characteristics highlighted in this volume.

The secular rise of political organization in the late nineteenth century then made diffusion slower but more successful. As organizational ties strengthened, the bounds of rationality loosened (cf. Simon 1976: 102–03, 240–41). Instead of using cognitive heuristics to draw their own inferences, more and more people looked to representative leaders for direction. These leaders had better access to information and greater experience in making decisions. Standing on firmer ground, they were less affected by the rash inferences suggested by cognitive shortcuts. While they deviated from comprehensive rationality as well, they had a better grasp of the constellation of political power and therefore could make more realistic decisions, even under conditions of uncertainty. Accordingly, organizational leaders waited for propitious circumstances before spearheading efforts to emulate foreign precedents. They did want to achieve similar goals, but led their followers into conflicts only when a good opportunity arose. Therefore, diffusion got under way more slowly, but ended up with greater goal attainment.

In sum, the emergence of political mass organizations concentrated effective decision-making in representative leaders who had greater capabilities for information-processing, relied less on cognitive shortcuts, and gave their followers more prudent guidance. Political-organizational development thus helps account for the deceleration but growing success of democratization waves – the other pole of the negative correlation stressed in this book. This core argument is depicted in Figure 2.1, which highlights organizational development as the main cause for the changing features of contentious waves.

As explained in depth in this chapter, additional repercussions of this secular increase in polities' organizational density reinforced these tendencies in the course of the twentieth century. In particular, organizational development came to reshape the stimulus side of diffusion. In polities populated by an ever wider range of organizations, dramatic revolutions were replaced by negotiated regime transitions as the main trigger of diffusion waves. These lower-profile efforts at effecting profound political change stimulated imitation attempts less precipitously; domestic organization leaders waited until the situation looked propitious. These slower emulation initiatives achieved a particularly high rate of success.

By developing this complex explanation, the second part of this chapter embeds cognitive-psychological micro-foundations in political-organizational macro-structures. It thus helps build a theory of politics that stands on firm empirical

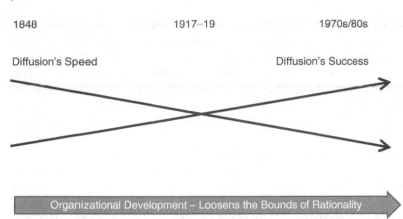

FIGURE 2.1 Organizational development reshapes diffusion.

ground but goes beyond the individualistic focus of cognitive psychology and does greater justice to the essential collective dimension of politics.

THE INSUFFICIENCY OF EXTANT APPROACHES

Network Approaches: Shrinking Distance among Countries

Diffusion studies often stress the role of networks (Rogers 2003: ch. 8), that is, the web of formal or informal connections through which various impulses flow (Emirbayer and Goodwin 1994; Ansell 2007; Kahler 2009; Christakis and Fowler 2009). In this view, the network's extension and structure and the location of different units account for patterns of emulation. For instance, an innovation adopted by a node that lies in the middle of the network should spread more quickly than one developed by a unit on the outskirts. Moreover, the denser the connections between various nodes, the faster and more widely waves of diffusion should advance.

Arguments about modernization and globalization are often added to account for broader trends in network development, especially the secular growth of transnational connections and the increasing density of all kinds of networks. Over the last two centuries, communication and transportation have improved enormously, and network linkages have multiplied and expanded. The "weak ties" whose "strength" sociologists extol (Granovetter 1973) – loose, non-intense connections through which most novel impulses spread – have proliferated. The globe has shrunk to a "small world" (Christakis and Fowler 2009: 19–29, 162–69), allowing information to travel almost instantaneously to the most remote places.

Therefore, an obvious prediction of network approaches is that over the course of history, diffusion processes will occur more frequently and unfold ever more quickly (Oliver and Myers 2003: 177, 186–91; see also Tarrow 2010: 208). Because the growing web of connections diminishes effective distances among countries, influences of all kinds should spread faster and farther. And because globalization erodes national distinctiveness and produces greater uniformity, the impact of foreign impulses on domestic structures and processes should grow as well; external models should more strongly mold internal politics and thus reproduce themselves. In the democratization literature, Huntington (1991: 101–02) advances this argument, which is also implied by Levitsky and Way's (2010: 43) emphasis on "linkage," understood as "myriad networks of interdependence ... to Western democratic communities." According to these lines of reasoning, diffusion should advance with increasing speed and ever greater success.

But the observed waves of regime contention and transition falsify the prediction of growing velocity. The revolutions of 1830 and 1848 (and even the protests triggered by the French Revolution of 1789: Timmermann 1989: 48, 369–77, 399, 537–44; Palmer 1959: 349–51, 424–26) spread faster than the conflicts set in motion by the Russian revolutions of 1917 and the third wave of democratization. In an era of slow communication and difficult transportation, political impulses diffused more quickly than in the age of CNN and easy air travel. Although the web of networks, including transnational political organizations, was incomparably denser in the twentieth century than in the nineteenth, challenges to established regimes spread with greater velocity in the latter. Surprisingly, globalization and the processes underlying it did not speed up the diffusion of regime contention. In sum, network approaches and modernization arguments cannot account for the historical trends in diffusion patterns.

Observable implications of network approaches about the main agents of diffusion are not consistently borne out either. According to these theories, the internationally most connected actors should spearhead emulation efforts. In fact, intellectuals and students, who are particularly attuned to novelty and curious about foreign developments, spearheaded the wave of 1848, which some scholars call "the revolution of the intellectuals" (Namier 1992).[1] But in 1917–19, leadership fell to professional politicians, especially party and union leaders, who did not have direct bonds to the protagonists of the triggering events, such as the Russian Bolshevists. For instance, the German Social Democrats, who took over the lead in the revolution of November 1918, were distant from and hostile to Lenin and his comrades, but the Russian October Revolution nevertheless helped induce them to push for their country's full democratization. Although the world had shrunk considerably during the intervening decades, the protagonists in 1917–19 had looser contacts to other polities than did their

---

[1] As discussed in Chapter 4, however, this label is inaccurate because broad cross-sections of people, such as artisans, workers, shopkeepers, professionals, housewives, and youths, participated on the frontlines of regime contention in 1848.

counterparts in 1848.[2] Network features do not explain the characteristics of diffusion across the various waves investigated in this book.

Can the modernization theories that inspire network approaches make sense of the historical increase in the success of democratic diffusion? Controversy continues to rage over this issue (Przeworski et al. 2000: 78–106; Boix and Stokes 2003; Doorenspleet 2004: 327–28; Epstein et al. 2006). While socioeconomic development significantly enhances the consolidation and survival of new democracies, recent statistical analyses suggest that its impact on the initial installation of democracy is much less clear (Teorell 2010: 5, 10–11, 57–58, 76; Mainwaring and Pérez-Liñán forthcoming: ch. 4). Given that the present investigation focuses on democratic transition rather than consolidation, the contribution of modernization theory is questionable. In sum, this line of reasoning has great difficulty accounting for the negative correlation between the speed and success of contentious diffusion.

The Rise of Nationalism: Greater Distance between Countries

Network approaches see an ever smaller world as better communication and transportation shrink effective distances among political units. Arguments about nationalism suggest the opposite: Political and cultural gulfs deepened as each nation became its people's primary anchor of identity and loyalty. Network approaches reflect the Enlightenment hope that universalistic reason, embodied in science and technical progress, brings the world together. Nationalism, by contrast, rests on the Romantic-era idea that historical-cultural particularities set different organic units apart. According to this inward-looking perspective, people's proper referent is their own nation. Therefore, they should question the applicability of external experiences and models and be averse to foreign imports.

In this view, rising nationalism posed increasing barriers to the diffusion of regime contention. For instance, nationalism fed the idea of a German *Sonderweg*, a special trajectory that diverged from materialistic Western civilization, embraced nobility, hierarchy, and order, and therefore rejected the plebeian chaos of democracy (Winkler 2000). Similarly, Slavophiles rejected Westernization in Russia. These particularistic ideas immunized nations against external influences and created intellectual and political closure.[3] In fact, emergent nationalism cut connections through which contention had diffused before. In the late eighteenth century, many foreigners, such as the French Marquis de Lafayette, the Prussian General von Steuben, and the Polish Colonel Kościuszko, fought in George Washington's ramshackle army of patriots; a few years later, both Lafayette and Kościuszko led uprisings in their

---

[2] This point is emphasized by Geyer (2010: 218–19).
[3] Smith 1993: 76–77; cf. Brubaker 1992. Marx (2003) also emphasizes the "exclusionary origins of nationalism."

home countries, and Lafayette continued to apply his American experiences to revolutionary causes in Europe throughout his lifetime (Kramer 1996: 102–9, 227–73; Markoff 1996: 26). Moreover, transnational connections among political exiles and secret societies of revolutionaries flourished from 1815 to the mid-1830s (Isabella 2009: ch. 1–2). But in the course of the nineteenth century, such wide-ranging linkages, border-crossing participation in regime contention, and personal borrowing from other countries' experiences became ever less common; intensifying nationalist loyalties precluded this footloose contention from the demand and supply side.

Arguments about nationalism, which gathered strength starting in the early nineteenth century, claim that immunity against foreign contagion grew over time. They therefore predict a steady slowdown in diffusion and a concomitant diminution of success. But this expectation of parallel trends diverges from the negative correlation between diffusion's speed and success highlighted in the introduction. In particular, over the last two centuries external impulses became more – not less – effective in spurring domestic transformations. Although nationalism intensified and found stronger adherence, political actors ended up replicating foreign precedents more. Despite the deepening divergence in popular loyalties and the emergence of hostility between countries, there was a tendency toward convergence in political regime type.

Arguments about nationalism do not only have difficulty accounting for changes in diffusion's success, but also in its speed. The single most dramatic wave of regime contention occurred in 1848, when nationalism was already intense. Although a crisis over the Rhine border in 1840 had inflamed German hostility toward France, for instance, just a few years later many Germans looked at France as a model of how to challenge repressive governments. Thus, despite the consolidation of national identities that began with the Napoleonic Wars, diffusion actually gained speed during these decades. The biggest deceleration occurred in the late nineteenth century, when nationalism continued its advance but did not achieve any qualitative breakthrough. In sum, the rise of nationalism cannot account for the inverse trends in the spread of political regime contention.

A closer look at the complex, multifaceted events of 1848 confirms that rising nationalism did not impede diffusion but was part and parcel of it. In Germany, Italy, and Hungary, national independence and unity were integral components of rebels' demands, together with political participation and liberalization as instituted in Belgium, Britain, and France. Political actors did not see the contradiction between nationalism and Western liberalism, between inward-looking self-discovery and openness to external influences that arguments on nationalism postulate.[4] Some Germans felt embarrassed that they again followed a French precedent, rather than acting on their own initiative (Varnhagen 1862: 264–70; Bayer 1948: 35–36) – but they did follow: Growing national pride did not block contagion from France.

---

[4] That nationalism not only foreclosed some types of linkages among polities, but also led to the establishment of others is examined on a global scale in Bayly (2004: ch. 6).

For these reasons, arguments about nationalism cannot explain the changing characteristics in the diffusion of regime conflict. As demonstrated so far, neither shrinking distances nor increasing barriers among countries account for the slowdown and increasing success of contentious waves; they cannot explain the negative correlation examined in this book.

World System Theory and Constructivism: The Power of External Impulses

Whereas network approaches and theories of nationalism emphasize common features of the international system, world system theory and constructivism stress qualitative differences between more powerful and advanced countries versus weak and backward nations. In this view, diffusion flows from the center to the periphery. The center promotes its innovations with material or ideational influence; countries outside the center, especially in the periphery, cede to this pressure or find the center's models attractive as instruments or symbols of modernity and progress (Huntington 1982; Meyer et al. 1997; Finnemore and Sikkink 2001; Gunitskiy 2010; Levitsky and Way 2010; Owen 2010; Torfason and Ingram 2010: 355–60; Narizny 2012). Because diffusion is conceptualized as a downward flow of impulses and models in a regional or global hierarchy, it has a strong vertical component and clear directionality.

Accordingly, the speed and success of diffusion depend on the point of origin: The center's innovations unleash more dramatic and effective waves of emulation than experiments in less influential, advanced, and prestigious countries, such as the semi-periphery. Patterns of diffusion should also vary with the concentration of hard and soft power in various regions or the world system as a whole. Hegemony gives rise to quick, powerful tsunamis, whereas multipolarity and balance produce modest tides of limited impact.

The waves of 1830 and 1848 indeed started in the most powerful and prestigious center country of that era, France, whereas the Russian revolutions of 1917 and the initial transitions of the third wave occurred at intermediate rungs in the world system: Tsarist Russia was a great power militarily but underdeveloped and backward in socioeconomic, political, and cultural terms; and Portugal, Greece, and Spain in the 1970s were semi-peripheral. But interestingly, France had limited direct influence over the rest of Europe, where four other great powers guaranteed a balance. After 1815, France did not command hegemony; and in 1830 and 1848, it did not use its power to promote the spread of regime contention (as it had done in the 1790s and early 1800s). Thus, French influence did not drive the explosive wave of 1848. It is even less plausible to attribute the relative success of the 1918–19 revolutions to Russian prowess; the country was racked by defeat in war, violent revolution, and secessionist movements and had no capacity to project power at that moment. For instance, Lenin and Trotsky were unable to support the struggling revolutionary government of fleetingly communist Hungary, which fell to foreign intervention.

By contrast, the United States commanded a great deal of hard and soft power over Latin America during the 1970s and 1980s; for instance, it had tremendous economic clout and longstanding connections to ruling militaries. When presidents Jimmy Carter and Ronald Reagan (the latter during his second term) embraced the promotion of democracy, world system and constructivist approaches anticipated a fairly quick transformation of the United States' "back yard." But despite President Carter's use of moral suasion and sanctions and President Reagan's later resumption of these pressures, serious challenges to dictators and actual transitions were years in coming. While the change in U.S. policy orientation clearly weakened authoritarian rulers and helped to sap their resolve, these effects were much weaker than world system theory and constructivist approaches would expect. In particular, if these approaches argue that France's mere prestige set in motion tsunamis among fellow European countries in 1830 and 1848, how can they account for the surprisingly slow and halting advance of the third wave of democratization in "peripheral" Latin America, right in the shadow of the "hovering giant" (cf. Blasier 1985) and within reach of the "talons of the eagle" (Smith 2008)?

In a more general perspective, world system theory and constructivism suggest a secular increase in diffusion's speed as political liberalism and democracy advanced over the last two centuries at the global level. Open struggles over political regime type started in the North Atlantic region, where countries had relatively equal status and were not tied into direct center–periphery relations. After Western Europe gradually established and consolidated democracy, the frontier of political regime contention moved east and south toward the periphery, including the former colonies of Latin America. As democratization moved down the global hierarchy, the developmental gradient between forerunners and promoters, on the one hand, and potential emulators, on the other, turned steeper.[5] If the postulate of a vertical flow were correct, the diffusion of political regime contention should therefore gather greater speed; the remaining holdouts would face increasing political, economic, symbolic, or moral pressure to fall in line with regional or global trends. But the secular slowdown of diffusion in Europe and Latin

---

[5] An alternative argument derived from world system theory and constructivism could highlight different waves' point of origin and claim that a precedent occurring in a core country has a more powerful impact than a similar event in the semi-periphery and periphery. But one of the few extant comparisons of different diffusion waves stresses that the Bismarckian social security system spread much more slowly from late-nineteenth-century Germany, by then a core country, than Chilean pension privatization diffused in the 1980s and 1990s; this semi-peripheral innovation spread significantly faster, even across world regions, especially from Latin America to Eastern Europe (Orenstein 2003). Other semi-peripheral innovations, such as the participatory budgeting initiated in the city of Porto Alegre, Brazil, have also spread to the core with surprising speed, stimulating a large number of replication efforts in Europe and North America (Sintomer, Herzberg, and Röcke 2008).

America falsifies this expectation and casts doubt on world system theories and constructivist perspectives.

Constructivism, specifically, does not fully capture the success of emulation efforts either. This approach conceptualizes diffusion as the spread of moral norms or ideational blueprints; it assumes that emulators replicate the original innovation in its substantive content. In this view, diffusion by definition produces convergence. But as explained in the introduction's definition of diffusion, the waves of political regime contention investigated in this book saw many instances of preemptive reform. That is, powerful actors on a number of occasions managed to forestall the full replication of a precedent by enacting a less profound reform. By making partial concessions, they erected a bulwark that took the wind out of the sail of demands to imitate the original experience. For instance, social-democratic leaders at the end of World War I in Germany tried by all means to sideline radical efforts to engineer a council system à la Bolshevist Russia; instead they pushed very hard for popular elections to a constituent assembly that would institute representative democracy. Similarly, a majority of European revolutionaries in 1848 embraced political liberalism and constitutional monarchy to avoid the proclamation of a republic and subsequent radicalization that had occurred in Paris, although it was the regime collapse in France that provided them with the impulse for challenging their own governments. Ironically, the downfall of a liberal, constitutional monarchy in France induced many emulators to push for precisely such a liberal, constitutional monarchy in their own countries! Thus, the Parisian events inspired them to act – but to act differently from the Parisian protagonists. Constructivism, which identifies diffusion with imitation and expects the spread of sameness, overlooks this striking disjuncture.

Certainly, however, international prestige and influence did affect the spread of regime contention. These factors made some countries' experiences and accomplishments more salient and appealing than those of others. Furthermore, developmental gradients created pressures for moving in the same direction as frontrunner countries. Most importantly, prevailing ideas and norms gave diffusion waves their broad direction. Above all, they explain why, during the long nineteenth century, these processes brought advances toward political liberalism and democracy, whereas in the interwar years, authoritarianism, corporatism, and fascism exerted a strong pull. Thus, world system theories and constructivism certainly help to explain significant elements of the diffusion of political regime contention.

But these lines of reasoning are of little help for understanding the important features of diffusion examined in the present book. For the reasons mentioned, world system and constructivist arguments cannot fully account for the changing speed and success rate across different waves of political regime contention. Above all, they do not foresee the negative correlation between these two trends.

Rational Learning: Autonomous Initiative of Domestic Emulators

Whereas world system arguments stress the proactive force of external impulses and depict the emulating units as reactive, learning theories advance the opposite view and attribute the main initiative to the emulators. In the prototypical version, learning proceeds rationally and is guided by the self interest of importing actors: They follow foreign impulses if cost/benefit analyses yield a positive balance.[6] As recipients make these evaluations in a rational fashion, their autonomous needs – not pressures from powerful countries – drive the spread of innovations. Emulators are in control and are driven in their replication decisions by self-regarding motives.

Rational learning suggests that emulation efforts, like other types of political action, are guided by assessments of the pertinent opportunities and risks. Actors will go ahead when benefits are likely to outweigh costs. This line of reasoning yields a prediction about the speed of democratic diffusion: People will act quickly when political regime contention looks particularly promising (cf. Weede and Muller 1998: 45); yet when in doubt, they will prudently wait for a better chance. Assuming that actors have a reasonable grasp of the actual constellation of power and can reliably ascertain their chances of success, rational learning suggests a positive correlation between diffusion's speed and success: People will act rapidly when their chances of goal attainment are particularly high; when they do not face a good opportunity, they will wait until chances improve. Rational choice certainly does not foresee a negative correlation between speed and success: Why would rational individuals rush into contentious challenges when failure is likely? Strict versions of rational learning that assume people have good information about the objective situation (e.g., Meseguer 2009) therefore cannot account for the negative correlation between diffusion's speed and success.[7]

Less stringent variants of rational choice recognize, however, that actors may not have a firm grasp of objective circumstances, especially the opportunities and risks of political regime contention. In the real world, cost/benefit calculations must rely on imperfect information, especially because challenges to established authorities face great uncertainty. The effective strength of the incumbent regime is unclear; it depends on backing from police and military and the ruler's own determination and skill in exercising power, which are difficult to gauge, especially in repressive nondemocracies (cf. Wintrobe

---

[6] For the sake of theoretical clarity, this book conceptualizes rational learning as the deductive approach derived from a few fundamental postulates about instrumental rationality (particularly well-explained in Tsebelis 1990: ch. 2); by contrast, empirical findings about people's actual patterns of cognition and decision-making give rise to the theories of bounded rationality discussed in subsequent sections of this chapter (see Thaler 2000).

[7] In their rationalist model of the likelihood of popular rebellion, Bhavnani and Ross (2003: 362–63) find that "repressive governments ... should be able to deter rebellion." Since this conclusion underpredicts rebellions, they are compelled to resort to "mistakes" to account for actual outcomes.

2007: 365–67). The breadth, intensity, and cohesion of the opposition are also shrouded in uncertainty due to prudent preference falsification (Kuran 1995) and the difficulty of overcoming collective action problems. To maximize their interests despite this fog, rational actors search for useful information and learn from developments occurring in other, similar countries and from the earlier experiences of their own nation. Accordingly, a successful change abroad can suggest that the time is ripe for undertaking a similar effort at home[8]; a failed attempt, by contrast, counsels caution.

This softer version of rational choice seems to offer a more promising explanation for the secular slowdown yet increased success of the diffusion of political regime contention. Given the limited achievements of the early revolutionary waves, rational learning over time prompted greater caution. Opponents of established regimes noticed that it was unrealistic to emulate external precedents immediately. Rather than rushing into action, they learned how to wait for a good opportunity to attain their goals. With this line of reasoning, rational choice accounts for the overall trends in the spread of democratizing impulses, including the negative correlation between speed and success.

But a closer look at specific waves and especially at the process of decision-making casts doubt on this learning theory as well, which presupposes only "weak requirements of rationality" (Tsebelis 1990: 24–31). In particular, emulative contention in 1848 arose from the third French Revolution; 1789 and 1830 had also triggered contagion. But these earlier rounds of challenges had yielded only temporary or limited success, at considerable cost. By 1848, the great risks and low promise of defying repressive governments had certainly become clear. Any careful cost/benefit analysis would have counseled prudence. How can rational choice then explain the striking velocity of contention's spread in 1848? Why did so many people disregard the obvious lessons of 1789 and 1830 and jeopardize their lives by protesting right after hearing about Louis Philippe's downfall? Following upon two not very successful waves of revolution, the rush to the barricades in 1848 diverged from rational maxims.

Instead, oppositionists in 1848 should have initiated challenges only where careful assessments found propitious conditions. But they did exactly the opposite: The news from Paris triggered spontaneous protests in a wide variety of settings, even under highly unpromising circumstances, as in the backward, repressive Danubian principalities of Moldavia and Walachia. Overenthusiastic masses threw rational caution to the wind; careful, thorough calculations, which the high stakes of regime contention made imperative, were conspicuous by their absence (Weyland 2009). Due to this puzzling rashness, the 1848

[8] A rationalist approach has special plausibility for the study of contention's spread inside a single country, as in Beissinger (2002): A government's response to one challenge provides a good indication of its likely response to other challenges.

wave swept across Europe quite indiscriminately. Emulation efforts did not occur selectively, as rational assessments would have counseled.

The content of lesson-drawing in 1848 does not suggest rational choice either. Paradoxically, the majority of challengers across Europe pushed precisely for the regime type that had just collapsed in France, namely a constitutional monarchy. In some sense, hard-core reactionaries, such as Austria's Clemens Metternich; the Prussian king's brother, Prince Wilhelm; and Russian tsar Nicholas drew a more logical inference from the overthrow of France's "citizen king," namely that this mixed system was inherently unviable and unsustainable (Varnhagen 1862: 261; Metternich 1883: 565–66, 592–93, 627; Haenchen 1930: 34; see Ruttmann 2001: 177–80). As liberal reformers felt inspired by Louis Philippe's downfall to institute the regime type that he had embodied, they relied on a rather twisted kind of reasoning – and the resulting wave of rebellions indeed ended largely in failure.

Most importantly, the process of actors' decision-making diverged starkly from the rules of rational learning. Especially in 1848, actors on both sides of the barricades did not base their choices on thorough, systematic assessments of opportunities and risks. The challengers, in particular, imprudently incurred tremendous risks by initiating and joining protests against regimes that had commonly applied brutal force. As Chapter 4 shows, careful deliberations were conspicuous by their absence. Instead, the news of Louis Philippe's overthrow quickly filled many oppositionists with optimism and enthusiasm; they jumped to the conclusion that they could accomplish a similar feat. The prevailing mood during this "springtime of the peoples" was not one of prudent calculation but of rash inferences that inspired excessively high hopes. In sum, the way people made their choices could not have been farther from the postulates of full rationality.

For all of these reasons, rational choice does not offer a convincing explanation of the processes and patterns of diffusion examined in this book. There is some indication that learning across waves played a role in the slowdown and increasing success of diffusion, but this learning does not look all that rational. In particular, the inferences drawn from the precedent events diverged from the norms of rationality. How can one square these diverse elements?

A NEW EXPLANATION: COGNITIVE HEURISTICS AMID ORGANIZATIONAL DEVELOPMENTS

Given the analytical insufficiency of extant explanations, this study proposes an alternative that rests on cognitive-psychological micro-foundations and highlights organizational macro-processes as the main cause of the changing features of democratization waves. Adding to earlier efforts to draw on bounded rationality (Simon 1955; Lindblom 1965; March and Simon 1993; McDermott 1998, 2004; Jones 2001; Jones and Baumgartner 2005; Weyland 2007; Bendor 2010), this book emphasizes how the emergence and spread of political organizations reshaped the operation and impact of cognitive mechanisms. In this way, it goes beyond a simple import of psychological findings, which focus on individual perceptions and choices, and elucidates collective action and strategic interaction, which are decisive for politics. After the following section establishes the micro-foundation of this theory, the subsequent sections explain the principal components of my macro-organizational arguments.

Bounded Rationality: Interaction of External Impulses and Domestic Emulators

As demonstrated in the preceding sections, neither world system theory and constructivism nor rational learning fully elucidates the diffusion of political regime contention. Promotion by the center and the initiative of emulators in the periphery are not alone decisive. The momentum of the external stimulus and the interests of the emulators do not determine diffusion on their own. Instead, they operate interactively. This book therefore proposes an approach that combines the appeal of the original model and the quest of the imitators: Recipients pursue their own interests in learning from external inputs, but their information processing is molded and distorted by the magnetism of foreign precedents.

Bounded rationality theoretically accounts for this interaction. This approach diverges from rational choice by highlighting the distortionary attraction and influence of the object of learning, and it differs from world system theory and constructivism by attributing initiative to the subjects of learning. The bounds of rationality mediate between these two poles. Specifically, foreign innovations can grab people's attention in recipient countries rather than being proactively sought out. Yet at the same time, the new model does not impose itself automatically; potential emulators assess it in light of their own interests. This assessment is distorted by characteristics of the model, however, and does not arise from recipients' interest calculations alone.

Bounded rationality rests on the solid empirical findings of cognitive psychology about actual human decision-making, not the ideal-typical postulates of rational choice. It highlights people's limited capacity to cope with overabundant information, especially under uncertainty and time pressure.[9] Since normal mortals cannot perform the comprehensive, systematic information processing prescribed by rational choice, they rely on inferential shortcuts to arrive at decisions and thus operate in fluid environments. But these shortcuts focus attention on some aspects while filtering out others, and they draw conclusions in simple and quick, yet not fully logical ways; therefore, they create the risk of distortions and biases. While these heuristics allow people to react to decisional opportunities and challenges and avoid overload and paralysis,

---

[9] These problems affect even business managers, who face strong performance incentives (Mezias and Starbuck 2008).

they can easily lead to mistakes and failures, especially in complex, rapidly shifting situations.

Reliance on cognitive shortcuts is especially pronounced under conditions of profound uncertainty – when established institutions, expectations, and calculations have lost their guiding force, when people face unexpected novelty and unpredictability, and when outcomes seem up for grabs. Waves of political regime contention can trigger such "eventful" situations (Sewell 2005) and constitute critical junctures, characterized by considerable contingency (Capoccia and Kelemen 2007; Soifer 2012). As preexisting decision rules fail to provide valid orientation, actors have to make up their minds from scratch, considering a multitude of fluid developments in their complex interaction. Under these confusing, if not chaotic circumstances, when the whole political ground is shaking and the passage of time seems to speed up enormously (cf. Becker 1999: 265–77, 289–90, 355), people are especially eager to resort to the crutches of cognitive shortcuts in a desperate effort to get a minimal grip. Time pressures preclude the gathering of solid information and deliberate decision-making; participants are flooded with contradictory news about fast-changing events (cf. Langewiesche 1998: 24–25) and lack the opportunity to ascertain its reliability. To navigate these unbounded situations, people feel compelled to draw on the mechanisms of bounded rationality.

Cognitive psychologists highlight two shortcuts, the heuristics of availability and representativeness (Kahneman, Slovic, and Tversky 1982; Gilovich, Griffin, and Kahneman 2002; Hastie and Dawes 2010: ch. 5). The availability heuristic shapes attention and memory recall and skews people's information intake and probability estimates. In a nutshell, drastic, vivid, directly witnessed events make a disproportionate impression on people's mind; by contrast, less stunning though equally or more relevant information is neglected. As people give disproportionate weight to striking appearance relative to actual importance, they deviate from rational calculations. Dramatic events have an excessive impact on people's perceptions and thinking, leading to an overestimation of their likelihood. After 9/11, for instance, many Americans avoided plane rides and went by car although that was much more dangerous; scholars estimate that 1,500 people died as a result (Gigerenzer 2006). In a similar vein, automobile drivers commonly slow down after seeing a car crash – although a single accident should not alter their cost-benefit calculations about speeding. But the shocking view overpowers systematic, rational considerations. It captures observers' attention and distorts their judgments; the object of learning shapes the subject's information processing.

The representativeness heuristic also causes deviations from rational judgments by basing inferences on apparent, even superficial similarities while disregarding relevant information, such as statistical base rates. One aspect of this multifaceted heuristic is that people have a tendency to draw excessively firm conclusions from limited data; they improperly assume that patterns found in small samples are representative of the whole population. Accordingly, an early stretch of success can imbue an innovation with the aura of inherent quality and make it look unusually attractive to a wide range of actors; a fully rational evaluation, by contrast, would consider the possibility that accidental factors contributed to the strong initial performance, which might soon give way to regression toward the mean. But the representativeness heuristic induces people to be overly impressed by a short run of data and to jump to conclusions about its significance. Once again, features of the object of learning distort the subject's inferences; the external stimulus influences its own reception in the interactive manner discussed at the beginning of this section.

The representativeness heuristic also leads observers to overrate the similarities between the forerunner and the situation that they themselves confront, and to underestimate the differences and their significance. These facile judgments make domestic circumstances appear similar to those that allowed for the precursor's original success. Accordingly, actors jump to the conclusion that the conditions for replication are given in their own country. They come to believe that their established regime is also weak; that internal discontent is widespread and intense; and that potential challengers are willing and able to mobilize collectively and to defy the forces of organized coercion. In other words, people in a variety of countries see the precedent as representative of the political situations they are facing, discounting important differences that a fully rational assessment would seriously consider.

Bounded rationality helps explain the observed patterns of innovations' spread. Due to the heuristics of availability and representativeness, a striking, impressive success has a disproportionate effect and grabs people's attention in other countries as well; and facile judgments of similarity fuel much stronger contagion than cautious rational learning justifies. As a result of these shortcuts, a dramatic precedent inspires the belief that challengers in a wide range of countries can achieve a similar feat, thus reshaping people's assessments of the feasibility and promise of confronting their own governments. Conversely, an unpromising rebellion that ends in catastrophic failure, such as the ill-fated Paris Commune of 1871, sends the opposite message (cf. Engels 1895: 17; Kautsky 1914: 285–87); interpreted via the representativeness heuristic, such failure discourages defiance elsewhere.

The mechanisms of bounded rationality, especially the heuristics of availability and representativeness, can thus explain tsunamis of diffusion that sweep with stunning speed beyond the limited range of similar political-institutional settings. They are crucial for understanding the wave of 1848, when the downfall of Louis Philippe triggered a plethora of immediate emulation efforts all over Europe. But because cognitive shortcuts inspire rash, ill-considered challenges of established regimes, aborted efforts and failures abound. Under the influence of the availability and representativeness heuristics, people rush into emulation efforts, often under distinctly unpropitious conditions. Therefore, many incumbents manage to suppress these protests and defeat uprisings. Cognitive heuristics thus elucidate the negative correlation between speed and success in the diffusion of regime contention, most striking in the aborted revolutions of 1848, when exalted initial hopes gave way to deep frustration and disappointment (Weyland 2009).

Insights on bounded rationality also capture people's decision-making process much better than alternative approaches, especially rational learning. As the wealth of primary documents show, participants in political regime contention commonly diverged from the rules of logic in defining their choices on this high-stakes issue. Given the tremendous danger of joining protests against repressive regimes, comprehensive rationality would counsel careful deliberation, a systematic evaluation of opportunities and risks, and an overall preference for caution. But thorough assessments of benefits and costs were conspicuous by their absence. People did not wait for solid information, but rushed into action on the basis of unfounded rumors.[10] Swept along by rash inferences that stimulated high levels of enthusiasm, critical masses of people threw caution to the wind.

The common resort to cognitive heuristics can also explain the outburst of emotions that characterized these "interesting times." As many participants and eyewitnesses of the 1848 wave noted (Varnhagen 1862: 211–16; Wolff 1898: 5, 21; Boerner 1920: 73–83; Schurz 1988: 100–01), news about the downfall of a seemingly powerful regime in another country often stimulates upsurges of strong feelings, such as wild enthusiasm and humanity-embracing joy. While these sentiments can threaten to overpower any semblance of rationality, they arise from the shortcuts of bounded rationality: They are unleashed when a foreign precedent suggests the rash inference that the domestic authorities are surprisingly weak as well and that the long-awaited chance for effecting a political transformation has finally arrived. As people jump to conclusions, they suddenly believe in unlimited political opportunities in their own country. This belief, produced by cognitive shortcuts, inspires tremendous excitement.[11]

As inferential heuristics explain the dramatic speed yet limited success of the spread of political regime contention in 1830 and 1848, what then accounts for diffusion's deceleration thereafter, as evident in the slower ripples emanating from the Russian revolutions of 1917 and in the unhurried advance of the third wave of democratization? Why did external triggers not induce twentieth-century oppositionists to jump on the bandwagon as quickly and unthinkingly as their forefathers had done? Why was nineteenth-century rashness followed by greater circumspection thereafter?

---

[10] Rudé 2005: 257. Traugott (2010: 193–95) argues that potential insurgents calculated the chances of success rather carefully and acted accordingly. But several episodes that he examines show, on the contrary, that "revolutionary zeal prevented [protesters] from heeding [a notable's] call for caution" and that another leader's cautious and prudent "opinion was ignored by the men in his company [and] he relented rather than break ranks with his men" (Traugott 2010: 194 and 195, respectively).

[11] Thus, emotions are not underlying causes, but intervening variables – contrary to Pearlman's (2013) interpretation of the Arab Spring.

Organizational Developments and Their Impact
on the Bounds of Rationality

As its main contribution to theory building, this book argues that organizational developments reshape the processing of political information and mediate the impact of cognitive mechanisms on political decision-making, which is a collective process. Cognitive psychology elucidates individual perception, inference, and choice, but political contention involves collective action and is therefore affected by organizational structures. The secular development of political organizations over the course of the last two centuries transformed the operation of cognitive heuristics and their repercussions for political decision-making in several ways, which the following sections explain. First, the very emergence of collective organizations profoundly reshaped the reception side of political diffusion, slowing down the advance of contentious impulses and giving them a higher rate of success.

By the nineteenth century, modernization and industrialization had produced masses of urban dwellers that were available for regime-challenging mobilization, and the rise of the territorial state had created an institutional arena for such contention (Tarrow 2011: ch. 4; Keane 2009: 459–62). But organizations that encompassed these people, especially above the local level, were incipient and inchoate in Central and Eastern Europe. Therefore, the decision whether to emulate external precedents and join protest and rebellion fell to individuals, who had only their friends, families, and other small, often informal networks to consult. These people had sparse, tenuous access to information, limited processing capacity, and minimal experience in political decision-making.[12] As a result, they were especially prone to rely on cognitive shortcuts and, defenseless against the resulting inferences, they tended to jump to conclusions without thorough, systematic deliberation, disregarding caution and rushing into action. Therefore, there was a strong chance that a stunning external precedent would induce a critical mass of people to engage in spontaneous emulation – and that many of these rash efforts would fail.

Specifically, a foreign success processed via the representativeness heuristic made opponents believe that their incumbent regime was also brittle and that discontented people would eagerly join challenges, just as in the frontrunner country. This overoptimistic updating of preferences drove more and more citizens of all walks of life into the streets. Because not only notorious "troublemakers" such as students (Huntington 1968: 369–74) protested, but also a cross-section of the population including shopkeepers, notables, artisans, professionals, workers, and even women and children, belief in the breadth and depth of discontent and in challengers' determination to withstand repression spread. Seeing the rapidly growing crowds, initially hesitant people came to

---

[12] To the present day, levels of knowledge among the mass public have remained strikingly low (e.g., Somin 2006), despite the much improved availability of information.

share this belief and decided to participate as well. A cascade of contention erupted, unleashed and propelled by cognitive shortcuts (cf. Kuran 1995: 74, 158–66, 180, 258; Kuran and Sunstein 1999). Thus, in inchoate societies, striking external precedents processed via inferential heuristics inspired critical masses of people to contest their rulers. By instilling excessive hope in the success of challenges, cognitive shortcuts helped to overcome collective action problems and to spark spontaneous collective action despite the absence of national-level organizations.

Yet when broad-based organizations arose, these unplanned outbursts of regime contention were replaced by more deliberate, targeted challenges, initiated and commanded by organizational leaders. In the second half of the nineteenth century, a momentous process of organization-building began, especially among poorer and middling sectors that sought sociopolitical inclusion (Tilly et al. 1975: 192–97, 212, 227, 237, 254). Social-democratic parties and unions came to envelop millions of workers in firm organizational structures and encompassing subcultures (Bartolini 2000; Eley 2002: ch. 1–2, 4). Catholic parties soon followed suit, and secular parties on the right and center eventually emerged as well. Employee and professional associations also grew to large scales. Common people now had leaders to follow, who guided and controlled collective mobilization and spearheaded regime contention.[13]

Whereas in the inchoate polities of the mid-nineteenth century, common people on their own had decided whether to challenge the established authorities, starting in the late nineteenth century, more and more people took cues and guidance from their leaders (cf. Popkin 1991; Lupia and McCubbins 1998; Ahlquist and Levi 2011). These organizational officials could draw on substantial access to information, experience in political calculation and decision-making, and contacts to other organizational leaders and the established authorities. Therefore, they had a much better grasp of the constellation of power and the prevailing opportunities and risks for forcing political change. Because organization leaders had a larger stock of knowledge (stronger "priors") and a greater capacity for obtaining and processing relevant news, their inferences and judgments were less profoundly shaped – and distorted – by cognitive shortcuts (cf. Jones 2001: 23, 82, 131; Mintz 2004). They better understood the depth and breadth of discontent with current rulers; the power capabilities, collective strength, and determination of the opposition; and the likely reactions of the government. This knowledge base, which was much more solid than what common people could muster (Simon 1976: 136–39, 166–68; Bendor 2010: 163–77), anchored leaders' judgments and left less room for cognitive heuristics. Because organizational leaders faced lower uncertainty and suffered from less "confusion" (Kurzman 2004), they relied less on inferential shortcuts. Standing on firmer ground, they did not grasp as much at straws (cf. Mintz 2004).

---

[13] For an interesting formal model on "the leader as catalyst," see Majumdar and Mukand (2010).

In general, bounded rationality is not invariant and uniform, but comprises a range of inferential patterns that deviate to different degrees from the strict standards of full rationality (cf. Forester 1984). While cognitive psychologists find individual variation, the aggregation of individual judgments in collective decision-making introduces further, even more pronounced differences. Organizational structures can enhance information-processing in several ways (Simon 1976: 41, 100–03, 240–41; Sah 1991: 70–71, 80–81, 86; Jones 2001: 23, 82, 131; Bendor 2010: 165–69; Secchi 2010: ch. 7–9). Although these insights emerge mainly from the study of bureaucracies and business firms (Landau 1969; Stinchcombe 1990; Sah 1991; Koh 1992; Heimann 1995; recent overview in Hodgkinson and Starbuck 2008b), several points are transferable to political organizations as well.

The division of labor gives organizations a much wider scope of attention than individuals (March and Simon 1993: 173; Bendor 2010: 165–66). Focusing on different aspects of the environment, subunits compose a more comprehensive picture of the setting (Simon 1976: 102, 166–69; Jones 2001: 133–35, 148–49, 159). Political parties, for instance, often have sections that deal with specific policy spheres, constituencies, or territorial areas. By extending and coordinating their information intake, organizations are therefore less at risk of neglecting relevant facts than ordinary people applying the availability heuristic. Specialization also allows for and breeds organizational competencies (Ansell 2011: 77–81) and technical expertise (Simon 1976: 136–38; Rosen et al. 2008), which lead organizational officers to question the superficial similarities highlighted by the representativeness heuristic and to consider relevant differences. While specialized knowledge is more essential for firms and bureaus, political organizations have also recruited and relied on experts, such as people trained in specific policy areas or pollsters and campaign consultants.

These organizational competencies and technical expertise, and the resulting broader, more systematic information processing help especially organizational leaders. These top officers also have a good deal of experience and considerable political skill, which make them less susceptible to the distortions caused by cognitive shortcuts (Hafner-Burton, Hughes, and Victor 2013) and allow them to better understand power constellations and identify promising conjunctures. These capacities, attested by a relatively high education level, for instance, are products of political recruitment (Schwartz 1969: 556, 568–69; Almond and Powell 1978: 123–40; Aberbach, Putnam, and Rockman 1981). The more solid the organization, the longer it takes ambitious aspirants to rise through the ranks, which increases future leaders' opportunities for learning and the organization's chance of identifying and eliminating unpromising candidates; German Social Democracy, for instance, tested its officers through a long sequence of positions. To pass these hurdles, candidates had to prove nimble and well-grounded, reasonably prudent and not too rash; intelligence and practical reason helped (see in general Mumford et al. 2007: 516–19, 537). The officials who managed to move up the ladder acquired a wealth of experience; learning from political advances and setbacks improved their aptitude.[14] For all of these reasons, organizational leaders tended to have a richer stock of knowledge and a greater capacity for calculations than average citizens. While intraorganizational learning and selective promotion in no way guaranteed full rationality, they helped to keep in check the facile inferences suggested by cognitive shortcuts.

These improved mechanisms of information-processing benefit all organizations, albeit to varying degrees. For instance, large size allows for greater specialization, more expertise, and longer testing of and learning by rising leaders. Additional contributions to the quality of information processing and decision-making depend on the type of organization, especially the difference between broad-based, internally diverse, and pluralistic organizations versus narrow, homogeneous, unity-seeking groupings.[15]

On one side of this spectrum, the mass parties and unions that emerged in the late nineteenth century comprised a variety of sectors with diverse political positions. To process the disagreements arising from this pluralism, broad-based organizations instituted mechanisms for internal discussion and deliberation. The reasonably open debates conducted in these fora, which ranged from executive committees to party conventions,[16] helped to weed out biases and mistakes (see in general Fearon 1998: 49–52; Mackie 1998: 79–92; less sanguine Brodbeck et al. 2007, and George and Chattopadhyay 2008: 364–67). Drawing on dissimilar experiences and advancing different interests, participants voiced divergent viewpoints and questioned one another. Therefore, argumentation tended to dig deeper, mitigating the facile inferences suggested by cognitive heuristics (cf. March and Simon 1993: 150–51, 202–3; Mercier and Sperber 2011: 62–63, 72–73; see also Mutz 2002: 116–18). Though limited by conformity pressures and the ideological commitments shared inside the organization, these deliberations allowed organizational leaders to achieve a better understanding of the political constellation.

Procedures for holding leaders accountable and obliging them to explain their decisions and actions further increased the chances for uncovering problematic

---

[14] For a useful general discussion of political learning, see Levy (1994).

[15] See in general Page (2007: ch. 6–8). The performance of organizations that fall in between these two poles depends on their level of diversity vs. homogeneity.

[16] German Social Democracy, for instance, had well-established fora for continuous internal debates about questions of tactics, strategies, and goals (e.g., Kautsky 1914: 127–55; Schönhoven 1985). Thus, contra Michels (1959), the party was actually not run by a unified oligarchy, as the serious conflicts among leaders over the party's role in World War I show, which erupted soon after Michels wrote and which in 1917 provoked the defection of a significant number of party leaders. For a nuanced discussion of Michels' strikingly categorical claims, see Rueschemeyer, Stephens, and Stephens (1992: 55).

judgments. Research shows that such representational mechanisms can lead to decision-making of higher quality.[17] The elected officials of broad-based organizations, whom I call representative leaders,[18] had a special incentive to process information carefully, evaluate the promise and applicability of foreign models, and assess whether the domestic opportunity structure was propitious for their emulation. As a result, they did not rush to replicate external precedents but waited for a good chance to do so successfully.

In contrast to these broad-based, internally pluralistic organizations that loosened the bounds of political rationality, small radical groupings that split off into cohesive, ideologically homogeneous sects were prone to engage in groupthink and suffer from particularly severe distortions in political judgment (Esser 1998; McDermott 2004: 249–55; Bénabou 2010; Schafer and Crichlow 2010; see also Bendor 2010: 179). For instance, proto-communist cells such as the far-left Spartacus Group in Germany in the 1910s, which sought "true unanimity in all decisive questions" (Liebknecht 1974: 697) and were averse to any compromise (Spartakus 1958: 356), were hothouses for cognitive shortcuts. The tendency to delegitimize or purge dissent stifled criticism and debate and gave problematic judgments free rein.

In such sect-like organizations, safeguards against misperceptions and cognitive biases are weak. The quest for homogeneity actually aggravates the tendency toward problematic judgments. For instance, psychological experiments demonstrate that while people generally "prefer supporting to conflicting information when making decisions," "homogeneous groups showed a particularly strong confirmation bias, which was clearly stronger than that of individuals" (Schulz-Hardt et al. 2000: 655, 658). Similarly, the rash inferences suggested by the availability and representativeness heuristics may reinforce each other and exacerbate distortions in judgments. Ideological sects thus operate with bounds on their political rationality that seem even tighter than those of inexperienced mass actors. Consequently, they may "get hooked on" some apparently successful external model and stubbornly pursue its replication against all odds, losing touch with reality, as the dramatic failures of the Spartacus Group in 1919 and of the armed wing of the Chilean Communists in the 1980s suggest (see Chapters 5 and 7, respectively).[19]

---

[17] Tetlock 1985: 314–321; Lerner and Tetlock 1999: 257–59, 262; Ryfe 2005: 57. These benefits depend on leaders not knowing their constituents' position (otherwise leaders opportunistically pander to those views) – a condition that seems fulfilled during uncertain, "confusing" episodes of regime contention.

[18] My concept of representative leadership is very similar to John Higley's definition of elites via "their strategic positions in powerful organizations and movements" (Higley and Burton 2006: 7), and my thinking about the historical emergence of the negotiated transition model (see Chapter 3 below) is influenced by his theoretical and empirical work (especially Higley and Gunther 1992).

[19] The same arguments apply to the guerrilla groupings operating in Latin America during the 1960s, which were inspired by the Cuban Revolution due to its "psychological immediacy and

In conclusion, organizational structures deeply affect the bounds of rationality; above all, internal pluralism and deliberative procedures yield better information-processing and decision-making of higher quality. Political
macro-factors thus shape the operation of cognitive micro-mechanisms.
Divergent from the methodological individualism underlying rational choice,
micro-foundations do not drive and determine macro-structures unidirection-
ally. Instead, macro-structures also mold how micro-mechanisms play out;
for example, organizational accountability affects leaders' judgments (Tetlock
1985: 298–307). The macro and micro levels interact thoroughly.

For these reasons, the speed and success of contentious waves depended
on the principal locus of oppositional decision-making – common people in
an amorphous, inchoate crowd (Rudé 2005) or representative leaders guiding
large numbers of followers. While both commoners and leaders are affected
by cognitive shortcuts, representative leaders are significantly less affected and
deviate less starkly from full rationality. Organizational ties can untie political
judgment and decision-making; as people are bound by broad-based organizations, the bounds of political rationality loosen (though they do not dissolve).
Drawing on their improved information-processing and political strategizing,
representative leaders guide affiliates and sympathizers with higher quality
assessments of external precedents and more promising ideas about applying
these lessons in their own polities. By following the suggestions, pleas, and
commands of their leaders, commoners act in ways that are less affected and
distorted by cognitive shortcuts.

Representative leaders guide organizational members through persuasion,
appeals to loyalty, or authority. Leaders who face accountability seek to explain
and justify their decisions. Followers are receptive to argumentation because
they expect leaders to define organizational strategy with some independence,
rather than mechanically reflecting the views of the bases (Fearon 1999: 60–63).
With their information access and experience, leaders then have a good chance
of convincing members that their course of action was reasonable (cf. Dewan
and Myatt 2008; Dickson forthcoming). When affiliates continue to have
doubts, loyalty induces many to accept and even support their leaders' decisions (Hirschman 1970: ch. 7). Last but not least, representative leaders command some degree of authority (cf. Wilson 1995: ch. 11), even if they owe their
position to competitive, democratic elections; in fact, bottom-up legitimization
can strengthen them. Leaders can use this authority to achieve compliance,
for instance by rewarding supporters and sidelining critics. Drawing on these
forms of influence, representative leaders can usually guide their affiliates and

temporal proximity," reflecting the availability heuristic. And, echoing the representativeness
heuristic, a "Communist party leader ... noted that 'The victory of the Cuban revolution spread
the illusion of a rapid and heroic triumph, leading to mechanical transplants'." (Wickham-
Crowley 1992: 33) On the role of cognitive shortcuts in these disastrous inferences, see
Wickham-Crowley (2012: 13–14).

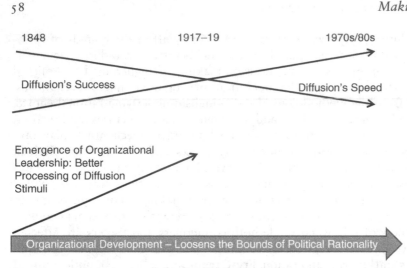

FIGURE 2.2 Organization reshapes diffusion's reception side.

sympathizers and ensure that their higher level of political rationality shapes the contentious actions of large numbers of citizens.

For all of these reasons, the enormous advance of popular organization starting in the late nineteenth century, exemplified by the growth of the social-democratic labor movement (Bartolini 2000; Eley 2002), underlies the notable deceleration in the diffusion of regime contention. The leaders of broad-based organizations have firmer ground under their feet than ordinary citizens as well as radical sects, who get carried away by waves of protest and surf them eagerly. Representative leaders, by contrast, have a better grasp of chances and risks and proceed with more realism; they do not act before a good opportunity for emulating an external precedent seems to arise. In the era of mass organization, regime contention therefore spreads more slowly but with a higher likelihood of success. As Chapter 5 below shows, this argument can account for the historical record of democratic contention in the twentieth century: Representative leaders tamed the mass impulses triggered quickly by the Russian revolutions of February and October 1917 and channeled popular pressures toward institutional reforms achieved by nonviolent means and legitimized by elections. This crucial step in my explanation is depicted in Figure 2.2, which highlights how organizational development reshaped the processing of external stimuli, that is, the reception side of diffusion.

Certainly, however, representative leaders are normal mortals and therefore subject to bounded rationality as well. While their decision-making capacity is less limited than that of common citizens and ideological sects, they are also affected by the heuristics of availability and representativeness to some extent. Therefore, they tend to overestimate the ease of following external precedents and act in ways that deviate from the commands of full rationality. Cognitive shortcuts have a special impact on leaders when they face a foreign event that deviates dramatically from their expectations and thus confounds or even shatters the assessments and calculations that leaders derive from their longstanding experiences. Since they have difficulty sizing up such a surprising occurrence and suddenly find the ground shaking, even representative leaders take significant recourse to inferential heuristics to cope with such a mental shock.

Chapters 5 through 7 document instances in which even longstanding party leaders initiated challenges under less than propitious conditions or overreacted to sectarian efforts to replicate a foreign model. For instance, German Social Democrats responded with excessive force to far-left attempts to emulate the Bolshevist capture of government power in October 1917. While hostile to the death, those two sides ironically acted out of the same belief that it was easy for radicals to grab power during revolutionary turmoil. This shared belief resulted from the representativeness heuristic and the rash inferences it drew from Lenin's success, which posed a striking challenge to Social Democracy's effective abandonment of revolution. By shaking up established patterns of thinking, this dramatic event prompted representative leaders to rely more strongly on cognitive shortcuts than they tend to do under normal circumstances.

Thus, representative leaders could be affected by cognitive shortcuts as well. But because their ample knowledge and long-standing experience prepared them reasonably well for many eventualities, they resorted to these crutches much less than ordinary citizens. And because their broad-based, pluralistic organizations had internal mechanisms for open discussion and deliberation, their judgments and decisions faced more scrutiny and were therefore less distorted by problematic inferences than was common in ideological sects. In sum, while the political rationality of representative leaders was bounded as well, it was comparatively less bounded and deviated less strongly from the standards of systematic information processing and logical inference.

One last points bears highlighting: What was decisive was the more thorough way in which representative leaders digested information, not the secular increase in the sheer quantity of information that resulted from the development of communication technologies and from societal modernization overall. In the world of bounded rationality, more information is not necessarily better. Instead, overabundance can actually foster, if not require greater reliance on cognitive shortcuts and thus lead to more problematic inferences and worse decision-making. Consequently, the world-historical growth in information access did not, as such, reshape the features of democratization waves, as the striking parallels of the Arab Spring of 2011 with the riptide of 1848 suggest (Weyland 2012a; see Chapter 8 in this volume). Only in polities where mass organizations emerged did representative leaders avoid getting carried away by dramatic precedents, proceed with prudence, and respond less rashly to external stimuli.

The Transformation of Diffusion's Triggers

The preceding section analyzed how the emergence of broad-based organizations, which started in the second half of the nineteenth century, reshaped the domestic processing of external precedents of political regime contention. In this way, organizational development transformed the reception side of diffusion. This part of my theory explained the notable difference between the revolutionary tsunami of 1848 and the less precipitous wave unleashed by the Russian revolutions of 1917. What then accounts for the additional slowdown and even greater success of emulative contention during the third wave of democratization in Latin America?

My theory highlights that further organizational development also transformed the stimulus side of diffusion. The main trigger of contentious waves changed; as a result, the force of the external stimulus diminished, and domestic actors gained greater room to maneuver and could wait for propitious moments before initiating emulation efforts. The tsunami of 1848 and the wave of 1917–19 were both detonated by the striking overthrow of long-standing rulers and the violent installation of a new regime. These stunning precedents unleashed powerful impulses for immediate emulation, which played out with full force in the inchoate polities of 1848 and which were tamed only with difficulty by organizational leaders in 1917–19.

By contrast, the most important trigger of the third wave of democratization in Latin America was Spain's pacted transition to democracy. This new type of precedent was much less dramatic and did not provide as potent a stimulus as violent revolutions. Because the Spanish example lacked the overwhelming impact of revolutionary triggers, domestic political forces were not immediately carried away. Mass actors remained largely unaffected, and organizational leaders initiated emulation efforts only when the internal power constellation looked promising. This fundamental transformation of the stimulus side of diffusion thus explains the further deceleration and enhanced success of the third wave of democratization in Latin America, as depicted in Figure 2.3.

Diffusion's features are not determined by the imitators and their choices alone; the nature of the originating event also plays a crucial role. Different types of stimuli set in motion different diffusion processes (Boushey 2010: ch. 3; Makse and Volden 2011). The signal matters, not only the reception. This section therefore explains how the input side of diffusion changed during the twentieth century, due to a further step in organizational development. In this way, it also elucidates how the present study can compare three contentious waves that seem to have disparate characteristics.

In the democratization processes under investigation, the originating events varied considerably, as is evident in terminology. The triggers in 1848 and 1917–19 were the revolutions in France and Russia, respectively, whereas the most important model for the third wave was Spain's pacted transition. Accordingly, regime contention in 1848 and 1917–19 is called revolutionary

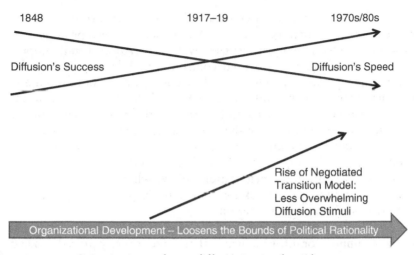

FIGURE 2.3 Organization reshapes diffusion's stimulus side.

and distinguished from the democratizations of the third wave, which were nonrevolutionary (for the latter point, see O'Donnell and Schmitter 1986: 11, 14). Yet rather than invalidating comparisons of these historically distant waves, this difference itself is part of my explanation because it resulted from the macro-structural development highlighted in this study, namely the formation of broad-based organizations. By substantiating this crucial point, my theory accounts for the evolution of diffusion triggers; in social-science jargon, it endogenizes this difference by explaining the shift from transgressive to contained contention (cf. McAdam, Tarrow, and Tilly 2001: 7–8). An apparent conceptual problem thus gives rise to an additional insight, indeed a cornerstone for a comprehensive explanation. Instead of comparing apples and oranges, my book explains how crab apples were domesticated into orchard fruits.

In a nutshell, the proliferation of political mass parties and wide-ranging interest associations and their spread across the ideological spectrum profoundly changed the predominant mode of democratic contention. Strong parties and associations had emerged first on the left, with the formation of social-democratic parties and their affiliated trade unions in the late nineteenth century. Yet eventually, political forces in the center and on the right responded to this left-wing challenge and formed stronger organizations as well. Parties of notables sooner or later extended their membership base and adopted greater institutional discipline. Gaining strength, these parties also gave minoritarian actors that commanded tremendous power capabilities, such as big business, large landowners, and to some extent the military, a formal voice in the system of interest representation. As a result, conflicts were fought out less and less through direct confrontation. Because most relevant actors could now have a voice at the table, they came to manage or resolve their divergences via negotiations.

Therefore, as firm, reasonably disciplined collective actors proliferated, the nature of democratic contention changed. Spontaneous street protests that could quickly turn into mass uprisings gave way to bargaining and compromise among political leaders, who used controlled mobilization merely for demonstrating their power capabilities. Such negotiated transitions, common during the third wave of democratization in Latin America, were much less risky than the insurgencies of 1830 and 1848 and the repercussions of the Russian revolutions; correspondingly, the rate of success that efforts to emulate these precedents attained was unusually high as well. Domestic actors initiated imitation efforts when the opportunity looked good; and a temporary lack of responsiveness or even an initial negotiation failure, which did not cause the tremendous costs and resentments of a repressed uprising, did not preclude a renewed effort to strike a bargain later on.

But while holding greater chances of success, negotiated transitions provided a much weaker stimulus for diffusion waves than revolutionary precedents had produced in organizationally unsaturated polities. Where a mass assault managed to dislodge an apparently powerful ruler, as in Paris in February 1848, this unusual success was much more dramatic and stunning than a transition engineered via bargaining and compromise. Such a striking overthrow therefore triggered a much quicker wave of imitation efforts; the force of this external precedent led to a tight clustering of diffusion. By contrast, a pacted transition inspires organizational leaders here and there, depending on the domestic situation. Therefore, it sets in motion a much slower and less clear-cut wave. In sum, the transformation of the main mode of democratic contention, which provided the signal for diffusion processes, explains the further diminution in speed yet increase in success that characterize the third wave of democratization in Latin America.

How, specifically, did organizational development produce this change in triggering events, and how did this transformation of the stimulus reshape diffusion processes in the world of bounded rationality? In the inchoate, amorphous polities of the mid-nineteenth century, crowd protests and mass assaults constituted the only viable option for challenging the established authorities. The absence of firm, broad-based organizations that could sustain collective action over time compelled oppositionists to try and overwhelm autocrats quickly through escalating street confrontation. The need to defeat the incumbent right away created strong incentives for raising the intensity and transgressiveness of contention and moving from mass demonstrations to violent attacks and full-scale insurrection. But such attempts to force immediate change held tremendous risks; many rebellions were defeated and backfired by provoking repression.[20]

---

[20] From 1815–1851, there were several revolts and uprisings in Paris, for instance – most of them unsuccessful (Mansel 2001: ch. 9, 13).

In the rare cases in which unorganized mass contention managed to unseat an autocrat, however, this unlikely achievement constituted such a stunning success that it turned into a powerful signal for oppositionists in other polities. Because the heuristics of availability and representativeness drew disproportionate attention to this dramatic event and made observers overestimate similarities with their own domestic situation, such a precedent provided strong impulses for sweeping emulation efforts. The force of this stimulus unleashed tsunamis. But the risks inherent in violent crowd contention, attempted rather indiscriminately in a diversity of settings, led to frequent failures. Thus, the striking characteristics of the originating events that prevailed before the era of mass organization help account for the speed of diffusion as well as its meager success.

As broad-based parties and interest associations formed, however, challengers acquired the capacity to maintain collective pressure over time and to calibrate and target it more carefully. Rather than having to rely on all-out confrontation designed to topple autocrats quickly, representative leaders were able to pursue their goals over the medium and long run and to apply influence in calculated dosages. Given the lower risks of this controlled strategy, oppositionists tended to back away from crowd protests and adopt gradualism and reformism, which often involved contacts and negotiations with the established authorities. Rather than pushing for an immediate, total victory in a desperate quest for all or nothing, challengers came to pursue their goals step by step. This moderation in turn elicited less repression from incumbents and thus reduced the risk and cost of failure.

The organizational foundation for reformist gradualism emerged first on the left side of the political spectrum with the emergence and steady growth of the social-democratic labor movement. But since centrist and right-wing forces did not have strong organizations, Social Democracy in the early twentieth century lacked reliable interlocutors with whom to negotiate a comprehensive regime change. Such inclusive bargains became feasible only as these moderate and conservative political forces and the societal interests backing them slowly but surely came to build greater organizational strength as well. Once the main political actors across the ideological spectrum had firm organizational representation, they could sit down and discuss their divergent interests and demands. To avoid the costs and risks of all-out confrontation, organizational leaders put a premium on compromise. While certainly no guarantee of success, such negotiations held a good chance of eventually forging a regime transition that was acceptable to all parties involved.

This favorable outcome, however, emerged from compromise and mutual concession. Therefore it amounted to a less clear-cut and stunning achievement than the dramatic overthrow of an authoritarian ruler. Because bargaining often unfolded behind closed doors among elites, including unaccountable sectors such as big business and the military, it seemed to establish limited forms of "democracy by undemocratic means" (Hagopian 1990). As a result, a negotiated transition constituted a much less powerful stimulus for emulation efforts elsewhere. Whereas the toppling of an autocrat had served as a powerful trigger for diffusion, a replacement based on compromise provided a weaker, muffled signal. Though substantively important and rationally preferable with its positive balance of benefits and risks, it was not the kind of clarion call that inspired a rash of imitation attempts. In the world of bounded rationality, negotiated regime transitions simply do not have the "overwhelming" force as triggers of diffusion waves that successful mass insurgencies had. They provided an especially limited stimulus for mass actors who relied heavily on the heuristics of availability and representativeness.

Representative leaders, who operate with less narrowly bounded rationality, did learn from these precedents; but since these leaders proceed with greater prudence, they acted on them only when the domestic opportunity structure looked propitious. As a result, a negotiated transition as in Spain inspired emulation efforts more slowly, but with a greater likelihood of success.

In sum, the transformation of the triggers of contentious waves helps account for the changing characteristics of these diffusion processes, especially their further diminution in speed and higher rate of goal attainment. The change in the main signal helps resolve the puzzle examined in this book by complementing the explanations focused on the reception side of diffusion. The macro-structural development emphasized in this study, namely the formation and proliferation of broad-based parties and interest associations, first reshaped the domestic processing of external impulses and then transformed these foreign stimuli as well. Through these two steps, organizational development brought forth the negative correlation between diffusion's speed and success. Whereas many scholars focus merely on one side of diffusion processes, mostly the reception side (cf. Boushey 2010: 62; Makse and Volden 2011), the theory developed in this book draws a more equilibrated and complete picture by analyzing the stimulus side as well.

It is noteworthy that changes on the input and reception side of diffusion came into play at different points in historical development. The waves of 1848 and 1917–19 were both unleashed by revolutions; they emanated from the same kind of precedent. Their differential features and outcomes resulted mostly from the transformation of the reception side, namely the rise of mass organizations in the intervening decades. By contrast, the further slowdown of diffusion evident in the leisurely pace of the third wave in Latin America was not caused by an additional strengthening of parties and interest associations; while such organizations spread across the ideological spectrum and thus brought more balance in polities' organizational density, in Latin America they rarely ever attained the institutional solidity that many European parties boasted. Instead, the additional reduction in diffusion's speed and the corresponding increase in its success resulted from the change in precedent event, namely the marginalization of the revolutionary option and the growing

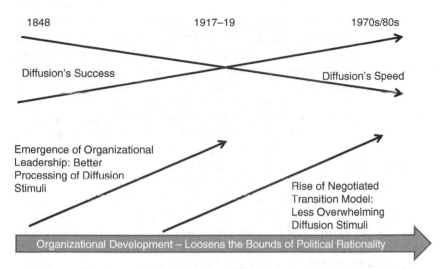

FIGURE 2.4 How organization reshapes diffusion.

predominance of negotiated regime transitions, exemplified by the Spanish model. Thus, the change in signal highlighted in the present subsection was mainly responsible for the special features of South American democratization. Figure 2.4 depicts the two main steps in my explanation and summarizes how organizational development reshaped the characteristics of contentious waves over the course of the last two centuries.

The Diversification of Diffusion

The proliferation of broad-based organizations across the whole ideological spectrum and the resulting transformation of the main triggers of contentious waves also led to the diversification of diffusion processes. Consequently, crisp, concentrically spreading waves gave way to complicated jumbles of currents and crosscurrents. In 1848, the French precedent had immediate, direct demonstration effects and stimulated imitation efforts all over Europe. In 1917–19, the Russian revolutions affected a wide range of observers as well; yet while they inspired the most radical groupings to attempt direct replication, they induced many moderate actors to forestall this outcome through preemptive reforms. Finally, during the third wave of democratization in Latin America, Spain's pacted transition constituted the main model, but significant sectors gravitated toward other foreign precedents, including Nicaragua's violent revolution. These heterogeneous sources of inspiration led to divergent courses of action and stimulated conflicts. As oppositionists pushed in different directions, a welter of undertows and whirlpools emerged. Therefore, the third wave of democratization unfolded in Latin America in a much more unshapely way than the tsunami of 1848 had advanced.

The increasing complexity of diffusion reflected the aforementioned changes on the reception side and the stimulus side of diffusion, which in turn resulted from the advance of broad-based organization. In regard to the recipients of external impulses, organizational development produced a variety of political parties and associations with different programmatic and ideological postures, which crystallized ever more clearly. In 1848, political actors had divergent orientations, but they were still vague, undefined, and fluid. Even among members of Germany's constituent assembly that met in Frankfurt's *Paulskirche*, coalitions and alignments shifted frequently as electoral politicians groped toward defining their own stance on the multidimensional issues that they suddenly faced (similar to France in 1848; see Breuilly 2000: 124). The secular rise of political organization and its spread from the left to the center and right entailed clearer and firmer definitions of ideological positions; politicians sorted into distinct parties and associations that were reasonably coherent in their visions and programs. Aligning along fundamental dimensions of cleavage, these parties embraced and propagated divergent goals and strategies.

The emergence of distinct ideological camps led political forces to gravitate toward different foreign precedents and to establish separate transnational affinities and connections;[21] after all, groupings with "shared mental models" are drawn to each other (Denzau and North 1994; Mantzavinos 2001: ch. 5; Jost, Federico, and Napier 2009). Accordingly, contentious waves turned from single-centered to multi-centric. Whereas in 1848, virtually every political actor was captivated by the dramatic events in Paris, in 1917–19 and especially during the third wave, political forces took inspiration from divergent external experiences. For instance, German Social Democrats were encouraged by the Russian February Revolution to push for full democracy, but saw the Bolshevist October Revolution as a deterrent example to avoid; far-left sects, by contrast, sought to imitate precisely Lenin's violent takeover of state power. Even more clearly, different forces in Chile's ideologically well-defined party system responded to dissimilar external precedents. Christian Democrats were impressed by Spain's pact-making; moderate socialists for a while took some hope from protests and regime collapse in Argentina; and communists sought to replicate the Sandinista insurgency in Nicaragua.

These divergent currents and crosscurrents of diffusion, especially visible during the third wave in Latin America, resulted on the reception side from the ideological differentiation of political forces. Of course, this diversification also presupposed a change on the input side of diffusion, namely a variety of external precedents and models. Distinct stimuli from this broader menu appealed to different domestic forces, depending on their ideological worldview. How did this diversity of foreign signals and stimuli emerge?

---

[21] In Europe, the left again took the lead in establishing transnational networks (e.g., Eley 2002: 86–93). For Latin America during the third wave of democratization, see Angell 2001 and Grabendorff 2001.

As the preceding section explained, the proliferation of broad-based organizations led to the prevalence of negotiated regime transitions over revolutionary mass assaults, especially in the initiatives of organizational leaders. Yet although these leaders commanded considerable clout and managed to guide large segments of the mass public, they never controlled all citizens, and they drew fierce resistance from radical sects. Therefore, the preference for pacted transitions could not displace all other options. In fact, slow, patient negotiations with their compromises and lack of a clear winner held only limited appeal in the world of bounded rationality. Whereas representative leaders prudently chose this low-risk strategy for effecting regime change, unorganized mass actors and radical sects were drawn toward bolder options, which seemed to allow for defeating autocrats decisively. As a result, mass protests continued to hold a good deal of attraction among some sectors, and fringe groupings sought to imitate what they regarded as successful revolutions. Thus, while representative leaders advocated negotiated transitions, the menu of emulative contention comprised alternative strategies as well.

Due to the variegated offerings on the input side of diffusion and the ideological crystallization of its recipients, diffusion processes changed from single waves to tumbles of surges, ebbs, and flows, which sometimes reinforced yet sometimes counteracted each other. Instead of having one source, they emanated from various signals that competed for attention. Correspondingly, domestic sectors differed ever more clearly in the foreign precedents from which they took inspiration. Demonstration and contagion effects thus multiplied and diversified. Whereas diffusion processes were predominantly monotone in the nineteenth century, they became polyphonic, if not cacophonous, in the twentieth century.

This diversification of diffusion contributed to its slowdown yet greater success. The uniform wake-up calls of the nineteenth century spurred challengers into quick action, but this rush often meant defying repressive governments with problematic means at inopportune moments. The downfall of Louis Philippe stimulated similar types of mass contention in a variety of settings; but conditions were often unpropitious, leading to frequent failure. Nineteenth-century challengers poured into the streets to protest and build barricades (cf. Traugott 2010), but when these uniform contentious tactics did not succeed, they had no fallback option.

In the twentieth century, by contrast, ideologically defined organizations responded to different signals that arose at various times. Depending on the distribution of influence among opposition forces, this diversity could slow down the spread of political regime contention. Disagreements over which model to emulate limited the backing that any contentious strategy garnered. Where organizational leaders were in control, they often sought to sort out this discord before initiating challenges. And where ideological sects rashly took the lead, broad-based, pluralist organizations tried to counteract this precipitation. As various groupings simultaneously pursued their own favorite approach, their tactics could get into each other's way. For instance, violent protests by extremist sectors could block moderates' efforts at negotiation. In this vein, the attempt of Chilean communists to spark a mass insurrection à la Nicaragua helped to undermine the peaceful demonstrations pursued in 1983–84 by the centrist and moderate-left opposition, which took some degree of inspiration from Argentina.

As the diffusion of contention diminished in speed, however, it tended to lead to greater eventual success. This accomplishment emerged from politically mediated learning, which benefited from the larger set of models appearing with the diversification of diffusion. This diversity often stimulated debates and deliberations, which gave rise to better outcomes because the advocates of different options highlighted the advantages of their preferred strategy and pointed to the problems with alternatives (Page 2007: ch. 6–8). Depending on their impact on the progress of political regime contention, some external models came to appear as unpromising, whereas other strategies and tactics made headway and found more support. Based on these experiences, a number of challengers abandoned their initial projects and switched to alternatives that seemed to hold better chances. In Chile, for instance, the center-left opposition gradually gave up its strategy of mass demonstrations, took encouragement from the Philippine transition of 1986, and contested the Pinochet regime in a constitutionally scheduled plebiscite, which it ended up winning. Thus, learning from political advances and setbacks sooner or later led challengers to converge on a promising option, which finally allowed them to triumph.

This groping toward a solution takes advantage of the variety of externally inspired options that different opposition groupings initially embrace. When all eyes focused on a single precedent, as in the nineteenth century, challengers disposed of only one instrument for attaining their goals. With all their eggs in one basket, they ran a considerable risk of failure. But once oppositionists had several irons in the fire, there was a greater chance of forging an effective weapon for bringing down an authoritarian regime. After all, the shared goal of dislodging a dictator provided a strong incentive for learning and some cooperation.[22]

This learning from political experience is not a purely intellectual enterprise, of course, and it does not reliably follow the rules of logical inference. Instead, it is mediated by political power and shaped by the (looser) bounds of rationality affecting representative leaders. First, some contentious tactics win out over others because they look more promising, but this promise itself reflects the balance of influence among ideologically diverse contenders. Learning involves assessing the power capabilities, determination, and tactical savvy of the government and of various opposition forces, all of which have reason to

[22] Despite the traditional cleavage between Peronists and anti-Peronists, even Argentina's opposition parties in the early 1980s formed a wide-ranging coalition, which drew up a number of programmatic agreements (Multipartidaria 1982).

dissimulate and bluff.[23] Arriving at a result is as much a question of negotiation and pressure as of perception and inference. Therefore, a strategy may emerge as the best option precisely because it has had the most adherents from the beginning, before any learning took place.

Second, this learning does not strictly follow the systematic procedures of comprehensive rationality but is affected by cognitive heuristics, which – as mentioned above – even representative leaders use to some extent.[24] Therefore, organized opposition forces do not process information in a neutral, unbiased fashion, but tend to gravitate toward recent, striking experiences to which they have an ideological affinity. The availability heuristic often skews attention. For instance, the solution to the impasse facing Chile's opposition in 1986, after the failure of mass demonstrations, emerged in part from the unexpected downfall of the Ferdinand Marcos regime as a result of electoral contestation – a success that made participation in Pinochet's plebiscite look promising. The surprising Philippine transition grabbed Chileans' attention and affected their judgments.[25] This lesson-drawing also presupposed an assumption of similarity between Marcos's Sultanistic regime (Thompson 1998) and the institutionalized Pinochet dictatorship – a typical, yet logically questionable product of the representativeness heuristic.

For these reasons, the experiential learning that occurs in the course of political regime contention tends to deviate from fully rational procedures, such as Bayesian updating.[26] Reliance on cognitive heuristics can yield rash inferences and misjudgments. Yet discussions among a variety of representative leaders, who bring their diverse perspectives to bear, can uncover the problems of some contentious tactics and realize the promise of others; interorganizational pluralism tends to have a similar salutary effect as the intraorganizational pluralism discussed in an earlier section (see in general Page 2007). These debates among various parties and associations, which can take considerable time, tend to give opposition efforts greater success. The ideological differentiation in the attraction to external precedents, another corollary of organizational development, thus helps explain the seemingly opposing tendencies of contentious diffusion, namely its simultaneous slowdown and growing success.

The Increase in Organizational Density and the Inward Shift of Political Attention

The secular process of organizational development had another repercussion that reinforced the notable slowdown yet greater success of contention's

---

[23] The resulting difficulties of learning from political and historical experience are stressed by Levitt and March (1988: 324–26, 333).

[24] Levy (1994: 291–94, 304–5) emphasizes in general that learning does not necessarily imply greater accuracy.

[25] The Uruguayan plebiscite of 1980, when a majority voted down a new constitution under a military dictatorship (a clear contrast to the Chilean "yes" vote that same year), also served as a foreign source of inspiration – a product of lesson-drawing less affected by cognitive shortcuts.

[26] See for a similar argument Schiemann (2007).

diffusion in 1917–19 and especially during the third wave of democratization in Latin America. The emergence and subsequent proliferation of broad-based organizations tipped the balance of political attention more and more toward the domestic arena. Consequently, external precedents made less of an impression on actors' judgments and calculations. As successful foreign events generated a weaker impulse for emulation, such efforts got under way only when the internal constellation of power looked promising. External precedents no longer triggered replication attempts immediately, but only when domestic opportunities opened up. This inward shift of political attention thus helps account for the negative correlation between diffusion's speed and success.

Before large-scale collective actors had formed, domestic politics was amorphous, fluid, and opaque; the distribution of political preferences and power capabilities was extremely hard to decipher. In the absence of broad-based organizations, who could know how widespread and intense political support for the established regime was; how willing oppositionists were to incur the risks of challenging the authorities and withstanding repression; and how capable they were of mobilizing and sustaining collective action? Because political forces were inchoate, valid and reliable information on internal developments was scarce. Therefore, actors tended to draw inferences from actual, visible changes that occurred elsewhere, such as the downfall of a neighboring regime. Because the domestic situation was inscrutable, common citizens and aspiring leaders looked for cues abroad. In the era of low organizational density and formless politics, they attributed disproportionate informational value to observable foreign precedents, which therefore exerted a substantial impact and triggered rapid emulation efforts.

This inferential approach was logically problematic, however: It privileged ease of observation over the relevance of the object of observation. Specifically, it assumed that hidden in the fog of domestic uncertainty lay a similar political opportunity as had just been revealed by the foreign event. Thus, the focus on external precedents entailed a heavy reliance on the availability and representativeness heuristics and exposed domestic actors to the distortions and biases inherent in these shortcuts. Dramatic, striking events impressed themselves on actors' minds; foreign successes were overrated in their significance and replicability, based on facile impressions of similarity between the precursor and the conditions facing potential emulators. These rash inferences derived from external events did not guarantee high-quality decision-making, and the resulting replication attempts achieved only limited success. In sum, before the secular advance of political organization, actors were trapped in domestic shapelessness and uncertainty, and were therefore eager to draw conclusions from regime changes abroad.

By contrast, political forces in organizationally denser societies had better information about the internal constellation of power and therefore displayed less interest in foreign developments. After collective organizations formed and then proliferated across the ideological spectrum, they engaged in observable interactions and established a track record on the political stage. As a result, domestic power relations became clearer and more predictable (cf. Przeworski 1991: 64–65). To assess future prospects, such as the likely fate of their regime, observers had an incentive to focus predominantly on the domestic situation. They now felt less need to draw indirect inferences from foreign developments, including gathering waves of regime contention. As more reliable information on the internal opportunity structure became available and uncertainty thus diminished, cognitive shortcuts held less sway; heuristic inferences could be cross-checked with more solid evidence.

Certainly, as the literature on third wave transitions stressed (seminal O'Donnell and Schmitter 1986: 3–5, 66, 70), even these processes of regime contention were shrouded in uncertainty. Therefore, domestic actors in the late twentieth century also took external developments into account and did apply cognitive shortcuts. But this level of uncertainty, and the compensatory tendency to take inspiration from foreign events, was much lower than before the organizational consolidation of polities, when profound "confusion" (Kurzman 2004) prevailed. After all, political parties, unions, and other interest associations now populated the political stage and established patterns of actions and interactions, which allowed for informed guesses about future developments. Compared to the nineteenth century, uncertainty diminished over the course of the twentieth century and became more bounded. As the domestic political ground turned firmer, actors had less reason to grasp at foreign straws, and the room for cognitive shortcuts to shape their thinking, calculations, and decisions narrowed.

This inward shift in political attention helps explain the changing features of diffusion processes. In amorphous, unshaped polities, people were impressed by external precedents, quickly jumped on the bandwagon of a gathering wave of contention, and challenged their ruler even when the domestic situation was actually unpropitious. As political organization advanced, by contrast, representative leaders came to base their decisions more on the domestic opportunity structure, which had become much clearer. External impulses turned into only one of several factors in the calculus of emulative contention, whereas they had supplied the main trigger before. This repercussion of organizational development contributed to the lower speed yet higher success of diffusion waves.

Indeed, the secular rise of organizations gave diffusion less force overall – a truly surprising finding in light of prevailing theories about globalization, which predict the opposite. The contentious riptide of 1848 constituted a much more obvious, dramatic diffusion process than the repercussions of the Russian revolutions and especially the variegated currents and eddies of the third wave. This unexpected result emerges clearly from the research conducted for this book, especially the testimony of participants and observers. The overwhelming impact of external triggers, especially the Parisian precedent, is patently obvious in 1848 (as in 1830). As Chapter 4 shows, actors of all political persuasions and positions of power, ranging from Austria's Prince Metternich, Berlin's military commander, and other aristocrats all the way to rebellious students, uniformly stressed the tremendous effect that the French events had on their thinking, feeling, and behavior. As one indication, people were addicted to the news about developments in Paris; whoever got hold of the most recent newspaper had to climb on a table and read aloud for all to hear (Streckfuss 1948: 24; Vitzthum 1886: 75).

By contrast, references to external precedents and their role in stimulating domestic emulation efforts are much less frequent in 1917–19 and especially during the third wave of democratization in Latin America. There certainly is conclusive evidence that foreign experiences mattered; actors of all stripes mentioned them and reacted to them. The Russian revolutions did have a substantial impact, and various external precedents, especially Spain's pacted transition to democracy, served as sources of inspiration during the 1970s and 1980s in South America. But compared to 1848, references to these foreign events are much sparser, and participants attributed less weight and impact to them. In fact, several former opposition leaders in Brazil and Chile reported in interviews that other countries' experiences played little role in their deliberations and decisions or characterized this impact as merely "atmospheric," rather than as a source of strong impulses and concrete inspirations (interviews with Correa 2007, Braga 2008, Dirceu 2008, and Franco 2008). Instead, the domestic constellation of power and the shifting relations among organized national contenders provided the principal base for their calculations and actions. External triggers mattered, but were heavily filtered through assessments of the correlation of internal forces.

In conclusion, as the world became "smaller" and globalization advanced, external factors paradoxically ended up having less – rather than more – impact (contra Huntington 1991: 101–02). The globalization literature debates whether external determinants have come to overwhelm internal actors and structures or not; controversy revolves around the extent to which global variables have increased in causal force. In regard to the diffusion of political regime contention, the present analysis finds the opposite: Over the last 200 years, foreign precedents have become less influential, whereas internal developments have acquired greater immunity and autonomy. When domestic politics are inchoate and therefore difficult to decipher, actors of all persuasions have particularly strong reasons to take cues from foreign developments. But as domestic politics takes shape, as collective actors emerge, proliferate, and establish observable patterns of interaction, internal developments become easier to read. This greater clarity about the domestic situation lowers the incentive to take a detour and draw inferences from external precedents.

The Complex Interweaving of Factors

The preceding sections have designed a theory that becomes increasingly complex as organizational development advances. While this macro-structural process provides the fundamental moving cause for the transformation of diffusion waves, it does not exert its causal force in a singular, linear way. Instead, the emergence and proliferation of broad-based organizations first reshaped the reception side of diffusion and then its stimulus side; moreover, it had additional repercussions that interacted with these primary effects in complicated ways. By the time the third wave of democratization unfolded in Latin America, this intersection of factors had become rather dense.

In inchoate polities, political impulses spread in a straightforward way. Accordingly, a dramatic foreign precedent quickly stimulated unorganized crowd action and set in motion a fairly uniform wave of challenges to autocratic rulers. Yet with the rise of broad-based organizations, a new type of actor emerged and came to moderate diffusion. Representative leaders now sought to filter the impact of external precedents, tame and guide contentious mass energies, and initiate emulative challenges only at propitious moments. At this stage, intraorganizational procedures that allowed for better information processing and decision-making made the crucial difference. This change at the reception side of diffusion accounted for the new features of contentious waves that appeared in Europe during the early twentieth century.

The further slowdown and increasing success that characterizes the third wave in Latin America did not, however, result from a linear intensification of this specific aspect of organizational development. That region's political parties and interest associations are not stronger and more encompassing than their European counterparts; in many cases they are weaker and have narrower constituencies. The New World has never had an equivalent to German Social Democracy of the early twentieth century. Instead, the third wave was shaped by other ramifications of organizational development, especially its spread across the ideological spectrum. As various organizations with different worldviews arose and the major sociopolitical forces thus gained their own organizational mouthpieces, interorganizational dynamics acquired particular importance. Above all, parties and associations entered into discussions and negotiations and acquired the capacity to conclude wide-ranging, binding agreements.

This outgrowth of organizational development brought a profound transformation of the input side of diffusion, namely the rise of the negotiated transition model. While representative leaders preferred this option due to its lower risks and greater chances of success, its nondramatic nature provided only a muted impulse for emulation efforts. Whereas revolutions had quickly unleashed contentious mass energies, Spain's pacted democratization provided a less powerful signal, which gave leaders the latitude to target emulation efforts to political opportunities. It was this indirect effect of organizational development that made the biggest difference for the third wave. The macro-structural change that provides the main causal thread for this study thus affected this diffusion wave as well, but through different mechanisms. Whereas in Europe during the early twentieth century, it reshaped first and foremost the reception side of diffusion, in South America during the late twentieth century it exerted its impact mainly on the input side, by opening up a new mode of contention.

In the aftermath of the Russian revolutions and especially during the third wave in Latin America, other repercussions of interorganizational dynamics also came into play. Parties' divergent ideological orientations and political strategies often prompted competition and conflict, which slowed down emulative contention. But by offering a wider menu of options, this diversity also allowed oppositionists to try out various strategies, learn via trial and error, and eventually settle on a particularly promising approach. A slower process thus led to greater success.

Furthermore, during the course of organizational development, political attention gradually shifted inward. With the emergence of firm collective actors, domestic politics became less fluid and indecipherable than it had been in the first half of the nineteenth century. And as these organizations established a track record and came to engage in routine interactions, it made ever more sense for domestic oppositionists to concentrate on internal politics and attribute less evidentiary weight to foreign events. This redirection of political attention brought a clearer focus on the relevant power constellation and political conjuncture, which discouraged precipitous imitation efforts and produced a higher rate of success.

All of these repercussions of organizational development made external impulses less overwhelming and gave structural factors and preconditions a more important role in shaping the spread of democratic contention. In inchoate polities, where external precedents tended to sweep up domestic oppositionists and trigger rash emulation efforts in a wide range of diverse settings, structural factors did little to condition the initiation of bold challenges – but this disregard for given political opportunities came to haunt the protagonists by severely limiting their chances of success. As organizational developments widened the bounds of political rationality,[27] the main instigators of emulative regime change considered the configuration of political forces more thoroughly. Through representative leaders' assessments and calculations, these structural parameters exerted more and more impact on democratization

---

[27] As political rationality became less tightly bounded, representative leaders may not have only been influenced by external precedents, but may have also used foreign models more strategically to promote their (preexisting) political goals. Common citizens and narrow sects were carried away by rash inferences and did not make deliberate use of foreign models, as the failure of their emulation efforts and the resulting costs demonstrate. Representative leaders, however, processed external inputs in a more active, deliberate way; as a reviewer argued, they may therefore have used these lessons to justify goals and strategies that they had already embraced before. In that case, external precedents would not have reshaped leaders' beliefs. But even if this conjecture, for which I found no evidence during my wide-ranging and intensive research, is correct, foreign models nevertheless could have a significant impact: Through the lessons promoted by representative leaders, they would have affected other politicians or the broader public. In that case, the process of diffusion would have taken an additional step, operating through the recipients of representative leaders' messages. This "democratic," partly mass-based mechanism of diffusion, recently examined by Linos (2013) in her study of social policy reform, constitutes an interesting area for further research.

waves, their speed and success. Consequently, objective reality came to shape contentious decision-making, not only determine its outcomes. Theoretically speaking, agency and structure, the two sides of my theory with its cognitive-psychological micro-foundation and its emphasis on macro-structural development, were integrated more closely.

CONCLUSION

Trying to explain the striking slowdown yet increasing success in the diffusion of political regime contention, this chapter has assessed a wide range of arguments derived from major theoretical approaches. But my extensive research about the waves of 1848, 1917 19, and the 1970s and 1980s suggests that transnational networks that grew in density with modernization and globalization; the rise of nationalism in the course of the nineteenth century; the differentials in hard and soft power invoked by world system theory and constructivism; and the learning modeled by rational choice cannot convincingly account for the negative correlation between the two diffusion trends and for the process of actors' decision-making. Above all, by highlighting one trend, established approaches cannot account for the other.

Specifically, arguments about modernization and globalization, world system theory, and constructivism predict increasing success but at the same time suggest a speed-up of diffusion, not the deceleration that my comparison of the three major waves of political regime contention finds. Arguments about nationalism, in turn, predict reduced speed but also diminishing success, again opposite to observed trends. Finally, rational choice postulates an inherent connection between speed and (the chance of) success, an expectation falsified by the inverse correlation found in this study. Process tracing also disconfirms strict rationalism: Participants in all three diffusion waves diverged substantially in their information-processing and choices from the postulates of inferential logic and rational decision-making.

A wealth of primary documents shows instead that actors on all sides of political regime contention regularly resorted to cognitive heuristics. These mechanisms of distinctly bounded rationality profoundly shaped their perceptions and calculations and caused substantial deviations from fully rational decision-making. Yet as my theory emphasizes, these micro-mechanisms played out differently depending on the political macro-context. In organizationally inchoate polities, as they prevailed during the nineteenth century, cognitive heuristics had full sway. In the absence of representative leadership, the choice on whether to challenge established governments fell to individual citizens, who had limited information access and little experience in making such high-stakes political decisions under tremendously uncertain circumstances. Therefore, these common people were susceptible to the rash inferences derived via cognitive heuristics from striking foreign precedents. The prevalence of bounded rationality explains why emulation efforts spread rapidly yet often happened at inopportune moments and therefore had a low rate of success.

The emergence of mass organizations in the late nineteenth century then accounts for the diminishing pace yet increasing success of diffusion waves, that is, the other side of the negative correlation between these two trends. The rise of representative leadership meant that the main decision about defying nondemocratic governments came to lie in the hands of experienced operators who had better information access and a higher processing capacity than common citizens. Standing on firmer ground, leaders were less influenced by cognitive heuristics; while they did rely on these shortcuts and therefore deviated from the postulates of full rationality as well, they had more opportunities to crosscheck the resulting inferences, especially where institutional procedures allowed for reasonably open discussion and debate. Therefore, leaders did not jump to conclusions about the replicability of striking, successful foreign precedents but waited for a good opportunity to launch their emulation efforts and defy established regimes. Accordingly, political regime contention spread with less speed but attained greater success.

After organizational development gave rise to representative leadership and thus reshaped the reception side of diffusion, it also ended up transforming the stimulus side and thus brought a further deceleration of contentious waves yet increasing success during the twentieth century. With the proliferation of political parties and interest associations, more and more challengers backed away from escalating street protests and mass insurgencies, and instead resorted to negotiation and pact-making when trying to effect regime transitions. As the principal model that propelled emulation efforts changed, the features of these diffusion processes changed as well. Dramatic, stunning revolutions spark quick, rash imitation attempts, but due to their haste they often fail. By contrast, pacted transitions that proceed via mutual concession and compromise do not inspire mass enthusiasm. Instead, they mostly offer lessons to representative leaders who send their broad-based organizations into emulative contention only when the time seems ripe. Consequently, diffusion proceeds more slowly, but has a greater chance of achieving its goals. This fundamental change in the nature of external triggers exerted a particular impact on the third wave of democratization in Latin America.

Two additional repercussions of organizational development reinforced the negative correlation between diffusion's speed and success. First, the crystallization of ideological positions that accompanied organizations' spread across the left-right spectrum produced a diversification of demonstration and contagion effects. Political parties and groupings gravitated toward different sources of external inspiration. As a result, they embraced distinct strategies and tactics of contention and received impulses for challenging their own government at different times. Since most organizations knew that they could not attain their goals easily, they sought to garner support from other organizations or waited for a particularly good opportunity before initiating contention. As a result, contagion advanced less quickly. And, while the pursuit of divergent emulation efforts could create complications and obstacles in the short run, it entailed higher chances of success in the medium run by bringing various options into play, stimulating diverse political experiences, and allowing for lesson-drawing. Sooner or later, a promising proposal for effecting regime change often emerged, found increasing backing, and ended up carrying the day. Thus, this repercussion of organizational development also contributed to diffusion's greater success.

Second, the emergence of collective actors and the definition of their ideological positions clarified the constellation of domestic power. The resulting reduction in uncertainty drew actors' attention predominantly to the internal front. External precedents, which provided comparatively valuable information at a time when domestic politics was inchoate and therefore shrouded in fog, became less important as the base for drawing inferences. Now, relevant actors could better assess internal opportunities and constraints and therefore did not act rashly under the impact of a foreign impulse.

All of these arguments elucidate the spread of political regime contention and account for the negative correlation between its speed and success. My new theory demonstrates that insights from cognitive psychology, which have already been applied to individual-level political choices, help explain collective action as well. For this purpose, cognitive micro-mechanisms need to be combined with macro-structures, as I do with my emphasis on organizational developments. Indeed, there is a profound interaction between these two levels. The emergence of political mass organizations not only sets the parameters for cognitive mechanisms, but affects their very operation as well: Organizational ties loosen the bounds of rationality. This interactive argument helps build a theory of politics that stands on the well-corroborated micro-foundation of bounded rationality and does justice to the complex macro-phenomena of politics.

3

Organizational Development and Changing Modes of Democratic Contention

This chapter examines the changing nature of the external precedents of political regime contention that set in motion the various diffusion waves analyzed in this book. As mentioned in Chapter 2, the last two centuries have seen a profound transformation in the modes of democratic contention prevailing in Europe and Latin America. In a glacial process, revolutionary assaults on the established political order have been replaced by negotiation and compromise as the predominant strategy for external, mass-based opposition forces that try to bring about regime change. In turn, this shift from transgressive to contained contention (in the terms of McAdam, Tarrow, and Tilly 2001: 7–8) has resulted from the emergence and proliferation of broad-based political organizations that my causal argument highlights. Thus, the macro-structural component of my theory accounts for this crucial change on the stimulus side of diffusion processes.

To set the stage for Chapters 4 through 7, which probe mainly alterations on the reception side, this chapter investigates the evolution of these triggers. It documents the sea change in the foremost diffusion stimuli in Europe and Latin America, from revolutionary uprisings in the first half of the nineteenth century to pacted transitions in the second half of the twentieth century. The rise of mass-absorbing parties and interest associations allowed and induced liberal and democratic challengers to back away from violent mass assaults against autocratic rulers, which carried considerable costs and held tremendous risks. To avoid these dangers, challengers came to prefer a reformist path that over time evolved into a strategy of negotiated transition. Consequently, the predominant form of democratic contention changed from bottom-up street protests to bargaining among political leaders (for Latin America, see Munck and Leff 1997). This transformation of the originating events ("signals") helped to diminish the speed of emulation waves while increasing their rate of success, especially in the course of the twentieth century.

As explained in Chapter 2, a mass uprising that succeeded in overthrowing a powerful autocrat – by nature a rare occurrence due to its inherent dangers – was a striking, stunning event that was bound to attract tremendous, widespread attention and to inspire high hopes of replication in line with the availability and representativeness heuristics. By contrast, negotiated transitions unfold in a gradual, nondramatic fashion, through "lame" compromises among political leaders rather than deeds of heroism (O'Donnell and Schmitter 1986: ch. 4; Flisfisch 1988: 327–71; Huntington 1991: 167–69; Corrêa 2005). Whereas a mass uprising yields clear winners, a negotiated transition ends up "without winners and vanquished," as the architect of the Spanish democratization, Adolfo Suárez, stressed (Suárez et al. 1986: 11). Because such a regime change involves concessions from all sides, it has a less clear-cut result. This unexciting mode of contained contention relies on often nontransparent bargaining among elites, including unaccountable powers-that-be. Since pacted transitions seem to establish "democracy by undemocratic means" (O'Donnell and Schmitter 1986: 38; Hagopian 1990), they are unlikely to make a strong impression and have a powerful impact on boundedly rational observers who rely on the availability and representativeness heuristics.

Furthermore, because negotiations require much less courage than efforts to dislodge repressive autocrats through escalating street protests, they tend to be more common.[1] This greater frequency further dilutes the impression that negotiated transitions make. Whereas a successful revolt erupting after a long stretch of political stagnation and quiescence, as in France in 1848 (or in Tunisia in 2010–11), is especially noteworthy and inspirational, efforts at negotiated transition undertaken here and there lack the same novelty and striking power. These more frequent attempts at democratization are less likely to spark the rash inferences suggested by the heuristics of availability and representativeness, grab observers' attention, and inspire a belief in easy emulation. While organizational leaders tend to grasp the importance of these precedents, appreciate their potential for producing solid change, and draw lessons from them, ordinary citizens are not swept off their feet. Negotiated regime change lacks the captivating impact that emanates from the overthrow of an authoritarian ruler by a mass rebellion.

In sum, the transformation in the predominant mode of democratic contention, from the bottom-up challenges prevailing in the early nineteenth century to the pacted transitions predominating in the late twentieth century, muffled the signal that could set in motion diffusion processes in Europe and Latin America. Whereas the overthrow of Louis Philippe in 1848 resembled a big rock tossed into a calm pond, Spain's gradual transition, the single most important trigger of democratization's third wave, looked like a pebble thrown into water that was already stirred up by other recent projectiles, such as transitions in Argentina in 1972–73 and Portugal in 1974 and the distension beginning in Brazil in 1974.

---

[1] On the infrequency of barricade fighting, for instance, see Traugott (2010: 230).

As a result, the third wave did not sweep across a continent in one month like a tsunami, as had happened in 1848, but unfolded over a decade as a slow but powerful confluence of various currents. The change in the nature of the signal that arose from the transformation of originating events profoundly altered diffusion processes, bringing lower speed yet greater success.

THE PREVALENCE OF REVOLUTIONARY EFFORTS IN THE NINETEENTH
CENTURY

The Predominance of Revolutionary Uprisings in the Absence of Mass Organization

During the first half of the nineteenth century, in most of Europe, crowd protests constituted the only feasible option for externally mobilized opposition forces seeking to effect political change. At that time, urbanization and modernization had assembled "critical masses" of city dwellers that could engage in regime-challenging collective action, but political parties and wide-ranging interest associations that incorporated these people into disciplined organizations had not yet formed. In such organizationally inchoate polities, challengers could rely only on massive popular assaults to pursue their goals and press incumbent autocrats to transform the existing regime. In the absence of broad-based organizations, oppositionists managed to overcome the collective action problem only episodically. Since they could exert effective political pressure only for a short while, they had to seek a decisive victory immediately.

Under these conditions, the only way for popular opposition forces to bring about political change was through massive street action, that is, the effort to force concessions through escalating protests and direct confrontation with the authorities and their repressive agents, the police and military. Since unorganized crowd mobilization is difficult to maintain for any length of time, it had a chance of success only if the challengers managed to overwhelm the established government quickly. If they encountered resistance, they felt a need to escalate the conflict and engage in violent confrontation, such as barricade fighting. Therefore, bottom-up challenges in inchoate polities were extremely risky, unpredictable in their outcomes – and rare in their occurrence (Traugott 2010: 230).

The absence of organizational leadership that could represent and commit the rebellious masses made negotiations infeasible. As Chapter 4 shows, even when princes tried to bargain with the contentious crowds besieging their palaces, they could not find a valid interlocutor; it was totally unclear who could authoritatively speak for the mass of protesters. Without broad-based organizations, there was no possibility of negotiation; fluid, amorphous masses cannot enter into any agreements.

The prevalence of explosive crowd mobilization as the main mode of democratic contention profoundly shaped the diffusion of impulses for political change. The nature of this signal helps account both for the amazing speed and the scarce success of the resulting waves of regime conflict. Mushrooming street protests that easily erupt in violence are dramatic, vivid events that immediately grab observers' attention. The availability heuristic induces a wide range of people to focus on outbursts that suddenly interrupt the dullness of normal political life, involve life-and-death struggles on the public stage, and decide the fate of important rulers. These instances of contention are tremendously novel and newsworthy, especially if they occur in a high-profile, prominent setting, such as Paris in the first half of the nineteenth century (Mansel 2001).

Moreover, if such an episode of spiraling contention proves successful in overthrowing a seemingly powerful ruler and forcing regime change, the representativeness heuristic leads many people in other polities to overestimate the significance and replicability of this single success. As explained in Chapter 2, they eagerly seek to imitate the foreign experience and proceed to challenge their own authorities as well. Due to this cognitive shortcut, a successful mass assault in one country can set in motion a riptide of emulation efforts elsewhere. The transgressive mode of democratic contention that predominated in Europe during the first half of the nineteenth century therefore had the potential to trigger tsunamis.

But the lack of organizational leadership and the crucial role of cognitive shortcuts in propelling the rapid spread of democratic contention to a wide range of settings also limited the probabilities of success severely. The chances for amorphous, unorganized, and leaderless crowds to defeat the police and military and to dislodge the established ruler were low in many polities (despite the institutional weakness of many states at that time). Even when governments, under duress, offered initial concessions to avoid further bloodshed and thus preserve their legitimacy, they retained command over organized coercion and thus maintained the capacity to exercise overwhelming power in the medium and long run. Unorganized protesters, however, were unable to sustain collective action. The initial upsurge of mobilization soon crested, and contentious crowds started to dwindle. Lulled into a false sense of security by the representativeness heuristic and equating princes' tactical concessions with the definitive victory achieved in the precedent experience, more and more challengers abandoned their fleeting commitment to participating in regime contention. When the rebellious masses began to withdraw into private life again (see in general Hirschman 1982: ch. 6), princes used their continuing control over the police and military to reassert their political predominance, slowly but surely. As the balance of power tilted again in their favor, they resorted to repression to prevent a recurrence of protests.

In sum, democratic contention via spontaneous escalating crowd protests provided the kind of political impulse that could spread quickly due to the availability and representativeness heuristics. But widespread emulation of this transgressive mode of challenging authoritarian regimes also held a high risk of failure. Given the absence of broad-based organization in most polities during the first half of the nineteenth century, this strategy constituted the only option for externally mobilized opposition forces that tried to force progress toward political liberalism and democracy at that time.

The Slow Emergence of Parliamentary Reformism

The principal exception to this amorphous mass contention that emerged in the first half of the nineteenth century was England, where a powerful parliament served as the central arena of constitutional decision-making and maintained this prerogative despite the mass challenge arising from the Chartist Movement. In this representative system, reasonably well-developed political parties succeeded in channeling the demands of relevant political forces. Because party organizations have long time horizons and can negotiate regime change, a gradual transformation based on a series of compromises was feasible. But precisely because the English strategy of successive suffrage reforms proceeded in a peaceful, nondramatic way, the steps along this path, such as the reform of 1832, did not grab the attention of many challengers in other European countries, despite their low costs and cumulating success. Surprisingly from a rational standpoint, these changes did not stimulate waves of emulation efforts, as the revolutions of 1830 and 1848 did. The availability heuristic explains why the nonconfrontational English reforms did not unleash the same inspirational impulses as the heroic French uprisings, especially at the mass level.

Leaders of the parties that eventually emerged in other European countries did learn from English gradualism, however. When the formation of party systems and the increasing attributions assigned to parliaments in more and more countries of Western and Northern Europe made imitations of the English precedent feasible, a growing number of gradual reforms, especially suffrage extensions, were adopted on the Continent starting in the late nineteenth century (Collier 1999: ch. 2).[2] The spread of democratic values helped propel this reform process (Freeman and Snidal 1982; Przeworski 2009: 292, 305–06), but until the burst of change triggered by the Russian revolutions and World War I (which Chapter 5 examines), it advanced in such a leisurely fashion that it does not qualify as a recognizable wave with compact temporal clustering and clear linkages among cases (cf. Kurzman 1998: 50–54). The reason for the low speed was that these changes resulted from lengthy parliamentary deliberations among elites, which do not spark enthusiasm among mass actors in other countries and therefore created limited pressures for emulation. In sum, a parliamentary model of gradual liberalization and democratization emerged

---

[2] This point is also highlighted by Congleton (2011: 252–61), though with a rather skewed emphasis on reform over revolution.

in the late nineteenth and early twentieth centuries (Share 1987: 531); but due to its nondramatic nature, it did not trigger sweeping waves of diffusion, as the revolutionary mode of democratic contention prevailing in the first half of the nineteenth century did.

THE RISE OF POLITICAL MASS ORGANIZATIONS AND ALTERNATIVES TO REVOLUTION

The emergence of political organizations in the second half of the nineteenth century slowly brought a shift from democratic revolution to reformist modes of contention and regime change in those European countries where mass mobilization had erupted and the politics of regime transformation could not be confined to parliamentary deliberations. In these countries, where in Dahl's terms (1971: ch. 3) inclusiveness preceded liberalization, the impulses that could trigger diffusion processes changed over time. This transformation of potential signals was not straightforward and uniform, however; it proceeded in twists and turns, driven by tensions and conflicts among the advocates of different strategies of political contention. Due to its attraction for boundedly rational individuals, revolution retained more followers than prudent rational assessments of this high-risk option would have counseled. Continued belief in the viability of this radical strategy and the dramatic impact that any successful revolution had on people applying the availability and representativeness heuristics constituted a serious challenge for the representative leaders of broad-based organizations who sought to chart a more moderate, reformist course. Therefore, tension and struggle over the transformation of modes of contention prevailed for decades.

Interestingly, both the advocates of revolution and of reform emphasized the need for political organization – but very different types of organization. Responding to the scarce success of spontaneous crowd challenges, those who wanted to force regime change through confrontational street action created small, tight-knit organizations; these conspiratorial cells sought to prepare and guide mass uprisings or take power through violent assaults as the vanguard of the people. By contrast, ever larger numbers of workers and other poor people joined broad-based socialist parties and unions that advanced their socioeconomic and political interests through a combination of controlled protests and negotiations. Although initially these mass organizations were rhetorically committed to revolution as well, in practice they tried to change the established political regime gradually from the inside through sustained, but self-limiting, contained contention.

This section examines first the rise of this reformist strategy, which came to include contacts and negotiations with supporters of the status quo. The subsequent discussion of revolutionary strategies highlights the challenges that this lingering alternative posed to the representative leaders of broad-based mass organizations, as the conflicts examined in Chapter 5 confirm.

The Rise of Mass Parties and of Reformist Strategies

The emergence of mass organizations, which after the repressive 1850s gathered steam in Central Europe from the 1860s (Bartolini 2000; Eley 2002), prompted a profound rethinking of the main approach to sociopolitical change. Where social-democratic parties and unions arose, especially in Central, Western, and Northern Europe, the new representative leaders began to move away from the strategy of mass assaults on the established order (seminal: Engels 1895; Bernstein 1991; see also Bouvier 2001: 900; Gildea 2001: 923–24). As these parties and unions recruited more and more members, integrated them into a dense network and all-encompassing milieu, and instilled a strong sense of discipline, they gained the capacity to sustain collective action and exert influence over the long run. Whereas unorganized crowds can force change only through spasmodic outbursts that carry tremendous risks and result in frequent failures, the ever more powerful labor movement could advance its demands through more promising and less dangerous strategies and tactics. Social Democracy applied sociopolitical pressure in calculated dosages to extract concessions step by step – not to overwhelm its adversaries through violent clashes.[3] Participating ever more widely in elections while also employing peaceful protests that were targeted on specific issues and that were carefully controlled by the leadership, it tried to effect change via negotiations and parliamentary action (Przeworski and Sprague 1986; Berman 2006: ch. 2–3). This gradualist strategy of contained contention allowed for corrections along the way,[4] avoided the risk of setbacks, preserved and further honed the organizational capacity built up over many years, and, with the steady growth of the labor movement, promised to bring one success after the other (Scheidemann 1921: 1–2).

In this vein, the most impressive mass organization emerging in Europe, the Social Democratic Party of Germany (SPD), emphasized electoral advances and parliamentary politics, despite its persistent rhetorical commitment to revolution. Party leaders effectively had no intention to embark on dangerous confrontations with the Imperial authorities, which would provoke repression and could destroy their principal political asset, organizational capacity. Emblematically, SPD president Friedrich Ebert assured the last imperial chancellor in the thick of the November Revolution of 1918 in Berlin, "I do not want [the social revolution]; indeed, I hate it like sin" (Baden 1927: 599; also reported by Scheidemann 1929, vol. II: 224). In even stronger terms, Gustav Noske (1920: 7), who hailed from the SPD's more conservative wing, claimed: "German Social Democracy had always rejected a violent revolution."

While backing away from forceful confrontation, the social-democratic reformism made possible by broad-based mass organization continued to

---

[3] Tilly (2008: 143) attributes the same kind of change in the "repertoire" of contention to the rise of what he calls social movements.

[4] On the benefits of a gradual strategy versus resolute efforts at comprehensive transformation, see in general Lindblom (1965: ch. 9).

rely on a bottom-up approach to democratic contention. Although unions commonly negotiated with business associations and although socialist parties participated in parliamentary proceedings and even maintained contacts with autocratic governments, a negotiated transition to democracy would have been difficult to effect because there were no organizationally solid interlocutors on the right side of the party system. Mass organizations with firm, lasting structures emerged first on the left. By the early twentieth century, the center and right still lacked disciplined organizations; with the exception of Catholic parties, institutionally fluid coteries of notables prevailed (Kirchheimer 1966: 178–80, 183–84). These loose groupings could not represent and commit powerful sociopolitical forces, such as conservative nationalists, backward rural sectors, big business, and the military.

For this reason, a democratic transition through a wide-ranging pact was not yet feasible. Social-democratic leaders could only enter into informal agreements with supporters of the old autocracy behind closed doors, as new chancellor Friedrich Ebert did in his secret accord with military head Wilhelm Groener in November 1918.[5] In sum, the organizational weakness of rightist and centrist parties precluded the wide-ranging compromises and mutual obligations that are decisive for a negotiated regime transition.[6]

The Lingering Attraction of Revolution

The gradualism and reformism embraced by broad-based parties and unions was not only hampered by the organizational deficit of the political right and center in the nineteenth and early twentieth centuries, but it also faced continuous challenges from the revolutionism of the radical left. Although the rise of mass organizations induced many advocates of sociopolitical change to abandon violent street assaults, small extremist groupings kept insisting on confrontational efforts to overthrow the established authorities. This revolutionist strategy remained appealing to sect-like cells of ideological radicals who reinforced each other's admiration for efforts to accomplish profound change quickly and who discounted the enormous risks of violent uprisings.

Revolutionaries did not simply want to wait for spontaneous mass uprisings, however, but were eager to spark such challenges. For this purpose, they

---

[5] German business and labor had strong and centralized peak associations, however, and therefore signed a formal agreement on fundamental socioeconomic issues – the famous Stinnes–Legien accord for a *Zentralarbeitsgemeinschaft* (Central Work Community) – right after the eruption of the November 1918 revolution (Feldman 1992: 521–30; Wehler 2010: 221–22).

[6] Collier (1999: 107–8) overestimates the significance and role of these disparate, partly informal, and not very effective agreements. For instance, the Ebert–Groener accord was a secret exchange between two leaders that did not fulfill its promise of guaranteeing the new government reliable military support. Instead, the army was dissolving by the day and the generals were losing control. That is the reason Gustav Noske felt compelled to use undisciplined right-wing volunteer units, the infamous *Freikorps*, to suppress the so-called Spartakus Uprising of January 1919 in Berlin.

needed organizations as well – but organizations that had to be tight-knit and homogeneous. Only highly committed activists were up to the dangerous task. Fears of detection and repression also counseled small size and precluded mass recruitment. And since firm cohesion and iron discipline were decisive, dissent was purged and ideological uniformity imposed. As explained in Chapter 2, this homogeneity and closure constituted a hotbed for groupthink that reinforced the rash inferences derived via the availability and representativeness heuristics, prevented these sects from exposing their ideologies to reality checks, and gave the commitment to revolution surprising staying power.

The confrontational efforts of revolutionary sects started with the incessant attempts of French radical Louis Auguste Blanqui to trigger the kind of uprising that had erupted spontaneously in 1830. Unimpressed by repeated failures, Blanqui and his select group of followers tried again and again to stir the masses into street contention (Gildea 2008: 48–56; Geary 2000: 135–36). Yet with the rise of broad-based organizations in Western, Central, and Northern Europe and the advance of many of those countries toward political liberalism and democracy, reformism looked ever more promising, and revolution slowly and haltingly lost support in these regions.[7] Confrontational strategies garnered a stronger following toward the underdeveloped east of the continent, where mass organizations were at best incipient and polities remained inchoate. Given the obstacles to reformist change, radical sects played a greater role in these backward and repressive settings (cf. Vössing 2011: 176–82).

The insurrectionist strategy developed in two basic directions, anarchism and Leninism. Anarchists hoped that high-profile attacks on rulers would trigger bottom-up rebellions, partly in reaction to the state repression provoked by their acts of terrorism. Spectacular bombings and assassination attempts were meant to stun the defenders and encourage the challengers of the established order and thus spark uprisings. Anarchists expected these striking signals to exert a spontaneous mobilizational effect, compensating for the lack of organizational linkages to wider sectors of the population.

Lenin, by contrast, had little faith in the latent revolutionary spirit of the masses and therefore created an organization that could take power on their behalf. This vanguard approach employed armed force to destroy the existing regime, grab power, and mobilize support from the working class thereafter. Whereas anarchists universally failed, Lenin was lucky and skillful enough to take advantage of the collapse of tsarist rule in World War I and lead his cadre party to power. This striking success gave the confrontational strategy of armed revolution, which by the late nineteenth century had looked increasingly obsolete, a tremendous boost in leftists' eyes (Carnoy 1984: 44–45; Hobsbawm 1996c: 74–75; cf. Owen 2010: 170–71). The availability heuristic drew widespread attention to the Bolshevist revolution, and in line with

---

[7] For the lingering impact of Blanquism on French politics, see Hutton (1981).

the representativeness heuristic, observers of all ideological stripes came to overestimate the ease of its replication, as Chapter 5 documents.

The risk of begetting a new and particularly fierce dictatorship that inhered in Lenin's vanguard strategy created unease even among left-wing revolutionaries, however. Most prominently, Rosa Luxemburg (1970) condemned vanguardism and set her hopes in the spontaneous insurrectionary energies of the masses. But what would induce significant sectors of the population to confront oppressive regimes? On this crucial point, Luxemburg took inspiration from the abortive Russian Revolution of 1905, in which mass strikes had escalated into fairly spontaneous challenges to the tsar and had forced important political concessions.

In sum, the emergence of political organization did not immediately lead to the abandonment of confrontational strategies for forcing sociopolitical transformations, especially in underdeveloped East Europe. Instead, revolution continued to look like a viable alternative to reformism, particularly in the eyes of radical left-wing sects. Revolution was far more striking and dramatic than reform; where it got under way (as in Russia in 1905) and especially where it achieved immediate "success" (as in Russia in 1917), it made a huge impression on a variety of observers and suggested the feasibility of replication, due to the heuristics of availability and representativeness. Because cognitive shortcuts suggested these rash inferences, they help explain why revolution continued to be perceived as a promising option, despite its enormous costs and risks. Whereas rational cost/benefit calculations strongly counseled a preference for reformism, especially in countries where mass organizations had emerged (cf. Przeworski 1985), inferential heuristics skewed actors' assessments. These shortcuts thus slowed down the transformation of the signals that set in motion diffusion waves.

Debates and Conflicts over Contentious Strategies

The retarding effect of dramatic precedents from backward polities came to the fore in the acrimonious mass strike debate that rocked German Social Democracy in the first decade of the twentieth century. This important controversy was triggered by external precedents, primarily the revolutionary uprisings of 1905 in Russia. On several occasions, mass strikes that stimulated broader popular mobilization pushed forward this thrilling attempt to transform Russia's rigid autocracy. Given the epic nature of these conflicts and the temporary success they attained, the availability and representativeness heuristics drew tremendous attention to these episodes. Leftists across Europe and even oppositionists beyond Europe (Kurzman 2008) took inspiration from these mass strikes.

A number of SPD left-wingers, most famously Rosa Luxemburg (1970), invoked the Russian example to advocate a more confrontational strategy for the party, such as the use of mass strikes to force the adoption of universal equal suffrage in Germany's subnational units, especially the huge and politically decisive Kingdom of Prussia. This mobilizational impetus encountered strong opposition from the party's organizational stalwarts, however, who did not want to jeopardize the labor movement's hard-won capacity for collective action in a dangerous confrontation with the imperial autocracy and its powerful supporters. In the eyes of most party and union leaders, mass strikes were unlikely to succeed; they were more likely to invite repression, which would set back the labor movement by years (Hughes 2009: 114–19). By contrast, continued pursuit of the reformist, institutional path held the strong promise of winning political power sooner or later; after all, the party had steadily increased its vote share and was about to become the strongest grouping in the imperial parliament (Kautsky 1914).

After the uprisings of 1905 had established Russia as the global center of revolution (Schulz 1980: 155; Harrison 2007), the tsar's overthrow in February 1917 and Lenin's power grab in October constituted even more dramatic and successful events that again triggered the availability and representativeness heuristics and served as a beacon for left-wing mobilization all over Europe. Amplified in their demonstration effects by these cognitive shortcuts, the Russian revolutions made such a powerful impression that left-wing radicals and even ordinary people in the West felt inspired to seek their emulation. Cognitive heuristics again prompted an overestimation of the significance of stunning change and put advocates of reformist gradualism on the defensive, although their strategy had much better prospects of success in most of Europe and was therefore preferable from a rational perspective.

As Chapter 5 analyzes in depth, the leaders of mainstream Social Democracy managed to contain the immediate mobilizational impulses emanating from the Russian revolutions in April 1917 and in January and February 1918. Instead, they exerted pressure for democratization at a more opportune moment, namely in October 1918, when the imperial authorities were reeling from Germany's defeat in World War I. But with long-standing mass discontent exacerbated by the severe deprivations of the war, the revolutionary option exemplified by the Russian precedent remained appealing and threatened a breakthrough in November 1918. Once again, however, SPD and union leaders quickly succeeded in channeling these bottom-up energies onto an institutional track by scheduling constituent assembly elections right away. Moreover, they defeated uprisings initiated by radical-left sects with a harshness betraying their own belief in the possibility of revolution, which the representativeness heuristic derived from the Russian precedent.

In conclusion, the wave of democratic contention in 1917–19 was characterized by a duality of models as potential triggers of diffusion. On the one hand, with the emergence of mass organization, reformist efforts to promote democracy had won ever larger numbers of adherents and had turned into the preferred strategy of the powerful social-democratic labor movement. But on the other hand, revolution continued to command determined support from tight-knit sects of leftist radicals. It also retained appeal among mass actors particularly susceptible to cognitive shortcuts, which disproportionately highlighted the Russian precedents. The Russian revolutions therefore inspired a number of attempts at uprisings that the mainstream Social Democratic Party and its union wing felt compelled to suppress while advancing their own reform demands. As a consequence of these mixed signals and conflicting impulses, the diffusion processes unfolding at that time had dangerous rapids and undertows.

THE PREDOMINANCE OF NEGOTIATION AND COMPROMISE
IN THE THIRD WAVE

The Spread of Organization and the Rise of the Negotiation Strategy

In the course of the twentieth century, mass organization further advanced in Europe and in more and more countries of Latin America as well. In particular, broad-based parties and associations spread across the ideological spectrum. In the late nineteenth and early twentieth century, it was mainly the political left that had formed firm, wide-ranging organizations; with the exception of Catholic parties in Continental Europe, right-wing and centrist groupings tended to consist of loose networks of notables. The resulting disadvantages in electoral competition, however, induced these sectors sooner or later to form mass parties as well. While not as cohesive or disciplined as the Social Democratic Party, these catch-all parties came to incorporate large numbers of voters. They represented other power capabilities as well, for instance, allowing business sectors to express their interests (Kirchheimer 1966: 184–95). Despite the absence of a clear programmatic orientation, even the electoral vehicles of populist leaders that arose during the early stages of mass mobilization often gained considerable solidity by sinking deep roots of loyalty among their followers, as Argentina's Peronist Party and Peru's American Popular Revolutionary Alliance (APRA) exemplify.

The proliferation of broad-based organizations consolidated the position of established collective actors as principal participants in politics and left little room for spontaneous crowds. In Europe and even in Latin America (especially South America), organizational leaders gained ever greater predominance on the political stage.[8] The increasing preponderance of organizations pushed ahead the transformation of the main mode of democratic contention. As demonstrated in the preceding section, the rise of broad-based parties and unions had produced a preference for gradualism and reformism. Yet because organizational capacity first developed on the left whereas the center and right side of

---

[8] Only in specific niches of the polity did less organized sectors retain a capacity for autonomous action. One of the principal niches is the university, where ideas of participation and spontaneity retained appeal. This exception accounts for the comparatively dramatic demonstration and contagion effects that drove the worldwide wave of student protests and other leftwing challenges of 1968.

the ideological spectrum remained institutionally fluid, negotiated transitions were difficult to conduct in the early twentieth century, especially where inclusiveness had outstripped liberalization.

With the proliferation of organizations thereafter, however, all of the major political forces and even important socioeconomic sectors acquired authoritative mouthpieces in the party system. The emerging balance in representation allowed for regime transitions via negotiation and mutual concession. Because most of the relevant sectors could have a voice at the table, ample compromises that undergirded nonconfrontational democratizations became feasible. Even powerful protagonists of authoritarian rule that would have to step aside from open political involvement in a new democracy, such as the armed forces, could find some articulation of their core interests on the right flank of the party system.[9]

Although the participants in negotiated transitions do not overwhelm their adversary and therefore cannot attain total success, organizational leaders found them preferable to street contention and mass rebellion because they held only limited risk. Based on this prudent calculation, representative leaders who tend to have wider bounds of rationality often held back their members when direct confrontations happened to arise. Therefore, the protests that sometimes erupted under authoritarian rule usually lacked the ample support that would have endangered the regime; during the third wave of democratization, bottom-up mobilization rarely succeeded in forcing regime change (O'Donnell and Schmitter 1986: 21; Huntington 1991: 146). In Brazil in 1968, for instance, mass contention spearheaded by students remained limited and therefore did not achieve success; instead, this crowd challenge backfired and provoked a significant aggravation of repression (Skidmore 1988: 73–84; Passarinho 1989: 126–29). This kind of failure in turn reinforced the preference for reformism and elite-level negotiations.

Precisely due to their limited costs and risks, such negotiations occurred with considerable frequency. Many opposition politicians were willing to maintain contacts with authoritarian rulers; some held conversations even with brutal dictatorships, as in Argentina during the late 1970s (Novaro and Palermo 2003: 181–86). Autocrats, in turn, were more likely to relinquish power via negotiation and compromise, which promised to safeguard their core interests, than to admit defeat in an open confrontation. Given their lower stakes, attempts at negotiated transitions were more common than successful efforts to force regime change through violent contention had been (Huntington 1991: 164–65).

---

[9] In their seminal comparison of different paths of democratic transition, Linz and Stepan (1996: 56–65) stress that broad-based organization is a necessary precondition for negotiations and pacts; similarly, O'Donnell and Schmitter (1986: 40–42) emphasize that for the political pacts that undergird democratization, organized political parties are the central negotiators.

This relative frequency, combined with their nondramatic nature, limited the impression that negotiated transitions could make on boundedly rational actors and reduced their potential to set in motion crisp waves of emulation. Elite-level bargaining and compromise were much less striking and newsworthy than the overthrow of French kings or Russian tsars had been. They did not constitute powerful signals and lacked the magnetism to attract widespread attention across borders, especially from common people. While organizational leaders in other countries took note, steps along the winding road of a negotiated transition were seldom stunning or vivid enough to grab the attention of ordinary citizens. Precisely because these drawn-out processes advanced in a more orderly fashion than the extraordinary revolutions of the nineteenth and early twentieth centuries, the heuristics of availability and representativeness did not make them look tremendously important and unusually promising. From a fully rational standpoint, their lower costs and higher prospects of success should have induced intensive learning; but due to their unexciting nature, reliance on compromise, and resulting mixed outcomes,[10] negotiated transitions did not make a big impression, nor did they stimulate enthusiasm among boundedly rational actors in other polities (as Chapters 6 and 7 document).

In sum, the further transformation of democratic contention affected the potential signals of diffusion processes and reshaped waves of democratization. Whereas the revolutionary outbursts of the nineteenth and early twentieth century had been highly unusual and had unleashed powerful demonstration and contagion effects, the containment and "normalization" of democratic contention during the twentieth century in Europe and Latin America limited the inspirational impulses emanating from any one of these more frequent attempts at regime change.[11] In the world of bounded rationality, where cognitive shortcuts govern information processing, a single lightning after a long night has a much bigger impact than a variety of sparks here and there.

---

[10] In his game-theoretical and historical analysis of the Spanish transition, Colomer (1998: 10; see also 17–18, 171, 177–81) highlights that this regime change produced a "rather mediocre democracy of low quality."

[11] Interestingly, in regions with inchoate polities such as Africa, the third wave of democratization unfolded much faster yet with lower success (as Chapter 8 discusses) – and one reason was the more dramatic nature of its trigger. The stunning collapse of communism provided the main precedent for the continent, and the immediately following outburst of bottom-up contention in Marxist Bénin shook up West Africa. More dramatic than a negotiated, gradual transition, which organizational weakness made infeasible on most of the continent (Bratton and van de Walle 1997: 82–88, 177–79), the ouster of Bénin's long-standing dictator quickly stimulated imitation efforts across the region. Interestingly, however, the preference of political elites for moderation and negotiation came to the fore and prompted the formation of "national conferences" to conduct and secure these precarious transitions. Lacking firm, broad-based organizations that would have authorized them as representatives, elites nominated in more discretionary ways (Joseph 1991: 18–19; Robinson 1994: 601–07) engineered fora for bargaining in this less legitimate fashion. These developments are analyzed in greater depth in the comparative section of Chapter 8 below.

Accordingly, the third wave of democratization did not start with a cannon shot like the overthrow of Louis Philippe in 1848 or of Tsar Nicholas II in 1917, but in the midst of musket fire coming from different sides. While the junior officer coup of April 1974 in Portugal is usually regarded as the opening salvo, it was actually preceded by the demise of an authoritarian regime in Argentina in 1973 and the decision of Brazil's dictatorship to initiate liberalization in early 1974. Moreover, it followed on the heels of military coups in long-democratic Chile and Uruguay in 1973 and was in turn followed by another coup in Argentina in 1976. Thus, at the time it happened, the Portuguese precedent did not particularly stand out; its significance is more obvious in retrospect than it was to contemporary observers.

The Portuguese revolution was also unusual because it was initiated from inside a core institution of the authoritarian regime, namely the military. A rebellion of junior officers, not mass protests or elite negotiations, forced dictator Marcello Caetano from office (Maxwell 1986: 109). Only after this intraregime combustion had disarmed repression did popular mobilization become feasible, which then helped to propel the political transformation. Thus, the initial step could not serve as an inspiration for the democratic opposition elsewhere: How could they induce military personnel to break rank and dislodge the chief executive? Thus, the very nature of the Portuguese transition limited its potential for triggering emulation efforts by democratic contenders elsewhere.

The Predominance of the Spanish Model of Pacted Transition

The precedent that had much more impact in Latin America was the pacted transition unfolding after the death of Spanish *caudillo* Francisco Franco in 1975 (Linz and Stepan 1996: 87–89; Higley and Burton 2006: 61–67).[12] This regime change proceeded via parliamentary bargaining and via compromises among political parties and encompassing interest associations (Share 1987: 533–44). Because it successfully dismantled a well-entrenched authoritarian regime and ushered in a viable full democracy, the Spanish process turned into the prime model of a negotiated transition. Certainly, its gradual advance and nondramatic nature prevented the Spanish case from capturing the attention of many ordinary citizens in other countries. But it did elicit great interest from organizational leaders, who – as explained in Chapter 2 – do not rely as heavily on the heuristics of availability and representativeness and who put more weight on considerations of substantive relevance. Accordingly, party leaders in a number of Latin American countries studied the Spanish precedent and sought to emulate the overall strategy or replicate specific aspects, as

---

[12] Given that most of Latin America's military regimes had repeated, often irregular turnover at the top, succession problems like that caused by Franco's death in Spain occurred quite frequently in the region.

Chapter 6 documents. This prototype of a pacted transition thus served as a significant impulse for the third wave in Latin America.

Because it was unexciting and inspired mainly representative leaders of political parties and broad-based associations, however, the Spanish transition did not unleash an immediate wave of emulation efforts.[13] Instead, its demonstration effects appeared at different times in different countries, depending on the constellation of power and the specific regime conjuncture prevailing in these diverse settings. For instance, the Spanish case influenced the Peruvian transition of the late 1970s, but had little impact at that time on Chile, where dictator Pinochet tried to institutionalize his regime with the constitution of 1980. Yet when the economic collapse of 1982–83 weakened Pinochet and allowed opposition parties to resurface, the Spanish model assumed importance in Chile. Moderate challengers advocated its emulation (Aylwin 1985) and it inspired a prominent albeit futile effort in 1985 to promote redemocratization through an ample National Agreement (Tagle 1995).

The nondramatic character of Spain's pacted transition not only forestalled an immediate emulation wave and prevented the tight temporal clustering of diffusion, but it also helps explain why the Spanish precedent never turned into the exclusive model of democratic contention, unlike revolution during the first half of the nineteenth century. In 1848, the availability and representativeness heuristics had focused all eyes on the stunning events in Paris and had made observers neglect other relevant precedents, such as the Italian uprisings of that year. The Spanish model, by contrast, did not capture the same outstanding attention, failing to outshine all other contentious experiences. Despite the great significance attributed to it by many organizational leaders, rival models also had supporters, especially among loosely organized popular sectors or narrow sectarian groupings, as Chapter 7 highlights. Therefore, Spain's precedent did not turn into the singular trigger of the third wave. That diffusion process, propelled by other interweaving influences as well, was more complex and decentered than the tsunami of 1848. As a result, the third wave formed a much less clear-cut wave.

In conclusion, the historical evolution of originating experiences, which reflected the momentous advance and spread of political organization, had a profound impact on waves of democratic contention. The changing nature of the triggering signals helps explain the diminishing speed and increased success of diffusion. Negotiated transitions, which came to win advocates as party organization proliferated across the ideological spectrum, lacked the striking features that – processed via the heuristics of availability and representativeness – could

---

[13] Yet because Spain's pacted transition did effect a complete regime change from authoritarian rule to democracy, it was more notable than the gradual steps toward political liberalism and democracy that more and more European countries negotiated toward the end of the nineteenth century and in the early twentieth century. The Spanish model therefore did prompt direct emulation efforts, whereas those reforms had not.

stimulate enthusiasm for emulation, especially at the mass level. Instead, this unexciting process of regime change drew interest mostly from the representative leaders of mass organizations, who sought to attain similar success in their own countries. These professional politicians, less bounded in their political rationality than ordinary citizens, looked for promising opportunities to proceed along Spanish lines.

The pacted transition model itself calls for an adaptation to prevailing circumstances: Contrary to revolutionary assaults, the initiative does not lie exclusively with the challengers, but requires receptivity from important supporters of the incumbent regime. It constitutes an interactive, not a unilateral mode of democratic transition. The opposition cannot single-handedly force negotiation (Share 1987: 533). Since incumbent autocrats are unlikely to be uniformly willing to bargain, this model can by nature not be emulated in a sudden burst. The fundamental change in the mode of the principal stimulus thus helps account for the unhurried advance of the third wave of democratization.

The Continuing Appeal of Transgressive Contention

Negotiated transition never turned into the only option for effecting regime change, however. Due to its inherently slow progress, its less than stunning nature, and its mixed outcomes, it did not manage to command monopolistic support. Instead, actors of various stripes continued to regard alternative modes of transition as viable, especially those that promised faster or more profound transformation, even at considerable risk. This latent or principled support provided the resonance for external precedents of this kind to make a disproportionately strong impression.

Accordingly, the collapse of Argentina's brutal dictatorship in 1982–83, which was accompanied by widespread protests, drew significant attention in South America, especially the Southern Cone. Although bottom-up contention did not play a great causal role in bringing down the Buenos Aires regime, which crumbled largely from internal tensions (Fontana 1987: 160–62, 186–87; Novaro and Palermo 2003: 469–72, 546–47), the Argentine precedent helped to stimulate mass demonstrations in the subregion. The availability heuristic highlighted this striking case of authoritarian failure and regime implosion, and the representativeness heuristic led democratic challengers in Brazil, Chile, and Uruguay to overestimate the similarities to the political conjuncture facing them. The Argentine "transition through rupture" (Share 1987; cf. Share and Mainwaring 1986; Huntington 1991: 142–49) thus helped to strengthen the conclusion that many people drew from the terrible economic meltdown caused by the Latin American debt crisis, namely that their own military governments were fragile as well. This inference fortified oppositionists' belief that determined street pressure could overpower these tottering regimes and force political transformations. These overoptimistic beliefs, based mainly on the domestic crisis, yet reinforced by distorted inferences from the Argentine precedent, provided impulses for the protests starting in mid-1983 in Chile and Uruguay and for the "direct elections" campaign of 1983–84 in Brazil (as Chapters 6 and 7 document).

Typically, striking, courageous mass contention and transition through rupture had more direct inspirational force than the subdued Spanish model of negotiated transition. Organizational leaders, however, worked hard to turn contestatory impulses away from direct confrontations with the incumbent regimes and channeled them instead into symbolic demonstrations of mass discontent in Chile and Uruguay and into pressure for a specific institutional reform proposal in Brazil. Despite these efforts to moderate citizens' mobilizational energies and guide them in prudent directions, these contentious initiatives had only mixed results. They uniformly failed to attain their immediate, concrete goals, such as Pinochet's resignation in Chile and the reinstitution of direct presidential elections in Brazil. But they did revive civil society (seminal O'Donnell and Schmitter 1986: 48–56), deepen tensions and divisions among the supporters of authoritarian rule, and thus prepare the eventual transfer of power, especially in Brazil. Thus, as in the earlier waves of democratization examined in this book, striking popular protests spread fairly quickly, but were not particularly successful. The Spanish model of a pacted transformation, by contrast, exerted demonstration effects slowly over the course of years, but ended up facilitating more effective transformations.

Remarkably, even revolutionary attempts to dislodge authoritarian regimes through armed assaults retained some followers among radical-left sects. This daring strategy had succeeded in overthrowing the Sultanistic dictatorship of the Somozas in Nicaragua. But this thoroughly personalistic form of rule (Booth 1998) constituted an exception in the Latin America of the 1970s and 1980s. The bureaucratic-authoritarian regimes of South America had brutally squashed the guerrilla bands that pushed the student radicalism of the late 1960s to its last consequences. Violent challenges had uniformly failed, merely provoking fiercer repression. Therefore, most opposition forces in the region regarded revolution as infeasible, dangerous, counterproductive, and clearly undesirable – a position also embraced by the scholarly literature on democratic transitions (O'Donnell and Schmitter 1986: 11, 14).

Leftist radicals in some countries, however, sought to keep the flame of revolution alive. Chile's Communist Party embraced this option in the early 1980s, inspired by the Nicaraguan "success." In line with the availability heuristic, this dramatic guerrilla challenge, which managed to spark a mass insurgency in 1978–79, attracted a great deal of attention (see Castañeda 1993: 104–11). Based on the representativeness heuristic, Chilean and international Communists vastly overestimated the replicability of the Sandinista example in Chile. Misperceiving the Pinochet dictatorship as a thoroughly personalistic, patrimonial regime, they jumped to the conclusion that violent forays could produce a similar explosion.[14] As Chapter 7 examines in depth, these efforts turned into a colossal failure, helping to undermine the protest strategy pursued by the moderate opposition from 1983–86 and giving dictator Pinochet, who was reeling from the economic catastrophe of 1982–83, a new lease on life.

The preceding discussion shows that during the third wave, the predominant model of negotiated transition faced competition from alternative modes of contention. This multiplicity of options, combined with the sober, unexciting character of the pacted model, helped to turn the third wave into a drawn-out sequence of changes that unfolded over years. Whereas the 1848 tsunami and even the wave of 1917–19 started with a big bang, the third wave got under way more slowly and much less dramatically with a series of muffled shots from various directions. Propelled by the high rate of success that negotiations and compromise ended up attaining, it gradually swelled to a powerful current, but continued to encounter eddies and undertows.

In sum, the fundamental albeit incomplete transformation of modes of democratization, which resulted from the emergence and spread of political organization, is important for explaining the changing features of democratic diffusion. As the triggering signal changed, the process of emulation changed as well. The rise of the negotiated transition model contributed greatly to the diminishing speed yet increasing success with which foreign precedents stimulated imitation efforts in a wide range of countries. The transfiguration of originating experiences thus helps account for the negative correlation between diffusion's speed and success that this volume highlights.

CONCLUSION

The present chapter examines the transformation of the stimulus for democratic diffusion, which helps account for the slower velocity and higher success rate of contentious waves in Europe and Latin America. As the theory of Chapter 2 emphasizes, the rise of broad-based organizations, first on the Old Continent and later in the New World, brought a shift in the predominant mode of regime contention in these regions, from revolutions to negotiated transitions – that is, from transgressive to contained contention. This change in the potential triggers of contentious waves reshaped diffusion processes profoundly. Instead of quick riptides that ended up producing only limited progress, as in 1848, strong currents came to prevail that flowed slowly but managed to push aside obstacles.

---

[14] In Brazil, by contrast, the incumbent military regime had avoided personalization, had decisively defeated all violent challenges, and had opened up paths for the opposition's electoral advancement (Weffort 1984: 63–67, 74–84; Motta 2007: 295–96; Reis 2007: 506–7). Therefore, the Nicaraguan revolution triggered no temptations of emulation, even among the radical left and the nascent Workers' Party (Partido dos Trabalhadores; cf. Keck 1992; personal communication from Daniel Nogueira-Budny, author of a 2013 PhD dissertation on the Latin American left, University of Texas at Austin).

In the early nineteenth century, the absence of broad-based organization meant that democratic contenders could rely only on violent mass assaults to effect political change. The difficulty of sustaining collective action meant that protests had to escalate quickly to have any chance of success. While this revolutionary strategy held a high risk of failure, such outbursts of conflict were dramatic and stunning, sending powerful signals to a wide range of observers in other countries. And on the rare occasion that surging street protests did attain success, many of these observers jumped to the conclusion that they could accomplish the same feat in their own polities. Rash, ill-considered, and initiated without serious assessment of the prevailing political opportunity structure, many of these emulation efforts failed, however.

Starting in the late nineteenth century, however, the rise and subsequent spread of broad-based mass organizations slowly and haltingly limited the recourse to direct confrontation. To lower the costs and risks of democratic contention, representative leaders preferred reformism and gradualism and eventually converged on a strategy of negotiated regime transition. Yet while this peaceful path to change held much higher prospects of success, it lacked the heroic, striking features of street protest and revolution. Moreover, precisely due to its limited danger, this negotiation strategy was pursued more frequently than mass rebellions. In the world of bounded rationality, all of these characteristics muffled the appeal of pacted transitions. Because this contained mode of contention did not constitute a very powerful signal for people relying on the heuristics of availability and representativeness, it did not stimulate mass enthusiasm. But organizational leaders drew important lessons and applied them to their own polities, giving their democratization efforts ever higher prospects of success.

In sum, the transformation of the originating events that could set in motion diffusion waves helps account for their changing features, especially diminishing speed and growing success. As the signal and stimulus changed, the process and its outcomes evolved as well. This transformation of the sparks of diffusion helps explain the negative correlation emphasized in this book.

The transformation of the predominant model of democratic contention proceeded in a tension-filled and halting way, however. The heuristics of availability and representativeness slowed down the embrace of the negotiated transition model. These cognitive shortcuts drew disproportionate attention to dramatic events, namely the revolutions that still occurred in some settings, and induced actors of various stripes to overestimate the feasibility of their imitation. In particular, the Russian precedents of 1917 seemed to suggest the continued viability of revolution, a strategy that had during the preceding decades lost support in the Western half of Europe. Given the renewed appeal of revolution, organizational leaders, even the heads of firm, broad-based organizations such as the German SPD, had difficulty directing mass enthusiasm into institutional channels in 1917–19; in fact, they betrayed their own fears about the feasibility of revolution by cracking down hard on its radical advocates.

The stark disagreements concerning the mode of transformation, which were especially pronounced in Central Europe, thus led to fierce conflicts among the challengers of authoritarian rule, which in turn help explain the birth defects of newly instituted democracies (as Chapter 5 discusses).

Only after political organization had spread across the ideological spectrum in subsequent decades, did negotiated transition turn into the predominant mode of democratic contention. In the second half of the twentieth century, therefore, representative leaders faced fewer radical challenges. Since the heuristics of availability and representativeness did not unleash an outburst of enthusiasm for these types of gradual transformation and a push for immediate imitation, leaders could tailor their efforts to promote political change to the prevailing opportunities and constraints. Consequently, they proceeded in an unhurried fashion – and attained a particularly high rate of success.

Because this chapter has explained the changing stimuli of these complex diffusion processes, the following four chapters focus mainly on the transformation in the reception of these stimuli. In historical sequence, they examine the three waves of democratic contention analyzed in this book. Accordingly, Chapter 4 investigates the riptide of 1848, which arguably constituted the most breathtaking diffusion process in the history of political regime change, at least before the Arab Spring of 2011. Chapter 5 dissects the wave triggered by the Russian revolutions of 1917, perhaps the most tortuous process, because the fundamental divergence over reform versus revolution prompted frontal conflict among the challengers of autocratic rule. The subsequent two chapters discuss the third wave in Latin America, first through a regional overview in Chapter 6. Chapter 7 adds an in-depth analysis of the lengthy Chilean transition, which saw a sequence of different emulation efforts and therefore constitutes a particularly instructive case.

4

The Tsunami of 1848: Precipitous Diffusion in Inchoate Societies

The swiftest wave of regime contention occurred in 1848: Within one month, the spark lit in Paris set much of Central and Eastern Europe ablaze (see recently Traugott 2010: 131–42). What propelled this wildfire? This chapter first assesses arguments derived from extant approaches, which highlight the role of networks, nationalism, international influence and prestige, and rational learning, respectively. As the mass of primary evidence about these dramatic events shows, none of these explanations is very convincing; while some can account for one aspect of the 1848 riptide or another, none of them manages to explain the coincidence of high speed and low success and the process of participants' decision-making.

My theory, which combines cognitive micro-foundations with organizational macro-structures, offers a more persuasive account. People's decisions on whether to risk emulating the French precedent diverged clearly from standard rationality and rested instead on the inferential mechanisms of bounded rationality. Rather than seeking solid information as a basis for their high-stakes choices, many people acted on the first scrap of news that became available; even unfounded rumors greatly affected the turn of events, as both enthusiastic students (Boerner 1920: 8, 84, 116, 122, 126–27, 149; Schurz 1988: 103, 112, 132) and military commanders report (Prittwitz 1985: 34, 49, 52, 60, 120, 127, 287; Hohenlohe-Ingelfingen 1897: 17, 22, 25–26, 43). People eagerly jumped to the conclusion that they could replicate the Parisian success and did not assess in any depth whether French lessons really applied to their own polity. Therefore, they rushed toward challenging their own authorities, even in unpromising settings that differed starkly from France due to their socioeconomic and political backwardness. As a result of this precipitation, many of these rebellions ended in failure.

This rashness prevailed because in the organizationally inchoate polities of the mid-nineteenth century, common people had to decide on their own whether they would join the gathering wave of protests. In February and March of 1848, there were no mass parties or trade unions in Central and Eastern Europe, and citizens thus lacked representative leaders from whom to take guidance or cues. Instead, normal mortals with their precarious access to information and their minimal experience in political decision-making were compelled to make up their own mind. Facing tremendous uncertainty in these fluid, fast-moving conjunctures, they relied heavily on cognitive shortcuts and were swept up by the logically problematic inferences suggested by the heuristics of availability and representativeness. The resulting deviations from full rationality account for the lightning speed but also the disappointing outcomes of this tidal surge.

Certainly, it is methodologically inconclusive to use a single case, the wave of 1848, for demonstrating that the absence of broad-based organization had a crucial causal impact on the characteristics of contention's diffusion in this instance; only the comparisons with later waves below can establish this point convincingly. But the present chapter draws the baseline for this analysis by documenting the lack of organizational density at that time and the haphazard ways in which common people made their choices.

ASSESSING ARGUMENTS DERIVED FROM EXTANT APPROACHES

The tremendous speed yet very limited success of the tsunami of 1848 seem to falsify the predictions derived from extant theories. Theories about border-crossing networks, which are expected to proliferate and grow with the continuous advance of socioeconomic and political modernization, have particular difficulty accounting for the velocity of contention's spread in the mid-nineteenth century. While communication and transportation had improved considerably during the early modern era, transnational connections nevertheless remained sparse and thin in 1848; certainly, they were much sparser and thinner than during the twentieth century, when regime contention spread significantly less quickly.

In 1848, most connections were confined to the flow of information, especially via newspapers (Langewiesche 1998: 12–17; Werner 2009: 45–48). Few links existed through which people could influence each other across borders and bring about contagious or coordinated collective action. At a time when there were no national-level political parties and interest associations, there obviously were no international organizations of this kind (Jørgensen 2012: 205), as they emerged in later decades, for instance with the creation of the Socialist International. Such regional or global networks undertook substantial efforts to promote democracy during the third wave in the late twentieth century – but paradoxically, these transition efforts spread much more slowly than in 1848.

Furthermore, contrary to charges from established governments, groups of exiles who had found refuge in liberal Paris were rarely instrumental in lighting the spark of rebellion in their home countries; only in the Danubian backwaters of Moldavia and Walachia did this kind of transnational connection play a significant role in igniting efforts to emulate the overthrow of Louis Philippe. In sum, network approaches and their combination with modernization theories are at a loss to explain the exceptional speed of the spread of political regime contention during the mid-nineteenth century.

Arguments about nationalism do not provide a convincing explanation for the riptide of 1848 either. Since the Napoleonic Wars, nationalism had been rising in Central and Eastern Europe. In Germany, for instance, a serious crisis with France over the Rhine border in 1840–41 triggered a strong upsurge of nationalism, which inspired the lyrics of the German national anthem. If nationalism immunized people against foreign precedents, one would certainly not predict that a few years later, so many Germans were willing to risk their lives in order to emulate the Parisian events. In fact, observers felt shame that their compatriots did not initiate the struggle for liberty on their own but instead followed the "archenemy," France. But these sentiments certainly did not forestall emulation efforts, which got under way at breakneck speed. In conclusion, nationalism fails to explain the force and velocity of the diffusion wave unleashed by the overthrow of Louis Philippe.

Certain notions of nationalism also suggest that patriotic feelings induce people to reject political liberalism and democracy as foreign imports; instead, they embrace the autocratic and corporatist traditions of their home country. This line of reasoning underlies the arguments about the German *Sonderweg* or Russia's resistance to Westernization. But the events of 1848 disprove this incompatibility assumption. Many revolutionaries in Central and Eastern Europe embraced *both* nationalism and liberalism: They demanded political freedom, constitutional rule, and parliamentary responsibility in the same breath as national independence or unification. Indeed, nationalism itself was not an autochthonous creation but spread partly in a diffusion process,[1] as is visible in the fact that so many European flags reproduce the basic structure of France's revolutionary *tricolore* by featuring three bands of color. In general, many Central European and even some Latin American oppositionists in the early to mid-nineteenth century imitated symbols of the French revolution, erecting liberty trees and singing the *Marseillaise* (Ruttmann 2001: 289–321; Sperber 1998: 64–74); Johann Strauss Jr., for instance, was arrested by the Austrian police because he had his orchestra play the French national anthem during the 1848 revolution. In sum, participants in these contentious episodes did not see a real conflict between nationalism and French-inspired efforts to push for greater political liberty. Theories of nationalism thus cannot account for political thinking and behavior during this contentious wave.

---

[1] This spread occurred soon after the emergence of nationalism in Europe, not only during the later import of nationalism by Third World countries, which Anderson (1991: ch. 6–7) highlights. See also Jørgensen (2012: 203).

Nationalism does, however, help explain the failure of most of these transformation efforts. In Central and Eastern Europe, challenges to existing governments opened up a Pandora's box of demands, including ethnic claims, resentments, and hostilities (Jaworski 1998: 40–48). The temporary weakening of state power allowed suppressed nationalities to raise their voices, for instance in Czechia, Hungary, and Northern Italy. In response, established authorities deliberately stirred up competing nationalist sentiments to split and weaken these challenges (as contemporary observers noticed: Schurz 1988: 118). To contain Hungarian demands for independence, for example, Austria's imperial government mobilized Croatian nationalism. Mixed population patterns and the unclear composition and extension of various nationalities opened up considerable room for disagreements, conflicts, and governmental manipulation efforts. In Germany, for instance, controversies over the size and shape of the nation state that the rebels of 1848 intended to found, especially the acrimonious debate over a *grossdeutsch* vs. *kleindeutsch* path to unification, fractured the revolutionary forces and contributed greatly to the failure of the *Paulskirchen* constituent assembly.[2] Thus, in political settings and historical conjunctures in which the nation state was at issue, processes of democratic diffusion faced great difficulties in attaining success (cf. Linz and Stepan 1996). In conclusion, the force of nationalism helps explain the widespread failure of the tsunami of 1848 (Malia 2006: 235–39) – but this effect makes the tremendous speed of this diffusion wave even more puzzling.

In regard to world system theory and constructivism, Paris certainly had special appeal as Europe's cultural capital and the historical seedbed of revolutions. Therefore, observers throughout Europe and even in Latin America were captivated by the overthrow of the French king; by contrast, the wave of uprisings that swept across the Italian states at the very beginning of 1848 elicited little interest and was dismissed as "baby revolutions" ("Revolutiönchen," Boerner 1920: 68; Hachtmann 1997: 118). Thus, international status and prestige, factors highlighted by constructivists, played a role in directing people's attention toward one precedent and filtering out others; in the terms of my theory, France's position in the global hierarchy selectively shaped the availability of the Parisian events.

But the process of diffusion in 1848 differed significantly from the picture painted by constructivism. Primary sources do not convey the sentiment that Central and Eastern European revolutionaries tried to keep up with frontrunner France; the motivation not to lag behind the advanced Western neighbor did not drive emulation efforts. In fact, most rebels did not want to replicate France's declaration of a republic but instead transform absolutism into a constitutional monarchy (Ruttmann 2001: 231); therefore, their constitutional

---

[2] Simms (2013: 216–18) highlights the concerns of other European great powers about German unification, which posed significant additional obstacles to the revolutionaries' success.

model was Belgium (cf. Elkins 2010: 989). They wanted liberalism, not democracy; and they saw liberalism not as a stepping stone on a gradual path toward democracy, but as a fundamental alternative (Sheehan 1995). Political liberals of the mid-nineteenth century rejected democracy, which in their view merely transferred undivided sovereignty from the king to "the people." Instead, they distrusted sovereign power as such and wanted to break it up through a separation of powers and contain it with checks and balances. Such a mixed constitution would tame the exercise of coercive authority and thus safeguard political liberty, their foremost goal. In sum, diffusion in 1848 did not entail the spread of identical values and was not driven by the desire to become like the French in political-constitutional terms, as constructivism's arguments about norms cascades and the imitation of "modern" forerunners postulate.

Instead, the impulses that spread in 1848 were primarily feasibility judgments – inferences about situational opportunities and probabilities, not normative maxims of appropriateness. Louis Philippe's overthrow suggested to observers across Europe that seemingly powerful governments may actually be weak and vulnerable to challenges; moreover, opposition may be surprisingly numerous and willing to stand up to repressive governments. Thus, the predominant thought derived from the Parisian precedent was not "We *should* challenge our own authorities" but "If the French can successfully confront their regime, we can do it too!" The regime collapse in Paris did not raise the standard of proper behavior that people in other countries felt compelled to follow; instead, it seemed to show what oppositionists elsewhere *could* accomplish in pursuit of their own goals. This type of conclusion is in line with the bounded rationality approach that informs the present book, not the normative logic of constructivism.

Regarding the more forceful instruments of influence emphasized by world system theorists, the rapid spread of rebellion in 1848 can certainly not be attributed to the export efforts of a great power. Contrary to initial expectations, France made no attempt to promote the diffusion of revolution, neither through military force (as it had done from 1793 to 1812) nor through secret agents (as conservative regimes claimed). The international constellation of power, which pitted France against four other European great powers, precluded any interference in other polities' affairs. Thus, foreign pressure played no role in propelling the tsunami of 1848. Solidarity among conservative regimes, however, helped extinguish the flame of revolution in 1849, especially in Hungary, Central Italy, and southwestern Germany; notably, France itself, which had by then taken a conservative turn under new president Louis-Napoleon Bonaparte, helped suppress the Roman Republic in the Papal States. Thus, coercion wielded by great powers drove the final nail in the coffin of several revolutionary efforts and thus contributed to the failure of the wave of 1848. But it played no role in its initial advance and certainly cannot explain the speed of this tidal surge.

Rational learning cannot account for the 1848 riptide either. Regime contention is dangerous because governments wield organized coercion. The autocratic states of the nineteenth century had few scruples to use brutal force against challengers, as they had consistently demonstrated during the preceding decades. For this fundamental reason, rational individuals should prefer caution and engage in conflict only when facing a good opportunity. The very mixed results that the rounds of challenges triggered by the French revolutions of 1789 and 1830 attained should have reinforced this preference for prudence. Accordingly, externally triggered regime contention should have spread very selectively to particularly propitious settings at especially promising moments, where and when careful evaluations of likely benefits and costs yielded a positive net balance.

Yet critical masses of people all over Europe disregarded rational calculations and eagerly supported risky challenges to repressive rulers, even under highly unpropitious circumstances; predictably, most of these ill-considered protests ended in failure. The indiscriminate and instantaneous advance of the 1848 wave disproves rational choice predictions about the pattern of diffusion. Regime contention spread to a striking variety of settings, ranging from socioeconomically advanced and political liberal Baden in the West to utterly backward Walachia and Moldavia in the East; even in Russia's totally closed polity, some conspiratorial circles sought to sow the seeds of revolution imported from France.[3] And all of these actors struck immediately after the Parisian precedent instead of waiting for a good opportunity. The very pattern of emulative efforts, especially their vast geographic scope, their striking temporal clustering, and their occurrence on the heels of the triggering events, contradicts the observable implications of rational choice, which expects differentiation in space and time in line with specific circumstances and corresponding opportunities and risks.

The process of decision-making also diverged starkly from standard rationality. Instead of basing their high-stakes choices on solid information, many people rushed into action based on the precarious news that happened to be available, including unfounded rumors (Boerner 1920: 8, 84, 116, 122, 126–27, 149; Haenchen 1930: 52, 76; Prittwitz 1985: 34, 49, 52, 60, 120, 127, 287). All eyes were glued to France, whereas the Italian revolutions received little attention although they arguably held more relevant lessons. After all, the Italian rebels had challenged the type of absolutist regimes that Central and Eastern Europeans were facing; by contrast, the French had just overthrown a constitutional monarchy, which most Central and Eastern European challengers intended to institute. What rational rhyme and reason was there to take inspiration from the downfall of one's preferred regime type rather than from

---

[3] Seddon (1984: 445–47). Poland, by contrast, was still too shell-shocked from the brutal suppression of the 1830–31 uprising to participate in this new wave of contention (Davies 2005: 251–55).

the contemporaneous efforts to establish it? Indeed, what if limited autocracy did not work, as hard-core conservatives such as Austrian chancellor Clemens Metternich (1883: 565–66, 592–93, 627); the Prussian king's brother, Prince Wilhelm (reported in Varnhagen 1862: 261); and the Russian tsar (Haenchen 1930: 34) inferred from the demise of "Citizen King" Louis Philippe?[4] That the collapse of a regime induced many people to try to install precisely that type of regime does not look very rational.

When deciding whether to engage in political regime contention, Central and East European oppositionists did not apply the careful, systematic approach prescribed by rational choice. Despite high stakes and grave risks, which would have counseled thorough assessments of likely benefits and costs, people eagerly jumped to the conclusion that they could replicate the Parisian precedent. They did not assess in any depth whether French lessons really applied to their own polity. Thus, they proceeded in hasty, haphazard ways, putting their lives on the line without much thought. The prevailing mode of decision-making was not one of dispassionate calculation, but of exuberance and enthusiasm unleashed by the facile belief that the French success could easily be replicated (e.g., Rellstab 1849: 17–18). A true, rational justification for this leap of faith was conspicuous by its absence.

All these considerations show that rational choice cannot explain the riptide of revolution that swept across Europe in 1848 and that reached distant Latin America as well. The notion of full rationality borrowed from economics would have to be stretched very far and very thin to include the inferential procedures and patterns of behavior that the 1848 revolutionaries displayed. As the following sections demonstrate, these thoughts and actions are captured much more convincingly with the concept of bounded rationality.

THE CRUCIAL ROLE OF COGNITIVE HEURISTICS

Instead of rational learning, cognitive shortcuts drove the spread of regime contention in 1848. Bounded rationality offers a better account of the way in which people in Central and Eastern Europe drew lessons from the overthrow of Louis Philippe. As mentioned in the examination of constructivism, what diffused during the "springtime of the peoples" were not norms and values but feasibility judgments (Sheehan 1996: 268), especially the belief that the chances for challenging the domestic government were good. And as the discussion of rational choice has just shown, these inferences did not emerge from careful, systematic reasoning based on solid evidence, but from the haphazard processing of selective perceptions. Participants in these events did not gather the relevant information and use it to assess opportunities and risks thoroughly; instead, they were captivated by one specific precedent while neglecting others,

---

[4] On the other side of the spectrum, Central European advocates of a republic raised the same question (Ruttmann 2001: 177–80).

and they jumped to conclusions about the replicability of this precedent in
their own polities. In sum, people deviated regularly and significantly from the
maxims of fully rational decision-making.

Two of the cognitive shortcuts documented by psychologists, the heuristics of availability and representativeness, played especially important roles
in shaping the thoughts and actions both of challengers and of supporters of
the established authorities. The availability heuristic guided and channeled
people's attention, skewing and limiting their effective information intake for
logically problematic reasons. The striking downfall of Louis Philippe in glamorous, advanced France made a deep impression on many observers; all eyes
were on Paris. These vivid, dramatic events had a disproportionate, excessive
impact on people's minds, as a wealth of primary documents shows – both
from youthful revolutionaries (Boerner 1920: 73–77; Streckfuss 1948: 23–27;
Schurz 1988: 99–101) and from aristocrats of different political persuasion
(Varnhagen 1862: 203, 211, 250–61; Prittwitz 1985: 13–17).

Berlin's military commander reported that "it is very difficult to describe
the tremendous impression that this news [from Paris immediately] caused ...
the large mass of Berlin's inhabitants [became] vividly excited" and faced a
"surprised and stunned government" (Prittwitz 1985: 13, 15–16; my translation, as in all quotations in this book). The court in Berlin was indeed dumb-
struck upon hearing the news of Louis Philippe's overthrow in late February
1848 (Streckfuss 1948: 23; Hachtmann 1997: 121, 124); Varnhagen (1862:
211) noted, "Immense was the consternation and panic of our nobility." The
confusion was exacerbated further by the declaration of a republic that immediately followed: "The distant thunderstorm had with its sequence of lightning
strikes instilled fear and terror, but this last blow was felt very close and everybody stared at it in torpor" (Varnhagen 1862: 212).

Students who turned into revolutionaries used similar terms: "The February
Revolution appeared like lightning from a fair sky .... How could I describe
the impression that these tremendous events had on me, on all of us .... I could
have embraced the whole world and shouted: Now we will be free as well!"
(Boerner 1920: 67, 73–74). Another student, Carl Schurz, who after the revolution's failure emigrated to the United States and rose through the ranks of the
Republican Party to become secretary of the interior, reported about the events
of February 1848 from Bonn, then part of the Prussian Rhineland: "I remember
to have been so completely captivated [literally: filled out] by these happenings
[the downfall of Louis Philippe and its immediate repercussions on his home
region in Western Germany] that I could barely direct my thoughts toward
anything else" (Schurz 1988: 101). Upon hearing the news of the new French
Revolution from a friend who barged into Schurz's study, "I threw down my
pen .... We ran down the stairs, into the street. Where now? To the market
square ... [which was] teeming with students.... What did they want? Nobody
really knew." The Parisian events stirred up these students, who wandered the
streets for hours, "without aim and without goal" (Schurz 1988: 100–01). They

did not act rationally, pursuing their interests via goal-oriented actions, but had been swept up by the availability heuristic.

The impact on Austria was similar. "On February 29 the first news of the Paris revolution ... electrified the Viennese .... Everywhere there was great excitement and turmoil. At every possible meeting point the educated and well to do gathered to talk politics and give vent to their bitterness against the government" (Rath 1957: 34). Prince Metternich's wife recorded in her diary that "this news created general consternation in Vienna" (Metternich 1883: 532). Another Austrian aristocrat reported that the reports from Paris caused "perplexity," "amazement at the so rapid and unexpected dethroning of the French King," "surprise," and "anxiety"; he likened the events to "one of the most terrible political thunderstorms, which nobody in the otherwise so tranquil imperial city could anticipate" (all in Hartig 1850: 171–72). And a Saxon diplomat in Vienna wrote in a letter on February 29: "You can imagine the sensation that the news of Louis Philippe's abdication, which arrived here this afternoon, caused. The whole city is filled with it," and added on March 5: "Here a somber, ominous mood reigns in all circles. Like a thunderbolt the Parisian Revolution shed light on the darkness of our situation .... The most doomful rumors are circulating" (Vitzthum 1886: 73, 75). A U.S. diplomat used similar terms, including the metaphor with which so many observers (e.g., Obermann 1970: 58) expressed the widespread shock: "The first intelligence of the new revolutionary movement in France came upon Vienna like a thunder-bolt from a clear sky, and caused a shock which vibrated through every nerve of her political system .... The imperial family [was] panic-stricken by the tempest which threatened" (Stiles 1852: 102). Thus, the downfall of Louis Philippe captured an enormous amount of attention in the Austrian Empire as well, made a strong impression on people of all political orientations, and shook the ruling circles.

Some people were not content to follow the Parisian news from afar but felt compelled to go to the source. A politically interested novelist who had the financial means was so captivated by the French events that within a day or two of hearing the news of Louis Philippe's abdication and the declaration of a republic, she immediately undertook the cumbersome trip to Paris and spent two weeks there to learn firsthand about the revolution, "the grandest event of our time," – until news of the Berlin uprising of March 18 induced her to return to her native Prussia.[5] During her encounters with other passengers on her boat and train rides in February and March of 1848, "Paris constituted almost exclusively the subject of our conversation" (Lewald 1969: 7; similar 9, 16). Thus, the cross section of people who happened to travel together was focused on the striking events in the French capital as well.

---

[5] Lewald (1969: 7, 11, 28, 66, 70, 74); the quote is from p. 28. On p. 11, Lewald mentions a progressive painter who was planning to take a similar trip to Paris in order to "see the popular uprising, the popular movement 'with his own eyes.'"

Even at the end of the world, in faraway Chile, "the French Revolution of 1848 produced a powerful echo." As an oppositionist reports about "the dethroning of a king ... this news produced general rejoicing in our country.... The revolution in Europe was thus almost a Chilean revolution" (Vicuña Mackenna 2003: 3–4; see also Vicuña 2009: 168–69). Thus, the breakdown of France's July monarchy exerted an unusual impact and turned into the trigger of a wave of imitation efforts that swept across Europe and reached Latin America as well. The availability heuristic is crucial in explaining the extraordinary impetus emanating from this precedent.

The perceptions underlying these psychological and political effects were highly selective, skewed by factors that were hard to justify. From a rational standpoint, the revolutionary wave that swept across Italy in January 1848 held much greater relevance than the collapse of Louis Philippe's liberal, constitutional monarchy. After all, the Italian revolutions challenged the kind of absolutist regimes that also prevailed in Central and Eastern Europe; thus, these uprisings had the same target and therefore offered more directly applicable lessons. But the Italian uprisings were largely ignored or dismissed as "Revolutiönchen" (baby revolutions, in the words of Boerner 1920: 68). Rational considerations cannot account for this neglect, which reflected the availability heuristic. Illogically, European oppositionists gravitated toward France, where the regime type that most of them wanted to institute, namely, constitutional monarchy, had just broken down.

This narrow and distorted focus reflected the availability heuristic. Given France's international prestige and its status as one of Europe's great powers, the demise of Louis Philippe attracted disproportionate attention, compared to the conflicts unfolding in some small, relatively insignificant Italian states. Moreover, Paris was widely seen as "the mother of revolutions"; after all, the revolutions of 1789 and 1830 had erupted from that epicenter. Accordingly, the third French revolution elicited tremendous interest. Moreover, the violent overthrow of a king affected people's thinking much more than Britain's suffrage reform of 1832. Although democratization in a number of European countries ended up advancing through a sequence of such gradual changes, these reforms lacked the drama of public protests and the sudden toppling of a government. The French events, concentrated in a few days, were much more vivid, exciting, and memorable than the careful British deliberations and choice; in line with the availability heuristic, they therefore grabbed people's attention. As explained in Chapter 2, the object of learning impressed itself on subjects' minds, rather than being sought out proactively.

As the availability heuristic channeled people's attention and drew it toward the demise of the Citizen King, the representativeness heuristic induced them to draw rash inferences from this selective information. Above all, critical masses of people quickly concluded that they could repeat the Parisian precedent in their own polity. Applying facile judgments of similarity, they inferred from this single event that their own rulers were also weak; that domestic opposition was intense and widespread; that potential challengers were willing and able to engage in collective contention; and that the established regime would easily cede to protest. Foregoing careful analysis, they saw France as representative of the political opportunities that they themselves faced. One case of striking success inspired the hope that similar feats could be accomplished throughout Europe.

It is notable that people held this expectation not as a preliminary, tenuous conjecture; on the contrary, they were firm in their belief and brimmed with confidence that it would come true. This excessive faith provides the clearest indication that the representativeness heuristic, not a rational assessment, drove this rash conclusion about the replicability of the Parisian precedent. Moreover, this belief was held not only by oppositionists, but by the members and supporters of the existing governments as well; authorities in Central and Eastern Europe also thought that Louis Philippe's fate foreshadowed their own. Thus, this belief was not a product of wishful thinking; it did not emanate from the hope to leave oppression behind and finally win freedom. Instead, the fact that actors on both sides of the barricades subscribed to this belief demonstrates that it resulted from a "cold," cognitive inference, not from moral fervor or political ideology. Finally, it was this belief that unleashed the tremendous outburst of emotions that made this "springtime of the peoples" so special. Wild enthusiasm and vibrant exuberance prevailed among substantial sectors of the population in March and April of 1848. These emotions presupposed the inference derived from Louis Philippe's demise that tyranny was doomed and that freedom was on its way; thus, these emotions were caused by the representativeness heuristic.

The inferences suggested by this cognitive shortcut and their effects on people's thinking and feelings appear in the diaries and memoirs left behind by observers and participants of various political persuasions. A student reported shortly after hearing about the Parisian precedent, "I knew *for sure* [my emphasis], Germany would have to follow, it could not lag behind" (Boerner 1920: 74; similar inferences reported in Prittwitz 1985: 1, 13–18). Student Carl Schurz drew a similar inference: "But since the French had now chased away Louis Philippe and proclaimed a republic, so *certainly* [my emphasis] something had to happen here.... Like some of my friends, I was gripped by the feeling that finally the great opportunity had arrived to win back for the German people its freedom and for the German fatherland its unity and greatness" (Schurz 1988: 100–01).

As a Berlin intellectual recapitulates: "The monumental impressions of the day [!] during which the news ... of a new revolution in France arrived turned people's minds revolutionary" (Wolff 1898: 5). Theodor Fontane (1920: 10), later a famous writer, then a pharmacist, reports: "Right after the February Days [in Paris] it began to ferment everywhere, in Berlin as well." In a similar vein, in Vienna on the very day when "the first news of the Paris revolution was published ... a placard was posted" in a prominent public place "reading: 'Within a month Prince Metternich will be overthrown!'" (Rath 1957: 34).

The representativeness heuristic stimulated not only individual willingness to participate in emulative collective action, but also public calls to engage in regime contention. A few days after the Paris events, a leaflet proclaimed: "France is a republic! For us the bell tolls as well! ... With courage and joyful hope we get/rise up and add to this free France, this free Switzerland, this free Italy a *free Germany*.[6] A moment has come how there will never be a more propitious one. Let us use it! Everywhere there is ferment" (in Obermann 1970: 56–57; similar 67). Another leaflet announced in Cologne, center of the Prussian Rhineland: "Encouraged by the glorious precedent of France, the German people finally dares as well to confront its princes ... in a manly fashion" (in Obermann 1970: 65).

As mentioned above, the externally inspired belief in the ease with which existing autocracies could be challenged did not result from wishful thinking, but was shared by the established authorities as well. Remarkably, arch-conservative Prince Metternich jumped to the same conclusion, exclaiming immediately after receiving news of Louis Philippe's downfall, "Oh well, it's all over!" (reported in Häusler 1979: 133). Similarly, aristocrats in Berlin responded to Louis Philippe's overthrow with shock and fear, commenting to each other: "Believe me, it will happen in the same way here as well!" (Varnhagen 1862: 214). In a desperate move to forestall these "dangers," the German Federation held an emergency meeting on February 29, a mere five days after Louis Philippe's downfall, prompted by "the magnitude and significance of the most recent events in France, whose repercussions on all of Germany in the most manifold and most important ways will be as immediate as profound" (meeting protocol reproduced in Fenske 1996: 45).

In regard to discontented sectors, the rash inferences suggested by the representativeness heuristic spurred spontaneous outbursts of regime contention by reshaping people's beliefs about the likely success of collective action. Forcing a political transformation suddenly seemed easy: "If the French can do it, we can do it too!" And support for a contentious challenge seemed widespread.[7] The daily increase in the size of the protesting crowds reinforced these rash inferences and induced ever more people to overestimate the chances of successful collective action. This "irrational exuberance" (cf. Shiller 2005) led critical masses of citizens to give up the prudent preference falsification that they had practiced for so long, reveal their actual rejection of the political status quo, and defy their

---

[6] In late 1847, a civil war in Switzerland had ended with the victory of pro-democratic forces; and in January 1848, a wave of uprisings had spread through Southern and Central Italy. But these episodes of regime contention did not unleash the tsunami of revolutions in March of 1848; it was triggered by the Parisian events, as its timing clearly shows. The earlier incidents then provided added inspiration for emulators in Central and Eastern Europe, but they had not had a noticeable influence on the overthrow of Louis Philippe either (e.g., Traugott 2010: 130).

[7] Some politically more experienced observers, however, were aware of the differences between France and Central and Eastern Europe. Accordingly, Lewald (1969: 35, 45–46, 70–78) emphasized that in Germany, the time was not ripe for instituting a republic.

rulers (cf. Kuran 1995: ch. 15–16; Marwell and Oliver 1993: ch. 4). As more and more people therefore saw their individual preconditions for participating in regime challenges fulfilled, a cross section of the citizenry streamed into the streets. While students and intellectuals were initially at the forefront of this erupting mass contention, especially in Vienna (Vitzthum 1886: 78–79), it was not long before people from a wide range of sectors joined, including artisans, journeymen, shopkeepers, professionals, workers, and even housewives and youths (for Berlin, see Hachtmann 1997: 173–82; for Vienna, Frank-Döfering 1988: 32–35). Thus, the uprisings of 1848 were far more than a "revolution of the intellectuals," contrary to Namier (1992). Not only did notoriously restless sectors such as students participate, but so did a broad sample of normally quiescent groupings. This fact demonstrated clearly how widespread and profound discontent was and how intensely many people longed for a political transformation. The sudden revelation of these preferences in turn induced additional bystanders to support the challenges and thus fueled the spiraling protests.

In conclusion, the inferences drawn via the availability and representativeness heuristics from the French success prompted the revolutionary enthusiasm that swept across Europe during this "springtime of the peoples." Facile, overconfident judgments fueled the dramatic speed of diffusion in 1848. As many people unthinkingly concluded from the Parisian events that they could accomplish a similar feat, they rushed to action and did not carefully assess whether the conditions were propitious for launching such a dangerous challenge (Weyland 2009: 409–16).

The Predominance of Cognitive Heuristics in the Absence of Organizational Leadership

These cognitive heuristics held sway and triggered a tsunami of regime contention because the protesters who began to pour into the streets soon after hearing of Louis Philippe's downfall lacked any broad-based, strong organization. While these emulative challenges were often preceded by reform demands submitted by small political clubs or existing estate representations, the sudden eruption of mass protest and its quick escalation to uprisings occurred spontaneously and without organized leadership. Thus, the revolution in Paris triggered a wave of regime contention that unfolded without prior mass organization and without links to preexisting elite associations (Wolff 1898: 25–26). In particular, the large majority of the population – workers, artisans, journeymen, small shopkeepers, and their employees – lacked any broad-based associations; trade unions, for instance, had not yet emerged (Miller and Potthoff 1986: 14).

Certainly, in the years preceding 1848, teleologically called *Vormärz* (pre-March) in German historiography, liberal notables had formed movements, clubs, and small-scale associations *(Vereine),* which had also begun to extend links across various polities, especially the German middle states, albeit tenuously (Sperber 1991: 92–94; Sheehan 1995: 56). Despite press censorship and serious restrictions on their activities, these groupings sought to exert influence over public opinion and state legislatures (Mommsen 1998: ch. 4). Leipzig firebrand Robert Blum, for instance, founded an "Oratorical Practice Society" in late 1845 that met weekly to discuss a host of issues, including history and politics; this "crypto-political" association sought to foment political education and prepare broader-based collective action and organization (Reichel 2007: 63–67). But these movements and associations were mostly confined to the *Bildungs-* and *Besitzbürgertum,* the educated upper middle class and the propertied bourgeoisie; they lacked connections, especially organizational linkages, to mass sectors, which remained largely inchoate.

For years, these elitist clubs and associations had advanced demands for political reform, especially the liberalization of autocratic rule and, where absolutism still prevailed, the move to constitutional monarchy. Yet since the time that princes had reconsolidated their control after the revolutionary wave of 1830, these groupings had made no headway because they faced stubborn resistance from incumbent governments and found little resonance and support among the mass public. Above all, these liberal efforts did not stir up any street contention, a political tactic that these clubs abhorred anyway.

In early 1848, right after the news of Louis Philippe's downfall arrived, reformist groupings in these clubs and in established legislatures and estate assemblies took advantage of the tremendous ferment that this stunning event caused and renewed their demands. But these moderate, liberal initiatives were immediately outflanked by the gathering storm of mass contention that was spearheaded by more daring sectors such as students (especially in Vienna) and that broke out spontaneously (see Schieder 1979: 15, 19–20; Sperber 1991: 166), driven by the optimistic inferences derived via the availability and representativeness heuristics.

In Berlin, for instance, an amorphous cross section of the citizenry began in early March to meet "under the tents" in a park outside the city walls, discuss political issues in informal assemblies, and draw up petitions. The government's indecisive response, oscillating unpredictably between belated concessions and arbitrary repression, then induced the growing mass of protesters to turn its contentious efforts ever more transgressive, resort to violence, and build barricades. This escalatory dynamic got under way without any organizational guidance or clear, firm leadership. In particular, the liberal clubs and associations did not stimulate or lead these demonstrations, protests, and rebellions – neither in Berlin nor in the other sites of imitative contention all over Central Europe. These groupings of notables lacked any roots in broader sectors of society and had no command over the heterogeneous masses that poured into the streets on their own initiative in a completely unorganized fashion.[8]

---

[8] Yet while the revolutions of 1848 were not spearheaded by political parties or other mass organizations, they stimulated the eventual formation of political parties by politicizing society and by providing incentives for the mobilization of large numbers of people (Langewiesche 1978).

Claims by the established authorities that foreigners, especially agents from France and exiles from Poland, coordinated and led the uprisings (e.g., Metternich 1883: 624–25) lack an evidentiary base as well. It is a common trope of governments to attribute unrest to foreign agitators, rather than to domestic problems. But even the agents of incumbent governments do not present any credible, convincing evidence that French or Polish exiles played a significant role in this wave of regime contention. For example, the military commander of Berlin, who wrote an extensive report about the March rebellion, does not offer any proof to back up these accusations (Prittwitz 1985: 45, 85). In fact, historians deny these charges based on police reports and eyewitness accounts (Streckfuss 1948: 42; Hachtmann 1997: 170–72). In conclusion, neither domestic nor foreign organizers prepared, spearheaded, or coordinated the mass demonstrations and protests that erupted all over Central Europe in March 1848.

Instead, this dramatic wave of regime contention arose from the outpouring of fleeting, shifting masses of people who came together without any organized guidance or leadership. It fell to individuals on their own or in small informal groupings to decide whether to join the regime contention that was gathering steam around them. As participating students and intellectuals emphasized (Wolff 1898: 25–25; Boerner 1920: 137–41; Streckfuss 1948: 58, 95, 129), variegated masses of people in Berlin, for instance, joined the growing protests spontaneously and engaged in violent contention "without planning and with excessive haste" (Hachtmann 1997: 158). As a revolutionary student stresses, "on March 18 [the height of the protests], we had to see – without a plan, without unity, without the most minimal organization – what we could accomplish with our meager means" (Boerner 1920: 137; similar 135–41). A variety of eyewitnesses and observers stress the unguided actions of shifting multitudes that were not centrally coordinated by established leaders (for Baden, see Real 1983: 45–48) – "a totally undisciplined and unorganized mass of people" (Streckfuss 1948: 58). Theodor Fontane (1920: 17–21) reports that for hours, he "let himself be carried away" by haphazard groupings, participating in a street fight here and wandering past a barricade there.

These amorphous crowds lacked any established leadership. Influential voices rose and faded from one day to the next. Whoever gave a rousing speech could stir thousands to action but lost support when an even more skillful orator appeared in the next assembly. As none of these aspiring leaders commanded solid support, it was unclear who represented the protesters (Wolff 1898: 11–25, 63–76; see in general Rudé 2005: 246–52). Therefore, the authorities were at a loss with whom to negotiate over potential concessions, as military commanders emphasize: Nobody could authoritatively speak for or reliably commit the rebellious masses (Rellstab 1849: 48–49, 62, 75–81; Hohenlohe-Ingelfingen 1897: 47–48; Prittwitz 1985: 264, 292, 321–22, 334–35; see also Haenchen 1930: 53). Due to this lack of organization and the absence of representative leadership, common people lacked a clear referent from whom to take cues.

Similarly, a participant in Vienna reports that there was "no planned coordination" guiding contention; when he sought "definite instructions, I erred; everybody did without any authoritative guidance what they regarded as right." People acted at the spur of the moment (reported in Bayer 1948: 24, 26–27). Another revolutionary complains about the "total political immaturity that reigned among the burghers of Vienna" and that hindered the efforts to organize a national guard after the barricade fighting (Kaiser 1948: 29). As a historian reports about one of the turning points of street contention: "The crowd expected the students to lead them, but apparently the students had made no plans.... At this decisive moment, when the popular movement might well have failed for lack of a clear-cut program of action, a young doctor ... fearing that the golden moment might slip away" gave a rousing discourse. "His speech ended the crowd's indecision and encouraged others to speak out" until "the crowd was filled with a desire for action" (Rath 1957: 59, 61). Yet the lack of organization prevented the contentious masses from formulating a clear set of demands when the government was willing to respond with concessions. "What the wishes were whose fulfillment could calm the storm was impossible to clarify due to the chaotic cacophony of voices" [*verworrenes Durcheinanderreden*] (Hartig 1850: 171–72). Thus, emulative contention in Vienna also unfolded without any clear organization and systematic leadership.

In these amorphous, fluid situations, common citizens had to decide on their own whether to join the gathering storm of protest or prudently stay on the sidelines. But these people lacked experience in making political decisions on high-stakes issues as well as good access to information and a strong capacity to process it, which representative leaders have due to their institutional position. As contemporary observers commented, "The broader population [in Berlin] was lacking any formation of political concepts and thoughts" (*Berliner März-Revolution* 1848: 15). To overcome this lack of understanding, revolutionary student Carl Schurz embarked on a crash course of historical, political, and philosophical readings, "especially the history of the French Revolution" of 1789, and studied "the problems of the day" via recent pamphlets and magazines: "In this way, I sought to clarify my political concepts and to fill minimally the very big gaps in my historical knowledge" (Schurz 1988: 107). Thus, only after participating in protests and embarking on intense "activities as agitator" (ibid.) did Schurz try to get a firmer grasp of the political situation; he had joined the initial outburst of contention without a solid base of knowledge that would have allowed him to perform systematic calculations of opportunities and risks.

Many ordinary citizens stood on similarly weak ground when the wave of contention propelled by the Parisian precedent approached their polity. To still their hunger for information, people eagerly awaited the newspaper; when the next copy arrived, they were so impatient to learn about the most recent developments that one person had to get up on a table and read aloud. In fact, a revolutionary who was also a bookseller complained in late March 1848 that his business was going badly because "nobody reads anything but newspapers" (Blum 1981: 59; see Werner 2009: 45–48; Jørgensen 2012: 210).

In general, people lacked reliable knowledge of the fast-changing political situation. News was sparse and incomplete (Vitzthum 1886: 87), and the papers spread a good deal of misinformation (examples reported by Lewald 1969: 70). Citizens had difficulty cross-checking the conflicting scraps of news that happened to appear. How widespread and intense was discontent with the existing regime? Were opponents willing to act – and withstand repression? Would the government offer concessions or dig in its heels? In inchoate societies without observable collective actors, common people had little capacity to assess these crucial parameters; protesting students and intellectuals report facing tremendous uncertainty (Wolff 1898: 3–4, 32–35, 56, 77, 81–84, 106; Boerner 1920: 73–84; Streckfuss 1948: 31–78). For instance, "dark rumors" swirled around (Boerner 1920: 81, 84; *Berliner März-Revolution* 1848: 16, 28, 46, 50, 54, 68), affecting people's decision-making (Wolff 1898: 32–35). Lacking firm ground and confronted with a torrent of rapidly evolving events (Haenchen 1930: 52, 76), they grasped at straws.

To make any sense of these complex and fluid developments and avoid decisional paralysis, citizens seized upon cognitive shortcuts and were highly susceptible to the distortions that the availability and representativeness heuristics can produce. Citizens' weak basis of knowledge and limited processing capacity left much room for inferential heuristics that drew disproportionate attention to certain vivid, dramatic events while keeping experiences, which were equally relevant, if not more so, off of people's radars; and that processed this selective information in quick yet problematic ways by suggesting simple but logically faulty conclusions (Weyland 2009).

In sum, the weakness of organizational ties led to particularly narrow bounds of rationality. The absence of representative leadership deprived common people of cues to follow. Due to the lack of collective organizations, all sides in these conflicts faced stark domestic uncertainty and eagerly looked abroad for any hint that they could glean. Actors as diverse as rebellious students (Boerner 1920: 67, 73–75), radical intellectuals (Streckfuss 1948: 23–25), established aristocrats (Varnhagen 1862: 203, 211–20), and autocratic military commanders (Prittwitz 1985: 13–18) therefore paid close, almost obsessive attention to the Parisian events. In atomized, amorphous polities, the spark lit in France produced a wildfire of regime contention (as modeled by Kuran 1995: ch. 15; Marwell and Oliver 1993: 63–75, 86–94, 182).

COGNITIVE HEURISTICS AND THE FAILURE OF POLITICAL REGIME
DIFFUSION

The speed of contentious diffusion in 1848 was matched by its high rate of failure. The underlying reason was that critical masses of people joined emulative challenges precipitously, without carefully assessing the domestic political opportunity structure; they initiated protests and rebellions indiscriminately all over Europe, even in unpropitious settings. Due to this rashness, the firestorm of conflict resulted in few actual, lasting regime changes. In the least propitious settings, such as backward Moldavia, protests were quickly suppressed. In more modern Central Europe, open contention induced the established authorities to make some political concessions and promises, which the rebels, under the impression of the Parisian success, mistook for definitive victories. But princes retained command over the forces of organized coercion, and as soon as popular mobilization began to recede, they gradually reversed reforms and tightened the reins of autocratic control again (see in general Rudé 2005: 259–62). As a result, few lasting advances toward political liberalism resulted from the tsunami of 1848. It swept across large parts of Europe with dramatic speed, yet without bringing much direct progress toward democratic development (Siemann 1985; Sperber 1994; Dowe et al. 2001).

Cognitive mechanisms that held particular sway in the absence of broad collective organization, especially the heuristics of availability and representativeness, account not only for the velocity of diffusion, but also for the meager success of this riptide of regime contention. In particular, the inference derived from the representativeness heuristic that the power constellation in much of Central and Eastern Europe was basically similar to the French precedent proved misleading. This overestimation of similarity stimulated quick emulation efforts even in settings that actually were unpropitious – a recipe for failure. Critical masses of oppositionists in other polities, viewing the Parisian success – a single occurrence that happened in a specific context – as representative of the rest of Europe, jumped to the conclusion that challenges to their own governments were also promising. But contrary to this facile generalization inspired by Louis Philippe's striking downfall, established regimes elsewhere proved much less weak, and oppositionists less powerful; there were a number of important differences between France and the rest of Europe, which undermined emulation efforts. Thus, contrary to the exaggerated belief in similarities suggested by the representativeness heuristic, divergence in political conditions prevailed (as emphasized by Hobsbawm 1996a: 10–11).

Moreover, the very overthrow of the Citizen King and the gathering tsunami of regime contention helped induce established authorities in the rest of Europe to respond more flexibly to challenges. In this way, they skillfully avoided Louis Philippe's fate, kept control of the means of coercion, and maintained the capacity to reassert their power as soon as popular mobilization started to ebb. Thus, in addition to the preexisting differences in political setting, power constellation, and mobilizational capacities, the French precedent itself prompted other princes to react differently to popular challenges. A successful regime overthrow in one polity not only has demonstration effects on oppositionists, but can also teach other governments how to forestall emulation. The overestimation of similarity arising from the representativeness heuristic certainly did not foresee these deliberate reactions to externally inspired challenges.

Crucial differences overlooked by oppositionists in Central and Eastern Europe concerned both the strength of established regimes and the unity and contentious capacity of the opposition. In regard to the political support base of governments, reliable command over the forces of organized coercion plays a central role (Skocpol 1979). In France, Louis Philippe had lost this control and therefore could not manage "to rouse the National Guard to his rescue" (Ellis 2000: 34). In Central and Eastern Europe, by contrast, princes did not encounter such defection; instead, they maintained firm command, especially over the military. The armed forces stationed in Berlin in March 1848, for instance, were eager to repress the popular uprising; reports of their ferocity and gratuitous brutality abound (Wolff 1898: 37, 46–48, 51–52, 57–58; Lewald 1969: 97–101). Unprecedented discontent in their ranks threatened to erupt only after King Friedrich Wilhelm IV decided to withdraw the undefeated troops and leave the capital temporarily to the rebels in order to avoid further bloodshed (Bismarck 1898: 25–30; see also Hohenlohe-Ingelfingen 1897: 49, 53, 55; Haenchen 1930: 58, 64). When revolutionary activism faded and popular mobilization predictably receded due to its lack of overarching organization, the king could count on the military to occupy the city again; in late 1848, he reconsolidated full autocracy.[9]

Similarly, the Austrian government maintained control over its armed forces and used them systematically to contain, encircle, and quash the foci of contention. While the imperial household beat a tactical retreat by leaving Vienna for a while to escape from the vortex of revolution, its experienced military commanders quickly suppressed uprisings in the provinces, especially Bohemia, Northern Italy, and then Hungary. Thereafter, in October 1848, they used the victorious troops in a savage assault on the capital as well, court-martialing and executing well-known rebels such as Robert Blum (Reichel 2007: 159–78). When Hungarians reignited the flames of revolution in 1849 and the Austrian military proved too weak to extinguish them, the emperor could count on military assistance from his fellow autocrat, the tsar of Russia, who was determined to maintain illiberal rule in Eastern and East-Central Europe.[10] As the example of the two great powers engulfed in emulation efforts shows, governments had solid command over their armed forces and were able to suppress challenges with force as soon as they regarded that as politically advisable. Contrary

---

[9] Within two weeks of the March 18 uprising, Prussia's Friedrich Wilhelm IV began to order troops back into Berlin, although he proceeded gradually in order not to provoke popular resistance (Haenchen 1930: 64–65).

[10] Princes' immediate intense efforts to coordinate their responses to the challenges triggered by Louis Philippe's downfall are amply documented in the letters that Prussia's Friedrich Wilhelm IV exchanged with a number of his counterparts across Europe, ranging from England's Prince Albert to the Russian tsar (Haenchen 1930: 25, 32–36, 39–40, 45–46, 61).

to the inferences suggested by the representativeness heuristic, the coercive foundation of their rule was much less precarious than Louis Philippe's.

At the same time that established regimes in Central and Eastern Europe proved significantly stronger than the king of the French, opposition forces were weaker and suffered from divisions and cleavages. Due to the West-East gradient in political modernization, civil society in France was more developed and better organized than its counterparts in Central and especially Eastern Europe.[11] Having undergone revolution, restoration, and renewed revolution for decades, the French had greater political experience than their neighbors to the east. Moreover, since 1830 France had enjoyed a liberal regime, which allowed for greater freedom of expression and association than the absolutism prevailing in most of Europe. As a result, levels of organization were higher than in the inchoate polities toward the east. All these factors allowed for broader-based, more successful, and more sustainable collective action.

By contrast, in the polities that saw emulation efforts, popular mobilization declined soon after the initial effervescence of contention, which in inchoate societies is, predictably, temporary. In Berlin, for instance, revolutionary enthusiasm quickly died down (Lewald 1969: 75–78); many people seemed to want the return of normality. The lack of firm overarching organization made it difficult for the remaining challengers to sustain pressure and project influence over the medium run. In fact, the efforts to create political organizations, which received a strong boost from the March revolutions, took time to come to fruition yet created problematic side effects in the short run because they split oppositionists along political-ideological lines. These divisions weakened the challengers and opened the door for divide-and-rule tactics by princes, who were gradually regaining political strength. As a result of all these problems, the only way for political liberals and democrats to fight back against the creeping advance of reaction was through renewed protests and riots. But the silent majority saw these renewed outbursts of political unrest as troublesome disorder. In conclusion, the dearth of political organization tightly limited the chances for emulative contention to achieve success.

Another difference from the French precedent and critical source of weakness afflicting opposition forces in Central and Eastern Europe was the absence of consolidated nation states, which turned "the national question" into a serious bone of contention and gave governments ample opportunities to apply divide-and-rule tactics. Whereas in France this issue played no role in the conflicts of 1848, it soon rose to the top of the political agenda in the rest of Europe, joining the regime issue. Demands for greater freedom also opened the door for ethnic claims and resentments, which raised a second, diagonal dimension of conflict and ended up dividing opposition forces – a problem that

---

[11] Some especially perceptive oppositionists were aware of this difference (Lewald 1969: 35, 45–46, 70–71, 78) and warned early about the creeping advance of reactionary forces (Temme 1996: 160).

the initiators of emulation efforts had not considered in their rash inferences and haphazard calculations. In Germany, disagreements over the path toward national unification, especially the inclusion or exclusion of German-speaking Austria, caused long delays in the *Paulskirchen* constituent assembly and limited support for the charter that the delegates eventually elaborated. And in the Habsburg Empire, bottom-up demands for ethnic autonomy (e.g., among Czechs) and top-down attempts to pit one nationality against another (e.g., Croats against Hungarians) split the challengers and allowed the imperial government to maneuver itself out of its precarious initial position and regain control. Taking their inspiration from France, where a nation state had been forged in earlier centuries, the initiators of emulative protests, under the influence of the representativeness heuristic, overlooked or underestimated these problems. While they saw a great deal of similarity to the French precedent, this crucial difference weakened them and contributed mightily to the widespread failure of this wave of political regime contention.

The representativeness heuristic also undermined the success of emulation efforts by inducing challengers to overrate the significance and staying power of the concessions that a number of Central and Eastern European governments initially made. Under the impression of the Parisians' easy success, oppositionists believed that they had also achieved clear, definitive victories that would have a lasting impact. They thought that the reformist cabinets that princes appointed under duress and the constituent assemblies that were elected constituted and sealed a permanent shift in the balance of power. Overestimating their own force and misinterpreting the withdrawal of the military from Berlin and Vienna as the capitulation of absolutism, they did not pay sufficient attention to the fact that the established princes retained political sovereignty and kept command over the instruments of coercion. While rulers had to compromise on the use of their power, they continued to control the main sources of power and therefore had the opportunity to return to their old ways when political circumstances changed. The fluidity of this situation made it imperative for the challengers to remain vigilant and maintain popular mobilization. Yet while some perceptive voices warned about the creeping advance of reactionary forces (Temme 1996: 160), many participants in the initial protests were lulled into an unjustified sense of security, believing that – like the French – they had already won the "war." Therefore, the upsurge of political engagement quickly ebbed, draining support from reformist forces; for instance, the citizen militias that were intended to counterbalance the military and thus protect opposition forces from princes soon suffered a stream of defections as citizens did not see the need for continued participation, preferring instead to concentrate again on their private pursuits. The remaining challengers therefore turned into easy prey for princes who gradually regained their political strength. The illusion of easy success, inferred through the representativeness heuristic from the French precedent, therefore ended up being a source of weakness.

Due to the predominant perception of similarities with the French precedent, challengers also did not foresee the possibility that Central and East European princes might learn from Louis Philippe's downfall and therefore respond differently and more skillfully to the gathering wave of protests. Certainly, however, the established authorities had every incentive to prevent full replications of the Parisian events. Because the French king's intransigence had triggered his overthrow, advisors to the governments of other European countries advocated a more flexible response to nascent regime contention. Princes often vacillated between repression and toleration of protests; Prussia's indecisive Friedrich Wilhelm IV followed a particularly shifty course during the first half of March 1848. But as the conflict intensified and violence erupted, princes soon interrupted the spiral of escalation by granting concessions and promising a transition from absolutism to constitutional monarchy; in particular, they appointed reformist cabinets that seemed to represent the moderate opposition, and they convoked constituent assemblies that were charged with rewriting the rules of the political game. In fact, the Danish king had more time to see the wave of contention coming and noticed the costly clashes in Vienna (March 13–15) and Berlin (March 18–19); on March 21, he therefore offered these changes to the crowds gathering outside his palace in order to preempt violence (Skovmand 1973: 97–103). Facing a much weaker civil society and disposing of overwhelming repressive capacity, the tsar of Russia also used a proactive strategy, squashing an externally inspired conspiracy of very limited scope and deterring any stirrings of protest with preponderant force.

All of these variegated responses differed from Louis Philippe's actions, but the other monarchs had the benefit of learning from his downfall – and the intention of avoiding precisely that outcome. With this purpose in mind, princes calibrated their reactions to the specific power constellation prevailing in their polity, especially their own strength. Thus, they deliberately diverged from the French precedent, a possibility not considered in the challengers' expectation of similarity. Through their flexible, differentiated responses, Central and East European rulers managed to save their skin. They also retained the loyalty of the military – and soon used it in most cases to roll back revolutionaries' early gains and reestablish full autocracy.

In all of these respects, the political settings and the course of events in Central and Eastern Europe proved distinctly different from those of the precursor, France. The perceptions of similarity suggested by the representativeness heuristic, which underlay the belief in the easy replicability of successful regime contention, proved misleading. The demise of Louis Philippe did not foreshadow the fall of the dominoes in the rest of Europe. Instead, fundamental differences in political circumstances limited the opportunities facing challengers toward the east, and princes scared by the French king's overthrow took steps to lower these chances even more. As a result, the protests and uprisings that critical masses of people in Central and Eastern Europe were eager to initiate and join ended up in a great deal of failure. The representativeness heuristic had inspired haste, which in turn made waste.

THE HISTORICAL SIGNIFICANCE OF THE FAILED REVOLUTIONS OF 1848

The prevalent failure of revolutionary efforts in 1848–49 raises the question whether this tsunami of contention had much historical significance: Does it really deserve the attention that it receives in this book, which analyzes it side by side with monumental events like the Russian Revolutions and world-spanning processes like the third wave of democratization?[12]

The underlying issue concerns the impact of massive political failure: Does a frontal but aborted or suppressed challenge to an autocratic regime make a difference in a country's political evolution? The ample literature on critical junctures and path dependence suggests a positive answer (e.g., Collier and Collier 1991): The outcome of a serious political crisis, which the 1848 revolutions undoubtedly constituted in many polities, often has important and lasting political consequences. If a confrontational effort at effecting profound change does not succeed, the result is usually not the status quo ante – it is not as if nothing had happened. Rather, the outcome of such a severe conflict often has tremendous repercussions for the power capabilities, interest definition, preferred strategies, and resolve of the contending actors, as well as for the institutional parameters and political patterns shaping their future interaction.

Specifically, if incumbents end up winning, as commonly happened in 1848, they try hard to prevent a recurrence of dangerous, costly challenges by weakening the clout, resource base, and organization of potential opponents and by restricting the political space in which they can operate (Breuilly 2000: 124). The Prussian king, for instance, tightened repression during the 1850s and thus prevented reform-oriented groupings from forming or acting. The royal house also sought to shore up its support base and ensure the loyalty of the armed forces. In fact, the experience of 1848 was so traumatic that even fifty years later, Kaiser Wilhelm II still urged his military to commit to forestalling a repetition of this menacing uprising! Thus, defeat in a major conflict can have a tremendous impact and shape a country's subsequent political trajectory.

Accordingly, many scholars have argued that German political liberalism never fully recovered from the failure of 1848. For instance, the inability of the mid-nineteenth century revolutionaries to forge Germany's unification left the national question unresolved and allowed conservative forces, especially Chancellor Otto von Bismarck, to use it as a wedge issue, divide political liberals, and further strengthen the Prussian military machine and the royal house.[13] Interestingly, Bismarck himself had cut his political teeth in the 1848 revolution

---

[12] I thank John Higley for raising this question forcefully.

[13] See for instance Winkler 2000: 130, 152–58, 167–95, 211–12, 215–17, 236–38. Even Sheehan (1995: ch. 8–10) admits these problems existed.

(Bismarck 1898), developing a special aversion to popular sovereignty and democratic politics, yet also learning that autocratic rule would have to absorb, domesticate, and defang participatory bottom-up energies. His resulting political strategy, a form of Caesarist authoritarianism (Winkler 2000: 174, 182–83, 191), greatly helped to cement *Hohenzollern* autocracy and keep Germany on a nondemocratic path for decades. In domestic politics, the monarchy remained predominant and unaccountable, confining Parliament to a subordinate position for a much longer time period than in similar European countries. This imposition limited the legitimacy of party politics and cemented executive hegemony up into the Weimar Republic, with fateful consequences for the survival of this fledgling democracy (Ertman 1999: 43–50).

In sum, the failure of the 1848 revolutions had a substantial impact on German history. This conclusion emerges from mainstream historical research and does not presuppose the structuralist or Marxist idea that a successful revolution is a necessary precondition for progress toward democracy. Moreover, it is not premised on similarly questionable assumptions about a country's "proper" road to modernity, which underlay the lengthy debates about an alleged German *Sonderweg* (special path – understood as an "historical aberration," Blackbourn and Eley 1984: 10). Regardless of this complicated and controversial issue (e.g., Blackbourn and Eley 1984 versus Winkler 2000), one can make a strong case that 1848 had crucial, lasting repercussions. The failure of transgressive mass contention and political regime conflict is by no means insignificant.

CONCLUSION

By applying insights on bounded rationality, this chapter explains the coincidence of dramatic speed yet scarce success during the revolutionary wave of 1848. Resorting to the heuristics of availability and representativeness, critical masses of people inferred from the striking collapse of Louis Philippe's rule that they could defy their own governments as well and achieve substantial advances toward political liberalism or democracy. The availability heuristic drew disproportionate attention to the Parisian events and led to a neglect of other experiences with political regime contention, such as the Italian revolutions of early 1848, which confronted absolutist governments similar to those prevailing in Central and Eastern Europe and therefore held greater relevance from a fully rational standpoint. Nevertheless, all eyes were directed toward the new uprising in the motherland of revolution, France. Moreover, the representativeness heuristic led people all over Europe to draw excessively firm conclusions from the Parisian success and to infer that they could accomplish a similar feat in their own polity; facile judgments of similarity derived via this shortcut induced them to rush into emulation efforts. For these reasons, a tsunami of regime contention swept across Europe in March of 1848, within one month of the triggering events.

But the inferences drawn via the heuristics of availability and representativeness proved to be problematic guides to action. The precipitous challenges they inspired encountered contextual conditions and government responses that differed significantly from the French precedent. The lessons derived from the Parisian events therefore did not lead to success in many instances. The established authorities proved stronger and savvier, and the opposition forces weaker and more divided, than oppositionists believed on the basis of Louis Philippe's easy overthrow. The French events did not prove nearly as representative of the situations prevailing in Central and Eastern Europe as this cognitive shortcut suggested. Therefore, emulation efforts frequently met with failure.

The operation of inferential heuristics thus helps explain one side of the negative correlation that characterizes waves of political regime diffusion, namely the association of high speed with low success. Acting with bounded rationality and disregarding the rules of prudence, challengers rushed into emulation efforts but rarely managed to accomplish their goals. They acted rather indiscriminately by challenging rulers all over Europe – but that meant that they struck in many settings that actually held limited prospects of success.

These tendencies prevailed because political organization was very incipient. Many people lacked organizational ties and therefore did not have representative leaders who would provide direction or cues. Common citizens therefore had to decide on their own whether to join in the mass demonstrations and protests that began to erupt under the impression of the French precedent. But these people had precarious access to information, being exposed to a variety of fast-changing news of dubious truth value; for instance, rumors often ran wild. Due to their lack of political experience, they also had little perspective and great difficulty making sense of this news. Therefore, they clung to cognitive shortcuts that allowed them to cope with decision pressure – yet at the risk of distortions and biases. Confronted with a political earthquake and surrounded by fog, these people were highly susceptible to the simplistic inferences derived via the heuristics of availability and representativeness; they lacked the solid base of knowledge and the information-processing capacity to cross-check the expectations suggested by the strikingly easy overthrow of the king of the French.

The preceding analysis also shows that cognitive-psychological mechanisms are crucial to explaining the distinctive characteristics of the riptide of 1848, especially its breakneck speed and disappointing failure. Bounded rationality provides the micro-foundation required to account for political macro-phenomena. This approach offers a more convincing account than alternative theories, including rational choice. Although the events under investigation lie far in the past, there is a great deal of primary source material with which to reconstruct people's perceptions and thoughts and thus document this finding.

The 1848 revolutions show the operation of cognitive heuristics in full force. The low level of organizational density gave the polity a fairly simple structure in which rulers, their institutional agents, and their elite supporters faced a mass public of individuals and small groupings. For emulative challenges to get under way, common people had to make up their minds largely on their own. Individual-level mechanisms such as cognitive heuristics thus came to the fore and can be observed in a direct, straightforward way. The decision-making process became more complex after more and more people joined political organizations, whose leaders then came to make the effective choices and lead the masses into action. How the emergence of political organization shaped the operation of inferential shortcuts and how waves of political regime contention changed as a result are the subject of the next chapter, which analyzes the international repercussions of the Russian Revolutions of 1917. Chapter 5 will add political-organizational macro-structures to the explanatory framework of this book and thus help build a theory of politics that rests on bounded rationality step by step.

5

The Delayed Wave of 1917–1919: Organizational Leaders as Guides of Targeted Contention

The Russian Revolutions of 1917 provided powerful impulses for political change in Europe and beyond (Hobsbawm 1996c: 65) and helped to trigger a number of contentious transitions to democracy. But this diffusion wave differed starkly from the riptide of 1848. Above all, it advanced more slowly but attained greater success in producing actual progress toward democracy. A year or more elapsed between the triggering events of February and October of 1917 and the suffrage reforms and overthrows of monarchies that a number of European countries experienced starting in late 1918. Why this delay in the initiation of externally stimulated regime contention? And why did the variegated attempts to cross the threshold to full democracy that eventually gathered steam reach their goals so often? What accounts for the distinctive features of democratic diffusion in the early twentieth century and the differences from the tsunami of the mid-nineteenth century?

The present chapter answers these questions by introducing organizational macro-structures into the micro-foundational framework applied in Chapter 4. The emergence of mass parties and trade unions in the late nineteenth century reshaped the operation of cognitive heuristics and affected their impact on political information-processing and decision-making; as a result of this interaction, the characteristics of democratic diffusion changed. Specifically, the rise of large-scale organizations took the effective decision about participating in emulative regime contention out of the hands of common people and transferred this responsibility to representative leaders, from whom many citizens came to take cues. Due to their institutional positions and the extensive political experience required for reaching them, these leaders disposed of much better information and had greater processing capacity than ordinary people. Having a firmer grasp of political developments and facing a narrower band of uncertainty, they relied less heavily on cognitive shortcuts, were less prone to rash inferences, and therefore acted less precipitously. Certainly, like all mortals, they also applied inferential heuristics, but the resulting conjectures and judgments were anchored by more solid information. Moreover, leaders had the opportunity to discuss these inferences with their advisors and their intraorganizational rivals. For these reasons, they acted with moderately bounded rationality – distant from the norms of full rationality, but also from the tightly bounded rationality that characterizes ordinary citizens and radical sects. It follows that mass parties and trade unions do not tend to respond to external precedents with immediate emulation efforts. Instead, they assess the constellation of power more carefully than common people do, and they wait for a good opportunity to proceed to political regime contention. For these reasons, in polities with broad-based organizations democratization waves spread more slowly, but these efforts have greater prospects of success. Profound change on the reception side of diffusion thus helps explain the negative correlation highlighted in this book.

The macro-structural argument substantiated in the present chapter implies that the type of political organization, especially the procedures for internal decision-making, profoundly affects the operation of cognitive heuristics and, consequently, the response to external stimuli. Organizations that allow for critical debate and pluralistic deliberation are well-positioned to widen the bounds of rationality and trace a fairly prudent course of action. By contrast, uniformity-seeking, sect-like splinters (cf. Geyer 1976: 94; Zarusky 1992: 84; Müller 2010: 173–85), which tend to be common at the extremes of the ideological spectrum, engage in "groupthink" (McDermott 2004: 249–55; Schafer and Crichlow 2010), give cognitive heuristics freer rein, and therefore embark on much rasher, ill-considered challenges. As the discussion below indeed shows, broad-based social-democratic parties that encompassed diverse tendencies, such as the (Majority) Social Democratic Party of Germany (Sozialdemokratische Partei Deutschlands-SPD),[1] acted with considerable prudence, based on a reasonable understanding of the prevailing opportunities and constraints; therefore, these mainstream parties managed to achieve many of their democratizing goals. Small circles of left-wing radicals, however, such as the proto-communist Spartacus Group in Germany, were "carried away" by

---

[1] In the course of World War I, an increasing number of SPD members and parliamentarians came to oppose the party leadership's support for the German war effort and formed their own organization, which in April 1917, influenced in part by the Russian February Revolution, created a separate party, namely the Independent Social–Democratic Party of Germany (USPD). Since pacifism was the USPD's only common denominator, the new party was highly heterogeneous in terms of ideology, strategy, and tactics (Moore 1978: 287); its members included long-standing moderates, such as revisionist Eduard Bernstein, who abhorred revolutionary adventurism (Bernstein 1998), but also ultra–radical firebrands, such as Georg Ledebour. For a while, the Spartacus Group, which in late 1918 founded the Communist Party of Germany, also found refuge under the USPD's broad tent. As a result of its stark internal divisions on most political and ideological issues, the party was often paralyzed, especially during the revolution of 1918–19 (Barth 1919: 64, 78, 89–90), rarely acted in any coherent fashion, and soon dissolved as its left wing joined the Communist Party whereas more moderate sectors reunified with the SPD.

the appeal of external models, sought to replicate them at all cost, and engaged in protests and rebellions at the first sign of an apparent opening. Due to this rashness, they mostly failed. Tragically, a number of them paid with their lives because mainstream Social Democrats and centrists – despite their better grasp of the situation – also relied on cognitive shortcuts to some extent: Under the impression of Lenin's easy power grab in Russia, they overestimated the likely success of far-left uprisings and therefore repressed these challenges with disproportionate force. Acting with the moderately bounded rationality described above, the representative leaders of wide-ranging organizations accomplished their goal of defending fledgling democracies from communist efforts to impose vanguard rule, but at the cost of unnecessary brutality and of problematic concessions to renascent right-wing groupings.

My theory emphasizes that the emergence of large-scale organizations reshaped the processing of political information and thus widened the bounds of rationality. In this view, the representative leaders of 1917–19 pursued similar goals as the inchoate masses of 1848, but in a less precipitous, more carefully planned fashion. An alternative interpretation claims that consolidated political organizations primarily seek self-preservation and therefore have a natural tendency toward risk aversion and moderation.[2] Theoretically speaking, however, it is unclear why organizations should be more intent on guaranteeing their survival than unorganized common people, whose real life, in flesh and blood, is at risk during contentious episodes. Empirically, organizational leaders do not tend to be risk-averse, but disproportionately risk-acceptant (March 1994: 51–52). Moreover, in the (pre-)revolutionary situation of 1918, broad-based political parties and unions made high-stakes choices that explicitly deviated from their organizational self-interests.

During the critical juncture of September–October 1918, for instance, the German SPD had to decide whether to share governmental responsibilities as a junior partner – at a time when defeat in a terribly costly war started by conservative sectors was imminent and when the established regime, the state, and even the nation were in danger of dissolution: Why bail out the sectors that had caused this disaster and "take over a bankrupt enterprise at this moment of

---

[2] See in general Wilson (1995: 9–11, 230); for the United States, Piven and Cloward (1979); for the pre–World War I SPD, see especially Michels (1959: part 6); and for the German revolution of 1918–19, see for instance Kluge (1985: 166). Michels's analysis is skewed by an unrealistic standard, namely "ideal democracy" identified with "the self-government of the masses" (Michels 1959: 11, 24), that is, direct democratic decision-making from the bottom up; any organization will fall short of that standard. Moreover, Michels is strongly influenced by the questionable "crowd psychology" of the turn of the century and has a predilection for strident claims (e.g., "the incompetence of the masses is almost universal"; "the rank and file are incapable of looking after their own interests," Michels 1959: 86), which betray a nonscholarly, ideological bent. In turn, Piven and Cloward's (1979) claims that only disruptive protest, not formal organization, can successfully bring change fails to consider the whole issue of collective action dilemmas à la Olson (1965).

greatest desperation?" leaders such as Philipp Scheidemann (1921: 176) asked. Party chairman Friedrich Ebert clearly framed the controversy: "If you privilege the interest of the party, you have to reject any governmental responsibility [at this point]; if, however, you think that the collapse of our country cannot leave us indifferent, then you need to examine very seriously whether we shall shoulder this risk" (quoted in Keil 1947, vol. 1: 448; see also Ebert 1926, vol. 2: 90–92). Clear majorities in both relevant party committees voted yes. Tragically, conservative and reactionary forces immediately took advantage of the SPD's decision to look beyond narrow organizational interests and associated the party with the crushing defeat and the onerous truce and peace conditions imposed by the victorious Entente. The party paid a high price – a risk it had knowingly incurred; organizational self-interest did not drive its choices during this crucial episode of political regime contention.

Similarly, the mainstream union confederation signed a basic compromise agreement with the employers' association right after the eruption of the November revolution despite the risk that "the reputation of union leaders could get discredited because they now, during this [revolutionary] movement, practically entered a coalition with the entrepreneurs." But union leaders concluded that it was "urgently necessary to achieve this agreement in the interest of the workers in order to avoid unemployment, destitution, and misery" (union document of December 1918 reproduced in Schönhoven 1985: 542–43). In their view, the pressing needs of the working population had priority over organizational self-interest.

In sum, the rise of organizations introduced a new level of decision-making about emulative regime contention. Whereas in 1848 ordinary people had to make up their mind about whether to follow external precedents, in 1917–19 many common citizens were followers of well-organized parties and unions and therefore received guidance from their leaders, who became the effective decision-makers. These representative leaders responded to external impulses for regime contention, but in a deliberate fashion that was attuned to the domestic power constellation and political conjuncture. Diffusion therefore diminished in speed, but increased in success. Certainly, however, not everybody belonged to broad-based, internally diverse organizations that proceeded with such prudence. A number of people had become distant from mainstream Social Democracy and escaped from its discipline, especially during the exceptional hardships of World War I, and some of them joined small sectarian groupings. More susceptible to cognitive shortcuts, these mass actors and sects were much rasher in responding to external precedents, yet they achieved limited success.

To document all these points and thus account for the wave of regime contention in 1917–19, which the following section discusses in conceptual and empirical terms, section 3 shows that the heuristics of availability and representativeness stimulated some impulses among mass actors and radical sects to emulate the Russian precedents right away. But as the subsequent section demonstrates, the leaders of broad-based organizations were less swept up by the simplistic inferences suggested by these shortcuts. Therefore, they channeled external impulses toward more orderly, institutional reform efforts undertaken at propitious moments. These steps toward democratization occurred with some delay from the external precedent and were often successful – the opposite of the 1848 tsunami. The last section offers evidence, however, that even these representative leaders operated with bounded – not full – rationality. While not as easily captivated by the availability and representativeness heuristics, they were still influenced by these shortcuts, deviated from strict rational standards in their judgments and actions, and overreacted to external impulses. In particular, they feared that radical-left efforts to emulate the Bolshevist capture of government power could come to fruition and therefore suppressed communist rebellions with excessive force.

THE NATURE AND CHARACTERISTICS OF DEMOCRATIC DIFFUSION IN 1917–1919

The Petrograd events set in motion intersecting waves of transformations, which ranged from direct efforts at imitation to preemptive reforms to forestall such contagion, especially via democratization. As the Russian Revolution of 1905 had done (Harrison 2007: 17–22, 34; Kurzman 2008), the February Revolution that overthrew tsarist absolutism stimulated mass mobilization for democracy. As leading Social Democrats stressed: "The Russian Revolution exerted a stimulating impulse on the oppositional movement and the popular mood in Germany" (Dittmann 1995: 508; see also 503), and: "After the overthrow of Tsarism in Russia, it turned into the general conviction in Germany that the days of Prussian autocracy were numbered as well" (Hoegner 1979: 21). With Russia's installation of a republic, Central Europe's semiabsolutist monarchies became democratization laggards, as even Germany's last imperial chancellor recognized (Baden 1927: 101–06; for Austria, Bauer 1923: 57). The Russian regime change therefore triggered popular demands for political and socioeconomic reform across Europe, as highlighted, for instance, by German Social Democratic Party leaders (Scheidemann 1929, vol. 1: 337–38, 342; Müller 1925: 96). An upsurge of labor protest engulfed several European countries, as well as nations in distant Latin America (Korzeniewicz 2000; Albert 1988: 237, 249, 252, 266–70). Restive masses demanded economic and social improvements and steps toward democracy, such as universal, equal suffrage.

Whereas the February Revolution unleashed democratizing impulses and provided inspiration especially for reformist sectors organized in broad-based parties such as the German Social Democratic Party, the October Revolution, which brought the communists' armed capture of power and subsequent suffocation of democratic advances in Russia, had divergent effects. The Bolshevist takeover turned into a model for narrow ideological sects, but became a deterrent example for the representative leaders who pursued determined yet prudent advances toward democracy.

The communist power grab immediately inspired sectarian groupings. It stimulated constant radical agitation starting in late 1917, triggered several attempts at direct replication that installed fleeting, precarious Soviet republics in Hungary, Slovakia, and Bavaria (Schulz 1980: 198–200), and spurred violent uprisings elsewhere, such as Berlin. Where radical revolutionaries temporarily succeeded, they provoked a ferocious backlash that swung the pendulum in the opposite direction. Indeed, Hungary was the first country to institute the kind of conservative dictatorship that proliferated during the interwar years (Oberländer 2001; Lorman 2006; Weyland 2010: 1164–69). Similarly, Bavaria turned into a stronghold of reaction, which provided fertile ground for Adolf Hitler to make his first attempt at seizing power in 1923 (Carsten 1988: 252–57; Winkler 2000: 396–98, 413, 431, 441–45; Wehler 2010: 401–03).

More important, however, was the indirect impact and deterrent effect of the Soviet precedent: The perceived risk of its spread induced centrist and moderate-left sectors to push for preemptive reforms and thus reinforced the democratizing impulse of the Russian February Revolution. Above all, broad-based parties sought to institute full democracy and thus immunize the body politic against the communist virus (Collier 1999: 78–79). The very radicalism and undemocratic nature of the October Revolution strengthened the determination of representative leaders to enact electoral and constitutional changes in a wide range of European countries (Bartolini 2000: 86–97, 106; Eley 2002: 152–57, 224–25), which brought the breakthrough to full democracy in Germany, Austria, Britain (Marwick 1965: 189, 203, 215; Garrard 2002: 79–80), Denmark (Hilson 2007: 11, 14–15), and Sweden (Verney 1957: 207–12; Scott 1988: 477–79; Collier 1999: 84–85) and additional liberalizing reforms in countries that were already democratic, such as Belgium (Collier 1999: 90; Lamberts 2006: 361–62) and Italy (Seton-Watson 1967: 511–12, 524–26, 547–48). Thus, the reformist response to the October Revolution, a deliberate political vaccination campaign, combined with the impact of the February Revolution to produce a powerful wave of pro-democratic regime contention.

As mentioned in the introductory chapter, the diffusion wave of 1917–19 differed significantly in its main features from the riptide of 1848. While some fairly spontaneous protests erupted right after the triggering events, such as strikes in Austria and Germany in April–May 1917 and January 1918, the leaders of broad-based organizations quickly tamed this bottom-up contention and kept it from turning into serious political challenges to the established authorities, which they regarded as unpropitious in the midst of total war. These representative leaders acted on foreign impulses and pushed forcefully for steps toward democratization only when the defeat of the Central Powers in World War I provided the opportunity. After the Russian precedents, there was a delay before externally inspired regime contention gathered steam.

Yet because representative leaders waited for the right moment, the democratizing wave of 1918–19 was much more successful than the mid-nineteenth century wildfire. Whereas in 1848–49 initial liberal concessions were quickly rolled back, 1918–19 saw the installation of full democracy in Austria, Germany, Britain, and Sweden and liberalizing measures in other European and even Latin American countries (Albert 1988; Korzeniewicz 2000). These democratic gains resulted not only from the war, but also from diffusion factors (Markoff 1996: 74, 85; Collier 1999: 77–79). The inspiration emanating from the February Revolution and the deterrent effect of the October Revolution played a crucial role. The democratizing wave of 1918–19 therefore affected not only vanquished Austria and Germany, but also victorious Britain, nonbelligerent Sweden and other neutral countries (Schmitt 1988: 40, 74, 121–22, 144, 190, 242), and uninvolved Latin America.

Diffusion's diminished speed but increased success emerged from the efforts of organizational leaders, who guided mass contention away from immediate outbursts and toward well-targeted challenges. In 1917–18, most officials of political parties and mass organizations, especially from the social democratic labor movement, tried hard to contain bottom-up protests, which they saw as unpromising and counterproductive due to the risk of a backlash. But when the constellation of power crumbled and a window of opportunity opened up, these leaders forcefully pushed their followers' reform demands. This calculated approach brought a slower spread of regime conflict, but more lasting transformations than the rash of uprisings in 1848. Representative leadership, which had emerged in the intervening decades, made a crucial difference. Above all, the massive social-democratic labor movement now encapsulated a large share of the urban popular sectors that had a particular propensity toward collective action. In the perceptive words of a leading participant: "Whereas in 1848 it was still an amorphous mass without political training and firmly organized party structures, by the outbreak of the World War the German people was organized in large-scale political parties whose purpose it was to put their stamp on politics" (Dittmann 1995: 632). As a result of this fundamental growth of organization, responses to external triggers became less spontaneous and more deliberate; less driven by enthusiasm and more realistic; and less rapid but more successful.

The following sections substantiate the three crucial aspects of this argument by discussing, first, spontaneous efforts to emulate the Russian precedents; then, the attempts of representative leaders to channel this mobilizational energy toward deliberate reform efforts undertaken at propitious moments; and finally, these leaders' overreaction to sectarian challenges stimulated by the Bolshevist success.

COGNITIVE HEURISTICS AT THE MASS LEVEL

As in 1848, many people were immediately impressed by a dramatic, successful external precedent. The Russian revolutions, besides raising hopes for peace, demonstrated the striking facility with which a long-standing autocratic dynasty could be toppled in February and a small determined minority could capture power in October. Some mass sectors that were not tightly controlled by social democratic leaders and that were encouraged by radical-left groupings quickly took inspiration from these external stimuli, eager to challenge their own governments. These ordinary workers, who acted rather spontaneously, had limited information and processing capacity and relied heavily on inferential shortcuts. As dramatic, vivid events that grabbed people's attention, the Russian revolutions were highly "available;" they made a disproportionate impression and stimulated considerable interest, for instance in Germany (Tormin 1968: 59–62). The "never-imagined ease and speed" with which the tsarist regime collapsed in February (Runkel 1919: 45) and the Bolshevists took power in October tempted people to jump to the conclusion that their own autocratic regimes were also giants on feet of clay: Why not confront them right away? Due to these foreign events, "the revolutionary idea was strengthened to such an extent that it explosively attained a breakthrough," a centrist observer emphasized (Runkel 1919: 45).

These immediate contagion effects of the Russian revolutions did not result from careful, rational cost/benefit calculations, but were fueled by the heuristics of availability and representativeness. Based on these cognitive shortcuts, the Petrograd events attracted tremendous attention and shaped the assessments and judgments of people of diverse ideological stripes. Many eyes were directed toward Russia, which the uprising of 1905 had turned into the global center of revolution (Schurer 1961: 463–67; Nettl 1969: 158; Schorske 1983: 28; see also Kautsky 1914: 142; Kurzman 2008). The stunning overthrow of a long-ruling dynasty in February and the bold coup by radical leftists in October constituted striking events that attracted great interest, especially from social democratic and socialist activists (Müller 1924: 79, 96; Spartakus 1958: 302–05; Liebknecht 1974: 358, 589, 679). As revolutionary shop steward Richard Müller (1924: 79) remembers, for instance, "The news from Russia was followed very attentively." And his colleague Emil Barth (1919: 18) commented with reference to early 1917: "The fertilizing impact of the Russian Revolution was now only beginning. Hope and desire moved through people's minds more strongly than ever. [Tsar] Nicholas and [*Kaiser*] Wilhelm, [Russia's chief general] Nikolaevich and [Germany's military leaders] Hindenburg-Ludendorff, didn't they practically call for a comparison? And what happened to those – could that not happen to these here as well?"

The social democratic press immediately announced the news of the February revolution in bold print on the title page and followed up with reports on the fast-changing events on subsequent days (Merz 1995: 134–39). Even large numbers of common people were struck by the Russian events. As Eric Hobsbawm (1996c: 59) reports, "According to the Habsburg censors [of mail to soldiers on the front], the Russian revolution was the first political event since the outbreak of the war to echo in the letters even of peasants' and workers' wives." In the same vein, a patriotic German sailor who left behind an extensive, famous diary was riveted by the news from revolutionary Russia (Stumpf 1967: 306–11). The initial reports that "a full-blown revolution" was "raging in St. Petersburg" immediately "engendered a number of lively debates in which skepticism alternated with overwhelming optimism" – similar to Carl Schurz's report from 1848. As soon as this sailor reached the next port a few days later, he visited a "reading room and ... studied the papers with great interest." They "were full of the Russian Revolution" (Stumpf 1967: 306, 308).

Reliable information on the complicated, fluid developments in Russia was sparse, however; even European leftists who sought to emulate the Bolshevist revolution lacked in-depth knowledge (Bassler 1973: 256, 260; Müller 2010: 160; see also Kautsky 1918: 73–74). A radical activist stressed, for instance, that "the news about the new Russia arrived in a rather meager fashion" (Müller 1924: 96). Top leaders of mainstream Social Democracy complained how deficient and defective, even plain false, the reports about Lenin's activities were that they received (Scheidemann 1921: 153–54). The civil war raging in the Soviet Union precluded any systematic gathering of information, and the ideological controversy about the communist experiment cast doubt on the objectivity of the eyewitness accounts that did reach the West (Zarusky 1992: 86–90). Direct contact between the Soviet leadership and left-wing groups in other countries was limited to a few individuals whose trustworthiness was questionable.

Yet although information was spotty, the epic Russian revolutions exerted an enormous effect on popular thinking; due to the availability heuristic, these striking events made a disproportionate, profound impact on people's perceptions and judgments. According to experienced political leaders, such as German Social Democrat Philipp Scheidemann (1929, vol. 1: 342), they helped to "alter ... the psychology of the people." A left-wing Social Democrat regarded the Russian February Revolution "as tremendous progress on the path toward liberty for Russia and the world" (Haase 1929: 141; see also 142–43). In the words of a revolutionary shop steward, "when the revolution and the overthrow of the tsar was reported from Russia, the workers gained new hope" (Müller 1924: 79).

The representativeness heuristic also shaped people's judgments. Due to the resulting overestimation of similarities, the facility with which Russian revolutionaries overthrew the tsar and later took power made people elsewhere believe that the autocrats ruling their own countries also stood on brittle foundations and that bold opposition efforts had good chances of success.[3] People across Europe therefore jumped to the conclusion that it was promising to challenge their domestic authorities as well (Eley 2002: 152; Morgan

---

[3] Even conservatives were impressed with the Russian Communists' "success" (Wirsching 2007: 147–56). As in 1848, this recognition across ideological frontlines demonstrates the operation of cognitive shortcuts, rather than mere wishful thinking on the part of left-wingers.

1982: 307–08). For instance, as revolutionary shop steward Müller (1924: 96) reported:[4]

The toppling of tsarist rule in March 1917 gave the revolutionary movement in Germany a concrete goal.... When on 8 November 1917 the German press reported the overthrow of the Kerenski government, the victory of the Bolshevists, and the victorious revolution of workers, soldiers, and peasants, there was no longer any doubt in the circles of oppositional workers about what was possible and necessary in Germany, and the reports of the German press about the Russian Revolution ... demonstrated the path and the instruments for the goal. Certainly conditions in Russia differed from Germany, but what the Russian peasant managed to accomplish should be even more feasible for the German industrial worker with his socialist training and organization!

A left-wing Social Democrat referred to the "breakdown of the tsarist regime" in a similar vein, claiming that "its immediate psychological impact on the mood of the German working class was enormous" (Dittmann 1995: 503). A radical socialist recalls in his memoirs: "The Russian [February] Revolution seemed to confirm all my [radical] ideas and expectations and stimulated my drive toward activity" (Geyer 1976: 57) and "The events in Russia were a powerful stimulus for the revolutionary illusions on the left of the German labor movement" (Geyer 1976: 62; see also 63–64, 95). Similarly, a Communist writes: "In Germany, since the February Revolution of 1917 all who had preserved some of the old [= radical leftist] ideals and goals had begun to become active" (Pieck 1959: 365). The sectarian Spartacus Group marveled that "the revolution in Russia won out so quickly within a few days," celebrated this "great historical drama," and derived an expectant question: "Russia frees itself. Who will free *Germany* ... ?" (Spartakus 1958: 302, 304, 305). Spartacus leader Karl Liebknecht (1974: 358) also highlighted the "tremendous importance of the domestic political repercussions/the internal changes in Russia on the other countries/the fact that Russia is no longer tsarist, for the internal political situation in all other European countries as well, especially Germany." Moreover, scholars observe that "the October Revolution in Russia stimulated among workers in Saxony a broad wave of sympathy" (Bramke and Reisinger 2009: 55).

Processed via the heuristics of availability and representativeness, the Russian precedents helped to stimulate strike waves,[5] which erupted in Austria and Germany in April of 1917,[6] immediately following the February Revolution, and in January of 1918, right after the October Revolution (Scheidemann 1929,

[4] Similar statements have been reported in Broué (2006: 90–98); see also Plättner (2012: 164).
[5] Historical analyses produced in communist countries, such as the volume edited by Albert Schreiner (1957: 7–8, 101–02, 143–44, 244–45) and the biography of Karl Liebknecht by Heinz Wohlgemuth (1975), put particular emphasis on the contagion effect from Russia. While these authors back up their claims with a wealth of documents, the present book refrains from relying on these writings due to their strong ideological biases.
[6] There were also strikes and a workers' uprising in Turin, Italy's industrial center, in August 1917 (Lill 2002: 363). Moreover, in the summer of 1917 the French army faced massive mutinies, in which the Russian Revolution seems to have played some role (Smith 1995: 192).

vol. 1: 342; Hautmann 1971: 34–49; Bassler 1973: 260; Lafleur 1976: 85–90; Feldman 1992: 334, 338, 443, 447–48; Dobson 2001: 167, 171, 369, n. 120; Eley 2002: 123, 137–38).[7] Thus, external triggers unleashed impulses toward mass contention within one month – as quickly as in 1848! This defiance in the thick of war pursued not only economic improvements, but also political goals such as universal, equal suffrage. While the material deprivations of the war and the ever more desperate longing for peace provided strong motivations for these challenges, long-standing demands for full democracy, activated and reinforced by the Russian precedents, also played a significant role (Wehler 2010: 124, 135–38).[8]

These strikes erupted rather spontaneously from mass initiatives, especially in 1917 (Feldman 1992: 337, 350). The informal grouping of revolutionary shop stewards who tried to coordinate these work stoppages responded to bottom-up pressures from the grass-roots. The vanguardist Spartacus Group (cf. Geyer 1976: 81), which sought to take advantage of the strikes by engaging in loud political agitation, had a very weak foothold among workers and therefore did not manage to influence the outbreak, course, or end of the strikes (Lafleur 1976: 85–88; Hoffrogge 2008: 41–43, 48, 64, 68; see in general Cronin 1980: 126–32, 144). Thus, the outstanding events of 1917 in Russia, processed via cognitive shortcuts, helped to trigger immediate mass contention, as in 1848. And because these bottom-up challenges were amorphous and unorganized, they did not manage to achieve important concessions and quickly petered out, particularly in 1917.

Given the disappointing outcomes of the strikes of spring 1917, the revolutionary shop stewards established a clandestine network to better prepare future contentious activities, especially in Berlin, their center of operation. This select group of activists played a greater role in unleashing the strikes of January-February 1918 (Müller 1924: 101–08; Geyer 1976: 64–65; see union documents reproduced in Schönhoven 1985: 414–44; also Bieber 1981: 450–53). Moreover, the sectarian Spartacus Group again sought to whip up labor unrest and turn it into revolutionary political challenges.

But even in this second round of massive stoppages, bottom-up pressure inspired in part by the Russian October Revolution played a crucial role as well (Barth 1919: 20; Feldman 1992: 443, 447–48). The tendency toward spontaneity[9] reflected the heterogeneous composition and organizational inchoateness of the industrial workforce after years of war. Because many regular workers who were long-standing union members had been drafted

---

[7] Hobsbawm (1996b: 65–66) highlights the stimulus that the October Revolution quickly gave to contention and protest all over the world.

[8] To take advantage of richer primary sources and a greater wealth of scholarly analysis, the following discussion focuses on Germany. The simultaneous strike waves in Austria followed the same pattern of bottom-up eruption and top-down containment by mainstream Social Democracy (Lafleur 1976).

[9] On the January 1918 strikes in Hamburg, for instance, see Ullrich (1999: 98–99, 152).

into the army,[10] a welter of women, young people, and recent migrants from the countryside now held factory jobs. These first-time workers were difficult to integrate into labor organizations and tended to act quite spontaneously (Moore 1978: 279–81; Bieber 1981: 450; Kluge 1985: 49; Canning 2010: 103–05). The need to operate under cover further hindered the efforts of the revolutionary shop stewards to build up a broad and firm network. Thus, this informal grouping helped to coordinate the strikes, but workers followed their lead because the shop stewards expressed bottom-up demands and grievances. Even in Berlin, these radical activists did not command discipline from the top down, but served as mouthpieces for popular beliefs and sentiments (Hoffrogge 2008: 41–43, 48, 64). The strikers' lack of organized leadership is evident in the fact that Social Democrat officials, who had not been involved in the strike decision, managed to take over control and quickly tamed this incipient mass contention, as the next section shows.

The strikers' lack of firm organization was even more pronounced in other cities. In Leipzig, with its strong concentration of workers, for instance, "The strikes always broke out against the wishes of union functionaries." In April 1917, right after the February Revolution in Russia, "ten thousand workers ... spontaneously walked off the job after hearing about the [bread] ration reduction," the final straw that broke the camel's back. "Not only did union leaders play no part in this action, they were totally uninformed" (Dobson 2001: 167–68). Thus, the decision to take to the streets and voice economic complaints as well as political demands arose from the mass level. Ordinary workers did not follow the guidance of representative leaders, but made up their mind on their own. As in Berlin, this independence reflected the decline of unions' hold over workers during the lengthy war, when many long-standing members fought at the front and were replaced by less organized segments of labor (Dobson 2001: 141; Kluge 1985: 48–49).

In sum, the outstanding Russian events of 1917, which common people, radical groupings such as the revolutionary shop stewards, and small-scale sects like the Spartacus Group processed via cognitive shortcuts, triggered immediate impulses for political contention, as it had happened in the mid-nineteenth century. This contagion advanced with amazing speed; within one month, both the February and the October Revolutions helped to stimulate contentious efforts that included political demands.[11] Thus, the velocity of this diffusion equaled the spread of the 1848 riptide. Yet as in that diffusion process, these grassroots challenges, while yielding some economic benefits, attained no

---

[10] This drafting of experienced workers was in part a reprisal against the strikes of April 1917. Targeting oppositional groupings and affecting some of the revolutionary shop stewards themselves (Müller 1924: 88–89; Barth 1919: 18), it limited the contentious network that these activists could build.

[11] In fact, the German mass strikes of late January 1918 were inspired in part by a strike wave in Austria that had erupted in mid-month, also partly in response to Russia's October Revolution.

political success. This failure is noteworthy because under the impression of the February Revolution, even established elites acknowledged the need for political reform. In April of 1917, the German kaiser, for instance, promised to transform the outdated, highly unequal electoral system of Prussia, the predominant component of the Reich. But this announcement was not followed by determined action, and the strikes did not manage to push the government toward forcefully promoting this change either.[12] In sum, as in 1848, efforts at political regime contention spread very quickly at the mass level, but failed to achieve their goals.

REPRESENTATIVE LEADERSHIP: WIDER BOUNDS OF RATIONALITY

A decisive reason for the political failure of this externally stimulated, bottom-up contention was that most leaders of organized labor, especially from mainstream Social Democracy, worked hard to contain these mobilizational impulses, subdue their political edge,[13] and end the strikes quickly by urging employers and the government to grant some material benefits (Scheidemann 1929, vol. 1: 341–43; Müller 1925: 17, 42, 80; Bailey 1980: 159, 163, 168; Eley 2002: 165). In these ways, representative leaders deliberately slowed down the diffusion of political regime contention in April 1917 and January–February 1918 because they regarded a head-on confrontation with the emperor as unpromising and "senseless" during total war (Ebert 1926, vol. 1: 364; see union documents reproduced in Schönhoven 1985: 351–53, 426–30, 443–44). Instead, top SPD politicians and trade union officials wanted to wait for the better opportunity to effect a regime transition that was bound to open up at the end of the war. At that time, they expected to reap the rewards for their cooperative stance during the struggle, convinced that "Germany's democratization had become inevitable since August 1914" (Hoegner 1979: 19). And if Germany were to lose, the imperial regime was likely to crumble, and power would fall to the SPD, as anticipated with striking foresight by SPD ideologue Karl Kautsky in 1914:

If we in Germany faced a situation in which Russia was in 1905 – a war ignominiously lost, the army in full anarchy, the peasantry in rebellion – then we would not need mass strikes ... to achieve, for instance, equal suffrage in Prussia [one of the SPD's core demands for democratization]: then the organizations of Social Democracy and the unions would look like the only unshakeable rocks in the general chaos; then the hitherto dominant circles would voluntarily relinquish their power and enter into the

---

[12] In September 1918, for instance, the social democratic union leadership complained bitterly to the imperial chancellor that the government had failed to push hard for the electoral reform proposals that the Prussian upper house was predictably obstructing (union document reproduced in Schönhoven 1985: 470).

[13] Ziemann (2011: 390) argues that in early 1918 there was "a potential for revolutionary transformation."

protective custody of Social Democracy to find refuge from the populace's fury. (Kautsky 1914: 202–03; paraphrase of his similar views from 1909 in Schorske 1983: 115)

The expectation that an opportune moment for challenging the kaiser's regime was bound to come induced the leaders of broad-based labor organizations to domesticate the spontaneous unrest triggered partly by the Russian revolutions in April 1917 and early 1918.

Contrary to mass sectors and small radical groupings, representative leaders thus did not get carried away by the heuristic inferences derived from dramatic external precedents. Instead, their broader base of knowledge, historical experience, comparative perspective, and greater capacity for deliberation and calculation made them question the immediate replicability of foreign events and highlight the differences that set apart their own polity from the frontrunner country (see in general Kautsky 1914: 126, 159, 161). Whereas the representativeness heuristic tempts people to overestimate similarities, leaders with their store of information are aware of diversity and do not jump to the conclusion that a foreign success can be imitated right away. Due to their institutional position, they have wider bounds of rationality and chart a path of greater prudence. Therefore, they put the brakes on spontaneous outbursts of mass contention, which they regard as dangerous and counterproductive.

The advantages in information-processing that representative leaders had over common people resulted from their organizational positions. As national-level officials of broad-based parties and unions, they had access to much richer and more reliable information than ordinary citizens, especially at a time when newspaper reporting was restricted by governmental censorship. Based on their wide-ranging organizational network and local representation in many neighborhoods, factories, and other units across the country, representative leaders had a good sense of the political strength of their own following and of party and union members' willingness to incur the risks of participating in political challenges. By the early twentieth century, the German SPD, for instance, had constructed a bureaucratic organization that systematically linked the central leadership with the local bureaus that the party had established throughout the whole country (Schorske 1983: ch. 5). The party also had close connections to societal associations, especially the massive socialist unions, which were wary of radicalism. The national leadership therefore commanded ample information about the political preferences and capabilities of the labor movement, a significant segment of society – indeed, the segment that had the greatest capacity for contentious collective action.

Furthermore, through their long-standing relations to other politicians as well as the imperial authorities, with whom they had for years maintained contacts, conversations, and negotiations,[14] Social Democrat leaders could also

---

[14] For instance, Social Democrat leaders held talks with government officials during the strikes of April 1917: "Topic: strike of ammunitions workers. What to do?" (Scheidemann 1921: 66–67).

assess the likely reactions of the main targets of their political demands and potential challenges. By participating in electoral campaigns and other political struggles, the party had accumulated decades of experience. In fact, many party and union officials had entered social democratic politics in their teens or early twenties; they clearly were professional politicians. In a well-organized, disciplined party and union movement, officials rose to the top step by step, after distinguishing themselves in several posts at lower organizational levels. This so-called ox tour gave those who managed to reach national office a vast stock of political knowledge and skills; candidates prone to misjudgments and faulty calculations had greater difficulty advancing.

Last but not least, throughout their organizational careers, these leaders were involved in constant discussions and deliberations and remained subject to scrutiny and accountability, even when they held top office. Despite its hierarchical structure, the SPD, for instance, had a pair of chairmen, not a single all-powerful president, and made important decisions via collegial bodies and steering committees. In particular, the party's position on crucial issues such as its stance concerning World War I and its participation in government in late 1918 emerged from intensive debates at which strong disagreements were voiced, considered from all sides, and then adjudicated via voting (descriptions in Scheidemann 1921: 6–8, 18, 174–76, 183). While the party tried hard to present unity toward the outside, it maintained a great deal of pluralism and diversity on the inside. This degree of internal democracy offered considerable opportunity for sorting out divergent viewpoints, subjecting perceptions and inferences to criticism, and weeding out rash judgments and overoptimistic proposals.[15] These well-institutionalized decision-making mechanisms thus provided safeguards against the unreflective reliance on cognitive shortcuts and broadened the bounds of political rationality.

Based on these organizational advantages in information-processing and decision-making, the party and union leadership questioned rash inferences suggested by the heuristics of availability and representativeness. Above all, they did not regard the Russian precedents as directly replicable nor see propitious conditions for challenging the kaiser and pressing their long-standing demands for full democracy immediately after the February and October Revolutions. Representative leaders thus diverged fundamentally from narrow sects prone to "groupthink" such as the Spartacus Group, which was captivated by the Soviet example and urged and promoted immediate imitation efforts.

Mainstream Social Democrats commonly stressed the differences between Russia and Germany, which in their view made the February Revolution not

---

[15] Regarding the mainstream union movement, documents reproduced in Schönhoven (1985: 414–37; 473–516; 539–98, 606–88) provide fascinating summaries of the extensive, intense, very frank, and sometimes conflictual debates among representative leaders about all important issues, such as the strikes of early 1918, SPD participation in government in late 1918, and the revolution erupting in November.

directly replicable and the October Revolution inapplicable to their own country. Two dissimilarities concerning class structure and political development struck them as especially important.[16] First, whereas Russia had a huge peasantry and tiny working and middle classes, Germany boasted an extensive proletariat that had steadily gained organizational capacity and political clout and that could also forge alliances with middle sectors (on this latter point, see Noske 1920: 58). Second, Germany's autocracy had opened space for reformist pressure from below, which would be endangered by all-out confrontation (see union documents of April 1917 and March 1918 reproduced in Schönhoven 1985: 346–47, 352, 439–44). Whereas the tsars had maintained repressive absolutism, the kaiser guaranteed the rule of law and free, fair, and – at the national level – equal suffrage, which had allowed the SPD to garner ever larger vote shares and win a plurality of parliamentary representatives in 1912. Accordingly, SPD chairman Ebert depicted the transition to full democracy as the culminating step of this political development and invoked the bloody Bolshevist Revolution with its undemocratic outcome as a deterrent example (Ebert 1926, vol. 2: 76; similar Scheidemann 1921: 1–2; see also Merz 1995: 175). Even left-wing Social Democrats admitted, "We cannot transplant the Russian example [specifically, the Soviet council system] to German conditions, but we need to learn from the experiences of the Soviet republic" (Haase 1929: 237; see also Müller 1924: 130).

Not swept away by the force of foreign precedents, mainstream Social Democrat officials judged the domestic opportunity structure as unpropitious for frontal challenges against the imperial authorities during 1917 and much of 1918. Several reasons induced them to call for caution and try hard to end the strikes of April 1917 and early 1918 (overview in Bieber 1981: 499–502). Given the ongoing war, nationalism, which enjoyed strong support in the working class as well, allowed the established authorities to bolster their power and discredit domestic challengers as traitors of the patriotic cause. Even labor leaders believed that open internal dissent would encourage Germany's enemies (see union document of April 1917 reproduced in Schönhoven 1985: 352) and that the walkouts, concentrated in the arms industry, were risking the lives of soldiers at the front, many of whom were workers and included their own sons.[17] Moreover, autocratic governments still

---

[16] Ebert (1926, vol. 2: 123–24) also highlighted the complexity of the German economy, which could not be run in the centralized fashion that Lenin was imposing in the Soviet Union. All these points originated in the social democratic revisionism of Eduard Bernstein and infused his own analysis of the 1918 revolution (Bernstein 1998: 237–38, 268). On these differences, see also Zarusky (1992: 30, 39, 43, 50, 54).

[17] For instance, his son, member of a submarine squad, told Social Democrat leader Wilhelm Keil (1947: 367) that he was aghast at the mass strikes of January 1918, which threatened soldiers' ammunitions supply. And in a letter to one of his sons, who was fighting in Northern France, Friedrich Ebert (1926: 364) criticized the April 1917 strikes because "they jeopardize you guys out at the front and boost the fighting spirit of our enemies." Tragically, Ebert lost two of his sons in World War I.

commanded tremendous repressive capabilities,[18] as union leaders impressed on their members (documents reprinted in Müller 1924: 182–84, 204–07, 211–12); this was especially true of the militarized regime that ran Germany starting in late 1916.[19] The government indeed announced that it would send defiant workers to the front and rigorously carried out this threat in mid-1917 and especially early 1918 (Feldman 1992: 339, 347, 450–55). Union and party leaders also feared a severe crackdown on their organizations, their main political asset, should they support challenges against the existing regime.[20]

For all of these reasons, Social Democratic party and union officials in Austria and Germany did not believe that in mid-1917 and early 1918 the time was ripe for large-scale worker mobilization, especially not for a contentious effort to transform the autocratic regime through political mass strikes. Instead, they strenuously tried to calm the labor unrest that the Russian revolutions helped to inspire at those moments. As they explained in their public pronouncements, speeches, and memoirs (Bauer 1923: 63–65; Ebert 1926, vol. 2: 348–52; Scheidemann 1929, vol. 1: 341–45; union document of March 1918 reproduced in Schönhoven 1985: 437–44; see also Lafleur 1976: 90–91), they insisted on waiting for a better opportunity to push for suffrage reform, the institution of parliamentary responsibility, and similar steps toward full democracy.

Leaders of majority Social Democracy therefore used their persuasive powers and appeals to discipline, which they had always highlighted as an organizational virtue (Bieber 1981: 510), to resolve both series of strikes quickly. In April 1917, mainstream unionists steered the work stoppages toward economic demands and away from political challenges to the imperial authorities (see union document of April 1917 reproduced in Schönhoven 1985: 352; Feldman 1992: 337). In early 1918, party chairman Friedrich Ebert and two other SPD officials joined the strikers' steering committee to influence their course directly; the initiative for this step came from striking workers themselves, many of whom retained trust in established labor leaders. As Ebert (1926, vol. 1: 352) later emphasized, "I entered the strike directorate with the determined intention to bring the strike to the fastest possible conclusion and

[18] In the enthusiastic voluntarism spurred by the Russian precedent, the sectarian radical left attacked and derided this argument (Spartakus 1958: 349–50).

[19] On the repression of left-wing Social Democracy from 1916 to 1918, see Schorske (1983: 308–12). While the military leadership did not command dictatorial powers (Wehler 2010: 108–09, 112–13, 119, 122, 163, 167), as some authors suggest (e.g., Feldman 1992: ch. VIII), it certainly held tremendous political influence and was prepared to use it in order to crush popular resistance.

[20] The fear that spontaneous mass strikes would provoke business retaliation or governmental repression that would severely damage the social democratic party and union organizations had a long standing. See, for instance, SPD ideologue Karl Kautsky's warnings in the famous "mass strike debate" triggered by the Russian Revolution of 1905 (Kautsky 1914: 117, 120, 123, 130, 134, 158). See also the general points advanced by Robert Michels (1959: part VI, ch. 1), which were derived mainly from the experiences of the German Social Democratic Party.

to avoid damage to the country." Once employers and the government granted economic concessions, the SPD politicians asked workers to return to their jobs and leave political demands such as general equal suffrage for reform efforts advanced via established institutional channels (Ebert 1926, vol. 2: 56–57). Thus, representative leaders pleaded for caution and prudence and tried to calm the contentious fervor that was rising at the mass level and was stirred up by ultra-left groupings (Feldman 1992: 449–54). They strenuously sought to make diffusion unfold differently than in 1848, namely with lower speed but greater success.[21]

Although the connections between workers and Social Democrat leaders had loosened during the war (see union document reproduced in Schönhoven 1985: 551; Bieber 1981: ch. 2; Wehler 2010: 111, 122, 135–36), they remained strong enough to give these appeals considerable resonance. When union and party officials drew on old loyalties and invoked their political experience and their reputation as advocates of popular causes, many workers acquiesced and turned away from challenges, especially on political issues. Even the newly recruited segments of labor that were populating factories during the war listened to the veterans of many earlier battles against business and the state. Governmental threats to suppress the strikes with force also suggested the wisdom of labor leaders' calls for caution. For these reasons, strikers soon concluded that the conditions for full-fledged regime contention were indeed unpropitious and resigned themselves to waiting for a better opportunity. As support for continued defiance dwindled, remaining diehards were increasingly isolated and felt compelled to give in as well. This realization sealed the strikes' fate; in mid-1917 and in early 1918, workers resumed production. Thus, representative leadership prevented externally stimulated mass contention from gathering steam at an unpromising time; the difference from the uncontrolled riptide of 1848 is noteworthy.

But this domestication of bottom-up mobilization led the radical fringe of socialist sects to resent the moderate leadership of mainstream Social Democracy even more intensely and to embrace Bolshevist-inspired revolution as the only promising strategy. Therefore, the network of revolutionary shop

---

[21] In similar ways, social democratic leaders had tamed contentious mass impulses triggered by foreign uprisings on earlier occasions. SPD ideologue Karl Kautsky reports such an instance with reference to the (eventually abortive) Russian Revolution of 1905: "When then a momentous event happened, the glorious October days in Russia [which brought an upsurge of political mass strikes], the whole working class of Europe felt electrified; that created a situation that had to be used for the struggle that was closest to our hearts, the struggle for better electoral laws for state parliaments .... But in this situation [upon encountering resistance to this effort], to give the struggle about electoral laws a turn [escalation] that could end with a [political] mass strike [as radical sectors led by Rosa Luxemburg demanded] would have been complete lunacy [that would have risked a] devastating defeat.... The party leadership and the whole party chose the [cautious] alternative, and they acted in this way completely in accordance with the situation and fulfilled their duty." (Kautsky 1914: 143)

stewards and the Spartacus Group began plotting protests designed to ignite an insurrectionary mass strike and overthrow the imperial regime.[22] As from mid-1918, the Allied advance on the Western front ever more clearly foreshadowed Germany's defeat in the war, the opportunity for such an assault on the autocracy seemed to be approaching. But the revolutionary shop stewards and the Spartacus Group did not manage to initiate or guide the mass contention of November 1918 that gave the imperial regime the coup de grace.[23] Instead, this storm of protests and uprisings began rather spontaneously before the start date that the shop stewards had set.[24] Moreover, this upsurge of contention merely finished the democratization process that the leaders of the majority Social Democratic Party had helped to achieve in October of 1918.

It is important to stress that by taming the strikes of April 1917 and early 1918, mainstream party and union officials did not intend to suppress demands for profound political reform, which they themselves had advanced for decades and repeated during the long years of World War I (see, e.g., Scheidemann 1921: 39–44, 64, 78–82, 158, 166–67, 175). Instead, they sought to channel these demands into their nonconfrontational strategy and then press them at an opportune moment. They made a first attempt in mid-1917, when in alliance with centrist "bourgeois" parties they demanded, among other changes, the parliamentarization of the kaiserreich, the crucial last step toward full democracy at the national level (cf. Ertman 1999: 43–44). The military leadership blocked this important reform effort, however, and Social Democrats avoided provoking a constitutional crisis in the thick of war.[25]

A much better chance to act on external precedents by pushing for democratization arose with military defeat at the front, which undermined the imperial regime, made its repressive capabilities crumble, and thus created a golden opportunity for a regime transition in late 1918 – exactly as SPD ideologue Kautsky had foreseen. Now "the time had ripened for social democracy to prepare the decisive attack on the old political regime," a centrist observer stressed (Runkel 1919: 51; 105).

Ceding to long-standing domestic demands from the social democratic movement and other reformist forces (see union documents reproduced in Schönhoven 1985: 378–84, 401, 470, 478, 510) and hoping to obtain better armistice conditions from Western democracies, the kaiser's government agreed to share power with democratic parties of centrist and left-wing orientation.

---

[22] These preparations are described in detail by Emil Barth (1919: 40, 47, 54–56), but with a vast exaggeration of the author's own role and its impact.

[23] Even Barth (1919: 56–59) admits and, in fact, highlights this point; Geyer (1976: 72; see also Bramke and Reisinger 2009: 61–64) confirms it for Leipzig, an industrial center with a heavy concentration of workers.

[24] Mainstream Social Democratic leader Philipp Scheidemann (1921: 209) highlights this fact in his refutation of Barth's (1919) self-important claims.

[25] Bieber 1981: 498; Winkler 2000: 348–51; Wehler 2010: 167. Of course, Social Democrats' caution drew acerbic criticism from radical sects (Spartakus 1958: 367–69, 379).

To induce the former opposition, including Social Democrats, to assume the burden of governmental responsibility at such a disastrous time and help administer the bankrupt empire, Wilhelm II had to offer important political and constitutional reforms (see Buse 1972: 239–40). Top-down concessions to organized bottom-up pressure and to U.S. president Woodrow Wilson's diplomatic missives transformed the autocracy into a parliamentary monarchy in October 1918, as the last imperial chancellor highlighted (Baden 1927: 365–66, 482–91; see also Miller 1978: 27–39). Targeted influence that party leaders exerted at the right moment helped to bring major steps toward democratization; thus, the prudent strategy pursued by mainstream Social Democrats during World War I achieved considerable success (cf. Collier 1999: 106).

In particular, the constitutional transformation of October 1918 guaranteed the parliamentary responsibility of the government. After the German Reich had instituted universal equal suffrage in 1871, allowing Social Democrats over the subsequent decades to win a plurality of parliamentary representatives, the unaccountability of the government to the legislature and its exclusive dependence on the emperor had been the main obstacle to full democracy at the national level (Ertman 1999: 42–49). The negotiated reform of October 1918, Social Democrats' reward for shoring up the stumbling state, overcame this hurdle. In the judgment of Social Democratic leaders, the constitutional change of October 1918 fulfilled their democratizing program and constituted "a turning point in Germany's history [and] the birthday of German democracy" (Ebert 1926, vol. 2: 75; see also 72–83; Noske 1920: 7; Scheidemann 1929, vol. 2: 209; Hoegner 1979: 35). Certainly, however, important hindrances still remained at the subnational level, especially the heavily skewed three-class voting system of Prussia, Germany's predominant unit.

Moreover, the reformed constitutional order did not find respect. Conservative military sectors quickly disobeyed the new party-based government, which was suing for an armistice, by ordering the Navy into one last battle to save its "honor."[26] This unauthorized and senseless command, effectively a coup attempt (Wehler 2010: 182–85, 194), prompted sailors not controlled by the social democratic labor movement (cf. Dittmann 1995: 552; Scheidemann 1921: 209) to engage in spontaneous protests.[27] Mainstream Social Democrats again sought to tame this bottom-up contention by sending their leading military expert to the coast to take control of the movement (Noske 1920: 8–24; Wette 2010). But with the crumbling of the empire, the spark had already spread among the hungry, war-weary population and set much of the country aflame. At this point, a full-scale revolution seemed imminent, and the revolutionary shop stewards and the Spartacus Group – heavily

---

[26] Late 1918 saw a broader debate about whether to engage in a "terminal battle," but the new government and the party coalition sustaining it rejected this risky idea (Geyer 2001: 502, 507).

[27] Even left-wing Social Democrats were surprised by the sailors' revolt (Haase 1929: 171; Barth 1919: 52); thus, they had not instigated it.

influenced by the Leninist precedent (Barth 1919: 62) – deliberately tried to fan the flames.

Concerned about the tremendous costs and risks of overthrowing the political and socioeconomic system at a time of severe deprivation and misery, Social Democratic leaders sought to moderate and channel this largely spontaneous mass contention into political-institutional reforms achieved via orderly, democratic procedures (Scheidemann 1921: 205, 210; Müller 1925: 42, 80; Miller 1978: 79–85; union document of December 1918 reproduced in Schönhoven 1985: 556–57). To forestall a replication of the Russian October Revolution, which radical-left sects promoted vociferously, SPD politicians hastily forced out the kaiser, assumed the government in a temporary coalition with the USPD, and enacted a range of additional political and socioeconomic reforms. These measures included the last few steps required to institute full democracy, such as the abolition of the Prussian three-class voting system and the extension of suffrage to women (Canning 2010). Moreover, as the first SPD chancellor emphasized, the party pushed hard for quickly electing a constituent assembly that would seal the transition to representative democracy (Ebert 1926, vol. 2: 120–24, 132–35, 147–49; cf. Barth 1919: 126, 129–30). In these ways, Social Democrats tamed the new outburst of spontaneous mass contention, took power, and effected the transition to democracy that they had long demanded.

Specifically, the SPD invoked the legitimacy arising from universal equal suffrage to build a pluralist, representative democracy. These moderate leaders wanted to avoid exclusionary class rule and therefore based the new political order on the participation of the whole citizenry, rather than the spontaneously mushrooming workers' and soldiers' councils, an obvious imitation of Russian soviets (Luxemburg 1970: 204–5; Dittmann 1995: 508, 566, 579, 587; Plättner 2012: 164; see also Landauer 2007: 190–91).[28] The SPD was determined to prevent a replication of the dual sovereignty that emerged in Russia in 1917,[29] where a provisional government faced ever more powerful militant soviets (Müller-Franken 1928: 13, 56–59, 66, 75–84, 213). Since the soviets had given Lenin's Communists a stepping stone, the SPD marginalized their German replicas politically and starved them financially. Whereas important advocates of a council system sought a "dictatorship of the proletariat" in a rather undemocratic fashion (Barth 1919: 25, 52, 77, 127; Müller 1924: 139; Müller 1925: 30, 79, 82–85, 89–94, 98; Geyer 1976: 78–80, 86, 94, 110–12; Kuckuk 2010: 68–73, 77),[30] Social Democracy insisted on standard

[28] Kolb (1979: 95) confirms the Russian inspiration. For an overview of the vague and fluid ideas about a council system held by various currents of the German left, see Kolb (1968).

[29] Mainstream union leaders were particularly adamant in opposing workers' councils, which they saw as a fundamental threat to union discipline and organizational command over workers. See union documents reproduced in Schönhoven (1985: 540–45, 609–30, 714–20, 734, 746).

[30] With the leftward shift of historiography during the "radical" 1960s, important authors claimed that the workers' and soldiers' councils held a direct-democratic potential and depicted them

notions of universal citizenship and full democracy that it had embraced for decades (Collier 1999: 106; Berman 2006: 14–16, 54–59). Therefore, it combated the radical council movement systematically and successfully. Moreover, it squashed an ultra-left uprising in Berlin in January 1919 (see next section) and suppressed similar rebellions elsewhere. To be safe from sectarian threats that were concentrated in large industrial areas, the freely elected constituent assembly gathered in the provincial town of Weimar, where an alliance of the SPD and centrist liberal and Catholic parties passed a highly democratic, progressive constitution.

As the preceding analysis shows, the representative leaders of broad-based organizations, especially mainstream Social Democracy, acted less impulsively than common people. They had a better understanding of the prevailing power constellation and the corresponding opportunities and risks. After the emergence of organizational leadership, external precedents of dramatic change spread more selectively, but with greater success.

Representative leaders have a more extensive radar and longer time frame than common people and radical sects, who are deeply affected by the availability heuristic with its disproportionate focus on immediate, vivid, directly accessible events. As leaders' attention is less narrowly confined, they consider factors and contingencies, benefits and costs that do not occur to regular citizens. In late 1918, for instance, SPD officials worried greatly that a full-scale revolution would disrupt the population's already strained food supply.[31] Based on their organizational position, access to information, and experience during the hardships of World War I, leaders foresaw this problem, which arose from the complexity of a modern, urbanized society (cf. Ebert 1926, vol. 2: 123–24; Bernstein 1998: 237–38); common people carried away by contentious impulses and sectarians engaging in groupthink did not consider this risk.[32]

Whereas the availability heuristic drew the attention of unorganized mass actors and radical sects to the Russian revolutions, representative leaders focused much less on foreign models and concentrated instead on the domestic power constellation. In the inchoate polities of 1848, all eyes were on France;

as an alternative to both liberal, representative democracy and to a communist dictatorship of the proletariat. Primary sources show, however, that a number of left-wing socialists, even outside the Spartacus Group (Pieck 1959: 422, 459; Nettl 1969: 448, 452; Weitz 1994: 35–36; Luxemburg 2012: 113) and the Communist Party, saw a clear dichotomy between "bourgeois" liberal, representative democracy versus a council system, which they identified explicitly with strict working class rule and a dictatorship (e.g., Müller 1925: 30, 79, 82–85, 89–94, 98), including – because much of the working class seemed to lack revolutionary consciousness – "the dictatorship of the minority" (Geyer 1976: 110).

[31] See many documents reproduced in Ritter and Miller (1975: 80–81, 84, 89, 94, 113).

[32] As another consideration that was beyond the scope of mass actors, Germany's organizational leaders knew full well that the Western powers, who could impose their will as winners in World War I, did not want Germany to fall to a Russian-style revolution (see, e.g., Landauer 2012: 173–74, 181), but instead saw the defeated country as an essential bulwark to Bolshevism (see recently Simms 2013: 319–22).

in 1917–19, by contrast, SPD and union officials took only limited inspiration from external impulses, instead basing their decisions primarily on internal opportunities and risks. Accordingly, documents from 1917–19 make significantly fewer references to revolutionary Russia than sources from 1848 made to revolutionary France (compare, e.g., Ebert 1926 and Scheidemann 1921 with Boerner 1920 and Varnhagen 1862). This fundamental shift in attention reflected the lower domestic uncertainty prevailing in polities of greater organizational density and the more solid knowledge commanded by representative leaders, which left less room for the availability heuristic.

Representative leaders' information access and experience also kept them from rushing into emulation efforts based on apparent similarities suggested by the representativeness heuristic; instead, they put stunning recent events in perspective and debated the applicability of foreign lessons inside their pluralistic organizations. Whereas the surprising downfall of the Tsarist autocracy and the amazing ease of the Bolshevist takeover induced common people and sectarian groupings to overestimate the replicability of the Russian precedents, representative leaders questioned these rash inferences because they realized the differences between Russia and their own country. German Social Democrats highlighted the greater strength of the working class and the constitutional advances of preceding decades, which allowed for democratic development and provided little rationale for a vanguard-led revolution with its enormous costs and risks (Kautsky 1918: 73–77; Ebert 1926, vol. 2: 120–24, 133; Müller-Franken 1928: 13, 75–78; Scheidemann 1929, vol. 2: 107, 124, 247, 262; Bernstein 1998: 237–46, 268). These leaders thus advocated political options foreclosed in the country that had unleashed the current wave of contention.

Besides grasping basic structural and institutional conditions, representative leaders also had a clearer sense of the power constellation and political conjuncture. Long-standing contacts allowed them to assess the determination, cohesion, and power of other political parties as well as the established authorities; through discussions and negotiations, they ascertained the government's likely reaction to challenges. In late 1918, for instance, SPD politicians frequently spoke with imperial officials and thus gained inside information that mass actors and radical sects lacked (Baden 1927: part 3; Scheidemann 1929, vol. 2: ch. 6; Ritter and Miller 1975).

For all of these reasons, the leaders of broad-based organizations are less strongly moved than ordinary citizens by inferences drawn via the availability and representativeness heuristics from a dramatic recent event and apparent success. Whereas common people and ideological cliques are captivated by a flash of lightning that fleetingly illuminates a specific scene, representative leaders have a better grasp of the whole landscape. Therefore, they act on external precedents when a good opportunity arises – and achieve a good deal of success, as evident in Germany's move toward full democracy in 1918–19. As representative leaders in other European countries acted in similarly prudent ways, the wave of regime contention triggered by the Russian revolutions clearly brought more advances toward democracy than the tsunami of 1848.

THE IMPACT OF INFERENTIAL SHORTCUTS ON REPRESENTATIVE
LEADERS

Despite their advantages in information access and capacity for calculation, however, representative leaders were affected by the availability and representativeness heuristics as well. Their political rationality was also bounded, albeit less narrowly than that of common people and ideological sects. The resulting distortions in judgment affected even leaders of pluralistic mass organizations that guaranteed criticism and debate.

Problematic inferences shaped especially these leaders' efforts to protect their prudent, reformist steps toward full democracy from the revolutionary attacks that sectarian groupings inspired by Lenin's power grab undertook. Radical sects that engaged in groupthink and were especially susceptible to cognitive biases tried to emulate the Bolshevist Revolution at all costs and incessantly advocated and promoted uprisings (Pieck 1959: 412–78; Liebknecht 1974: 643, 646, 662, 677–79, 681; Weitz 1997: 84; Pesendorfer 2012: 83–86, 152–56, 166). To defend the nascent democracy that they were carefully nurturing, centrist and Social Democrat leaders suppressed these hyperactive efforts. Yet they applied disproportionate force because they also inferred from Lenin's success that communists could easily capture power. This pervasive fear (extensive documentation in Merz 1995) triggered a strong reaction. Thus, the representativeness heuristic inspired fierce struggles, especially by prompting sectarian adventures, but also by leading representative leaders to combat these ill-considered rebellions with excessive brutality (Nettl 1969: 443–61; Wehler 2010: 206–09, 398–99).[33]

The stunning October Revolution skewed the inferences of a wide variety of political leaders, albeit to distinctly different degrees. Since radical leftist sects such as the Spartacus Group (cf. Geyer 1976: 81, 94; Dittmann 1995: 475) were particularly subject to cognitive distortions, they jumped at any apparent opportunity to imitate this precedent and tried to grab power,[34] as

---

[33] In his comprehensive analysis of the "German revolution," Kluge (1985: 93–94) highlights both types of actors' deviations from rationality. He takes radical leftists to task for their "illusionary infatuation with grabbing power" but also criticizes mainstream Social Democracy for its "irrational" reliance on repressive forces. Zarusky (1992: 92–95) offers a nuanced assessment of the rationality issue.

[34] Occasionally, even a center-left leader fell prey to the belief in the easy replicability of revolution. In this vein, Dutch socialist Pieter Troelstra, a long-time moderate, got carried away by the Russian Revolution and its impact on neighboring Germany and impulsively proclaimed in late 1918 "that the working classes would now take power. But no one had prepared for such a revolution, and the socialist leader was soon forced to back down" (Blom 2006: 428). This ill-considered initiative created widespread distrust and hurt his party for years.

during the "Spartacus Uprising" of January 1919 in Berlin (Bernstein 1998: ch. 12), the Council Republic of April 1919 in Munich,[35] and the Hungarian Soviet regime of mid-1919 (Tökés 1967). Any rational assessment of the existing power constellations would have counseled caution. But the representativeness heuristic prevailed.

Consequently, these sectarian groupings fell prey to "political fever;" their "sense of responsibility ... lay buried in the effervescence of illusions," as a left-wing socialist observed (Müller 1925: 35–36). In Berlin, Rosa Luxemburg herself complained about her comrades' "somewhat childish, half-baked, narrow-minded radicalism" (cited in Nettl 1969: 475). Spartacus leader Liebknecht (1974: 588–89) stressed that "the Russian Soviet Republic ... stirs up those left behind [in the world revolution], fills vacillators with courage, and boosts everybody's energy and determination by a factor of ten." Seeing the SPD-led regime as equivalent to the Kerensky government (Liebknecht 1974: 623) that Bolshevists had overthrown in October 1917, he tirelessly called for emulation (Liebknecht 1974: 582, 643, 646, 662, 677–79, 681, 688–90; see recently Pesendorfer 2012: 166–67). As soon as a power vacuum seemed to open up in early January 1919, he sought to take over the government by assault (Nettl 1969: 478–83; similar for Bremen, see Kuckuk 2010: 67–68). This ill-prepared imitation attempt (cf. Barth 1919: 132) was quickly crushed and cost Luxemburg and Liebknecht their lives.

Despite this disastrous outcome, three months later, radical leftists in Munich also made a violent power grab, inspired by Lenin's success as well as its recent emulation in Hungary, which proclaimed a revolutionary Soviet Republic in March 1919. An intellectual leader of this sectarian effort wrote in a public letter to Lenin, "On March 21, the news of the declaration of the council republic in Hungary hit here like a bomb .... Speakers in popular assemblies found enthusiastic approval for their plea to emulate the Hungarian example." "The positive news from Budapest ... multiplied the Communists' activism" and helped to give rise to "the anticipation that the Bavarian Soviet Republic was an ideal goal that could be achieved in short order" (Mühsam 2007: 140, 142; see also 145, 148–49, 151, 175). Left-wingers indeed installed such a radical council system within a couple of weeks. As the Central Revolutionary Council of Bavaria proclaimed in its official announcement of this move, "the Bavarian Council Republic follows the example of the Russian and Hungarian peoples" (reproduced in Schmolze 1978: 271). The new leadership indeed took many inspirations from these precedents (Neubauer 1958: 88–90).

As another protagonist reports, the precipitous establishment of a Soviet-style system was driven by the facile belief that "what succeeded in Russia must be successful here as well" (Toller 2009: 86; similar Schmolze 1978: 335). Soon, "decisive political influence was won by a few Russians, merely because

[35] Neubauer 1958. This radical experiment received an additional impulse from the pro-communist regime that held sway in Hungary in early 1919 (Kluge 1985: 132–33).

their passport certified them as Soviet citizens. The grand deeds of the Russian Revolution bestowed each of these men with a magic glow; experienced German Communists looked up to them as if blinded" (Toller 2009: 110). The leader of this bold revolution, German Communist Eugen Leviné, proclaimed, "We'll proceed as in Russia," for instance, through the forced requisitioning of foodstuffs (Toller 2009: 94). In fact, however, the exiled state government, with national help, proceeded as in Berlin: The forces of order brutally suppressed this rash experiment, which even its protagonists in retrospect regarded as overly precipitous and premature (Mühsam 2007: 167, 174) and as a huge mistake (Toller 2009: 96, 112). The same sequence of events repeated itself in some other cities, such as Bremen (Kuckuk 2010: 69–78). Thus, sectarian leaders were especially caught up in cognitive shortcuts, drew problematic inferences, and initiated regime contention under hopeless conditions – repeatedly.

Although representative leaders had access to better information and a greater capacity to cross-check their inferences inside pluralistic organizations, it was, ironically, a similar belief in the potential replicability of the Bolshevist Revolution that induced centrist and Social Democrat leaders to crack down hard on far-left sects. Due to the Russian precedent, communist uprisings elicited exaggerated fears and heavy repression that, from a rational viewpoint, was out of proportion with the actual threat. In Germany, the precarious new republic faced dangers from right and left; given the preponderance of power capabilities, the threat from conservative politicians, bureaucrats, military, and business was more serious. While radical leftists constantly engaged in noisy street action, their real power bases were slim because mainstream Social Democracy encompassed large segments of the popular masses in firm organizations. Commanding limited support, the revolutionary left never had a realistic chance of success. But the scary Russian precedent and sectarians' penchant for invoking it with slogans like "All power to the councils!" (cf. Noske 1920: 61) induced even representative leaders to overestimate the communist threat (as documented exhaustively by Merz 1995; see also Gallus 2010: 27–30; Wehler 2010: 206–09, 398) and respond with unnecessary brutality. Judgments influenced by the heuristics of availability and representativeness account for this puzzling overreaction – which held sway not only in Europe, but even in faraway Argentina during a "tragic week" of severe repression in January 1919 (Rock and dos Santos 1971: 178–83, 213).

In Germany, many prominent SPD politicians saw Bolshevism as a significant threat that they concentrated on combating. Philipp Scheidemann, for instance, frequently referred to this danger (Scheidemann 1929, vol. 2: 225, 243–46, 262–63, 279–84, 291–93; cf. Baden 1927: 580). When the SPD took over power, he promised to the last imperial chancellor, "My party will take care that Germany will be spared Bolshevism" (reported by Müller-Franken 1928: 78). Acting on this pledge as a top official of the new revolutionary government, Scheidemann supported the military repression of the "Spartacus uprising" of January 1919, arguing that without this crackdown, "the Bolshevist wave would have swept away all the barriers we had constructed with such trouble to ensure the life of the democratic Republic" (Scheidemann 1929, vol. 2: 284). Similarly, first Social Democrat chancellor Ebert exclaimed: "The German workers should look at [Bolshevist] Russia and be warned!" and condemned the "putschist [armed-revolutionary] tactics" of proto-communist sectarians (Ebert 1926, vol. 2: 123; similar 76). And an SPD delegate in the Weimar constituent assembly highlighted his party's great accomplishment "that the German revolution did not follow the example of the Russian" (quoted in Matthias 1972: 115; see also Hoegner 1979: 36; Dittmann 1995: 557).

Thus, despite its information access, processing capacity, and experience, the SPD leadership was also affected by cognitive shortcuts to some extent. Overrating the replicability of the Bolshevist precedent, it overreacted to leftist uprisings and granted excessive concessions to reactionary forces, such as the old military and new irregular militias (Bassler 1973: 245–47; Bernstein 1998: 182, 201–02, 222). While the SPD with its prudent strategy managed to institute and safeguard the majority's preference for representative, liberal democracy, the distortions arising from inferential heuristics did cause problems.[36] The new regime emerged with birth defects that weakened it from the beginning and contributed to its eventual downfall.

Why did SPD leaders prove more susceptible to cognitive shortcuts in combatting radical sects, while responding with prudence to spontaneous mass contention and successfully pursuing the long-standing goal of full democracy? Correspondingly, why did they process the impulses emanating from the Russian February Revolution more rationally than the repercussions of the Bolshevist coup of October 1917? Given the Social Democrats' experience with a conservative monarchy, the tsar's downfall did not come unexpected, and the German SPD was well-prepared to take over the reins of government in case of a similar event at home, as the Kautsky quote above shows. Moreover, their long-standing organizational efforts were meant precisely to ensure a smooth, orderly takeover; the labor movement leaders were used to guiding, disciplining, and domesticating mass sectors. For these reasons, taming the spontaneous strikes of April 1917 and January–February 1918 and preparing for steps toward democratizing reforms was an integral part of their organizational repertoire. The political rationality honed in decades of political experience was prepared to deal with these issues.

By contrast, the October Revolution constituted more of a shock that fundamentally threatened the reformist political strategy traced for so long by Social Democrats. That a rather small band of sectarian revolutionaries could grab power with the force of arms stunned these representative leaders and caused a particularly striking impact: It made a much stronger impression on them than the overthrow of the tsar. No wonder that party leaders in their public speeches, internal debates, and memoirs referred much more frequently

---

[36] The resulting missed opportunities to effect a more thorough and therefore lasting democratization of Germany are assessed in particular depth by Moore (1978: ch. 11).

to the October Revolution than the February Revolution. Because the SPD had effectively foresworn violent revolution, it was now "caught on the wrong foot." Party leaders were mentally unprepared for the – in their eyes – terrible surprise of a successful armed takeover, which greatly boosted the appeal of revolution among the radical left. Moreover, they did not command the organizational instruments or power resources to deal with this shock. Mass organizations are skillful at guiding and taming contentious impulses that arise from the bottom up, but are rather helpless against armed challenges. During the "Spartacus Uprising," for instance, SPD leaders were in despair about their vulnerability to violent attacks. Lacking adequate defensive capabilities of their own, these leaders were prone to overestimating radicals' chances of success. For these reasons, they were more susceptible to the exaggerated inferences that the representativeness heuristic derived from the Bolshevist power grab. As a result, representative leaders who proved quite apt at keeping cognitive shortcuts at bay in pursuing their own, long-elaborated strategy did fall prey to inferential heuristics in responding to unexpected sectarian challenges.

To conclude, the leadership of broad-based organizations had generally less narrow bounds of rationality than ordinary people. Therefore, they achieved greater success in 1918–19 than unorganized mass actors – who are especially susceptible to the availability and representativeness heuristics – achieved in 1848. But because representative leaders were also affected by these inferential shortcuts, their success remained limited. The resulting difficulties, which are common in new democracies, have received enormous emphasis in the German case due to the later breakdown of the Weimar Republic and the disastrous successor regime. But it would amount to retrospective determinism to see this catastrophe as foreordained by the mistakes of 1918–19.[37] The contentious wave of 1917–19 brought several effective transitions to democracy – much more progress than the tsunami of 1848. Representative leaders' prudence led to greater and less fleeting goal attainment, whereas the rash enthusiasm of the "springtime of the peoples" ended mostly in frustration and failure. Speed and success correlate inversely in the diffusion of regime contention. The emergence of pluralistic organizations and their representative leadership, which broadened the bounds of political rationality, brought less haste and more advances toward democracy.

CONCLUSION

The preceding analysis shows how organizational macro-developments came to affect the operation of cognitive micro-foundations and how this interaction reshaped the diffusion of political regime contention. Because the emergence of representative leaders widened the bounds of political rationality and

---

[37] Canning (2010: 85–86) similarly argues that the accomplishments of the 1918 revolution deserve proper recognition.

prompted a more thorough assessment of domestic opportunities and risks, striking foreign precedents lost their overwhelming force and no longer triggered immediate emulation efforts. As a result, the wave of 1917–19 advanced with much lower speed but greater success than the riptide of 1848.

In the mid-nineteenth century, stunning foreign events had unleashed quick contagion effects because mass actors had been largely unorganized and had therefore been highly susceptible to inferential shortcuts. As a result, they had rushed into imitation attempts without much concern for the prevailing power constellation – and these efforts had frequently failed, as Chapter 4 demonstrated. In inchoate polities, cognitive heuristics operated in an unfettered fashion, molded political decision-making, and strongly influenced its outcomes – which were disappointing. In the absence of organizational macro structures, the micro-foundation of my theory accounts for the tsunami of 1848.

To explain the wave of 1917–19, however, this micro-foundation needs to be complemented by macro-structures; politics now was more complex. By the early twentieth century, a new type of political actor had appeared on the scene. The formation and secular growth of broad-based organizations, whose prototype was the massive, encompassing social democratic movement in Germany, brought the rise of representative leadership. Due to their institutional position and political experience and due to procedural mechanisms for internal debate and criticism, these leaders enjoyed better information access and processing capacity, and their judgments and decisions suffered less from distortions and biases. While they were impressed by epic foreign events, such as the Russian revolutions, they did not initiate immediate imitation attempts, but evaluated the domestic opportunity structure to strike at the most propitious moment. Diffusion therefore slowed down, but tended to bring more success.

The emergence of representative leadership thus widened the bounds of political rationality. Organizational macro-developments profoundly influenced how cognitive micro-foundations shaped contentious decision-making. As political society turned less amorphous and more differentiated, better-endowed leaders came to guide mass action and kept contentious fervor arising from inferential heuristics in check. This macro-micro interaction introduced a crucial layer of complexity into my theory. It explains why a foreign spark did not immediately ignite an explosion, but spread in more differentiated, context-dependent ways.

The preceding analysis demonstrates this complex layering of micro- and macro-factors, of cognitive impulses and organizational restraints. Ordinary people not firmly controlled by broad-based organizations responded to the Russian revolutions in similar ways as their forebears had done in the mid-nineteenth century. Directly exposed to the heuristics of availability and representativeness, they eagerly sought to emulate these stunning precedents by starting strikes in April 1917 and January 1918. These immediate outbursts resembled the rush to imitative contention that an inchoate citizenry undertook in March of 1848.

But now, after the creation of broad-based parties and unions, representative leaders called for prudence and domesticated this bottom-up contention. Because they had a better understanding of the constellation of power and faced less uncertainty than ordinary individuals do, they relied less heavily on cognitive shortcuts and therefore assessed the prevailing opportunities and risks more carefully. Therefore, they insisted on waiting for the proper opportunity to emulate these external precedents and worked hard to persuade mass actors to end their spontaneous strikes. In these ways, they helped prevent a repetition of the 1848 wildfire – and of its disappointing results.

Representative leaders channeled externally inspired contentious energies into institutional reform efforts. With the political opening arising from Germany's impending defeat in World War I, this prudent strategy indeed brought a transition from semiabsolutism to parliamentary monarchy in October 1918. And when reactionaries quickly sought to reverse this regime change and a new wave of mass contention erupted in response, Social Democrats again took the lead, forced additional reforms, and contained this revolutionary outburst, especially by holding elections for a constituent assembly. Thus, organizational leadership was decisive in guiding and controlling mass actors and in engineering a transition to full democracy. Acting with less tightly bounded rationality, party and union officials ensured that foreign impulses transmitted through cognitive shortcuts were processed with a great deal of political success.

Certainly, however, representative leaders are mere mortals and apply cognitive shortcuts as well. Therefore, they can be overly impressed by a dramatic foreign event and overestimate its replicability. If this precedent is contrary to their own goals, they seek to prevent its emulation by all means. Accordingly, Social Democrats squashed Bolshevist-inspired uprisings by ultra-leftist sects, although this repressive campaign led to atrocities and required an illogical alliance with right-wing forces.

By substantiating these arguments, the present chapter shows how bounded rationality operated after the emergence of large-scale organizations and how this interaction of cognitive micro-foundations and political macro-structures shaped the diffusion of political regime contention. After Chapter 4 demonstrated the importance of bounded rationality through an examination of the riptide of 1848, the preceding investigation demonstrated that it is not uniform, but can be more or less tight in its bounds. The extent to which cognitive inferences deviate from full rationality varies, depending on the principal locus of decision-making. Compared to the severe constraints facing ordinary individuals who decide on complex, fluid political issues on their own, the representative leaders of broad-based, pluralistic organizations have wider bounds of rationality. This interaction of cognitive micro-foundations and organizational macro-structures contributes to the secular slowdown yet increased rate of success in the diffusion of political regime contention that is evident when comparing the waves of 1848 and 1917–19.

The preceding analysis demonstrates how organizational development reshaped the processing of information about external precedents, that is, the reception side of diffusion. While facing a similar stimulus as their fore-fathers in 1848, namely the revolutionary overthrow of an autocratic regime, representative leaders in 1917–19 responded differently, namely with much greater prudence. They initiated emulative regime contention less rashly but therefore achieved full democratization. Over time, however, other facets of organizational development also led to a transformation of the stimulus side of diffusion through the emergence of the pacted transition model. As politi-cal organizations multiplied and covered the ideological spectrum, all major sociopolitical forces came to have mouthpieces in the party arena. Therefore, they could work out their disagreements and conflicts via negotiation and com-promise, a much less costly and risky strategy than mass assault and uprising. By analyzing the third wave of democratization in Latin America, the next chapter shows how the resulting change in external triggers brought a further slowdown of diffusion processes, yet gave imitative regime contention even greater success.

6

The Slow but Potent "Third Wave" in South America: The Prevalence of Negotiated Transitions

The preceding chapter explained why the wave of regime contention unleashed in part by the Russian revolutions unfolded less precipitously but with greater success than the tsunami of 1848. My analysis demonstrated the importance of organizational development for the domestic processing of external triggers. In 1917–19, representative leaders, especially Social Democrat Party politicians and unionists, responded to the foreign precedent of a dramatic revolution with much greater deliberation and prudence than unorganized, leaderless crowds had during the mid-nineteenth century. Rather than rushing into challenges to autocratic governments, they waited for a promising opportunity, which the end of World War I provided. This crucial change at the reception side slowed down diffusion, but led to greater progress toward democracy.

The third wave of democratization spread through Latin America at even lower speeds yet with particularly high success; emulative contention ushered in regime transitions in country after country, sooner or later. This diffusion process gathered momentum in Portugal, Greece, and Spain in 1974–75, but then took a few years to cross the Atlantic Ocean. In South America, regime contention erupted in Bolivia and Peru in 1977, Ecuador in 1978, Argentina in 1982, Brazil, Chile, and Uruguay in 1983, and Paraguay in 1987. Democracy was instituted in Ecuador in 1979, Peru 1980, Bolivia 1982, Argentina 1983, Uruguay 1984, Brazil 1985, Paraguay 1989, and Chile 1990. While the demise of authoritarian regimes among next-door neighbors, from Ecuador to Paraguay, suggests direct contagion effects, the dominoes fell much less quickly than in 1848. But only two contentious efforts failed, in Bolivia 1978–80 (Whitehead 1986a) and Chile 1983–84 (see Chapter 7), and both countries managed to democratize soon thereafter. Compared to 1848, the third wave thus occupies the opposite pole in the negative correlation between diffusion's speed and success[1]; its scores on these two dimensions differ significantly from the revolutions of 1917–19 as well.

To account for diffusion's further slowdown and even higher goal achievement after 1917–19, the present analysis of the third wave in Latin America complements Chapter 5's argument about changes on the reception side of diffusion by highlighting a profound transformation of the stimulus side, which was caused by additional advances in organizational development, as explained in Chapter 3. During the twentieth century, broad-based parties and associations, which had first emerged among the left, spread across the ideological spectrum. Consequently, centrist and right-wing forces gained the capacity to advance their interests and apply their power capabilities via interorganizational bargaining as well. Negotiation and compromise therefore turned into the predominant mode of democratic transition. Most oppositionists backed away from frontal challenges, especially revolution, which carry tremendous risks and frequently end in failure; instead, they preferred bargaining with its lower costs and better prospects of success.

Such negotiations cannot be initiated at will, however, because they involve bi- or multilateral transactions. While oppositionists demonstrate their urgent demand for regime change through peaceful protest and other forms of contained contention, they have to wait for receptivity from the authoritarian regime and its supporters. Moreover, bargaining itself is a drawn-out process. Greater success therefore went hand in hand with lower speed in this wave of democratization. In these ways, the transformation of external stimuli through the rise of the pacted transition model accounts for the further move along the negative correlation of diffusion features that is evident in the unhurried advance of democracy in South America during the 1970s and 1980s.

While negotiated transition constituted the main model during the third wave in the Western hemisphere, this kind of external precedent does not serve as a dramatic signal that grabs people's attention. In the real world of bounded rationality, the appeal of this strategy of compromise is muted. Unexciting in process and slow in progress, it does not unleash mass enthusiasm, thus stimulating a rash of emulation efforts. Instead, it is mostly representative leaders who learn from such a precedent; and they apply its lessons and initiate attempts at regime change only when they see the time as ripe. In line with the political influence of these leaders, the change in diffusion's main trigger, evident in the importance of Spain's pacted transition as the principal model for Latin America, was decisive for the particularly leisurely pace, yet widespread success of this sequence of democratization processes.

Yet as discussed at the end of Chapter 3, pacted transitions did not displace all other options on challengers' menu. Instead, cognitive heuristics helped to

---

[1] To highlight the wide reach and high success rate of the third wave in Latin America, Drake (2009) calls it a "tsunami." In terms of speed and sweep, however, the third wave differed greatly from a tsunami, as the striking contrast with the riptide of 1848 shows.

maintain the appeal of rationally less promising modes of contention, such as mass protests and even revolution. When a seemingly successful precedent occurred, such as the Argentine protests of 1982–83 or the Nicaraguan revolution of 1979, crowds or ideological sects were eager to undertake similar efforts. Representative leaders, of course, sought to tame this spontaneous contentious energy, limit its transgressive edge, and channel it into more contained and controlled challenges; and they tried hard to isolate and marginalize the advocates of insurrection and violence. Thus, the diversity of transformative strategies and the variety of external precedents embraced by different political forces meant that the reception side of diffusion continued to play an important role; the leaders of broad-based parties and unions struggled on several fronts, even more than in 1917–19. Their main goal was to ease out autocrats, but they also sought to enlist and discipline their constituents and other mass actors and to marginalize radical sects.

The diversity of external catalysts for diffusion processes and their fairly thorough processing by representative leaders[2] meant that the third wave in Latin America was much more heterogeneous and fragmented than earlier waves had been, especially the flash flood of 1848. With the slow unfolding of this multifaceted, polychromatic process, contagion and demonstration effects among emulating countries – that is, secondary diffusion – came to play a greater role as well. Whereas in 1848, all observers had primarily looked at the "overwhelming" precedent of France, in the 1970s and 1980s not only did Spain serve as a source of inspiration, but so did regional variants of pacted transitions or alternative models, such as the crowd protests erupting in Argentina in 1982. This variety of precedents slowed down emulative contention by spurring disagreements and even conflicts among challengers, but it also offered them a broader menu of options that allowed for learning through trial and error. As the representative leaders of opposition forces sooner or later abandoned or marginalized unpromising alternatives, they tended to converge on a strategy that held special promise in their country. Learning from political experience thus helped to produce a particularly high rate of actual transitions toward democracy. The second section below therefore examines how the diversity of modes of contention and the secondary diffusion processes inside Latin America contributed to the slower speed and greater success of the third wave.

Another factor helped to improve the prospects of emulative regime contention in Latin America during the late 1970s and 1980s, namely the promotion of democracy by developed countries, especially the powerful United States. Such vertical influence had not played a significant role in 1848, when France did not try to export its revolution; and in 1917–19, Russia's Bolshevists were too weak to give their export efforts real impact. But the "hegemonic" United

---

[2] The impressive range of foreign experiences that Chilean oppositionists studied is mentioned in Castillo (1991: 16–18, 59, 148–50, 158, 166, 169, 179, 181).

States did command great clout in Latin America, and European countries also had some means of influence. While the United States had historically accepted authoritarian rule in Latin America and had actively supported dictators out of concern over communism during the Cold War, President Jimmy Carter redirected foreign policy to push for human rights and democracy; and after a relapse into anticommunism during his first term, Ronald Reagan resumed democracy promotion in the mid-1980s.

However, this push from countries at the top of the global hierarchy was not the engine propelling the third wave in Latin America. Despite the tremendous power of the United States, Carter's high-profile efforts did not trigger a rash of democratic contention. In fact, a disproportionate number of actual transitions occurred not under Carter, but – ironically – after Reagan's repudiation of his predecessor's initiatives and during his renewed cooperation with dictators. U.S. pressure produced few direct effects in the short run. But over time, the influence of developed countries did contribute to the success of emulative democratization in Latin America. In particular, the United States and its European allies guided Latin American oppositionists toward moderation and negotiated solutions, and they sought to restrain military rulers from using repression to stifle challenges.

By substantiating these arguments, the present chapter explains the distinctive features of the third wave in Latin America, which my comparison with other diffusion processes puts into stark relief. Analyzing the third wave is not an easy undertaking because the diversity of modes of democratic contention and the differences in their domestic reception, the role of secondary diffusion, and the impact of vertical pressures made this democratization process much more complex, multifarious, and decentered than the tsunami of 1848 or even the wave of 1917–19. The intersection of various foreign inputs and their processing by divergent domestic forces created complicated interaction effects and tremendous entanglement; and the different mix of these factors also led to considerable dissimilarity across cases (see in general Morlino 2012: 106). While a comprehensive, thorough investigation would require a book of its own that examines each country separately, I single out one particularly drawn-out and interesting case for in-depth analysis in Chapter 7: Chile exemplifies with singular clarity the main themes highlighted so far, especially the role of different options for emulative contention, developed country pressures for redemocratization, and political learning that eventually arrived at a strategy crowned with success.

In the present long and unavoidably complicated chapter, the heterogeneity of the third wave makes a focus on South America advisable. In this region, broad-based societal and political organization, the causal factor highlighted in my theory, was particularly common.[3] By contrast, civil and political

---

[3] The role of broad-based parties and unions in controlling and channeling contentious mass mobilization is obvious in cases as diverse as Peru during the late 1970s (Sanchez 1989: 152–55, 166, 205–6) and Uruguay in the mid-1980s (Gillespie 1991: 135, 141–42, 149, 154, 166, 174).

societies in most of Central America were much more inchoate.[4] Moreover, in that region U.S. clout continued to be predominant, almost overwhelming (Levitsky and Way 2010: 130–31), leaving little room for the horizontal influences that are characteristic of diffusion. As a result, effective transitions to democracy in Central America emerged from international negotiations such as the Esquipulas Peace Process, rather than from demonstration and contagion effects. In fact, the civil wars of the 1970s and 1980s created additional complications for democratization and further differences from South America (Lehoucq 2012: ch. 2–3). Last but not least, earlier U.S. efforts to impose limited, problematic forms of democracy ("electoralism," Karl 1990: 14–15) in Central American countries such as El Salvador make it difficult even to date transitions – a conceptual problem that is much less acute in most of South America. For all of these reasons, the following analysis concentrates on this region.

THE PRIMARY MODEL: SPAIN'S NEGOTIATED TRANSITION

The third wave did not arise from one single, outstanding catalyst, but from three contentious processes clustered closely together, namely the Portuguese revolution of 1974, the collapse of the Greek colonels' regime in the same year, and Spain's negotiated transition following upon the death of *caudillo* Francisco Franco in 1975. The demise of authoritarian rule in Southern Europe attracted considerable interest in South America and drew ample media coverage, for instance in Brazil (Abreu 2005: 57). Observers in the region paid attention right away and examined these precedents. Due to long-standing historical connections and ongoing linguistic and cultural links, the Portuguese revolution was especially "available" in Brazil,[5] as was Spain's pacted transition in the whole region; the meltdown of the military dictatorship in "distant" Greece entered less on Latin Americans' radar screen (e.g., *Veja* 1974) and had little political impact.[6]

The precedents of Portugal and Spain represented distinct modes of democratic contention – transgressive versus contained – and inspired

---

[4] As Díaz Cayeros and Magaloni (2013: 245) emphasize, Mexico's belated democratic transition played out in idiosyncratic ways, because its dominant-party regime differed considerably from the military dictatorships of South America. Moreover, international actors exerted "only marginal influences" (ibid.).

[5] The Portuguese revolution was immediately reported in Brazil with long articles in the main news magazine *Veja*, with pictures on the title pages and the captions – in my translation – "Portugal – The End of a Dictatorship," *Veja* 295, May 1, 1974, and "Portugal – The Beginning of Democracy," *Veja* 296, May 8, 1974. A stream of articles kept up with developments in the former mother country during subsequent weeks.

[6] As an exception, Argentina's Raúl Alfonsín in 1982 elaborated a transition proposal inspired by the Greek experience (Novaro and Palermo 2003: 470–71).

different sectors of challengers in South America. Spanish democratization was a model of top-down initiation and elite negotiation and turned into the preferred option of many representative leaders, especially moderate oppositionists such as the center-right wing of Chile's Christian Democrats (M. Aylwin 1980; P. Aylwin 1985; Huneeus 1985; Arriagada 2002: 87–89). While more left-leaning political forces initially embraced strategies that relied much more on popular mobilization and bottom-up challenges, the political strength and resilient support commanded by many military governments sooner or later forced a convergence on negotiation and compromise and induced more and more oppositionists to support or at least acquiesce in the emulation of the Spanish model. Thus, as representative leaders came to understand the opportunities and constraints that regime contention faced in South America during the late 1970s and 1980s, they took their inspiration mainly from Spain's pacted transition. The Portuguese revolution constituted a more exciting regime change and quickly elicited attention from boundedly rational actors. But its slide into radicalism scared powerful forces on both sides of the regime divide in Latin America. More basically, its initiation by an intraregime military uprising precluded its replication: Oppositionists had no way of starting such a rebellion. Therefore, the Portuguese precedent had a much lower impact on Latin America than the gradual transition pursued by its Iberian neighbor.

The Limited Repercussions of the Portuguese Revolution in Latin America

The April 1974 rebellion of junior officers brought down Portugal's decades-old authoritarian regime, which had in the 1930s served as an inspiration for Brazilian autocrat Getúlio Vargas. This coup, which unleashed popular mass mobilization and set in motion an ever more deep-reaching, left-leaning revolution, had an immediate effect on Brazil's military dictatorship, which came to fear a similar bottom-up explosion. The Portuguese revolution gave an additional boost to the plan of new president Ernesto Geisel (1974–79) to start a careful, gradual "decompression." After the harsh repression under General Emílio Médici (1969–74), Geisel intended to let off steam and thus forestall dramatic challenges. As the Portuguese precedent highlighted the danger to avoid, it strengthened Geisel's determination to pursue slow liberalization against the resistance of military hardliners (Maxwell 1986: 131–32).

But the impact of the Portuguese revolution on Brazil's incipient transition was limited. The fundamental decision to soften the dictatorship had already been made before the Lisbon events, under Geisel's predecessor. Because violent attacks by left-wing sects had by then been squashed (Geisel's comments in D'Araujo and Castro 1997: 287; Stepan 1988: 33), the predominant currents inside the Brazilian regime saw the time as ripe for prudent liberalization (Gaspari 2003: 255, 321–23, 396; Skidmore 1988: 160–71). Thus, Geisel's policy of distension was already under way when the officers' rebellion in the

by observers (Fuentes, De la Dehesa, et al. 1989), it was the subject of more sustained study and analysis than had been common of precedents during the earlier waves of democratic contention investigated in this book. For instance, Mariana Aylwin, the daughter of a leading Christian Democrat and later president of Chile, Patricio Aylwin, wrote a substantial report about the Spanish case in 1980, highlighting its success (M. Aylwin 1980: 48, 57, 73); and a scholar close to Chile's Christian Democratic Party authored a long book about the centrist party led by the main architect of the Spanish transition, Adolfo Suárez, and about its contributions to the negotiation process (Huneeus 1985).

Given a wealth of personal links, professional connections, and exile experiences, numerous Latin American political leaders had firsthand knowledge of the Spanish transition and served as channels of information transmission. They presented the Spanish case in their publications and drew lessons for their own countries (e.g., Bernales 1986: 49, 56–57, 77–78). Party leaders who spent their exile in Spain, such as Chilean Christian Democrat Andrés Zaldívar (interview 2007), provided frequent pieces of information and advice; Chilean socialist Erich Schnake was particularly close to Spain's socialist prime minister Felipe González (Schnake 2004: 315–16, 327–30), who had been the main opposition leader during the Spanish transition and whose endorsement of this negotiated process (Share 1986: 180–87) gave it additional appeal, especially for left-wingers. González also took it upon himself to give South American politicians recommendations drawn from his country's experiences. At the inauguration of Argentina's new democratic president Raúl Alfonsín in late 1983, for instance, he questioned the protest strategy pursued by the Chilean opposition at that time and urged a more moderate approach via negotiation – along Spanish lines.[10] Just a few months later, moderate Christian Democrat Patricio Aylwin invoked the Spanish example and publicly embraced the same position (P. Aylwin 1985: 150, 153). Finally, Latin Americans invited leaders of the Spanish transition to learn about that experience and obtain firsthand advice. In this vein, both Uruguay's opposition parties and Chile's Christian Democrats brought Spanish centrist Adolfo Suárez, who had taken the crucial steps in dismantling the Franco regime, for extended consultations and public meetings in mid-1984 and late 1986, respectively.[11] In Chile, Suárez reinforced the opposition's decision finally to give up the protest strategy (see Chapter 7) and, instead, to contest autocrat Augusto Pinochet inside the institutional

---

[10] Interview with Garretón 2007. González gave similarly moderate, conciliatory advice to the many Uruguayan oppositionists with whom he also met on this occasion (*Opinar* 1983c). At a Socialist International meeting held years before, González had already advocated "a cautious, patient and pragmatic approach to authoritarian regimes in Latin America" (*LAPR* 1978). In late 1983, an intellectual of the Spanish Socialist Party, interviewed by a Chilean news magazine, also advocated moderation and *concertación* (interviewed in Rodríguez 1983: 34).

[11] On the Uruguay visit, see Gillespie (1991: 174, n. 32) and *La Democracia* (1984). Suárez also talked to many Latin American oppositionists at Raúl Alfonsín's presidential inauguration in Buenos Aires in December 1983. See, for instance, Lara Curbelo (1983).

framework created by the dictatorship (Fundación Eduardo Frei 1986; Suárez et al. 1986; Guillier 1986).

Due to all these diffusion channels and learning processes, "Spanish democratization ... was immensely relevant to and influential in Latin America" (Huntington 1991: 102). As Uruguay's first post-authoritarian president Julio Sanguinetti (1985–90) said (in Boeker 1990: 91), "The Spanish transition was a very important event which inspired us." Spain exemplified the mode of regime change via political and socioeconomic pacts among organizational leaders whose historical emergence Chapter 3 discussed. This model of contained contention, codified by the transitions literature in political science (especially O'Donnell and Schmitter 1986: ch. 4), helped to inspire several transition efforts in South America. In Chile, for instance, a wide range of opposition forces and moderate supporters of the Pinochet regime, upon the instigation of the Catholic Church and with backing from the United States, designed an *Acuerdo Nacional* in 1985. But fearing that negotiations about regime change would isolate him politically, the dictator rejected this emulation effort rudely. Brazilian redemocratization rested on more successful transition agreements established in 1984, based on mutual assurances and informal bargains between opposition leaders, conservative politicians, and generals behind closed doors.[12] Peru's military president Francisco Morales-Bermúdez (1975–80) also conducted a transition along Spanish lines,[13] convoking a constituent assembly in 1978,[14] and holding formal and informal conversations and negotiations with political parties and some unions.[15]

Specific aspects of the Spanish democratization process also found advocates in South America. For instance, the constitutional court created by Spain's constituent assembly in 1978 elicited tremendous interest from a hispanophile

---

[12] On these contacts, with a reference to Spain, see Cardoso (2006b: 97–99); on the written agreement signed by four political leaders, see discussion by one of the signatories, PFL Senator Marco Maciel, in Albuquerque and Durham (1987: 56–58); on the informal, nonpublic assurances given by the opposition's presidential candidate Tancredo Neves to various military leaders, see Passarinho (1989: 139–40, 171) and Silveira (2001: 38); on all these agreements, see also Bruneau (1992: 263–65) and Skidmore (1988: 251). In 1984, Neves mentioned Spain's Pacto de Moncloa as a positive example (Corrêa 2005: 23).

[13] Bolivian President Hugo Banzer wanted to initiate a similar kind of transition, but quickly lost control of the process, which ended up unfolding with many twists and turns from 1977–82 (Malloy and Gamarra 1988: 95–96, 117, 122–39).

[14] Although Fernando Belaúnde, leader of the Popular Action Party and president both before and after the military regime (1963–68, 1980–85), rejected participation in the constituent assembly, the main site of negotiation, he himself proposed a transition pact in 1979–80, inspired by the Venezuelan "Pacto de Punto Fijo" of 1958 (Sanchez 1989: 168, 174–75).

[15] Prieto Celi 1996: 183, 200, 202, 247, 251; Sanchez 1989: 130–31, 158–60, 177–80, 184–88; Dietz 1992: 241–47. On the frequent talks between military officials and civilian politicians, especially APRA leader Víctor Raúl Haya de la Torre, see interviews with Morales-Bermúdez 2009, Silva Ruete 2009, Barrón 2009, and García Belaúnde 2009. Based on these conversations, Haya, as president of Peru's Constituent Assembly, replaced the charter's draft section on the armed forces with the version elaborated by the military itself.

politician, Javier Valle-Riestra, who used his seat in Peru's constitutional convention of 1978–79 to push with enormous energy, great eloquence, and eventual success for the emulation of this innovation (Valle-Riestra 2009: 45, 68, 83; interview with Valle-Riestra 2009; see also García Belaúnde 1996: 114; Ortiz de Zevallos 1989: 100–1; interview with García Belaúnde 2009). According to a leading constitutional lawyer, Peru's whole new charter was based essentially on the Spanish model, which as the most recent product of European constitutionalism was on lawyers' minds (interview with Quispe Correa 2009). A deputy in Peru's constituent assembly personally knew the main architect of the Spanish charter and thus obtained a host of relevant materials, which he brought to Lima (interview with Barrón 2009). In fact, it seems that the Spanish constitution of 1978 had a broad influence on the definition of constitutional rights and judicial procedures in a wide range of Latin American countries (Haro 2005; Brinks and Blass 2009).

In sum, the example of Spain substantially affected the third wave in South America.[16] But this diffusion process differed from the earlier waves of democratic contention, especially 1848. Rather than making a big impression on the mass citizenry, the Spanish experience was transmitted and processed primarily by representative leaders, who operated with wider bounds of political rationality. These organizational officials proceeded with greater prudence and waited for a propitious political conjuncture before embarking on emulation efforts. For these reasons, attempts to act on lessons from this pacted transition did not cluster closely in time, as had happened especially in 1848. Instead, the first emulation efforts in South America, which occurred in Peru in 1978, were years apart from the Brazilian agreements of 1984 and Chile's *Acuerdo Nacional* of 1985.

Because Latin America's authoritarian regimes, especially the bureaucratic-authoritarian variant predominant in South America, were institutionally solid and often enjoyed the backing of important societal sectors, opposition leaders lacked the capacity to initiate a transition on their own; to have a realistic chance of success, they had to wait for a move toward political liberalization undertaken by the dictatorship itself, as in Brazil and Peru (cf. O'Donnell and Schmitter 1986: 19–21), or take advantage of a sudden crisis, such as the economic collapse befalling Chile in 1982–83. Thus, efforts to emulate Spain's strategy of negotiation usually did not happen at a time of the opposition's choosing; instead, opposition leaders had to choose the right time. While challengers' embrace of moderation and compromise helped to soften authoritarian

---

[16] The transitions in Ecuador and Uruguay also advanced via pacts (Isaacs 1993: 118–24; Gillespie 1991, especially ch. 7–8). Even in Argentina, party leaders sought a negotiated transition in 1981 (Quiroga 2004: 261–66) – before the defeat in the Falklands War weakened the military regime so much that the opposition came to regard concessions as unnecessary (Quiroga 2004: 329–33; Fontana 1987: 173–76, 188).

coalitions, dictators retained veto power; the opposition's offer of negotiations tried to unclench their fist, but could not force their hand.

The very clout of many outgoing military regimes, which were impossible to drive from power through street protests or violent insurgencies,[17] turned the Spanish model of crafting a transition via elite-level negotiations into the most promising option available to South American opposition leaders. The Iberian experience showed that a regime change was feasible even under considerable constraints. Interestingly, this important case of success made Latin American politicians overestimate the chances of replication in their own country. As Chapter 2 argued and Chapter 5 showed, even the leaders of broad-based organizations are affected by the representativeness heuristic, despite their looser bounds of rationality. In this vein, Chile's moderate opposition spent a good deal of political capital on the *Acuerdo Nacional* of 1985. Leaders of various stripes set high hopes in this effort to launch a Spanish-style transition through negotiation (interview with Molina 2007), although dictator Pinochet had categorically disavowed the cautious steps toward a political opening and conversations with the opposition that his own newly appointed interior minister Sergio Onofre Jarpa had undertaken in 1983–84. Indeed, Pinochet flatly rejected the *Acuerdo Nacional* as well.

Thus, inspiration in the Spanish case did not automatically bring success; the representativeness heuristic could lead even Latin America's representative leaders astray.[18] However, efforts to emulate this precedent certainly held better prospects than transgressive modes of democratic contention, such as mass protests. Political learning from Spain's pacted transition thus helps account for the high rate of success that regime contention during the third wave in South America achieved. The reliance on negotiation, which made it impossible for the opposition to force the initiation, progress, and successful conclusion of such a transition, also helps explain the slow unfolding of this diffusion process. The higher chances of goal achievement inherent in this elite-driven democratization strategy thus went hand in hand with low speed. The cross-regional dissemination of this transition model, which depended on organizational leadership, thus underlies the coincidence of these two diffusion features that sets South America's third wave so far apart from the disappointing

---

[17] Instead, authoritarian leaders claimed that disruptive challenges from the bottom up (would have) strengthened their determination to maintain power. See, for instance, the interviews conducted by Prieto Celi (1996: 170–71, 213) with Peru's last military president Francisco Morales-Bermúdez, and by D'Araujo and Castro (1997: 383, 390–93) with Brazil's Ernesto Geisel.

[18] Moreover, even the moderate Spanish case served as a deterrent for some ultra-conservative politicians. Jaime Guzmán, for instance, a leading ideologue of the Pinochet regime, engineered the constitution of 1980 in a way to "avoid Franco's 'great mistake'" of not resolving the problem of political succession (Huneeus 2007: 396). The Chilean military was also determined to avoid the subordination to civilian authority that Spain's new democracy had established (Weeks 2002: 396–401).

tsunami of the mid-nineteenth century and even the mixed wave of the early twentieth century.

SECONDARY DIFFUSION IN SOUTH AMERICA: ADDITIONAL SOURCES OF INSPIRATION

Because the primary trigger of the third wave – the precedent of Spain – did not have an overwhelming impact in Latin America, there was room for other contentious experiences to attract attention as well. And because emulation efforts unfolded slowly, secondary diffusion among South American neighbors could come into play. The additional precedents from which opposition forces could learn included variants of negotiated transitions. After all, negotiations by nature involve adjustments to a country's particular circumstances. Therefore, emulation of the Spanish precedent went beyond mere replication; it did not proceed uniformly, but in country-specific versions. For instance, Peru's convocation of a constituent assembly, a parallel of the Spanish strategy, differed from Brazil's reliance on a sequence of legislative and executive elections to effect a very gradual transfer of power.[19] With the emergence of these diverse transition strategies, other countries could learn from intra-regional adaptations of the Spanish model, not only from the original.

Moreover, the sober, unexciting strategy of pacted transition never turned into the exclusive mode of regime contention during the third wave, as Chapter 3 explained. Instead, there continued to be political space for alternatives, especially massive crowd protests, as they erupted during the crumbling of Argentina's totally discredited dictatorship in 1982. While the causal contribution that these demonstrations and strikes made to the demise of Argentine military rule is questionable,[20] this bold defiance sparked the availability heuristic and elicited interest in other Southern Cone countries.

Due to the variety of contentious options that could serve as sources of inspiration, the third wave was more heterogeneous than the riptides of 1830 and 1848. Secondary diffusion acquired greater importance; rather than merely reinforcing the emulation of the original precedent, it came to offer a more

[19] On Brazil, see Lamounier (1989: 55–72). These differences were significant to important politicians. On the one hand, Fernando Belaúnde, leader of a major party and Peru's president from 1963 to 1968 and 1980 to 1985, argued "that a new constitution was unnecessary and that presidential and legislative elections should instead be held immediately" (Dietz 1992: 243). On the other hand, Brazil's major opposition party in the early 1980s, the Partido do Movimento Democrático Brasileiro (PMDB), demanded a constituent assembly (Leonelli and Oliveira 2004: 31–32, 40–41, 66, 72), but the incumbent regime blocked this effort in order to retain control of the transition process.
[20] Fontana 1987: 160–62, 186–87; Novaro and Palermo 2003: 469–72, 546–47; Quiroga 2004: 332. By contrast, Munck (1998: 139–46) postulates an important impact. But while the military's loss of legitimacy in the eyes of civil society played an indirect role, protests as such did not.

extensive menu for challengers. Therefore, oppositionists did not all converge on the same external model; instead, based on their ideological orientations, various groupings advocated and tried out different strategies. As a result, contentious diffusion during the third wave turned into a complex mingling of currents and cross-currents.

Moreover, two empirical patterns suggest learning among neighboring countries. First, statistical investigations commonly find robust evidence of secondary diffusion. Emulation decisions across the border seem to increase a country's propensity to follow those precedents.[21] Second, the geographical sequence of the South American transitions looks like a classical fall of dominoes. Democratization advanced among contiguous countries and rippled step by step across the continent. After Ecuador reestablished democracy in 1979, neighboring Peru did so in 1980, then Bolivia in 1982, Argentina in 1983, Uruguay in 1984, Brazil in 1985, and Paraguay in 1989. Contagion and demonstration effects seem to have crossed borders directly. These statistical findings and spatial patterns make it important to investigate secondary diffusion during the third wave in South America.

The Uneven Strength of Secondary Diffusion

Despite these indications, my ample field work, which included archival research and numerous interviews in Chile, Peru, and Brazil, yielded surprisingly limited evidence of direct cross-border diffusion (similar statistical finding in Teorell 2010: 82, 88–89). With the important exception of the Argentine mass mobilizations and "transition through rupture" in 1982–83 (Share 1987; cf. Share and Mainwaring 1986; Huntington 1991: 142–49), the variety of contentious efforts and regime changes in South America had only minimal if any direct impact on oppositionists in the region. Mass publics and especially organizational leaders were aware of democratic contention among their neighbors, but usually attributed little relevance to these events.[22] In fact, even attempts to analyze intraregional experiences thoroughly and establish direct contacts with their protagonists to gain firsthand knowledge were surprisingly infrequent.

Peruvian politicians of various orientations attributed very little importance to the experiences of neighboring countries (interviews with Barrón 2009, Diez Canseco 2009, Morales-Bermúdez 2009, Negreiros 2009, Pease 2009, and Valle-Riestra 2009). For instance, they clearly knew about the

[21] Wejnert 2005: 67, 72–73; Brinks and Coppedge 2006; Gleditsch and Ward 2006; Mainwaring and Pérez-Liñán (forthcoming: especially ch. 4). Surprisingly, however, Teorell (2010: 80–83, 86–89) finds that this effect is entirely due to diffusion processes in sub-Saharan Africa, not in Latin America or Eastern Europe, where evidence of direct neighborhood effects looks so obvious.

[22] In Paraguay, however, the opposition that suddenly mobilized in mid-1987 called for an *Acuerdo Nacional* (*Análisis* 1987b) and formed an *Asamblea de la Civilidad* (*Análisis* 1987a), using terms coined by the Chilean opposition. Perhaps U.S. involvement (see *Análisis* 1987b) mediated this transfer.

democratic transition under way in Ecuador from 1977–79, but they do not report taking inspiration from these events although they underwent a similar process during the same time period, which included a constituent assembly as well. Instead, their new charter was much more influenced by Spain (interview with Valle-Riestra 2009). The troubled experiences of Bolivia, which during the late 1970s also sought to reestablish democracy (*Caretas* 1979; Muñoz 1980; Whitehead 1986), had even less impact, especially in propelling Peru's transition. Instead, the military regime in Lima saw Bolivia's chaotic stop-and-go pattern as a deterrent – an instigation not to relinquish power too quickly, but to insist on an orderly, negotiated transition that strictly followed its institutional timetable.

In Brazil, the gathering wave of democratic contention and regime change in the vicinity also had few repercussions. The country's transition was very slow and gradual, clearly controlled by the incumbent military governments, which continued to enjoy a good deal of civilian support. Bottom-up challenges therefore had few chances to deflect this transition from the trajectory determined from the top down. Certainly, the surprising electoral victories of the official opposition in 1974 and 1982 and the massive strikes of 1978–79 (Alves 1985: 143–44, 192–210, 227–30; Lamounier 1989: 65, 61–62, 71) pushed the process beyond the military's original intentions, but even these challenges drew flexible, fairly savvy responses that preserved a great deal of governmental control (Martins 1986: 82–91; Duncan Baretta and Markoff 1987: 46–53). Because the domestic opposition had limited room for making a significant difference in the regime's liberalization and democratization project, lessons drawn from other contentious experiences in South America rarely came into play.

In one significant instance, however, secondary diffusion did make some difference. The mass demonstrations for direct presidential elections starting in 1983, in the context of a severe economic crisis and the exhaustion of military rule, were influenced by the wave of protests sweeping across the Southern Cone at that time. The Argentine precedent, in particular, drew attention and served as an additional inspiration for protagonists and participants in this *Diretas Já* campaign (Cardoso 1983; Mir 1983; Nader 1983; Nader and Meirelles Passos 1983; Nogueira 1983). For instance, a democratic politician from Argentina was invited to a mass rally in Southern Brazil; his testimony of the struggle for free, democratic elections was uplifting and moving to the crowd (Leonelli and De Oliveira 2004: 345). Overall, in the words of important party politicians, the Argentine example provided "atmospheric" reinforcement for bottom-up contention in Brazil (interviews with Braga 2008, Dirceu 2008, and Franco 2008; see also the caricature reproduced in Rodrigues 2003: 22).

In fact, a turning point in the *Diretas Já* campaign, after which it became the largest mass mobilization ever witnessed in Brazil, arose directly from Buenos Aires. In the second half of 1983, relatively small crowds had demonstrated for direct elections; even in São Paulo in November, only about 15,000 people turned out, a much smaller number than the 100,000 expected by the event's sponsors (Kotscho 1984: 13). But then, Governor Franco Montoro attended the inauguration of President Alfonsín in December, and the outpouring of Argentines demonstrating their enthusiastic support for the new democracy made an overwhelming impression on the São Paulo Governor (São Paulo, Governo do Estado 1987: 50; Leonelli and De Oliveira 2004: 367; see also Kotscho 1984: 20–21). He was so encouraged that he pushed single-mindedly for organizing a huge mass rally in front of São Paulo's cathedral in January 1984, overriding the skepticism and calls for caution that many representative leaders of his own party – typically – voiced. As later president Fernando Henrique Cardoso recalls, "All realistic calculations indicated that the conditions for such a rally were not given" (Cardoso and Toledo 1998: 60; see also 58–59). But inspired by the Argentine precedent, Montoro threw prudence to the wind and insisted on pushing ahead. This demonstration drew 250,000–300,000 people, far more than expected. That success in turn boosted the *Diretas Já* campaign to much greater prominence (Cardoso and Toledo 1998: 58) and helped it take center stage in Brazilian politics for months (interview with Dirceu 2008). As mass mobilization took off, other opposition leaders came to throw their political weight behind the campaign (interview with Braga 2008). Huge rallies proliferated across the whole country, culminating in a gathering of 1.2–1.5 million participants in São Paulo in April 1984. As this episode shows, the Argentine success exerted a significant impact on neighboring Brazil through the dramatic, vivid experience of an important leader, who was overwhelmed by the heuristics of availability and representativeness.

Despite this amazing spark, however, Brazilian opposition leaders did not rush into a mechanical imitation of Argentine mass mobilization. Instead, they marshaled this bottom-up pressure for a specific institutional target. Whereas the protests in Argentina (and then Chile) simply pushed for an end of the dictatorship, the Brazilian *Diretas Já* movement supported a constitutional amendment designed to replace the indirect presidential elections instituted by the military regime, which disadvantaged the opposition, by a direct popular contest. As is typical, the representative leaders of broad-based organizations tamed contentious bottom-up energies unleashed in part by a striking external precedent, channeled them toward institutional reform to take advantage of an electoral opportunity opened up by the government, and thus avoided an all-out confrontation with a particularly powerful authoritarian regime, which in their eyes could have provoked a dangerous backlash (Cardoso 2006a: 147). Once again, however, the military government managed to prevent this alteration of its transition plan through a combination of carrots and sticks; an insufficient number of deputies voted for the direct election amendment in Congress (overview in Skidmore 1988: 240–44).

The massive but domesticated bottom-up contention of 1983–84, inspired in part by the Argentine mass mobilizations, had only an indirect effect by helping to undermine the cohesion of the military's civilian support coalition. The resulting internal divisions then allowed for the defeat of the governmental candidate and the indirect election of a moderate opposition leader as prospective president in 1985 (Corrêa 2005). This notoriously cautious winner, Tancredo Neves, had been wary of the mass mobilization during the direct elections campaign and had preferred negotiations with the incumbent regime. Thus, even the indirect effect of the *Diretas Já* movement did not bring a great departure from the withdrawal project of the outgoing military regime.[23]

In sum, during Brazil's lengthy transition process, there was little democratic diffusion from neighboring countries overall. Yet toward the end of this path, the Argentine precedent did help to propel redemocratization, albeit in a limited way.

Chile underwent South America's last transition from authoritarian rule, after a particularly lengthy and tortuous struggle for regime change. Due to this delay, there were a number of regional experiences that could have served as sources of inspiration during some of these twists and turns. Once again, however, leading politicians of different persuasions and from both sides of the fence reported that most events in neighboring countries had little impact (interviews with Correa 2007, Martínez 2007, Núñez 2007, Vodanovic 2007). These representative leaders were clearly aware of regime contention in South America, but did not pay much attention or attribute great importance to these experiences.

In fact, Chilean politicians had surprisingly weak contacts and connections to neighboring countries. For instance, although Chile's Socialist Party had similar populist origins as Peru's American Popular Revolutionary Alliance (APRA) and had maintained fairly close links during the 1930s and 1940s, Chilean Socialists claimed that in the 1980s the two parties had no connections whatsoever (interview with Vodanovic 2007). Similarly, leading politicians did not seem to know neighboring countries or be known there. For example, Christian Democrat Patricio Aylwin, later the first post-transition president (1990–94), allegedly had never visited Bolivia (interview with P. Aylwin 2007).[24] And when Chilean oppositionists invited Raúl Alfonsín, the Argentine Radical Party leader who received the presidential sash from the outgoing dictatorship in December 1983, they had the impression that it was his first visit across the Andes, ever[25]; in turn, Chileans at the reception held to honor Alfonsín asked each other, "¿Quién es este gordito?" – "Who is this chubby fellow?" (author interview with an important opposition politician, Santiago, July 2007; similar Silva Cimma 2000: 399). As these anecdotes suggest, even after repression and exile had forced many oppositionists into foreign countries, leading

---

[23] Tragically, Neves died before taking office, bringing his coalition partner, a former supporter of the military regime, to power.

[24] By contrast, Gabriel Valdés (2009: 283), who had served as Chile's foreign minister, reports various connections to politicians from Peru and other Latin American countries.

[25] Novaro and Palermo (2003: 518) highlight the "isolationist tendencies of Argentine parties," which leaders such as Alfonsín tried to overcome from the early 1980s onward – but, it seems, with limited success.

democratic politicians had little familiarity with their counterparts across borders.[26] Although a democratization wave was sweeping across the region, not much direct learning from neighbors occurred.

As in the Brazilian case, however, there was one exception when a striking upsurge of democratic contention in the Southern Cone did have some impact on Chile. The protests erupting in Argentina in 1982, which gave the coup de grace to a tottering military regime and helped to seal a "transition through rupture" in 1983, provided a bit of reinforcement for the mass demonstrations that started across the Andes in 1983. While the decomposition of the Argentine dictatorship,[27] which prompted this strong bottom-up challenge, had a peculiar cause, namely defeat in the Falklands War, the Pinochet regime had just suffered an equivalent fiasco: The neoliberal economic model that it had imposed with great fanfare as the core of its "refoundational" project (Garretón 1989) had crashed in 1982, causing an unprecedented 14 percent drop of GDP and sky-high unemployment rates. This economic catastrophe stimulated tremendous social discontent and seemed to sound the death knell for the dictatorship, as the thrashing by Britain had done in Argentina.

As a result, the courageous Argentine protests and subsequent democratic election and festive inauguration of President Alfonsín attracted attention across the mountains in line with the availability heuristic; despite press censorship, Chilean news magazines mentioned these events in their reports. Moreover, the representativeness heuristic highlighted similarities in the regime conjunctures of Argentina and Chile; the crumbling of the Argentine dictatorship strengthened the belief that Pinochet's hold on power was also endangered. As a result, crowd contention in Argentina had some demonstration and contagion effect on Chile, reinforcing the monthly protests undertaken from mid-1983 onward. These mass demonstrations, which initially found a surprising degree of adherence even in areas that had been sympathetic to the Pinochet government, shook the regime to the core, allowed for opposition parties to reappear on the political scene and resume their proselytizing and organizational efforts, and thus became the first step in Chile's long struggle for redemocratization. Diffusion among neighbors thus had some impact on democratic contention in Chile, although the emulative protest strategy did not achieve its goals, as Chapter 7 shows.

This analysis of secondary diffusion during the third wave in South America yields two distinct findings. On the one hand, most contentious experiences in the region did not serve as direct inspirations for neighboring countries.

[26] After Argentina restored democracy, however, a number of politicians sought to help their neighbors achieve the same goal. In early 1984, for instance, youth groups from the main Argentine and Chilean parties held a meeting right on the border to promote democratization (*Análisis* 1984).

[27] As Barany (2012: 151) highlights, however, the Argentine regime did not collapse, but managed to ensure a reasonably orderly, albeit rapid transition.

On the other hand, the Argentine crowd protests of 1982–83 did provide some additional impulse for similar challenges in the Southern Cone.[28] The following subsection examines the reasons for these different phenomena. Why did the Argentine precedent matter when several other potential sources of learning in the region elicited only minimal interest?

Reasons for the Differential Impact of Intra-Regional Precedents

The impact of the Argentine "transition through rupture" and the neglect of other regional experiences that were mostly variants of the pacted transition model à la Spain reflected the imbalance in the political appeal of different modes of regime contention discussed in Chapter 3. Rational calculations made negotiations and compromise look most promising in countries where military regimes commanded a good deal of institutional strength and political backing. But cognitive shortcuts highlighted more directly the courageous and exciting demonstrations and the striking disintegration of the regime in Buenos Aires. The availability heuristic focused attention on the massive, bold defiance against a brutal dictatorship and the subsequent amazing victory of model democrat Raúl Alfonsín (see Cavarozzi 1986: 45–48). These citizen mobilizations were visible and dramatic, whereas the internal decomposition of the military left fewer public traces.

The Argentine regime's demise also lent itself to an epic story of success. A dictatorship that had brutally terrorized society, ambitiously sought to transform the economic development model, and tried to fulfill the long-standing nationalist aspiration of regaining the Falkland Islands was suddenly put on the defensive and suffered assaults from all sides. This striking reversal of fortune made the autocracy look like a giant on feet of clay that would tumble as soon as it was challenged. In line with the representativeness heuristic, the Argentine transition through rupture helped to instill hope in citizens chafing under repressive regimes elsewhere that they could accomplish a similar feat. The Argentine precedent thus provided an additional spark for contentious mobilization in neighboring countries.[29]

The inferences derived via cognitive heuristics are not fully valid guides to political action, however. The protests inspired in part by the Argentine case in Brazil, Chile, and Uruguay did not achieve their specific goals, although the tremendous economic problems afflicting these countries in the wake of the debt crisis provided enormous fuel for the fire. Contrary to oppositionists' high hopes, street contention proved incapable of dislodging authoritarian rulers. No other

---

[28] For reports about and repercussions of the Argentine precedent on Uruguay, see *Opinar* (1982), *La Democracia* (1983), Lara (1983), and Pasquet Iribarne (1984).

[29] In Uruguay, this impact was predominantly indirect: Protests took their primary inspiration from the mass demonstrations in Chile (Blanco 1983b; *Opinar* 1983b; Gillespie 1991: 125, 130 n. 9; see also Ricaldoni 1983), which in turn gained an impulse from the Argentine precedent.

South American military regime was internally as fragmented as the Argentine dictatorship and so weakened by failure on all fronts. Despite its defeat in the constitutional referendum of 1980 (Corbo 2007: 31), the Uruguayan dictatorship retained a good deal of strength (Gillespie 1991: 76); Pinochet could rely on the centralized hierarchy and institutionalist tradition of Chile's armed forces, especially his firm command over the army, to survive the apparent collapse of his neoliberal economic model; and the Brazilian regime blocked the *Diretas Já* movement and maintained indirect presidential elections, although rising conflicts among its supporters cost it the victory in that contest. Thus, the protest strategy that took some inspiration from the Argentine success did not encounter similarly propitious conditions elsewhere. Southern Cone regimes were too strong to capitulate or fall to mass challenges.

As representative leaders sooner or later learned from the limited success of confrontational approaches, the less heroic strategy of negotiations with the incumbent generals held greater promise. Rather than having to abandon power without reliable guarantees, as their Argentine counterparts did,[30] the Brazilian, Chilean, and Uruguayan regimes had the clout to impose restrictions on the opposition and managed to extract formal or informal concessions. Facing governments that maintained considerable strength, challengers had better reasons to learn from Spanish bargaining than from the unusual Argentine case. But halting progress on a long and winding road, which often moves two steps forward, one step back, was less dramatic and attention-grabbing than the Argentine transition through rupture. The availability heuristic therefore did not highlight these relevant experiences, limiting their impact on neighboring countries. During the long years that Chile's intellectually sophisticated opposition searched for ways and means to ease out dictator Pinochet, it rarely considered the Uruguayan case, for instance, where a civil-military pact engineered a transition years before Chile achieved redemocratization.

Moreover, negotiated transitions do not achieve the clear-cut success that crowd protests hope to achieve and that the Argentine demonstrations seemingly produced. Bottom-up mass contention seeks to dislodge the authoritarian regime and allow for a new start. The Argentine generals had indeed not managed to impose conditions on the incoming democratic government. By contrast, pacted regime changes cannot create such a clean break with the past. They rest on compromise and involve a give-and-take in which the opposition needs to accommodate core demands of the military and its civilian supporters in order to persuade the armed forces to relinquish power. These pragmatic concessions are unpalatable and may even run up against fundamental moral principles, especially when the extremely complicated and controversial issue of human

---

[30] Despite their weakened position, even the Argentine generals managed to negotiate a deal with some sectors of the Peronist Party, which had won every open election since 1946 and therefore seemed likely to take power in 1983 as well. Only the unexpected victory of Radical candidate Raúl Alfonsín left the armed forces completely unprotected (Vacs 1987: 30–31).

rights violations is involved. Because negotiations do not bring full success, such transitions do not look very appealing to boundedly rational actors. For all of these reasons, this rationally preferable mode of democratic contention elicited less direct, immediate interest than the more exciting protest strategy.

But the experiences of Argentina's new democracy, which used its fresh start to embark on some rather bold initiatives, also demonstrated that success is in the eyes of the beholder, of course. Whereas the Chilean opposition took some inspiration from Argentina in its effort to force out the Pinochet dictatorship with crowd protests, Chile's incumbent regime also learned from a striking precedent across the Andes – and dug in its heels with greater determination. The Alfonsín government supported the efforts to put the former military *Juntas* on trial for the gross atrocities and other misdeeds committed under their command. This courageous move toward transitional justice sent shock waves through the authoritarian regimes of the Southern Cone (*LAWR* 1984a, 1984b), especially Chile (as Chapter 7 discusses in depth). In line with the representativeness heuristic, many uniformed agents and civilian supporters of these dictatorships feared a repetition of this bold precedent in their own country (on Uruguay, see Schumacher 1984; Gillespie 1991: 127, 183).[31]

To forestall this risk, civilian and military hard-liners pushed for staying in power as long as possible and rejected any concessions to the democratic opposition. This episode shows that the example of a new democracy that is especially successful in the eyes of pro-democratic forces does not automatically guarantee further democratization in neighboring countries. Instead, the prosecution of former authoritarian rulers in one country can serve as a deterrent for incumbent autocrats elsewhere and make them more reluctant to relinquish control of the government.[32] Fundamental disagreement over what constitutes success is another reason for the limited role of neighborhood effects during the third wave in Latin America.

As this investigation of secondary diffusion inside South America shows, many experiences of democratic contention and transition in the region lacked the dramatic features and unambiguous success that would have sparked the availability and representativeness heuristics and prompted noticeable demonstration and contagion effects. Only the striking mass mobilizations in Argentina and their apparent success provided inspiration for democratic forces in the Southern Cone; and while bottom-up challenges did not attain their intended goals in Brazil, Chile, and Uruguay, they did strengthen the opposition's hand in subsequent negotiation efforts, most clearly in Brazil and

[31] This fear of retribution predated the Argentine precedent, affecting, for instance, Bolivia's stop-and-go transition efforts in the late 1970s and early 1980s (Malloy and Gamarra 1988: 133, 136, 144) as well as Peru's smoother democratization process, as various very knowledgeable political leaders stressed (author interviews, Lima, July 2009).

[32] This anticipated reaction and resulting deterrent effect is not discussed in Sikkink's (2011: 148–50) brief examination of the impact of prosecutions on democracy.

Uruguay. Except for the repercussions of the Argentine precedent, however, the apparent falling of the authoritarian dominoes in South America was less a product of direct cross-border impulses than of common inspiration in the Spanish example – and of the democracy promotion efforts of influential First World nations, which the following sub-section examines.

VERTICAL PRESSURES FROM POWERFUL DEVELOPED COUNTRIES

To what extent did exhortations and pressures from the United States and European countries contribute to the sequential unfolding of the third wave in South America, especially its comparatively slow speed and high success? This "vertical" influence exerted by powerful, advanced countries over weaker, developing nations is a new factor for this study that had not played a major, systematic role in the two earlier waves of democratic contention examined above. In 1848, France did not forcefully spread revolution, contrary to the experiences of the revolutionary wars of the 1790s and the Napoleonic era of the early 1800s. In 1917–19, the Soviet Union's efforts to export its revolution proved ineffectual, failing to prevent the quick demise of the communist experiment in Hungary in 1919. Only President Woodrow Wilson's democratizing pressure on the German Empire had a substantial impact in helping to trigger the constitutional reform of October 1918, which was, however, quickly swept aside by the immediately following November Revolution. In sum, the waves of 1848 and 1917–19 were predominantly horizontal diffusion processes among autonomous units; they played out mostly in Europe, which during the long stretch of time between the Napoleonic Wars and the Cold War lacked an established hegemonic power with the leverage to impose its regime preferences.[33]

The third wave in South America differed because after the global advance of democracy in earlier decades, it unfolded in a "dependent" region; the frontline of democratization had moved downward in the global hierarchy. During the 1970s and 1980s, the United States commanded a great deal of influence in the continent and came to use it to promote political liberalization and democracy during the presidency of Jimmy Carter (1977–81) and the second term of Ronald Reagan (1985–89). Whereas the United States had played no role in Latin America in 1848 or in South America in 1917–19, it had started, during World War II, to exert pressure on Latin America to move toward democracy. The years from 1944 to 1946 had indeed seen a mini-wave of democratization in the region for which the United States' impending victory over fascism and national-socialism served as an inspiration (Bethell and Roxborough 1992; Rock 1994; Mainwaring and Pérez-Liñán, forthcoming). In fact, the United

[33] This lull in forceful regime promotion is reflected in the data compiled by Owen (2010: 2, 15–21); many of the relatively few cases listed between 1815 and 1948 were efforts by "reactionary" powers to suppress democratic contention among their neighbors.

States forcefully promoted democracy in several South American countries, especially Brazil and Argentina, where unusually free and fair elections were held in 1945 and 1946. Even at that time, however, U.S. pressure did not always achieve its goals; for instance, it strengthened rather than weakened nationalist populist Juan Perón in Argentina, who soon established an authoritarian regime. Moreover, the United States switched its course in 1947–48; with the beginning of the Cold War, the concern for political stability and anticommunist solidarity came to override the preference for democracy and induced U.S. foreign policy-makers to accept and even support authoritarian rulers in the region (Bethell and Roxborough 1992; Rock 1994).

After Vietnam and Watergate had prompted a serious questioning of the legitimacy of U.S. foreign policy, President Carter took up initiatives originating in Congress and turned the promotion of human rights into a principal banner of his presidency (Smith 1994: ch. 9; Sikkink 2004: ch. 3, 6). Using U.S. leverage, the new chief executive pressed Latin American dictators to stop torturing political prisoners and sought to ensure free, clean, and fair elections. These demands, advanced quite openly and baldly, as their Latin American targets stressed (Pinochet 1998: 20–24, 175–79, 234–35; Arancibia and de la Maza 2003: 389–92; interview with Cáceres 2007; Hugo Medina in Boeker 1990: 83), prompted a nationalist backlash from a number of military regimes. Even weak countries such as Guatemala simply canceled cooperation agreements that the U.S. sought to use to exert pressure (for Guatemala, see Smith 1994: 245; for Brazil, D'Araujo and Castro 1997: 349–53; for Chile, Sigmund 1993: 110). In fact, civilians, even some oppositionists, were moved or felt compelled to reject U.S. imposition and defend national sovereignty (Skidmore 1988: 196–97; Sigmund 1993: 113; Novaro and Palermo 2003: 184–85, n. 9). As a result, except for small changes such as the dissolution of Chile's main intelligence agency followed by its immediate recreation under a new name, President Carter's pro-democracy efforts had limited effects in the short run. Above all, they did not manage to alter the regime trajectories of South America's full-scale dictatorships in any direct way. During his term in office, Carter's efforts made little visible difference in most of South America.

The U.S. president did have some success, however, in reinforcing an ongoing transition in Peru (Abugattas 1987: 132). General Francisco Morales-Bermúdez had already announced his willingness to hand over power to civilians,[34] but U.S. encouragement strengthened his determination to proceed toward a political opening and to stipulate a clear timetable (Manrique 1977, 1978; Prieto Celi 1996: 176–79). Since the Peruvian military regime had never been very repressive and since it had already initiated redemocratization, the audience costs of complying with U.S. exhortations were low. Moreover, Peru was in unusually dire economic straits, as vividly described by its former economy

---

[34] Morales-Bermúdez claimed (interview 2009) that he made the decision for a regime change in May 1976, that is, before Jimmy Carter appeared on the international political scene.

minister (Silva Ruete 1982). The ambitious development policies pursued from 1968 to 1975 had caused an early debt crisis that made the country dependent on aid from the International Monetary Fund. Since the United States held veto power in the IMF, it had much greater leverage over Peru than it did over other South American countries.[35]

While only rarely effective in the short run, Carter's democracy promotion had significant medium-term effects, however, which slowly but surely helped to propel the third wave of democratization in South America and to make it more successful than the waves of 1848 and even 1917–19 had been. The high-profile advocacy of the U.S. president encouraged opposition forces in many countries and gave their difficult efforts a morale boost. Organized in fairly broad-based parties that operated openly or clandestinely, these challengers did not immediately embark on bottom-up mass contention, but waited for good opportunities to push for redemocratization, which often arose from internal tensions and conflicts inside the authoritarian regimes (seminal O'Donnell and Schmitter 1986: 15–21). President Carter also helped to prepare such top-down openings by putting human rights ahead of anticommunism, which many military regimes had invoked to justify their rule. The clear shift in the hegemon's posture sapped dictators' legitimacy and reinforced the desire of soft-liners to withdraw from politics,[36] especially where left-wing radicals and guerrilla forces had been defeated (or had not yet burst onto the scene, as in Peru).[37] Thus, U.S. exhortations propelled and reinforced governmental liberalization measures that increased political space for opposition efforts and moved South American countries, however slowly, toward democracy.[38] Last but not least, Carter's pressures laid the seed for later transitions by inducing dictatorships to respond with institutionalization efforts that exposed them to some form of electoral accountability. Accordingly, the military regimes in Uruguay and Chile designed constitutions that foresaw plebiscites – which allowed for opposition victories in Uruguay in 1980 and Chile in 1988.[39] As dictators' defeats

[35] According to Peru's economy minister of the time, the IMF softened its stance because the country was steadily moving toward democracy (interview with Silva Ruete 2009).

[36] The shift in the U.S. stance also had a "psychological impact" on the democratic opposition (interview with Alva Orlandini 2009), giving it encouragement.

[37] Peru's last military president, Francisco Morales-Bermúdez, told the author (interview 2009) that the one factor that would have prompted him to interrupt the transition process was if the terrorist threat from the Shining Path had appeared under his government. But the Shining Path undertook its first major attack only on the day of the transitional election in 1980 (see also Prieto Celi 1996: 255–57).

[38] In Bolivia, Carter's admonitions helped induce dictator Hugo Banzer to call presidential elections (*LAPR* 1977; Whitehead 1986: 57; Malloy and Gamarra 1988: 95–96), which set in motion a process that after several years of troubles and travails led to democracy.

[39] Arguably, Carter's pressures contributed to the institutionalization of the Chilean dictatorship via the constitution of 1980 (Sigmund 1993: 110; similarly for Uruguay, see Gillespie 1991: 68, 188), which foresaw a plebiscite on the continuation of President Pinochet's rule for the end of the decade. Because this plebiscite offered the institutional opening through which the

prepared the ground for redemocratization, U.S. influence had a delayed and indirect but important effect.

In most cases, however, U.S. pressures bore fruit only under Carter's successor Ronald Reagan, who, ironically, pulled back from determined democracy promotion immediately after taking office and instead embraced military regimes during his first term (for Argentina, see Quiroga 2004: 255, 276; for Chile, Sigmund 1993: 132–39). Because some of these authoritarian rulers, such as Argentina's and Uruguay's dictators, were tottering already and because other transition processes were well-advanced, as in Brazil, Reagan's temporary reversal did not halt the unfolding of the third wave, but merely delayed it in some instances. In fact, the Republican president himself felt compelled gradually to resume Carter's efforts to push for democracy and pursue this goal fairly consistently during his second term (Carothers 2001). Reagan's anticommunist policy in Central America over time boxed him into this corner. After all, how could he criticize left-wing Nicaraguan Sandinistas as undemocratic while he cooperated with right-wing nondemocrats in South America (Muñoz and Portales 1991: 71, 83, 94; Peceny 1999: 146; Kornbluh 2003: 418, 420)?

To defang this criticism, the Reagan administration started in 1985 to exert consistent pressure on the rightist Pinochet regime in Chile, the main surviving dictatorship in South America. New ambassador Harry Barnes ostentatiously demonstrated his support for the opposition, and various U.S. emissaries urged the dictator's military and civilian supporters to restore democracy (Boye 1985; Sigmund 1993: ch. 7). Governmental and nongovernmental actors from the United States as well as from several European countries then gave Chile's center-left opposition coalition a great deal of logistical, financial, and political backing, which was critical to defeating General Pinochet in the 1988 plebiscite on his continuation in power (as Chapter 7 discusses in depth). Thus, powerful developed countries assisted Chile in advancing on its long and winding road back to democracy.

In sum, vertical pressures on authoritarian regimes and support for opposition forces helped to propel regime contention in South America and contributed to the high rate of democratic transitions. U.S. influence proved important in Peru in the late 1970s and in Chile in the second half of the 1980s. It also had slower and less visible effects in other transitions by bolstering democratic groupings and by weakening the determination of authoritarian forces to cling to power. While the United States brought the greatest clout to bear, European countries were more consistent in their efforts during the 1980s

democratic opposition finally, after many failed efforts, managed to dislodge the dictatorship, democracy promotion by the U.S. president, which brought little success during his term, contributed indirectly to the Chilean transition – many years later. This argument has been advanced by leaders of the Chilean opposition (e.g., Lagos 1995: 45–46) and by scholars (Hawkins 2002: 3, 106–39).

and used some particularly effective instruments for democracy promotion. The German party foundations, for instance, had a broad network of contacts in South America, through which they avidly channeled resources and advice to oppositionists (Grabendorff 2001: 217–18). In this vein, the social democratic Friedrich Ebert Foundation provided crucial sustenance to moderate socialists in Chile (Friedrich Ebert Stiftung 2007) and reinforced their deradicalization, encouraging them to move away from street protests and combat the dictatorship through its own institutions; this externally supported strategy shift produced the eventual victory in the plebiscite of 1988.

In these ways, vertical influences contributed to the success of democratic contention during the third wave in South America. By supporting oppositionists and advising them on how best to challenge military rulers, governmental officials and nongovernmental organizations from the First World assisted these groupings in achieving their principal goal. Moreover, by persuading regime soft-liners to relinquish power and by constraining hardliners from sabotaging or reversing transition processes, they helped to tip the balance in favor of redemocratization.

Overall, however, considering the tremendous clout of the Northern giant, these efforts had surprisingly limited effects in South America (Carothers 2001: 142; Mainwaring and Pérez-Liñán, forthcoming: ch. 4, 7),[40] as the disjuncture in the timing of U.S. initiatives versus actual regime transitions shows. President Carter's strong push for human rights and democracy achieved little direct, visible impact during his term in office, while President Reagan's reversal, fortunately, did not do much damage. Despite its enormous economic and political influence, the "hegemonic" United States could not impose its regime preferences on "peripheral" South America; this comparatively weak region did not cede easily or quickly to U.S. demands. Only in its immediate "back yard" in the circum-Caribbean did the United States achieve great impact, as its important contributions to the transitions in the Dominican Republic (Wiarda 1989: 437, 449) and the Central American countries show (Peceny 1999: 184; Mainwaring and Pérez-Liñán, forthcoming: ch. 4, 7). But even there, its coercive capacity was limited and not very effective, as evident in the long years of intense but contained hostility toward the socialist regimes of Nicaragua and, of course, Cuba. The regional hegemon could remove autocratic rulers and enforce democratization only when it was prepared to use overwhelming military force, as in the invasions of Grenada (1983) and Panama (1989); yet it was rarely prepared to go that far.

In conclusion, U.S. power did not drive the third wave in Latin America, especially in the southern subcontinent; above all, it did not overwhelm or

---

[40] For Chile, this point is highlighted by Sigmund (1993: 145, 148, 160, 205–6) and Purcell (1987). Even Smith, who stresses the U.S. promotion of democracy, writes: "As with many other cases, Washington's influence on Chile's transition to democracy was no more than marginal" (Smith 1994: 294).

override the diffusion processes examined above.[41] While vertical influence played a role, a great deal of room was left for horizontal stimuli, especially in South America.

In fact, there seem to be interesting interaction effects: External pressures often need internal preconditions to be effective. Above all, domestic tensions and divisions provide crucial opportunities for foreign influence to make a difference. When a military regime commands strong support because it combats radical violence and "chaos," as in Argentina right after the coup of 1976 (Novaro and Palermo 2003: ch. III 1–2), it is impervious to foreign exhortations, even demands to respect the most fundamental human rights. But when significant domestic opposition has formed and taken the initiative to challenge authoritarian rulers, foreign countries can effectively support these contentious efforts and raise the cost of repression by incumbents. In these ways, external democracy promotion assists broader segments of the citizenry and their organizational leaders against oppressive governments, joining an ongoing battle over liberty, participation, and representation, rather than stirring up nationalist sensitivities by appearing to hinder a government in its fight against the "enemies of the people." As President Carter's success in supporting an incipient transition in Peru and the Reagan administration's contribution to the plebiscite victory of the Chilean opposition suggest, vertical influence is most efficacious in helping to bring internal efforts to a successful conclusion (similar Patricio Aylwin in Boeker 1990: 51). In regard to the features of diffusion processes examined in this book, pressures by powerful countries enhance the eventual success of emulative regime contention, but do not greatly affect its speed.

THE PROCESSING OF DIVERSE IMPULSES BY REPRESENTATIVE LEADERS

In line with my overarching theoretical argument, the preceding sections have examined the input side of diffusion and shown that the third wave in South America emanated from various external impulses. Most important were the precedent of Spain's pacted transition, contentious experiences inside the region, especially the Argentine protests, and pressures from influential Western countries, particularly the United States. This diversity of foreign stimuli offered democratic opposition forces a broader menu of options than were available to challengers in 1848 and 1917–19, when violent revolution constituted the outstanding, overwhelming trigger for diffusion processes. This variety meant that oppositionists had some choices; which strategy they embraced would, in turn, affect the eventual outcome and shape the success of democratic contention. This chapter started by analyzing the stimulus side of diffusion; it now needs to

---

[41] The same conclusion applies to the "color revolutions" that occurred in the post–communist world in the early 2000s (Bunce and Wolchik 2011: 234–40, 291–94, 306, 318–19), examined in Chapter 8.

discuss the reception side, which played a crucial role in the 1970s and 1980s as well.

Chapter 3 attributed the rise of the pacted transition model to further steps in organizational development, whose earlier stages had, from the late nineteenth century onward, first reshaped the reception of external stimuli (as Chapter 5 demonstrated). In the twentieth century, as broad-based organization spread across the ideological spectrum, regime change via negotiation and compromise became feasible, and political forces of various stripes came to converge on this strategy of political transformation because it carried lower risks than bottom-up crowd challenges.

After Europe had taken the lead, Latin America also experienced a good deal of organizational development, stimulated in part by European models and by emigrating activists. As oligarchical rule gave way to mass politics, fairly broad-based organizations, especially political parties, emerged in more and more countries, especially in South America. While they rarely built the comprehensive organizational networks or achieved the firm discipline that European Social Democracy boasted, parties and interest associations in many nations managed to encompass a significant part of the politically active population. Even populist vehicles founded by personalistic leaders could over time capture popular loyalties and acquire strong roots, as the Peronist Party did in Argentina and APRA in Peru. As a result, South American nations, especially the major countries, achieved a reasonable degree of organizational density (Kaufman 1977: 115–19, 130–35; Lavareda 1991: ch. 6; Dix 1992; Roberts forthcoming). Rather than acting spontaneously as parts of amorphous crowds, ordinary people and their informal networks tended to look to representative leaders for cues and guidance on how to participate in politics, especially when it came to risky contentious initiatives.

Bureaucratic authoritarianism sought to suppress or destroy these mass organizations, most brutally in Argentina and Chile, or artificially recreate and control them, as in Brazil. While the core structures and leadership cadres of these parties and unions survived in clandestinity or exile, their linkages to and hold over their popular constituencies weakened. By destructuring civil societies and atomizing individuals, dictatorial repression recreated some potential for spontaneous crowd action to erupt if the regime ran into trouble. These antiorganizational efforts of military rulers were more intense in countries where preexisting party systems had been stronger, as in Chile, Uruguay, and Argentina[42]; they tended to be less thoroughgoing and fierce in nations where party systems had been weaker or more fragmented, as in Bolivia, Brazil, Ecuador, and Peru. The differential force of authoritarian

---

[42] The military regimes of those three nations also imposed determined neoliberal reforms. By causing unemployment and boosting the informal sector, these measures helped to weaken broad-based parties and especially trade unions.

coercion thus had a leveling effect on organizational density across South America, compressing earlier frontrunners to the middling rungs of other nations.

Given the intermediate level of organization prevailing during the 1970s and early 1980s and the diversity of political parties along the ideological spectrum, the variety of precedents that characterized the third wave prompted a great deal of debate, disagreement, and even conflict among opposition forces. These discussions centered on whether a bargaining strategy à la Spain or crowd contention à la Argentina were more promising. Prudent calculations suggested a preference for negotiation and compromise, premised on the belief that the institutionally solid dictatorships reigning over most of South America could not be brought down through direct confrontation and mass assault. But cognitive shortcuts drew attention to the kind of bottom-up mass challenges exemplified by the Argentine protests and instilled hope in forcing transitions through rupture. Even many representative leaders were tempted to embrace the protest strategy when their country's military regime faced particularly dire straits, as the Pinochet dictatorship did in 1983. Moreover, political-ideological competition among challengers, including the radical efforts of narrow ideological sects, could induce some leaders to advocate more forceful contention, such as mass demonstrations; after all, opposition groupings were not only trying to dislodge dictators, but were also rivaling with each other. These different political goals gave rise to complicated calculations that could induce organizational leaders to promote transgressive contention despite its risks.

These disagreements among politicians contributed to the slow speed with which the third wave advanced in South America. The variety of contentious options and diversity of opposition forces limited the support that any one of these strategies could initially command; consequently, challengers were reluctant to embark on regime contention or had difficulty getting it off the ground. Efforts to win concessions from regime soft-liners looked unpromising when street protests erupted and threatened escalation and confrontation, which could play into the hands of hard-liners. Representative leaders who wanted to follow the Spanish precedent therefore discouraged transgressive crowd action; they sought to domesticate contentious energies erupting from the bottom up and channel them into contained demonstrations that could serve as bargaining chips for their pact-making. Advocates of mass protests, by contrast, inveighed against consultations with government officials, which they feared would divide and weaken the democratic opposition. Thus, adherents of these divergent strategies of emulation worked at cross-purposes, which slowed down progress toward democracy.

These kinds of disagreements surfaced especially in the early 1980s, when the debt crisis shook South American autocracies to the core and when the Argentine protests helped to suggest that massive demonstrations and strikes could indeed bring down authoritarian rulers.[43] As mentioned in the section on secondary diffusion above, the Argentine example elicited interest in the Southern Cone and reinforced the belief of a number of oppositionists that mass mobilization constituted a promising alternative to the Spanish model. As a result, there were efforts in Brazil, Chile, and Uruguay to turn the spiraling protests into fundamental challenges to the incumbent regimes. But even politicians who spearheaded this contention did not advocate all-out confrontation, as in the insurgencies of 1848. They shied away from the incalculable risks inherent in such all-or-nothing efforts, which could easily backfire. And of course, the continuing advocates of Spanish-style negotiation urged caution as well.

For these reasons, representative leaders of various stripes deliberately contained contentious impulses and prevented them from turning into frontal attacks against the established regimes. Instead, they channeled the antiauthoritarian effervescence into nonviolent demonstrations of discontent, as in Chile and Uruguay, or directed them toward popular pressure on behalf of institutional reform, as in the campaign for direct presidential elections in Brazil. Thus, even opposition leaders who embraced the protest strategy softened its bite to lower the danger involved in directly defying repressive dictatorships.

This street contention drew a great deal of spontaneous support from broad sectors of the population, who were eager to emerge from the political suffocation enforced by authoritarian repression (seminal O'Donnell and Schmitter 1986: ch. 5). Many common citizens made fairly independent participation decisions because organizational linkages had temporarily weakened under the dictatorship. Consequently, convokers of these mass rallies were frequently surprised by the turnout; more people attended than politicians had ever expected. In Santiago in mid-1983, countless citizens banged pots and pans at the appointed time, even in the smart neighborhoods where President Pinochet used to enjoy strong support; and in Brazil in early 1984, the direct election campaign drew record crowds. The belief that military regimes were weak and could be forced to grant a political transformation prompted large-scale participation.

But as skeptics, especially partisans of negotiation and compromise, had predicted, crowd protests failed to force dictators' hands and thus did not achieve the specific goals that politicians had aimed for. As discussed in this chapter, authoritarian rulers proved more resilient than advocates of the protest strategy had surmised. Therefore, sooner (as in Brazil and Uruguay) or later (as in Chile) opposition forces returned to the negotiation strategy and tried to move

[43] In Brazil, for instance, discussions among opposition leaders continued throughout the many months of the *Diretas Já* campaign, as especially left-wing observers such as Rodrigues (2003) highlight. Even fiercer debates raged in Chile from 1984 to 1986 over the protest strategy, as Chapter 7 discusses.

authoritarian rulers toward democratization through mutual concessions and accommodation.

In sum, the temporary preference given to the protest strategy turned out to be a detour that arguably slowed down the advance toward democracy, especially in Chile (see Chapter 7). The diversity of external precedents helps explain why the third wave took considerable time to unfold in South America. The variety of options made it difficult for democratic challengers to settle on any one strategy. And the option that opposition forces, under the impression of the Argentine precedent, temporarily chose did not manage to accomplish its goals. Therefore, it was discarded as more and more democratic leaders switched (back) to Spanish-style negotiations, however begrudgingly.

Over the medium and long run, however, the experience of mass contention strengthened the hand of opposition leaders in dealing with military rulers and their civilian supporters; in this way, it contributed to the eventual success of negotiation efforts. The protests demonstrated how broad and intense discontent with authoritarian rule was. The generals noticed the depth of their isolation from society, which reinforced their willingness to relinquish government power so as to protect the military as an institution. Moreover, opportunistic elements among conservative politicians realized that it was high time to jump ship. In this vein, important sectors of Brazil's ARENA (Aliança Renovadora Nacional), the official party backing the dictatorship, split off in 1984 and formed a "Liberal Front" that allied with the moderate opposition and paved the way for a regime transition. Thus, while mass demonstrations could not force dictators from office, the incontrovertible information they provided about the distribution and intensity of political preferences (cf. Kuran 1995) induced important members of the authoritarian coalition to adjust their strategies and consent to a transition or facilitate it by switching sides. By confirming the strength of the opposition's demands and by softening up its adversaries, protests indirectly and eventually contributed to the success of the Spanish-inspired negotiation strategy.

In conclusion, the sequential emulation of different external precedents by opposition forces helps account for the particularly slow advance, yet high success rate of the third wave of democratization in South America. As challengers faced a menu of externally provided options, the way they processed them – that is, the reception side of diffusion – deeply shaped regime contention and its outcomes. Specifically, the eruption of the Argentine protests, whose appeal reflected the availability and representativeness heuristics, helped to draw opposition forces temporarily away from the strategy of negotiation and compromise à la Spain. While contentious street action did not achieve its goals, the demonstration of massive discontent ended up strengthening the opposition's hand when it returned to the bargaining table.

THE LIMITED IMPACT OF EXTERNAL STIMULI IN SOUTH AMERICA'S
THIRD WAVE

The preceding sections show how the variety of external precedents and
their complex domestic repercussions set the third wave apart from the other
two diffusion processes analyzed in this book; specific features of the input
side and the reception side help account for the particularly slow but successful advance of emulative regime contention in South America during the 1970s
and 1980s.

In addition, there was a fundamental change that contributed to diffusion's
low speed and high success – the opposite of what happened in 1848: External
impulses overall now had a surprisingly limited impact on domestic politics. As
foreign precedents did not exert great force, they did not propel quick emulation efforts, but left national politicians considerable latitude to act on external
lessons when they regarded the internal situation as propitious. The difference
to 1848, when the Paris events literally overwhelmed discontented citizens and
autocratic authorities in Central and Eastern Europe, is remarkable.

In 1848, political actors and observers of all stripes, ranging from students
and common citizens to aristocrats and kings, were eager, almost obsessed with
getting the latest scrap of news from France. In South America during the 1970s
and 1980s, by contrast, political leaders and mass publics paid much less attention to external precedents of all kinds. Politicians associated with the opposition as well as the outgoing regime commonly report in their memoirs and in
personal interviews that foreign stimuli did not strongly affect their thinking
and decision-making.[44] Their statements from the thick of regime contention,
such as speeches and contemporaneous interviews, confirm this surprising fact:
They referred infrequently to foreign experiences and invoked their lessons
even more rarely.[45]

The unexpectedly sparse interest in foreign events and their limited impact
on internal politics, which fly in the face of common images of globalization

[44] The evidence is so overwhelming that it is difficult to highlight any specific source, but easy
because virtually any source will serve. For instance, Leonelli and Oliveira's (2004) exhaustive, 639-page account of Brazil's *Diretas Já* campaign, which features an outstanding, thorough name index (pp. 619–39), mentions Raúl Alfonsín, whose stunning election victory in
Argentina fell in the time period covered, only twice. Similarly, Prieto Celi's (1996) book-length
interview with Peru's last military ruler, Francisco Morales-Bermúdez, rarely refers to external events, except foreign policy challenges. Moreover, Chile's political leaders interviewed in
Arancibia's (2006) massive volume of 696 pages mentions foreign precedents and models very
infrequently.

[45] This lack of references to external precedents was not due to a general reluctance of decision-
makers to admit foreign influences, driven by the desire to boost one's own importance and to
claim creativity. Instead, many experts who had prepared Chilean-style pension privatization
in Latin America during the 1990s openly stressed that they had taken "90 percent [of the new
system] directly from Chile" (Weyland 2007: 117) and justified this eager imitation by arguing
that there was no need to "reinvent the wheel."

as a process that threatens to overwhelm domestic factors, reflected the organizational macro-developments highlighted in this volume, namely the emergence and proliferation of broad-based parties and interest associations; accordingly, this trend was clear in 1917–19 already, when participants in regime contention made substantially fewer references to foreign developments than in 1848. The formation of collective actors with public programs and considerable track records turned internal politics more observable and predictable than in the era of low organizational density with its occasional, unforeseeable eruptions of fluid, amorphous crowd contention. As the visibility of politics increased and uncertainty diminished, political actors, especially representative leaders, came to base their contentious activities first and foremost on the internal opportunity structure. Foreign events merely provided an additional input; they were no longer the main push factor, as had been the case when domestic politics was inchoate and therefore inscrutable.

As mentioned, during the 1970s and 1980s, a wide range of collective actors populated the political scene in South America. Parties and interest associations announced their goals, and their past course of action offered further indications of their probable future behavior. The main participants in the political game were fairly visible, especially after authoritarian regimes took initial steps toward liberalization and political parties reappeared from clandestinity. Consequently, a good deal of information on the domestic distribution of political preferences and the constellation of power was available. While there still was considerable uncertainty on the specific moves that different actors would make, as the transitions literature stressed (especially O'Donnell and Schmitter 1986: 3–5), politics was much more predictable than at times of low organizational density, when collective action was fluid, fleeting, and episodic and when fundamental "confusion" (Kurzman 2004) therefore reigned.

As a result, political leaders and ordinary citizens had an incentive to focus primarily on internal developments. Because the domestic fog was much less dense than in 1848, external precedents held less importance. In the mid-nineteenth century, foreign events had constituted the only observable phenomena; therefore, they held substantial evidentiary value, compared to the undecipherable shadows that abruptly entered and faded from the domestic political scene. In South America during the late twentieth century, by contrast, important observable actors populated the stage, so it made most sense to concentrate on them directly. External events could still offer clues and therefore continued to elicit some interest, especially from representative leaders with their wider bounds of rationality. But foreign precedents now had a limited impact because politicians, both from the opposition and the authoritarian government, had good reason to focus mostly on domestic politics, especially the cooperative or conflicting interactions among the organizations that had emerged.

The consolidated identities and track records of internal collective actors also made the specificities and peculiarities of domestic politics more obvious and thus highlighted the corresponding differences from regional neighbors. For instance, the *Partido do Movimento Democrático Brasileiro*, the *Unión Cívica Radical* of Argentina, the Christian Democratic Party of Chile, and APRA and *Acción Popular* in Peru all were the main centrist or center-left challengers of military regimes – but how different they were! Whereas in the amorphous polities of 1848, scarce information and high uncertainty prompted an overestimation of similarity in line with the representativeness heuristic, political leaders and even common citizens in South America during the 1970s and 1980s were quite aware of the particular opportunities and challenges they faced. My interviewees frequently stressed the special characteristics of their own authoritarian regime and of the local opposition; when asked, they highlighted the unlikeness of neighboring experiences (e.g., interviews with Correa 2007, Martínez 2007, and Núñez 2007). In sum, as the night of political inchoateness had long passed and observable actors were occupying the political stage, oppositionists took only limited inspiration from shining foreign precedents, instead basing their decisions on whether and when to emulate an external model primarily on internal developments. Diffusion still mattered, but it was filtered much more thoroughly through the domestic opportunity structure.

Due to this fundamental inward shift of political attention, representative leaders responded to external stimuli for regime contention much less precipitously than the crowds of the nineteenth century. While they were inspired by successful challenges in other countries, they did not rush to emulate but worked hard to prepare a promising course of action. For instance, they tried to tame the spontaneous mass impulses strengthened by the Argentine protests, channeling them into peaceful demonstrations or institutional reform efforts. These prudent efforts to act on foreign lessons took advantage of the political openings allowed by dictators in withdrawal and adapted popular challenges accordingly. Where the established regime was strong but flexible, as in Ecuador, Brazil, and Uruguay, the principal opposition forces proceeded via negotiation and used mass demonstrations merely as bargaining chips; where a dictator was particularly obstinate, as in Chile, they sequentially tried out various strategies and finally settled on contesting the regime in the plebiscite that it had constitutionally scheduled. This country-specific approach, which diverged from the uniform street protests and subsequent barricade fights of 1848, helped guarantee a high rate of success.

CONCLUSION

This chapter explains why the third wave in South America constituted less of a clear-cut, well-behaved wave than the other two diffusion processes examined in this book, especially the tsunami of 1848: It did not emanate from a singular, powerful trigger, spread uniformly, and advance concentrically with tight temporal clustering. Instead, it arose from several intersecting currents and crosscurrents, flowed past eddies, sandbars, and even whirlpools, and slowly emptied through a delta of meandering sidearms into the sea. Thus, while eventually reaching its destination, this diffusion process was much more multifaceted and variegated, decentered and fragmented than the revolutionary waves of 1917–19 and especially of 1848.

The most distinctive reason was that the main impetus did not emerge from a dramatic revolution that grabbed everybody's attention, but from the Spanish experience of a negotiated transition, which was too gradual in process, nondecisive in outcome (with its pacts and compromises), and sober and unexciting in nature to elicit widespread enthusiasm via the heuristics of availability and representativeness. The Spanish model therefore did not trigger a rash of emulation efforts. Representative leaders realized its promise and sought to act on its lessons, but only when the specific circumstances inside their own country looked propitious. Because Spain did not captivate many people and monopolize their attention, there was room for other precedents to make an impression as well, both from outside and inside South America.

In regard to this secondary diffusion among emulating countries, the heuristics of availability and representativeness gave the striking mass mobilization in Argentina, widely seen as an important factor in the downfall of a brutal dictatorship, political appeal. At a time when authoritarian regimes were reeling from severe economic crises, the exciting Argentine precedent helped to inspire protests that temporarily put Spanish-style negotiations on the backburner. As more and more representative leaders argued, however, mass challenges to military rules did not achieve their goals. Therefore, opposition forces sooner or later returned to the bargaining table. While the irruption of the Argentine precedent helped to slow down transition efforts, it ended up strengthening the hand of opposition negotiators by demonstrating the extent and intensity of discontent with the dictatorship; in this way, it contributed to the success of the third wave.

Democracy promotion by developed countries, especially the powerful United States, further augmented the chances of success. These vertical pressures, which did not play a significant, systematic role in 1848 or 1917–19, reflected advances in modernization, which had moved the frontline of democratization downward in the global hierarchy. After the "core" of the world system had consolidated democracy, it used its influence to extend it to the periphery; from the mid-1970s onward, the "hegemonic" United States did so ever more consistently in its sphere of influence, including South America (and especially Central America). Interestingly, these efforts did not attain quick results, as the disappointing balance sheet of President Carter's term in office shows. But in the medium run, they did help persuade military rulers to relinquish power and encourage challengers to push for change, especially with moderate means. While contributing to the beneficial outcome of the third wave, the promotional activities of developed countries introduced additional complexity by intersecting with other sources of diffusion and by varying across country and over time (e.g., with President Reagan's twists and turns).

This variety of stimuli pushed toward the same end goal, namely democracy, but it often prompted disagreements and even conflicts in the short run. Many representative leaders regarded negotiation and compromise as most promising from a realistic perspective, whereas mass actors were more attracted to the sporadic precedents of crowd protests. Sooner or later, the former position prevailed, leading to transition efforts that were by nature adjusted to the power constellation and political conjuncture of each country. Thus, even pacted transitions came in different variants – hence the delta metaphor used in this chapter. In fact, the fundamental shift of attention toward domestic developments, which reflected the rise of broad-based organization, reinforced the tendency of challengers to adapt emulative regime contention to the specific situation of their country. They took external experiences and lessons into account, but were not swept off their feet, as the revolutionaries of 1848 had been. Foreign precedents mattered, but they were far from overwhelming, despite the advance of globalization.

For all of these reasons, the third wave represents a diffusion process that was – rather diffuse.

7

Crosscurrents of the Third Wave: Interorganizational Competition and Negotiation in Chile

Chapter 6 demonstrated the noteworthy complexity of the third wave in Latin America, especially by focusing on the input side of diffusion and highlighting the confluence of diverse external stimuli. This variety of options in turn intersected with the ideological differentiation of political organizations, which shaped the reception side of diffusion. As various political groupings gravitated toward different external precedents and models, disagreements and conflicts arose over the best strategy to follow. The resulting discussions hindered opposition unity and slowed down the advance of emulative regime contention. But the availability of various strategies also allowed for learning from political experiences and thus enhanced the chances that democratization efforts would eventually come to fruition. As unpromising options sooner or later lost support, large sectors of the opposition came to embrace an approach that managed to dislodge the dictatorship. External backers of democratization helped to create this opposition unity, a crucial precondition for effective pressure on authoritarian rulers. In sum, the broader offerings at the input side of diffusion, the debates over their domestic processing, and the gradual convergence among opposition forces help explain the particularly slow speed but also the high success of the third wave in South America.

The case that most clearly exemplifies the special features of this diffusion process, especially on the reception side, is Chile. That country had long had a well-structured, programmatically oriented multiparty system that covered the whole ideological spectrum, from the hard-core right to the radical left. Accordingly, different political forces found different external models appealing; in fact, what some politicians admired as a model, others abhorred as a deterrent. Chile's transition thus reveals with particular clarity the discussions and conflicts at the reception side of diffusion, which Chapter 6 mentioned only in brief overview. For the present effort in theory-building, the Chilean case is especially instructive because it sheds bright light on the interorganizational dynamics discussed at the end of Chapter 2; the causal mechanisms at work and their complex interweaving appear with particular clarity in this case. The following analysis of Chile's tortuous transition constitutes a plausibility probe for that part of my complex argument.

At the same time, there was a range of foreign precedents and models that Chilean oppositionists could draw from. The country's transition efforts started late, in 1983. By that time, several democratization processes in Southern Europe and Latin America had already unfolded and could serve as sources of inspiration (Garretón 1991: 219). In fact, Chile's democratic forces faced a particularly obstinate adversary, General Augusto Pinochet, who sought to refound the polity and gained solid sustenance for this long-term project from the institutional strength and hierarchical structure of the armed forces. Chile's transition therefore took many years, exposing the country to various external stimuli, including new precedents such as the Philippine transition of 1986. Thus, there was ample grist for the mill of interorganizational discussions and negotiations.

The Chilean transition also offers a particularly fruitful comparison with the revolutions of 1848 and 1917–19 because both the ideological left and right associated democratization with profound socioeconomic transformations. Conservatives and reactionaries feared, and socialists and communists hoped, that democratization would end Chile's neoliberal experiment and bring back economic nationalism, state interventionism, and social redistribution. For both sides, the Chilean transition seemed to involve not only political regime change, but also controversial socioeconomic issues. Therefore, an in-depth analysis of the Chilean case may help to allay the conceptual concerns over the relationship between democratization and (attempted) revolution discussed in the introductory chapter.

Last but not least, there is an important pragmatic reason for focusing on Chile, namely a wealth of information. The comparatively recent unfolding of the Chilean transition and the remarkable longevity of the country's political elite allowed me to interview numerous top leaders from both sides of the regime divide; several were already in their eighties when I spoke to them in 2007, such as Patricio Aylwin and Sergio Onofre Jarpa, and some have since died, namely Edgardo Boeninger and Enrique Silva Cimma. Furthermore, Chile's Universidad Finis Terrae has carried out a comprehensive oral history project on the military regime, the complicated transition, and the new democracy. This monumental effort has yielded several books of interviews with political leaders of various stripes (Arancibia et al. 2002; Arancibia and de la Maza 2003; Arancibia 2006; Fernández Abata et al. 2013). I also gained access to dozens of transcribed interview tapes from the university's Centro de Investigación y Documentación en Historia de Chile Contemporáneo.[1] Because many of

---

[1] I greatly appreciate the generous cooperation of CIDOC's head Francisco Bulnes, who gave me access to these transcripts. Due to the terms set by CIDOC's interviewees, I do not cite or quote from these unedited and often very frank documents.

Chile's political leaders have also published their own reflections on the transition or their political memoirs (e.g., Lagos 1985, 2012; Allamand 1993, 1999; Fernández 1994; Boeninger 1997; Arriagada 1998; Aylwin 1998; Pinochet 1998; Silva Cimma 2000; Muñoz 2008; Valdés 2009; Tironi 2013), the documentary base for analyzing this regime change is exceptionally rich.

THE ORGANIZATIONAL BASIS OF DIVERSE EMULATION EFFORTS IN CHILE

The complex processing of various external stimuli during Chile's lengthy process of regime contention rested on the spread of broad-based organizations across the ideological spectrum that had occurred in the course of the twentieth century – first in Europe, and then in South America as well, especially in Chile. As mentioned in Chapters 2 and 3, firm, disciplined mass organizations had initially formed on the left, with the foundation and growth of the social democratic labor movement, which exerted powerful, sustained pressure for democratization starting in the late nineteenth century. Due to its ideological roots in Marxism, Social Democracy was also most affected by the Russian Revolutions of 1917, which provided the main, singular stimulus for emulation efforts and preemptive reforms at that time.

In subsequent decades, the center and right of the political spectrum created stronger mass organizations as well. Even in many South American countries, a more ideologically balanced set of broad-based parties and national-level interest associations arose with the arrival of mass politics, sooner or later. While not as programmatically oriented as European Social Democracy, a wide variety of political organizations publicly signaled their ideological postures, and a growing number established international linkages with like-minded parties, in Latin America and beyond; even populist parties such as Peru's APRA had connections across borders. This crystallization of political positions and corresponding insertion in transnational party networks, such as the Socialist International, induced these diverse political groupings to gravitate toward different foreign experiences. Whereas in 1848 and even in 1917–19, relevant actors had uniformly been impressed by a single precedent – whether they embraced or abhorred it – during the third wave, parties and associations of different ideological orientation took inspiration from different external sources.

In Chile, which has long boasted Latin America's most wide-ranging and ideologically defined party system, this differentiation of diffusion processes was particularly clear and visible. Many of the country's Christian Democrats were attracted to Spain's pacted, gradual transition; moderate socialists and other center-leftists temporarily drew some inspiration from Argentina's transition through rupture for their efforts to force a regime change through bottom-up mobilization; and radicalized Communists tried to prepare or instigate a popular insurgency à la Nicaragua to drive the dictatorship from power.

At the same time, the hard-core civilian right (which soon formed its own party, *Unión Demócrata Independiente* – UDI) rejected negotiations à la Spain precisely because they had brought democratization; and the military feared an Argentine-style transition by rupture because it had paved the way for prosecuting human rights violators in uniform.

With this ideological differentiation, the diffusion of political regime contention became multifaceted and complex. Therefore, as Chapter 6 explained in general and the present chapter investigates in depth for the Chilean case, different foreign impulses got in each other's way and temporarily hindered the advance of regime contention. Only when political learning, mobilization, and power clearly established one strategy as most promising and marginalized the others, did large parts of the opposition finally unify. Only then did the push for a democratic transition gather sufficient strength to make headway. And as competing options were sorted out through debates and conflicts among opposition forces, a majority of challengers settled upon a particularly promising strategy that eventually achieved success.

The lengthy process of regime contention and transition in Chile is especially instructive because opposition groupings tried out a diversity of strategies and tactics and engaged in rich, fascinating debates over their advantages and disadvantages, benefits and risks. Ample democratic sectors tried during the severe socioeconomic crisis of 1983–84 to bring down General Pinochet through mass protests inspired to some extent by neighboring Argentina. But the dictatorship survived this bottom-up challenge, partly because radical leftists incited violence and thus provided a pretext for continued repression. After years of frustration saw a broad "national agreement," renewed protests, terrorist attacks from the far left,[2] and a futile campaign for free elections, the opposition begrudgingly decided to play by Pinochet's rules. Reassured by a striking new experience, namely the unseating of Philippine dictator Ferdinand Marcos through an electoral challenge in 1986, they entered a constitutionally scheduled plebiscite in 1988 and finally won. Whereas various forms of transgressive contention modeled on different external precedents had failed, opposition leaders managed to defeat the authoritarian ruler by moving to contained contention and marshaling their organized followers for an institutional contest.

A point made toward the end of Chapter 6 bears reiteration, however: None of the external precedents that helped stimulate and shape democratic contention in Chile had a decisive impact on the process and outcome of this halting transition; in particular, none of them altered the direction of the country's path back toward democracy in a major way. These foreign sources of inspiration clearly mattered for the process of regime change, reinforcing some contentious efforts while directing attention away from others, at least temporarily. But these stimuli from the outside did not make a great difference.

---

[2] I use "terrorism" not pejoratively, but as a scholarly concept, like, for instance, Sánchez-Cuenca and Aguilar 2009.

At each twist and turn in this lengthy process, internal factors were more important and determined the fundamental contours for opposition strategies and their results. External influences were of secondary importance – just as the "classical" transitions literature has claimed (O'Donnell and Schmitter 1986: 18–19).

THE BEGINNING OF CHILE'S TRANSITION AND THE EXAMPLE OF MASS MOBILIZATION IN ARGENTINA

Chile's democratic opposition was under siege during the first ten years of the Pinochet regime. The brutal coup of September 1973 ushered in a period of intense repression that drove centrist and especially leftist political parties underground. Trying hard to protect some nuclei of leaders and maintain at least a skeleton of organizational structures, these groupings were unable to challenge the authoritarian regime in any direct way. Pushed to the wall, they could not run an effective campaign for the plebiscite on Pinochet's tailor-made constitution of 1980 and therefore did not manage to prevent the institutionalization of the dictatorship. Moreover, during the late 1970s and the beginning of the 1980s, the government enjoyed a good deal of domestic support because it had stabilized the runaway inflation unleashed by the Allende administration and had, after a severe adjustment crisis, engineered a temporary economic boom.

That boom came to a crushing end in 1982, however, when Chile's GDP dropped by a catastrophic 14 percent and unemployment skyrocketed to around 24 percent of the workforce. Exacerbated by the Latin American debt crisis, this collapse destroyed the regime's performance legitimacy and boosted socioeconomic and political discontent. The economic meltdown gave the democratic opposition the opportunity to resurface. During the difficult first decade of the dictatorship, political leaders from these groupings had taken a number of initiatives to overcome the profound polarization and fierce conflict of the late 1960s and early 1970s. Through meetings and cooperative ventures inside Chile and abroad, Christian Democrats, moderate sectors of the Radical Party, and "renovating" factions of Socialists[3] had begun to establish connections and lay the ground for joint activities directed against the Pinochet regime (Arrate and Rojas 2003: 232–33; interviews with Boeninger 2007 and Correa 2007; Serrano 2009: 75). At the same time, the radical wing of the Socialist Party was forming a coalition of its own with small ultra-left sects and the Communists, who were advocating "all forms of struggle," including political violence (Álvarez 2008).

---

[3] This renovation of Chilean socialism, which brought a move away from the political radicalism of the 1960s and 1970s and an abandonment of Marxism-Leninism, is amply documented in Núñez (1991b) and analyzed in Walker (1990), Roberts (1998), and Arrate and Rojas (2003: ch. 7–8).

Thus, new lines of division emerged among Chile's fractious set of challengers, whose divergent ideological commitments to comprehensive projects of socio-political change led to incessant debates and hindered broad cooperation throughout the transition – a crucial obstacle to successfully challenging the dictatorship and, for years, a serious hindrance to stronger U.S. pressure on the dictatorship. Above all, many Christian Democrats vetoed collaboration with the Communists, partly in order not to discredit the opposition in the eyes of centrists and moderate supporters of authoritarian rule, whom they sought to win over. The renovating Socialists, by contrast, faced competition from more left-leaning factions of their own party and from the Communists; therefore, they were more willing to include the far left in the opposition coalition. In the early 1980s, the Socialist Party was divided into up to eight [!] currents, and thus debates and conflicts among the diversity of opposition forces multiplied (as covered thoroughly in Arrate and Rojas 2003: ch. 7–8).

It was in this domestic conjuncture – a severe socioeconomic crisis under-mining support for the dictatorship – that various nascent opposition group-ings initiated regime contention in May 1983 by calling for monthly protests, which drew enormous participation from a cross section of the population; in fact, turnout was much more massive than the organizers had dreamed. This bottom-up challenge, which seriously shook the Pinochet government (author interview with a former regime insider, Santiago, July 2007), had mostly domestic roots, namely economic deprivation, unemployment, and poverty. External demonstration and contagion effects also played some role, however. By early 1983, it was clear – and Chilean news media amply reported – that a wave of democratic transitions was advancing in South America. Andean neighbors Ecuador, Peru, and Bolivia had already shaken off military rule in preceding years; Brazil had held free legislative and gubernatorial elections in late 1982, a crucial step in its gradual regime opening (*abertura*); and the Uruguayan dictatorship, which had suffered an amazing defeat in a constitu-tional plebiscite in 1980, was stumbling (Maira 1984: 296–303; interviews with Arrate 2007, Garretón 2007, and Molina 2007). Thus, a regional wave of democratization efforts was under way, turning Chile, which had always been a political leader and innovator in South America, into a laggard; the opposition was painfully aware of this historical anomaly, called attention to it, and sought to rectify it (e.g., speeches reproduced in Ortega and Moreno 2002: 49, 76).

The most direct external stimulus emanated from right across the mountains: In 1982–83, Argentines were protesting massively against their military regime, which felt compelled to relinquish control and restore democracy without man-aging to extract reliable guarantees from the incoming civilian forces. Given the atrocious human rights violations committed under the autocracy, which made military personnel especially fearful of retribution after redemocratization, this failure was striking; it signaled the tremendous weakness of the outgoing dicta-torship. But although this debility arose from the disastrous performance and severe divisions inside the armed forces, cognitive shortcuts directed attention to the large-scale crowd protests, which were more visible. Presidential contender Raúl Alfonsín, who visited Chile in April 1983 and met with a wide range of opposition politicians, also attributed his country's march toward democracy more to multiparty efforts and public demonstrations than to the Falklands War, the direct trigger of the Argentine regime's demise (Blanco 1983a: 58; on this meeting, see also Silva Cimma 2000: 398–99, and interview with Silva Cimma 2007). For these reasons, Argentina's transition through rupture attracted interest and, in line with the representativeness heuristic, provided an additional impetus for oppositional mass mobilization in Chile.

Contagion from Argentina was intensified by the transition elections of late 1983, which the most democratic candidate, Raúl Alfonsín, won decisively, in an amazing victory over the long-dominant, but not very democratic Peronists (Bitar 1983b; *Cauce* 1983; Geis 1983a, 1983d; *Mensaje* 1983; Rossi 1983; Santibañez 1983a, 1983b). The "success" of the Argentine protests in bringing these elections, Alfonsín's stunning triumph, and his high-profile inauguration as president, which again drew hundreds of thousands of enthusiastic citizens into the streets of Buenos Aires, provided further inspiration for the Chilean opposition (Almeyda 1984: 7–8; Maira 1984: 297–99; Lagos 1985: 179; interview with Silva Cimma 2007; Lagos 2012: 59). For instance, exiled Socialist leader Sergio Bitar (1983b: 36; similar Bitar 1983a) ended his analysis of the Argentine elections with the following reflections: "For the Chileans this experience is of prime importance.... Argentina also demonstrates that the move to democracy can be rapid and orderly.... The conditions are hope-inspiring (*esperanzadoras*). This is a boost for democracy in Chile and a strong stimulus for us [exiled politicians]."

Occurring across the border, the Argentine mass mobilization, democratization through rupture, and preparation of elections were cognitively available to Chileans, as numerous media reports suggest (Cavallo 1982, 1983; Cárdenas 1983; Frank 1983; Pinochet de la Barra 1983; Yopo 1983).[4] While Chile has remained fairly isolated from the rest of Latin America, the long-standing love-hate relationship with its neighbor helped to draw attention to the dramatic Argentine events.[5] This apparent case of success reinforced the impression that bottom-up challenges during the severe socioeconomic crisis were promising. Chileans therefore became even more confident in their belief that protests could force out Pinochet as well; even moderate, center-left Christian

---

[4] Interestingly, the socialist-leaning magazine *Análisis* ran more reports about the Argentine protests than *Hoy*, which was close to Christian Democracy; *Hoy* focused more on the election of Argentina's first democratic president, Raúl Alfonsín. This observation confirms my argument that different political groupings gravitate toward different (aspects of) foreign precedents and models.

[5] In a long analysis of Argentine history and politics, the leader of the more radical wing of the Socialist Party, Clodomiro Almeyda (1984: 3), emphasizes how exile experiences have brought Argentines, Chileans, and Uruguayans much closer together.

Democrats therefore demanded Pinochet's immediate ouster as the first step toward a democratic transition (Ortega and Moreno 2002: 41, 67, 81; Cavallo et al. 2008: 463–73). In sum, the availability and representativeness heuristics helped to turn the Argentine precedent into an additional stimulus for Chilean protesters, further strengthening the domestically rooted impulses for regime contention. Oppositionists were eager to act on their socioeconomic and political grievances and frontally defy the brutal dictatorship, hoping to replicate Argentina's success.

There was room for mass mobilization and spontaneous citizen participation in Chile because authoritarian repression had weakened organizational leaders' control over their constituents. Historically, party leaders had enjoyed firm command over members and affiliated associations such as trade unions. But under the dictatorship, these cadres lost touch with many members, who therefore had to decide on their own whether to join protests or not. At the very inception of regime contention in Chile, cognitive heuristics therefore held disproportionate sway and contributed to the relatively quick eruption of protests inspired to some extent by the Argentine demonstrations.

Driven by domestic causes and reinforced by the external stimulus, the upsurge of disaffection in Chile prompted several contentious initiatives in 1982–83. A wide-ranging, heterogeneous group of mid-level politicians and associational leaders formed a new movement (Proyecto de Desarrollo Nacional – PRODEN) that sought to spearhead opposition (Carvallo 1982; Geis 1983c; Acevedo 1983); copper workers led by a young, inexperienced upstart wanted to call a general strike to challenge the Pinochet regime head-on; and radical-left groupings were itching to engage in violence, hoping to spur a popular insurrection. The impetus for these challenges arose mainly from the bottom up (Puryear 1994: 76–79; Schneider 1995: 159). Broadly similar to the strike waves of 1917–18, mass actors – temporarily released from representative leaders' control due to the suppression of parties – were eager to act on their socioeconomic and political grievances and, inspired in part by a neighboring precedent, sought to bring down the authoritarian regime.

Many leaders of Chile's centrist, center-left, and renovated Socialist parties, however, who were forming an alliance similar to Argentina's *Multipartidaria*,[6] advocated greater caution (Aylwin 1998: 228; Arrate and Rojas 2003: 335; Serrano and Cavallo 2006: 190; see also comments by union leader Arturo Martínez in Ortega and Moreno 2002: 136). These politicians had access to better information, a broader perspective, and long-standing experience and were therefore less affected by cognitive shortcuts. As a result, they saw the risks

---

[6] Geis (1983b: 6). Socialist leader Sergio Bitar (1983a) referred to the "Multipartidaria argentina" as an "experience valid for Chile," urging Chile's opposition parties to "advance much more in a constructive dialog, with the creation of options and concrete measures for accelerating the return of democracy." During the first half of 1983, news reports commonly used the name coined in Argentina to refer to this nascent *Alianza Democrática* (e.g. Blanco 1983a: 57).

of uncontrolled protests and general strikes,[7] which were difficult to sustain at a time of sky-high unemployment. Moreover, transgressive contention could play into the hands of extremists on both sides of the ideological spectrum and thus hinder rather than further a democratic transition (Ruiz-Tagle 1983: 314).[8] The Chilean dictatorship rested on a powerful, institutionalized military and could not be brought down through a direct, massive confrontation. The only chance was to provoke divisions inside the regime that would lead less hardline generals and moderate civilian rightists to withdraw their support from President Pinochet and back a return to civilian rule.

To open up such a gulf inside the authoritarian coalition,[9] the opposition hailing from the center to the renovated left, which created the Democratic Alliance in mid-1983, had to calibrate protests carefully: Street demonstrations needed to show how widespread and intense citizens' discontent with the authoritarian regime and their longing for democracy were, but they needed to avoid the specter of polarization, confrontation, and chaos that had triggered the 1973 coup. It was crucial to get large numbers of Chileans to reveal their clear preference for regime change and exert strong symbolic pressure, but to refrain from any effort to force the government out directly, especially through violent attacks.[10] For these reasons, mass contention had to be channeled into orderly forms that documented its force but kept it within limits.[11]

Therefore, party leaders, who sought to regain their hold over the mass membership, gradually took control of the protest movement and marginalized more spontaneous groupings such as PRODEN (Ortega Frei 1992: 211–19, 242; Garcés and de la Maza 1984: 30–35; Arrate and Rojas 2003: 334–40; Verdugo 1983b: 9–10; Carvallo 1983: 9; Aylwin 1998: 243–44). To avoid risky unrestrained mobilizations such as a general strike, they helped devise a strategy of periodic peaceful protests that were meant to publicize widespread discontent but avoided a showdown with the military regime (Ortega Frei 1992: 226–29; Cavallo, Salazar, and Sepúlveda: 2008: 449, 451). By channeling contentious bottom-up energies, political parties thus tried to take center stage and reestablish the predominance over Chilean civil society they had traditionally had (Zapata 1985: 222). Yet initially, representative leaders, who

[7] What the regime truly feared was a targeted shutdown by the transport sector, which had been crucial in bringing down the Marxist government of Salvador Allende (interview with Jarpa 2007).

[8] Interestingly, these concerns also reflected lessons that some politicians drew from an outstanding foreign experience, namely the suppression of the Solidarity Movement in Poland (Arriagada 2002: 88).

[9] Even an autocrat as predominant as President Pinochet depends to some extent on military and civilian support that he cannot completely control (see in general, Svolik 2012).

[10] See the interesting discussion of several "methods of nonviolent action" and of the role of violence in Schock (2005: 38–48).

[11] Arriagada (2002: 88) maintains that the opposition derived this lesson in part from the experiences of the Polish Solidarity Movement, which spearheaded amazingly massive mobilizations in 1980–81, but was suppressed in late 1981.

had found it difficult to stay in touch with their constituents under the brutal dictatorship, were surprised about the extent of popular participation in the demonstrations; when the hour for the monthly pot-banging arrived, deafening noise erupted all over Chile's cities, even in middle class neighborhoods where support for Pinochet had formerly been strong (Verdugo 1983a).

While advocating prudence, leaders of the Democratic Alliance, especially renovated leftists impressed by the upsurge of socioeconomic discontent, were also affected by cognitive inferences drawn in part from the Argentine precedent.[12] The neighbors' striking success provided some reinforcement for unrealistic hopes in the imminent fall of Chile's dictator. Even important sectors of moderate opposition parties, such as the Christian Democratic current led by Gabriel Valdés, got carried away and embraced the protest strategy (Ortega Frei 1992: 201; Tironi 2013: 124–25). In fact, the new coalition of opposition forces advanced highly ambitious demands, especially Pinochet's immediate resignation.[13] Convinced of the regime's weakness, impressed by the depth of domestic disaffection, and inspired to some extent by the advancing Argentine transition, they tried to force a rupture.

As regime insiders stress (Fernández 1994: 189–92, 201–2; also interview with Rodríguez 2007), the dictatorship was indeed in a very precarious position, and its survival seemed doubtful. This weakness constituted a clear opportunity for the opposition, if it proceeded in a savvy and skillful way (see Allamand 1999: 45). But by pushing so hard, the Democratic Alliance overplayed its cards, antagonized moderate supporters of the dictatorship that offered negotiations (Allamand 1999: 45–46, 66; Arancibia et al. 2002: 317–20, 366–69; Arancibia and de la Maza 2003: 363–64; see also *Realidad* 1983), and inadvertently helped Pinochet reconsolidate his faltering grip on power (Arancibia and de la Maza 2003: 362–64). The experienced politician the dictator appointed as his new interior minister to weather the crisis, Sergio Onofre Jarpa, was taken aback by what he perceived as the opposition's radicalism (interview with Jarpa 2007). In his conversations with the Democratic Alliance, he felt unable to acknowledge the demand for Pinochet's departure (Verdugo 1983b: 7–8). As these consultations failed to make headway and the monthly protests continued, Jarpa faced mounting criticism from regime hard-liners, who incessantly tried to undermine his cautious liberalization measures. As soon as President Pinochet had managed to reconsolidate his internal support and reassert the regime's strength, he cracked down with a new state of siege in late 1984 and then dismissed Jarpa. As a result, the Chilean opposition did

---

[12] Ricardo Núñez, Manuel Antonio Garretón, Raimundo Valenzuela, and Sergio Molina mentioned the impact of the Argentine regime disintegration (interviews 2007).

[13] Ortega and Moreno (2002: 41, 67, 81); Boeninger (1997: 301). The moderate leader of the Radical Party reports in his memoirs (Silva Cimma 2000: 411) that he regarded this demand as "very bold" and argued against it, but to no avail. A moderate socialist made a similar point (author interview, Santiago, July 2007).

not manage to take advantage of the opportunity created by the tremendous socioeconomic and political crisis of 1983. They failed precisely because they undertook the same kind of effort that seemed to achieve success in Argentina, namely to bring down the dictatorship through mass demonstrations.

THE NICARAGUAN MODEL AND THE FAILURE OF MASS PROTESTS IN 1983–1984

Another crucial reason for the protests' lack of success was continuing disagreement among the challengers of the Pinochet regime – a decisive source of weakness. Above all, the Democratic Alliance failed in its efforts to keep the monthly demonstrations under control. Instead, far-left sectors and radical sects used the protests to promote violence. Inspired especially by the recent revolution in Nicaragua, where a mass insurgency had dislodged a right-wing dictatorship, Chilean Communists and their Russian, Cuban, and East German supporters sought to prepare a popular uprising in Chile as well.[14] Applying the heuristics of availability and representativeness, these groupings hoped that the striking Nicaraguan success could sooner or later be replicated in Chile.[15] Therefore, party cadres in Santiago's poor neighborhoods took advantage of the opposition protests to build barricades and incite street battles with the police and military (Schneider 1995, Rojas Núñez 2011: 29–32, 274–75, 289, 293–94); and in 1983, a guerrilla organization directed by the Communist Party (Peña 2013), the Manuel Rodríguez Patriotic Front (Frente Patriótico Manuel Rodríguez – FPMR), initiated a campaign of terror against the dictatorship, especially its agents of repression (Arrate and Rojas 2003: 353–55).

The narrower, more close-knit, and ideologically homogeneous these groupings were, the more radical and violent their activities. The Communist Party, which had traditionally enjoyed a good deal of working class support in Chile, sought to lay the ground for a future mass uprising (and subsequent socialist revolution) by recruiting radical youths through direct confrontations with the forces of repression; as the dictatorship cracked down rather indiscriminately with brutal raids of whole neighborhoods (*allanamientos*), more and

---

[14] Martínez Muñoz (2004: 98, 154–64, 186–93), Samaniego (2002: 8, 11, 13, 18), Bravo Vargas (2010: 84–85, 95, 110, 127, 182–83, 189), Rojas Núñez (2011: 197, 202–07, 227), Pérez (2012: 8–11); Pérez Silva (2012: 214, 217, 225–28, 235–36, 241). Other successful recent "liberation struggles" also provided inspiration (Samaniego 2002: 10, 18; Álvarez 2006: 136–41), but Nicaragua, where a number of Chilean Communists participated in armed combat during the 1970s and 1980s (Álvarez 2008: 34, 56; Rojas Núñez 2011: 112–42, 150–53; Pérez 2013), stood out. A far-left sect that had always been more violence-prone, the Movimiento de Izquierda Revolucionaria (MIR), also took inspiration from the Nicaraguan success (Pinto and Leiva 2008: 89–91).

[15] Samaniego (2002: 11) forcefully denies simple copying from the Nicaraguan success, but without providing evidence of adaptation to Chile's specific circumstances. Rojas Núñez (2011: 44–47, 58–59, 81–82, 357) reports communists' beliefs that their contentious mobilization could undermine the dictatorship.

more people from the popular sectors would be driven into the Communists' arms, so they hoped. The smaller cells to the far left went much further by undertaking more and more bombings, kidnappings, and assassinations that targeted especially police and military personnel. Typically, these sects constituted hotbeds of groupthink (see for instance Rojas Núñez 2011: 53–54) where the rash inferences suggested by cognitive shortcuts reinforced each other, prompting particularly ill-considered (though meticulously planned) challenges to the autocracy.

The belief derived from the representativeness heuristic that the well-institutionalized Chilean dictatorship resembled the thoroughly personalistic, even Sultanistic Somoza dynasty in Nicaragua (cf. Booth 1998) would not have withstood careful analysis (as highlighted by moderate socialists, e.g. Vodanović 1988: 51–54).[16] The corresponding hopes that a guerrilla struggle and subsequent mass insurgency, which had toppled the anticommunist regime in Central America, could also bring down its Southern Cone counterpart was wildly unrealistic. It reflected a clear overestimation of similarities between two rather different cases, a typical product of the representativeness heuristic. The Nicaraguan success induced radical leftists to jump to rash conclusions; and the rasher the conclusions, the more tight-knit and sect-like these groupings were.

Communist violence, especially the monthly street battles in poor neighborhoods, created an enormous dilemma for the democratic opposition (Arriagada 1998: 169–95). On the one hand, the specter of chaos facilitated the Pinochet regime's efforts to shore up support;[17] as shantytowns burned, middle-class neighborhoods stopped protesting (Allamand 1999: 72). Ever larger sectors of the Democratic Alliance realized sooner or later that the protest strategy was unsuccessful and even turned counterproductive (Puryear 1994: 103–09; Boeninger 1997: 301–02, 330; comments by Enrique Silva Cimma in Ortega and Moreno 2002: 71; Arrate and Rojas 2003: 371; Fernández Abata, Góngora Escobedo, and Arancibia Clavel 2013: 227). Yet on the other hand, the noncommunist left did not dare to abandon bottom-up mobilization in order not to relinquish poorer mass sectors to the Communists and drive them toward Nicaraguan-style insurgency. One of the principal leaders of the renovated Socialists, Ricardo Lagos, framed the options in late 1983: He wanted to bring the exit from authoritarian rule "à la Argentina and not à la Nicaragua" (Lagos 1983: 28; Lagos 1985: 179). Because dictatorial repression had loosened the connections between party leaders and their constituents, leftist politicians worried that their withdrawal from protests would allow Communists to

---

[16] On the connection between institutionalization and personalization in Pinochet's dictatorship, see Rouquié (1986: 116–17).

[17] See the assessments of moderate rightist Andrés Allamand (1989: 65) and of *Junta* member Fernando Matthei in Arancibia and de la Maza (2003: 362, 385). Also see interview with Fernández (2007). Even Bermeo (1997: 310), who challenges the transition literature's "myths of moderation," admits that transgressive contention backfired in Chile in 1983.

capture their followers (author interview with an opposition leader, Santiago, July 2007; see also Fernández Abata, Góngora Escobedo, and Arancibia Clavel 2013: 223–24). The democratic left therefore felt compelled to persist with protests much longer than a realistic assessment of their prospects for bringing down the dictatorship advised.

The failure of the transition effort of 1983–84 shows that even experienced representative leaders with command over information and processing capacity could be affected to some extent by problematic inferences arising from the heuristics of availability and representativeness, both directly and indirectly. In regard to direct effects, the Argentine transition through rupture helped make centrists and moderate leftists overly optimistic during the severe socioeconomic crisis shaking the Pinochet regime, by suggesting the promise of the bottom-up strategy and contributing to unrealistic demand-making.[18] As for the indirect repercussions of cognitive shortcuts, the particularly ill-considered Communist efforts to provoke an insurrection à la Nicaragua trapped left-leaning sectors of the democratic opposition in the protest strategy even after its low chances of success had become apparent. Representative leaders, who had a more realistic understanding of opportunities and risks, felt compelled to compete for support with ideological groupings and radical sects that – under the impression of the striking Nicaraguan success – had a distorted view of the power constellation in Chile.

This paradox – that actors operating with wider bounds of rationality face the need to accommodate the biases afflicting people swept up by inferential heuristics – has broader theoretical significance. Rationalists claim that enlightened minorities can guarantee rational outcomes in the aggregate even if most actors cannot perform rational calculations; in this view, people who calculate better compensate for the limitations of many others (Tsebelis 1990: 34–35). But at the beginning of the Chilean transition, the opposite happened: A misguided minority compelled a more realistic majority to persist in an unpromising, counterproductive course of action. Due to political competition, inferences derived via cognitive heuristics can shape the processes and outcomes of regime transition even if they affect only small numbers of people directly.

In conclusion, these discussions and conflicts among the wide range of challengers of authoritarian rule show how the diversity of foreign models slowed down the advance of regime contention in Chile. The fact that centrist and renovated-left opposition sectors rejected political violence precluded the mass insurgency à la Nicaragua that the Communists advocated, while the violence that the radical left perpetrated helped to undermine the protest strategy inspired in part by Argentina. Moreover, competition among left-wingers prompted the continuation of mass mobilizations even after their diminishing political returns had become obvious. This persistence in turn hindered the

---

[18] Moderate Christian Democrat Patricio Aylwin, who always preferred negotiation efforts, advances this point in his account of Chile's struggle for democracy (Aylwin 1998: 257).

switch to a mode of contention that more moderate opposition forces saw as holding greater promise, namely the negotiation and compromise that had yielded a successful transition in Spain. As different groupings of challengers sought to emulate divergent foreign models, efforts at regime contention in Chile resembled a tumble of crosscurrents.

RETURN TO A NEGOTIATION STRATEGY À LA SPAIN

Moderate sectors of Christian Democracy, especially the wing led by Patricio Aylwin, had always been skeptical about the prospects of bottom-up mobilization. They knew that the military regime maintained a good deal of support among crucial sectors and that it rested on solid institutional foundations; therefore, it could not be toppled via crowd contention. Instead, these sectors had long admired Spain's pacted transition (interviews with M. and P. Aylwin 2007, Boeninger 2007, and Zaldívar 2007), which showed that authoritarianism could be dismantled from the inside, with the begrudging acquiescence of many of its erstwhile backers. To understand this negotiation strategy and derive lessons for Chile, Aylwin's daughter Mariana studied the Spanish case in a long report (M. Aylwin 1980), and other scholars linked to moderate Christian Democracy conducted even more extensive and thorough analyses (Huneeus 1985).

In the late 1970s and early 1980s, these moderate sectors did not see the slightest chance for initiating a negotiation effort. At that time, authoritarian rule was bolstered by apparent economic policy success, and the fear of communism sparked by the Allende government was still fresh. Therefore, the Pinochet regime managed to push forward its own institutionalization and to monopolize the elaboration of a new constitution, blocking any input from broader political sectors. The alternative proposals developed by the Group for Constitutional Studies, which twenty-four lawyers ranging from the center-right to the center-left had formed, found no receptivity. These legal experts, among them Patricio Aylwin, looked closely at Spain, which had sealed the dismantling of its authoritarian institutions through a constituent assembly (interviews with P. Aylwin 2007 and Vodanović 2007). While these deliberations did not affect outcomes at a moment when the Chilean dictatorship was doing the exact opposite, namely cement authoritarian rule through its new charter, they laid the ground for later negotiations and cooperation among civilian politicians by establishing contacts and strengthening connections across earlier ideological frontlines (Serrano and Cavallo 2006: 182–85; Serrano 2009: 73–75).

A new negotiation effort slowly took shape starting in 1984, after several rounds of mass protests had failed to topple the dictatorship. At a time when political polarization was intensifying and violence was on the increase, adherents of negotiation and compromise advocated ever more strongly a change of course. Most prominently, Patricio Aylwin argued in a political seminar in mid-1984 that the opposition should step back from challenging the regime's legitimacy head-on and instead seek to change the institutional framework of authoritarianism from the inside through negotiation efforts. Aylwin (1985: 150, 153; Aylwin 1998: 264) explicitly recommended Spain as a model to emulate.[19] External actors also counseled moderation. Notably, at the inauguration of Argentine president Alfonsín in December 1983, Spain's new prime minister, Felipe González, personally urged the leading opposition representatives from Chile to give up protests and move to negotiations (interviews with Garretón 2007, Lagos 2007, Núñez 2007, Silva Cimma 2007, and Vodanović 2007; see also Figueroa 1985: 61 and interview with Correa 2007). The fact that this charismatic Socialist leader, who had been in the opposition during the Spanish transition, endorsed and advocated this model gave it additional appeal, especially in the eyes of Chile's renovating Socialists (see Schnake 2004: 303, 315–16, 327–30). González's impressive performance in government, especially his achievement of democratic consolidation and social policy reform,[20] also helped to convince a slowly growing number of Chilean leftists of the promise of a pacted transition strategy.[21]

Although these domestic and foreign calls for prudence drew criticism from the advocates of crowd mobilization (cf. Aylwin 1998: 265; Serrano 2009: 80–81; Ortiz 1985: 181–83), they helped garner support for an attempt to broker a broad agreement with moderate supporters of the authoritarian regime that would hopefully pave the way for a negotiated transition, as it had done in Spain. By reaching out to open-minded conservatives and regime soft-liners, this compromise strategy would reassure powerful sectors that redemocratization would not endanger their core interests and values. At the same time, it would isolate hardliners, especially dictator Pinochet, and leave them little choice but to acquiesce in a transition, however begrudgingly.

Under the auspices of the Catholic Church, a trio of centrists, including Christian Democratic leader Sergio Molina, started in early 1985 to patiently meet with a wide variety of important politicians, ranging from conservatives who were sympathetic to the military regime (Allamand 1999: 90–103) to moderate socialists. Months of conversations slowly unearthed affinities on fundamental political principles, especially democracy, and constructed points of consensus on how to move away from authoritarian rule (Zabala 2007: 39–73; Avetikian 1986; interview with Molina 2007). For instance, the thorny issue of human rights violations was treated with caution as participants insisted on strict procedural justice and foreswore politicization and "revenge" (Zabala 1995: 101, 140). The U.S. government, which had long advocated

---

[19] Some moderate Socialists also endorsed the Spanish model at that time (Flisfisch 1985: 14–15).
[20] See Maravall (1995). Spanish democracy had suffered a serious threat during the coup attempt of February 1981 (Cercas 2010).
[21] From an outside perspective, Boeninger (interview 2007) highlighted the impact of Felipe González on the long-standing "strong debate" (interview with Arrate 2007) among Chilean Socialists over the advantages and disadvantages of the Spanish model.

a Spanish-style strategy of moderation and negotiation (Muñoz and Portales 1991: 59, 62, 78), supported this effort to arrive at agreements (Sigmund 1993: 155–58; Kornbluh 2003: 445–47; Zabala 2007: 44–45); for instance, it invited several participants to a conference and official briefing in Washington, DC, that strengthened the emerging consensus (interview with Lagos 2007; see also interview with Jarpa 2007; Cavallo et al. 2008: 517–18).

In August of 1985, the politicians involved in this ambitious attempt to construct a broad, solid foundation for a negotiated return to democracy signed a National Agreement, which they publicized widely and forwarded to the military government in the hope of starting conversations. With the help of the German embassy, proponents of this *Acuerdo Nacional* even managed to convince members of the military *Junta* to ask the president to consider this proposal and engage the opposition (Arancibia and de la Maza 2003: 371–74; Zabala 2007: 66; Cavallo et al. 2008: 545–46, 549–50; see also interview with Molina 2007).

By establishing such a wide-ranging consensus, especially by bringing together centrist and leftist oppositionists with conservatives and regime softliners, this initiative diminished long-standing distrust and hostility, prepared later cooperation across ideological camps, and thus laid the basis for Chile's eventual transition to democracy. A vast range of political groupings committed to this goal and indicated their willingness to work out their differences through reasonable compromises and fair procedures.[22] This determination ended up having a crucial impact on the preparation and conduct of the constitutionally scheduled plebiscite of 1988. In particular, regime soft-liners and conservative politicians who had supported the *Acuerdo Nacional* helped to block the manipulation efforts of President Pinochet's inner circle (Allamand 1999: 157–66).[23] Their insistence on clean procedures was decisive for enabling the democratic opposition to win this contest.

But in the short run, in 1985, the subscribers and backers of the National Agreement did not receive the positive response they had hoped for. Hardcore supporters of the dictatorship, such as Unión Demócrata Independiente (UDI) ideologue Jaime Guzmán, attacked the *Acuerdo* as vague and questioned what its proponents regarded as its main strength, namely the cooperation among politicians of diverse orientations (Guzmán 1991; Boeninger 1997: 311; Zabala 1995: 103, 121–22). Less reactionary conservatives, such as Pinochet's former interior minister Sergio Onofre Jarpa, also disliked this initiative because they continued to distrust even the moderate opposition,

---

[22] Center-right leader Andrés Allamand (1993: 44–68) developed a broader concept of "a democracy of agreements" (*la democracia de los acuerdos*), highlighting the *Acuerdo Nacional* as the precursor.

[23] On the lasting political impact of reaching out to moderate rightists with the *Acuerdo Nacional*, see also interview with Lagos (2007), who focused on the constitutional reform negotiations of 1989.

preferring continued military rule to ban the danger of communism (see Jarpa's comments in Arancibia et al. 2002: 371–73; see also Allamand 1999: 90, 99). Most importantly, the dictator himself was unwilling to cede one inch, and his hierarchical command over the armed forces allowed him to resist any political pressures.[24] He stubbornly insisted on the timetable enshrined in the 1980 constitution, which guaranteed his dictatorial rule until the end of the decade and foresaw a plebiscite on its further continuation for 1988 only.

Pinochet's iron determination thus blocked this attempt to start a negotiated transition. The Spanish-style strategy requires receptivity from the regime side, which it did not find to a sufficient extent in Chile, especially from the dictator himself. Contrary to Francisco Franco during the Spanish transition, Pinochet was still alive – and very powerful as well as very obstinate. Even a personal appeal by Santiago's cardinal could not induce him to talk to the proponents of the *Acuerdo Nacional;* the dictator rudely rejected the churchman's plea.

A crucial reason why Pinochet was so adamant about staying in power and why he continued to command strong military support was the fear of retribution for the atrocities committed under authoritarian rule. This concern became especially salient in late 1985 because the human rights trials that Argentina's new democracy had initiated (cf. Pinochet 1998: 154–55) were moving toward convictions; former authoritarian leaders were facing the ignominious prospect of long, even lifetime prison sentences. In line with the availability heuristic, these striking events across the Andes made a tremendous impression in Santiago and caused consternation and alarm at the very core of Chile's authoritarian government. As the published revelations of *Junta* member Fernando Matthei suggest (Arancibia and de la Maza 2003: 375–80) and my interviews corroborate, the Argentine trials had a devastating impact on Chile's armed forces and their leading civilian collaborators.[25] To impress the threat of a replication in Chile on his closest collaborators, President Pinochet summoned his ministerial cabinet and the military *Junta* to an unusual joint session, at which he had the final plea of one of their Argentine counterparts, Admiral Emilio Massera, read aloud. The defendant was outraged that those who had, in their eyes, successfully defended the fatherland against the danger of communism would now be punished by those they had saved – a complaint that supporters of the Pinochet dictatorship came to repeat over and

---

[24] During a political conflict in 1984, Pinochet had threatened *Junta* member Matthei that his army would forcefully take over the air force, which Matthei commanded (Jarpa in Arancibia et al. 2002: 340).

[25] One of my interlocutors who had worked for the Pinochet government confirmed the basic outline of Matthei's account; another one literally gasped for air when I asked him about this scene; and two others disqualified Matthei with a vehemence and venom ("Matthei is a liar!!!") that speak for themselves. Unfortunately, as the special archivist of the Library of Chile's National Congress confirmed in July 2007, there is no record of this exceptional meeting in the official proceedings that Chile's *Junta* kept.

over again.[26] When, in the high-profile meeting in Santiago, Matthei allegedly questioned the Argentine (and Chilean) regime's justification for torture and forced disappearance, namely the need to fight a "war against subversion," Pinochet and his supporters were even more shocked.[27]

Until the very end of the authoritarian regime, hard-liners predicted that Chile's democratic opposition would emulate the Argentine precedent and seek "revenge" against the winners of this internal war. Alluding to an even more drastic act of retribution against a military president, namely an opposition lynch mob's hanging of President Gualberto Villarroel outside the presidential palace in neighboring Bolivia in 1946, Justice Minister Hugo Rosende would show members of the authoritarian regime the plaza in front of Chile's presidential palace: "Do you see that lamppost over there? That's where they will hang you! And since I am less important, they will hang me on the lamppost behind it. But they will hang us all!" (as reported by Carlos Cáceres in Serrano and Cavallo 2006: 179; transcripts of confidential CIDOC interviews; interviews with Cáceres 2007 and Fernández 2007). Rosende used to tell the dictator himself: "They will lock you in a caged circus wagon and parade you up and down the *Alameda*," the main avenue in downtown Santiago, which passes right behind the presidential palace (reported in interview with Rodríguez 2007; similar Hawkins 2002: 166).

While Minister Rosende invoked an even more dramatic precedent from an earlier time period, the tremendous fear of retribution for the dictatorship's egregious human rights violations was activated by the cognitive availability of the Argentine trials. As mentioned in Chapter 6, President Alfonsín's support for prosecutions had immediately sent shock waves through the Southern Cone, including Brazil and Uruguay (*LAWR* 1984a, 1984b). Given the magnitude of atrocities in Chile and the ongoing repression in the mid-1980s, the Chilean military was highly concerned about the demonstration effect emanating from the Argentine case. Calmer voices, including *Junta* member Fernando Matthei, pointed to the differences, given the much greater clout of the Chilean armed forces by contrast to their multiply defeated Argentine counterparts (Cavallo et al. 2008: 549). But the representativeness heuristic made many supporters of the dictatorship see strong similarities and therefore anticipate a replication of the Argentine trials.

The intense fear of prosecution under democracy cemented Pinochet's determination to step down as late as possible and to refuse any significant concessions to the opposition (Arancibia and de la Maza 2003: 386). The human rights issue was a principal reason for the ongoing intraregime discussions on

[26] I heard this line of reasoning, often advanced with considerable emotional charge, in several of my interviews in Santiago in July 2007. Military leaders in other Latin American countries made the same argument, for instance Brazil's former army minister Leônidas Pires Gonçalves (in Leal 2008).

[27] Matthei in Arancibia and de la Maza (2003: 376). In 1989, however, the air force commander himself threatened "the most grave consequences" if the incoming democratic government were to pursue Argentine-style prosecutions (quoted in Huntington 1991: 216–17).

a potential perpetuation in office beyond 1988 (Espinosa 2008; see Kornbluh 2003: 423–27, 450–52). Fearful of punishment, hard-liners advocated postponing the plebiscite that the 1980 constitution foresaw for that year (as reported in Fernández 1994: 215–16). After the severe crisis of 1982–83 had been overcome and opposition protests had died down, they saw no reason to risk losing power by submitting to a popular vote. Remarkably, these voices were still heard after the dictator had lost the 1988 plebiscite. Although it would have constituted a flagrant violation of Pinochet's tailor-made charter, they called on the dictator to cling to power. In fact, Pinochet himself initially intended to disregard his plebiscite defeat, claim special powers, and continue to rule in open breach of his own constitution (NSA 2013: documents 6–8).

But conservative politicians and regime soft-liners, many of whom had supported the *Acuerdo Nacional,* refused to go along with these insinuations and plans. Over the years, less dogmatic supporters came to mark their political distance from the hard core of the autocracy (Boeninger 1997: 324–26, 343, 347). Their vigilance was crucial for guaranteeing a reasonably fair plebiscite and for blocking efforts to overrule the opposition victory; for instance, Air Force Commander Matthei frontally opposed Pinochet's demand for extraconstitutional powers on the night of the vote count (NSA 2013: document 8). The opposition's commitment to moderation and compromise, indicated by the 1985 agreement, combined with ever stronger pressures from developed countries, convinced more and more center-rightists and even right-wingers that the risks of returning to democracy were lower than the political and economic costs of illegally maintaining power, as will be explained in greater depth below.

THE FAILURE OF INSURRECTIONARY VIOLENCE
AND ITS DOUBLE-EDGED IMPACT

As the preceding section showed, the resistance of regime hardliners and President Pinochet's own fear of retribution blocked concessions to the democratic opposition during the mid-1980s; in particular, the National Agreement signed by a wide range of civilian politicians, including moderate conservatives, failed to prompt any step toward democratization by the authoritarian government. Because the Spanish-inspired negotiation strategy thus did not make headway in the short run, the advocates of mass mobilization and even the proponents of political violence gained renewed strength. The opposition still had not found a strategy that its diverse currents could agree on.[28]

At that point, the Communist Party, still pursuing its Nicaragua-inspired campaign of violence, prepared a frontal attack on the dictatorship.[29] Its Manuel

---

[28] The great diversity of opposition groupings in early 1986 and the variety of foreign precedents that they considered is emphasized in Paulsen (1986a, 1986c).
[29] The responsibility of the Communist Party for the attempt on Pinochet has recently been confirmed by party leader Guillermo Teillier (interview in Peña 2013). See also Rojas Núñez (2011: 27, 53, 204, 311) and Pérez (2012: 8–11).

Rodríguez Patriotic Front imported a huge amount of weaponry from Cuba and distributed it to safe houses all over Chile. Most daringly, in September 1986 a group of *guerrilleros* made an assassination attempt on Pinochet that almost succeeded. This burst of violence and the discovery of the weapons caches had a counterproductive, deterrent effect, however. It strengthened the authoritarian regime, which had long emphasized the danger of communism. More importantly, the enormous size of the arsenal and the heavy weapons it included profoundly scared the democratic opposition and cast serious doubt on Communists' democratic credentials. These arms were meant to outfit a large-scale military force and to give Communists coercive control over any post-authoritarian government (Sigmund 1993: 161–62) – exactly as had happened in Nicaragua (Gorman 1982). What means would other opposition forces have to prevent Communists from claiming "vanguard rule," establishing a new dictatorship, and disregarding the interests, desires, and values of the majority of the citizenry?

Disturbed by Communist violence and deeply concerned about their true intentions, the centrist and left-wing opposition finally drew a clearer dividing line that marginalized the radical left, especially its armed sects.[30] The Christian Democrats, who had long vetoed the participation of Communists in the center-left opposition alliance, definitively reaffirmed this exclusion. More importantly, the renovated Socialists, who had long wavered between their ever more unconditional democratic convictions and their old loyalties to and continued competition with the Communists, came to condemn and reject the use of political violence and distanced themselves from the undemocratic, vanguardist approach of the Communists (Vodanović 1988: 51–54). In a crucial open letter of late 1986, the leader of this current, Ricardo Núñez (1991a: 227, 231), called the Communists and other far-left sects the biggest obstacles to opposition unity, denounced revolutionary projects, and also declared the exhaustion of the protest strategy, which a leading Socialist intellectual had already criticized in an influential confidential memo.[31] The line in the sand that the renovated Socialists drew in turn forced the more radical factions of the Socialist Party to abandon their equivocations over political violence, move away from their long-standing alliance with the Communists, and shift toward an approximation with the moderate left. This belated moderation resulted in their inclusion in the center-left opposition alliance and culminated in the eventual reunification of the Socialist Party in 1989.

---

[30] Numerous opposition politicians highlight the failed attempt on Pinochet as a crucial turning point (comments in Ortega and Moreno 2002: 53, 137–38, 154, 215, 254; interview with Correa 2007).

[31] To my knowledge, José Joaquín Brünner's "notes for discussion" (September 1986) have never been published, but their main points are summarized in Bulnes (1986) and Arrate and Rojas (2003: 386), and Aylwin (1998: 317–18) quotes some sentences.

The categorical rejection of violence by the democratic opposition and the ever more widespread questioning of crowd protests meant the definitive abandonment of transgressive contention. The solidity and strength of the authoritarian regime made a confrontational effort to defeat the military through mass mobilization in the streets simply unrealistic, as Christian Democrats had long argued and as even many renovated Socialists had come to realize. The political jolt arising from the assassination attempt and the resulting realignments among the left thus led to a significant broadening of support for negotiation and compromise. The long-standing disagreements among the opposition finally began to diminish (interviews with Lagos 2007 and Silva Cimma 2007).

To reinforce this ever firmer consensus among democratic forces – the product of years of experiential learning (Garretón and Espinosa 2000: 43) – Christian Democrats invited the architect of the Spanish transition, former prime minister Adolfo Suárez, for a high-profile visit in December 1986, during which he explained the crafting of this democratization process and, together with his Chilean commentators, including Ricardo Núñez, discussed lessons for Chile.[32] A host of other external actors, both governmental agencies and nongovernmental organizations, also supported the move toward moderation and concertation. The German party foundations (Friedrich Ebert Stiftung 2007) and the U.S. National Endowment for Democracy (NED), for instance, provided generous financial assistance as well as political advice, which more or less subtly recommended negotiation over confrontation (Pinto-Duschinsky 1991: 40, 50, 60; Hofmeister 1999: 35, 37, 40; interview with Valenzuela 2007; Altman, Toro, and Piñeiro 2013: 207–11). Chilean socialists, who had long looked down upon European Social Democracy as a sellout to capitalism (as reported in Schnake 2004: 259, 308, 314–15, and interview with Lagos 2007; see also Puryear 1994: 30), now reversed this stance and joined the Europe-dominated Socialist International (Arrate and Rojas 2003: 421). Thus, foreign influence, especially from prestigious and resource-endowed developed countries, reinforced the trend toward moderation that had been set in motion domestically.

In the short run, however, the opposition's newfound commitment to negotiations found no receptivity from the top of the authoritarian regime. Strengthened by the domestic backlash against Communist violence, which prompted the Reagan administration in the short run to ease its pressure on the dictator (Muñoz and Portales 1991: 79–80), Pinochet continued to reject any concessions. But interestingly, the Communist attack and preparation for civil

---

[32] Videotape of Suárez's speech and Chileans' comments, Fundación Frei (1986); Suárez et al. 1986; Guillier 1986; interview with Boeninger 2007. On Núñez's positive reaction, see Altman, Toro, and Piñeiro (2013: 208). In Uruguay in mid-1984, Suárez had participated in a similar high-profile "seminar on negotiated transitions to democracy, at which politicians from all parties were quite visible" (Gillespie 1991: 174, n. 32).

war induced domestic sectors, including moderate supporters of military rule, as well as the U.S. government, to see the dictator's obstinacy more and more as a risk to Chile's political stability in the medium run. The stubborn refusal to move toward democracy, especially Pinochet's clear intention to perpetuate his rule far into the 1990s, was bound to fuel the political disaffection and ideological polarization that fed support for the hard left, including the communist guerrillas. Interestingly, the U.S. foreign policy establishment now came to fear a Nicaraguan or Salvadoran scenario, where right-wing stubbornness and left-wing pressure for profound change had unleashed a spiral of polarization and fueled escalating violence. The resulting civil wars had brought a Marxist government to power in Nicaragua and continued to threaten centrist or right-wing administrations in El Salvador, which despite heavy U.S. support proved unable to defeat leftist guerrillas (Falcoff 1986: 833–34, 839, 846–48; Purcell 1987: 2–3, 11; Muñoz and Portales 1991: 72, 78–79; Sigmund 1993: 133, 151–58; Kornbluh 2003: 418, 445–47).

For these reasons, the Reagan administration started to push ever more strongly for Chile's return to democracy via the plebiscite that Pinochet's own constitution foresaw for 1988. A transition effected through the institutional framework created by the military regime itself would be nonconfrontational and lay the ground for a new civilian regime that would be acceptable to all sides and lead Chile out of the dangerous slide into polarization. Given increasing external pressures – not only from the United States, but from a wide range of European and Latin American countries as well – moderate conservatives and regime soft-liners also viewed Pinochet's obstinacy increasingly as a problem and embraced a fair plebiscite as a real test of the political viability of continued authoritarian rule (author interview with an important regime official, Santiago, July 2007). If the regime's candidate won, he would have popular legitimacy to govern for another eight-year term; but if he lost, these sectors would accept defeat and relinquish power. This commitment among moderate supporters of the dictatorship, for which the wide-ranging discussions and compromises culminating in the *Acuerdo Nacional* of 1985 had laid the ground, meant that the plebiscite had to be conducted as a clean, procedurally unobjectionable contest, without manipulation or fraud (Arancibia and de la Maza 2003: 389–92).[33]

Thus, by indicating the danger associated with ideological polarization and political confrontation, far-left violence eventually helped to move powerful domestic sectors and the regional "hegemon" United States toward

---

[33] The downfall of Ferdinand Marcos's dictatorship in the Philippines, which the next section discusses, contributed to this softening of Pinochet's support. To regime-backers, this striking event showed that U.S. support was unreliable: Although the United States for many years had helped to sustain Marcos – like Pinochet – as an ally in the global struggle against communism, it quickly dropped this old friend when he faced a determined democratic challenge – so their interpretation (interviews with Errázuriz 2007, Fernández 2007, and Rodríguez 2007; cf. Pinochet 1998: 235).

acquiescence in and stronger pressure for democratization, respectively (see in general Mainwaring and Pérez-Liñán, forthcoming: ch. 4). For a while, the street battles promoted by the Communist Party and the terrorist acts committed by the FPMR strengthened the hand of the authoritarian regime and undermined more promising efforts at democratic contention, such as peaceful demonstrations of discontent and negotiation efforts. But over time, it became clear that the dictatorship could not manage to guarantee "law and order" and defeat this violence; on the contrary, fierce repression triggered more violence, as the attempted magnicide and huge arsenals showed. This failure inverted the political repercussions of leftist violence, turning it into a stimulus for democratization.[34] The same outcome prevailed in the case that colored U.S. perceptions of the Chilean stalemate in 1986–87: In the Salvadoran civil war, the failure of the U.S.-supported government to destroy the guerrilla through military means eventually prompted a peace deal and the installation of democracy (Wood 2000: 5, 80–82, 198–202; Lehoucq 2012: 72, 83–86).

This change in the political impact of radical-left violence in Chile is a striking instance in which a factor that for years had hindered efforts at regime change, namely the ill-considered attempts to replicate the Nicaraguan "success," ended up making a positive contribution to a democratic transition. Regime contention in Chile followed a long and winding road, but finally arrived at its destination. In a broader perspective, this paradoxically salutary impact of Communist violence resembles the deterrent effect that the Bolshevist power grab of 1917 in Russia and the overeager emulation efforts in other countries, such as the incessant revolutionism of Germany's Spartacus Group, had in inducing representative leaders to spearhead preemptive reforms and transitions to full representative democracy. As Chapter 5 showed, this radical-left pressure led German Social Democrats to push hard for early elections to the Weimar Constituent Assembly. In Chile, a broadly similar challenge from a leftist sect induced domestic supporters of authoritarian rule, moderate opponents, and external democracy promoters to converge on the 1988 plebiscite as a fair and honest decision mechanism for deciding the country's political future.

THE PHILIPPINE MODEL AND THE OPPOSITION'S INSTITUTIONAL STRATEGY – AND SUCCESS

How and why, exactly, did the opposition decide to enter the plebiscite, and then manage to win it? Neither one of these steps was a foregone conclusion. On the contrary, the question of whether to participate in this contest had long divided the democratic forces, even the centrist Christian Democrats (interview with Martínez 2007). Many challengers feared that the dictatorship would seriously

---

[34] These opposite effects of violence, which played out sequentially in Chile (as in El Salvador), are discussed by Schock (2005: 44–48, 157–58) and Bermeo (1997: 316).

skew the playing field and leave barely any room for opposition campaigning. With such manipulation and coercion, Pinochet had engineered an overwhelming victory in the 1980 referendum on his constitution. Important opposition sectors now suspected a repetition of that traumatic experience. Therefore, they were reluctant to participate in a popular consultation that – they feared – would be virtually impossible to win and that would instead provide artificial "legitimacy" for a prolongation of authoritarian rule (e.g., Correa and Sanfuentes 1987; Maira 1987; see also Lagos 2012: 4, 67).

Based on these concerns, many democratic forces rejected the upcoming plebiscite, in which the dictator himself was likely to stand, and demanded free elections instead, which would probably be fought among civilian candidates (Geisse and Gumucio 1987). In their eyes, an open, fully competitive contest would be decisive for restoring democracy in Chile. Interestingly, savvy conservatives, such as young center-rightist Andrés Allamand and stalwart Sergio Onofre Jarpa, latched on to this proposal. These moderate regime supporters calculated that free elections would offer a right-wing candidate much higher chances of winning than a plebiscite that forced voters to make a binary choice for or against the military regime. Whereas the plebiscite bundled all the votes of the heterogeneous opposition on the "no" option, free elections held the prospect of splitting the opposition vote among several candidates, which could allow the regime's standard bearer to emerge victorious with a plurality (Allamand 1999: 128–30, 132; interview with Jarpa 2007; see also Arancibia and de la Maza 2003: 388–89 and Fernández 1994: 216, 228). Democratic leaders were aware of this political risk, but pushed for free elections out of principle (Boeninger 1997: 324–25, 341). Ironically, President Pinochet did them the favor of vetoing the free elections proposal and insisting on the plebiscite, which he hoped to win as he had in 1980.

Because the opposition had not made much headway with the variety of contentious efforts undertaken in prior years, its leaders slowly and begrudgingly moved toward the conclusion that the plebiscite might offer the only possibility for ending the dictatorship. Since 1983, they had bet on a number of strategies, inspired by different foreign precedents, but had failed to bring significant advances toward democratization. Learning from political experiences eliminated one option after the other and prompted a gradual convergence on the effort to beat the dictatorship at its own game by contesting it in the polls. Preparation for the plebiscite also induced a wide range of challengers to focus on a specific political decision – defeating Pinochet – on which they strongly agreed; it made them deemphasize their broader sociopolitical projects, on which they continued to diverge. The resulting unity was cemented through a closer alliance, the *Concertación de Partidos por la Democracia,* which indicated in its very name the embrace of moderation and negotiation – "concertation."

But would the opposition coalition have a realistic chance, given that the regime controlled the whole state apparatus and could use manipulation and fraud to claim victory? Interestingly, a recent transition halfway around the globe eventually helped to alleviate these concerns and bolster the decision to participate in the plebiscite. In early 1986, Philippine dictator Ferdinand Marcos tried to steal an election, but this blatant fraud triggered domestic protests and strong international pressure, provoked a split inside the military, and in these ways enabled the democratic opposition to take power. This striking fall of a personalistic right-wing dictator, who looked similar to Pinochet, was widely covered in the Chilean media[35] and drew attention from the educated public and political leaders (Ortega Frei 1992: 337, 355–56; interviews with Molina 2007 and Rodríguez 2007; Tironi 2013: 185–86). Due to a highly embarrassing diplomatic incident with the Philippines a few years earlier (Cavallo et al. 2008: ch. 27; Muñoz 2008: 113–17), Marcos's fall had particular salience in Chile and activated the availability and representativeness heuristics among opposition forces desperate for a way out of their political dilemma. Immediately after this stunning event, a reporter noted (Paulsen 1986b: 4): "The Chilean opposition this past week could not avoid making political decisions with one eye looking at the East, at what happened in the Philippines."

Consequently, the surprising Philippine success, in which mass protests played a decisive role in defeating a dictator (as emphasized by Hales 1986 and Paulsen 1986b: 4), helped quickly stimulate a renewed bout of crowd demonstrations in Chile in early 1986 (Mönckeberg 1986: 4–5; Huntington 1991: 158; interview with Molina 2007). But when this bottom-up pressure just as quickly proved futile again, representative leaders drew more sophisticated lessons from this case of democratic contention, which had erupted after an election called by the authoritarian regime. This more thorough and comprehensive analysis of the Philippine episode suggested to Chilean opposition leaders that participation in the 1988 plebiscite may hold considerable promise. The success in the Pacific archipelago demonstrated that democratic forces could defeat an authoritarian regime in the polls, and if the government tampered with the results, domestic and international pressures would force it out.[36] Upon analyzing the process of Marcos's downfall in greater depth, Chilean politicians inferred that they could take advantage of the 1988 plebiscite to terminate the Pinochet dictatorship.[37]

---

[35] For instance, the major news magazine *Hoy* devoted its title page, editorial, and first article to the Philippine events and their "lessons" for Chile (*Hoy* 450, 3 March 1986, 5–7).

[36] Cortés Godoy (1987: 338–39); Huneeus (1987: 317); interview with Arriagada 2007; Valdés (2002: 25); Puryear (1994: 132). Marcos's striking downfall showed regime supporters that the United States could quickly drop a long-standing ally; they feared that Pinochet was next in line (Fernández 1994: 209; interviews with Fernández 2007 and Errázuriz 2007).

[37] Besides the Philippine precedent, the democratization via elections in Brazil and the defeat of the Uruguayan military regime in the constitutional plebiscite of 1980 suggested this lesson as well (Figueroa 1986; Vaccaro 1987: 13; Aylwin 1998: 332).

After cognitive shortcuts quickly drew Chilean oppositionists' attention to the Philippine events and representative leaders started to derive lessons from them, the United States also came to encourage and finance systematic efforts to learn from this precedent. Since President Reagan in the mid-1980s had turned toward more forceful democracy promotion (Hawkins 2002: 144–48), the new National Endowment for Democracy (NED; see Carothers 2001: 127–29, 136–39) strongly supported the Chilean opposition (Sigmund 1993: 169–74, 177, 207). Specifically, it highlighted the Philippine success to foster participation in the plebiscite. With NED funding, activists from the Pacific island grouping visited Chile and a delegation of Chilean democrats traveled to Manila to learn about successful voter registration and election supervision (*Hoy* 1987; NDI 1989: 5–9; interview with Arriagada 2007; Tironi 2013: 185–86). This thorough information-gathering allowed the Chilean opposition to draw many useful ideas from the Philippine experience and adapt them to their own needs.[38]

In preparing for the plebiscite with NED and Soros Foundation support, the Chilean opposition also used opinion polls that reliably ascertained people's political preferences and vote intentions, and focus groups that allowed for a deeper understanding of voters' attitudes, concerns, and hopes (Puryear 1994: 134–53; Huneeus 2007: 417–21). These surveys and studies were conducted in part by experienced U.S. consultants, who also trained Chileans (Tironi 2013: 153, 183–204, 218). With this technical advice from abroad and the comparatively solid base of knowledge provided by opinion polls and focus groups, the representative leaders of the Chilean opposition were shielded against the distortions in judgment that the availability and representativeness heuristics can cause. After all, the Marcos regime was sultanistic and therefore more brittle than the highly institutionalized Pinochet dictatorship (Thompson 1998). Instead of overestimating the similarities and rushing to simple imitation, Chile's democratic challengers studied the Philippine precedent thoroughly, drew careful lessons from it, and calibrated their efforts to the opportunities and constraints provided by Pinochet's plebiscite. For instance, they organized a much more wide-ranging vote-monitoring effort than their Asian counterparts had undertaken (interview with Lagos 2007).

All these debates and discussions played out among the opposition's representative leaders, who also spearheaded the preparations for the plebiscite. In the late 1980s, the political initiative clearly lay with party politicians, not their mass followers (Oxhorn 1994: 55–56; Schneider 1995: 192). Whereas in 1983, bottom-up pressures had helped to induce even moderate party leaders to sign off on the protest strategy, now these politicians undertook sustained efforts to mobilize their constituents, register them as voters, and ensure their turnout in the plebiscite (Arriagada 1998: 247–56). The shift in the arena

---

[38] Interview with Lagos 2007; Fernández 1987; Muñoz (2008: 186–87). On the Philippine experiences that were of interest for Chileans, see Kessler (1991: 205–11).

of contention – from the streets to the polls – favored organizational leaders who could guide the participatory energies of centrist and leftist citizens into procedural channels (see in general O'Donnell and Schmitter 1986: 57–58). As is typical of polities with a good deal of organizational density, political leaders prevailed, except for the temporary irruption of striking precedents of apparently successful protests. The crucial role of representative leaders, whose information-gathering was enhanced by external support, in turn accounted for less distorted learning and a process of decision-making that reflected wider bounds of political rationality.

Certainly, however, opposition politicians tailored their activities to popular concerns and moods in order to increase their chances of defeating the dictatorship. For instance, U.S. consultants (Castillo 1991: 42–43), including pollsters who had conducted surveys during the Philippine transition (Soza 1988; Valdés 2009: 320–21; Tironi 2013: 189, 192; see also Cortés Godoy 1987: 341–42), discovered that fear continued to grip many Chileans, making them wary of the untested opposition (Soza 1988; comments by Eugenio Tironi in Ortega and Moreno 2002: 161–63; Lagos 2012: 95–97; Tironi 2013: 188–204). These advisers therefore urged the democratic forces not to highlight the Pinochet regime's repression and human rights abuses, which would only reinforce this fear. Instead, they advocated a focus on the future with a message of hope and optimism. Accordingly, the NO campaign designed brilliant TV ads focused on the light-hearted slogan, "La alegría ya viene" (happiness is about to come). Even Pinochet supporters acknowledged the effectiveness of this propaganda compared to their own (see Allamand 1999: 154; author interview with important Pinochet supporter, Santiago, July 2007; Boeninger 1997: 343). This episode (analyzed in depth by Tironi 2013: ch. 18–22) shows the important role that external support for the Chilean opposition, inspired partly in the Philippine success, played in the run-up to the plebiscite of 1988.

Foreign assistance was also crucial in helping the domestic opposition construct a countrywide system of election-monitoring and parallel vote tabulation, which was decisive for preventing fraud (Gamarekian 1988; interview with Molina 2007; Cavallo et al. 2008: 648–49). These efforts were capped by a high-profile delegation of external observers, who witnessed the plebiscite firsthand; fittingly, this group was led by the mastermind of the Spanish transition, Adolfo Suárez (NDI 1989: v-vi, 9–12). Moreover, when suspicions arose that the dictatorship might nevertheless tamper with the results or simply disregard a negative outcome (Arancibia and de la Maza 2003: 401–04), the United States as well as European and Latin American countries exerted heavy diplomatic pressure to forestall this danger (Sigmund 1993: 174–77, 207; Kornbluh 2003: 423–27, 450–52). As argued in Chapter 6 the "vertical" influence of powerful developed nations had a particularly important impact in preventing the interruption of an ongoing transition process; while foreigners often have difficulty prompting the initiation of regime change due to nationalist sensitivities, they can significantly reinforce its momentum once it has gotten under way by providing financial and technical assistance and exerting diplomatic clout.

In addition to a wide gamut of external actors, domestic conservatives and soft-liners in the armed forces, including a majority of the military *Junta,* had also come to reject manipulation and fraud. For the reasons explained during my analysis of the *Acuerdo Nacional* of 1985 and the backlash against Communist violence in 1986, moderate right-wingers insisted on fair parameters for the plebiscite and helped prevent the government from skewing competition decisively against the opposition. Similarly, they accepted the defeat that voters handed President Pinochet on October 5, 1988. When the government equivocated on that dramatic night and rumors ran wild, both former interior minister Jarpa and *Junta* member Matthei publicly acknowledged the opposition victory in order to stop the shenanigans (Kornbluh 2003: 425–26, 451–52; see also Edgardo Boeninger in Boeker 1990: 41–42). And when the dictator pushed for emergency decree powers, Matthei and other *Junta* members refused this demand in order to block any extra-constitutional perpetuation in power (NSA 2013: documents 6–8).

In conclusion, after unsuccessfully trying to oust the dictatorship in a variety of ways, democratic challengers in Chile finally achieved their goal by entering an institutional arena that the dictatorship, in its quest for legitimacy and institutionalization, had opened up itself (Hawkins 2002: ch. 4–5). The opposition strategy, prepared by the National Agreement of 1985, was informed by the stunning Philippine precedent, which cognitive shortcuts put on Chileans' radar screens, but which representative leaders, with encouragement and support from the United States, studied in considerable depth and adapted to the political conjuncture prevailing in their own country.

THE TRANSITION NEGOTIATIONS OF 1989

The clear victory in the plebiscite made the *Concertación* look like the probable winner of the upcoming presidential elections of 1989. Thus, a change of government was finally within sight. But would it also bring a real transformation of the political regime, given that the 1980 constitution enshrined serious restrictions on popular sovereignty and assigned a tutelary role to the military? The opposition was eager to use its political momentum to wring important concessions from the authorities. Yet the majority of the *Concertación* preferred prudent negotiations à la Spain and refrained from frontally challenging the dictatorship. To lay the ground for a stable democracy, it preferred limited change based on a broad compromise, rather than pushing for a more decisive break and risking renewed polarization and conflict (Viera-Gallo 1989: 17–18) – which had prompted the traumatic destruction of Chilean democracy in 1973.

After the defeat of Pinochet's self-perpetuation effort, the regime begrudgingly agreed to manage the transition to democracy via negotiations. Excessive inflexibility could have exposed its tailor-made institutional framework to politically irresistible demands for a profound, comprehensive overhaul via a constituent assembly; in fact, the amendment procedures enshrined in the 1980 constitution were not watertight (Uggla 2005: 58–59). Moreover, the opposition victory of October 1988 meant a strong mandate for change; therefore, stubbornness would have weakened the political prospects of the right-wing parties, which would from now on have to carry a growing share of the burden of protecting the dictatorship's legacies and safeguarding its old personnel. Therefore, the moderate conservatives assembled in *Renovación Nacional* (RN) supported modifications (Allamand 1999: 170–79; Jarpa in Arancibia et al. 2002: 399–401), although the hard-liners in UDI offered determined resistance (Boeninger 1997: 347–49).

But while willing to concede some changes, the Pinochet government was determined to maintain restrictions on the new democracy in order to guarantee the continuity of its market-oriented economic model and, above all, to prevent the ascendant civilians from prosecuting the armed forces for human rights violations.[39] Although Argentina's new democracy had been forced by several military rebellions to scale down its punitive efforts considerably, the fear of perceived "revenge" still ran high among hard-liners, as analyzed above (see also Fernández Abata, Góngora Escobedo, and Arancibia Clavel 2013: 257–60). Pinochet himself certainly had much to account for.

These mixed motives gave rise to a tough bargaining process in 1989. Although the opposition was cautious in its demands for modifications in order to pave the way for a smooth transition to democracy, President Pinochet and the military *Junta* fought many changes tooth and nail and vetoed several. After protracted negotiations (chronicled in Uggla 2005: 59–65), a compromise emerged that softened some of the constitutional constraints imposed on popular sovereignty, but that also guaranteed important institutional safeguards for the military and its civilian backers.

What were the main changes (overview in Heiss and Navia 2007: 172–83; detailed documentation in Geisse and Ramírez 1989: 23–178)? The Pinochet regime had sought to strengthen the legislative clout of right-wing forces by stipulating the appointment of nine senators, in a body with only twenty-six elected members. The *Concertación* proposed and *Renovación Nacional* accepted the elimination of this stranglehold on democratic representation. But the dictator dug in his heels. Finally, a compromise emerged, namely, an increase in the number of elected senators to thirty-eight, which diluted the relative weight of their designated colleagues.[40] The reforms also gave civilians

---

[39] Both a regime insider and an opposition leader stressed (interviews, Santiago, July 2007) that the human rights issue, while never discussed openly, really was the fundamental problem shaping the divergent positions in these negotiations.

[40] According to Patricio Aylwin (comments in Ortega and Moreno 2002: 220–21; similar interview with Martínez 2007), RN agreed to support additional changes during the first democratic

equal representation on the National Security Council (originally designed to be dominated by the military) and turned its decisions from binding constraints on democratically legitimated authorities into "opinions" for these authorities to consider (while the sabers might be rattling, of course). Other important modifications eliminated restrictions on political pluralism, especially the proscription of "Marxist" parties, and strengthened guarantees of a range of political rights. Last not least, the protection of human rights, as stipulated in the international conventions signed by Chile, was enshrined in the constitution (Ensalaco 1994: 416–17).

In exchange, the *Concertación* agreed to close the above-mentioned amendment loophole and to give the rules governing military affairs the status of "organic constitutional law," which hindered future changes. The Pinochet regime soon took advantage of the latter concession and used its legislative powers during its waning days to cement the autonomy of the armed forces from civilian oversight – including legal prosecution. In fact, the rules passed by the dictatorship over the years withheld from the incoming president the right to dismiss the commanders of the armed forces. This limitation meant that the new democratic government would have as the army commander breathing down its neck none other than General Pinochet!

Besides agreeing to specific constitutional amendments, the democratic opposition made a big political concession in these negotiations: It effectively accepted the validity and legitimacy of the constitutional framework imposed by the dictatorship. After many challengers had questioned this institutional architecture for years, their efforts to bring it down as a part of their broader projects of sociopolitical transformation had uniformly failed. Learning by experience turned them more realistic and induced them to focus on political regime change. Therefore, they acquiesced in using Pinochet's reformed constitution as the legal scaffolding for the new democracy. The hope soon to enact another round of important changes helps explain this acquiescence,[41] which paved the way for a smooth exit from the dictatorship.

CONCLUSION

Chile's lengthy, tension-filled regime transition exemplifies the great complexity of the third wave of democratization. In particular, this case highlights the impact that ideological diversity among political parties and other groupings had on the emulation of foreign precedents. The variety of external sources of inspiration – the main topic of Chapter 6 – gave rise to frequent disagreements among the challengers of authoritarian rule, which slowed down the initiation,

---

government, but then reneged on this deal. Allamand (1999: 185–88) reports this episode from his perspective.

[41] It then took sixteen years, however, until most of the remaining restrictions on popular sovereignty and democratic governance were eliminated at the end of Ricardo Lagos's presidency in 2005 (Funk 2006).

advance, and progress of regime contention; after all, opposition unity is a crucial precondition for success. But the wider range of offerings also led to a learning process that, after many twists and turns, brought a convergence on a particularly promising foreign model, which finally helped the democratic opposition defeat the dictatorship. Thus, while Chile took a long and winding road toward redemocratization, it ended up with success – the typical combination of diffusion features during the third wave in South America.

The preceding analysis substantiates the claim of Chapter 6 that the third wave arose from various external stimuli – quite different from the single primary spark that propelled the tsunami of 1848. While important domestic sectors and foreign actors embraced a negotiation strategy à la Spain, alternative modes of contention also exerted considerable attraction. Protests and mass mobilization inspired in part by Argentina temporarily held such appeal, and popular insurgency and armed struggle à la Nicaragua did so in a more lasting fashion, albeit for smaller groupings and radical sects. The broad menu of foreign models, a distinguishing feature of the third wave in general, nurtured particularly pronounced disagreements among Chilean challengers because of the wide-ranging ideological diversity of domestic organizations and groupings. Because different collectivities in Chile's programmatic multiparty system held clearly defined, widely divergent positions, they also established transnational linkages to different ideological families (such as the Socialist International), and they gravitated toward different foreign precedents of regime contention.

As their underlying cause, these distinct connections and affinities reflected a corollary of organizational development, namely the crystallization of divergent political standpoints discussed toward the end of Chapter 2. As organization spread across the ideological spectrum, a broad gamut of parties and associations emerged, which in Chile – more clearly than in other Latin American countries – covered the whole range from right to left (Garretón 1991: 221–22). In line with their preferred approach to politics, these variegated groupings were drawn toward different foreign precedents and models. Moderate Christian Democrats embraced Spain's pacted transition and urged its imitation; moderate leftists and renovated Socialists for a while took some inspiration from Argentina's mass protests; and far-left groupings and radical sects were fired up by the Nicaraguan revolution. Contrary to the earlier diffusion processes examined in this book, domestic political forces thus disagreed not only over whether to emulate a foreign precedent, but over which precedent to follow. In Chile, these debates and conflicts played out with particular clarity; but they are visible in other Latin American cases as well, for instance in the discussions over Argentina-style mass protests versus Spanish-style negotiations among Brazilian opposition forces during the *Diretas Já* campaign (Rodrigues 2003: 20–21, 44, 62–64, 74).

These disagreements over the most promising foreign model slowed down the diffusion process but also contributed to its eventual success. In regard to this reduced speed, it took time for specific options to gather a critical mass of support, and divergent options pursued simultaneously by different groupings hindered each other. Such mutual obstruction occurred during the mass protests of 1983–84, which drew moderate opposition sectors away from the negotiation strategy and which soon faltered due to the political violence incited and perpetrated by Communists.

But since there were various foreign models at play, it became more likely that one of these inputs would end up offering promising lessons for combating the dictatorship effectively. If the Chilean opposition had only one iron in the fire, as the revolutionaries of 1848 with their wager on unorganized crowd protests did, the risk of failure would have been much higher; the most similar mode of contention employed in Chile, the mass demonstrations of 1983–84, indeed failed to bring down authoritarian rule. But the Chilean opposition disposed of a broader set of options, and after experimenting with several of them, it eventually settled on an effective strategy for dislodging the dictatorship. With the slow convergence on a negotiation strategy and the additional ideas provided by the novel Philippine precedent, party politicians ended up designing an approach with which they defeated the dictator from inside his own "special-ordered" institutional framework and then transformed the constitutional architecture to open space for the return to democracy.

The variety of initial options stimulated even more open and critical debates among different political parties and groupings than the discussions that go on inside broad-based, pluralistic organizations (discussed in Chapters 2 and 5). While various collectivities, especially far-left sects, were ideologically committed to their preferred models, the repressive setting of the Pinochet dictatorship provided a hard reality check, which facilitated a reasonably clear assessment of success or failure. As a result, the debate over the best contentious strategy turned into a learning process (Garretón and Espinosa 2000: 43–44), conducted predominantly among representative leaders. While certainly not purely intellectual, but shaped by political power and refracted by competitive interests, this lesson-drawing cross-checked facile analogies and rash inferences and weeded out the starkest distortions and biases caused by cognitive shortcuts. In these ways, the protracted discussions in Chile over the proper contentious strategy and the most useful foreign model ended up yielding particularly wide, loose bounds of political rationality.

In all of these ways, the multiplicity of external inputs and their ideologically differentiated processing by Chilean opposition groupings contributed both to the slow advance and the high rate of success that distinguish the third wave from the other diffusion processes examined in this book, especially the riptide of 1848.

8

Theoretical Conclusions and Comparative Perspectives

The flourishing diffusion literature has documented that external impulses matter and begun to explore why they matter, but it has not yet analyzed the substantial differences in the patterns and features of diffusion processes. Examining this issue, the book highlights a counterintuitive finding: Over the last 200 years, there has been a striking slowdown in the spread of political regime contention in the Western world – despite faster communication, easier transportation, and denser global networks. Surprisingly, the most dramatic wave of conflicts over regime change occurred early in democratization history, namely in 1848. By comparison, the much-discussed "third wave," sometimes called a "tsunami" (Drake 2009: ch. 7) due to its momentous impact, unfolded in Latin America at a rather glacial pace from the mid-1970s to the early 1990s (Markoff 2009: 58), very different from the true tsunami of 1848.

At the same time, the success of externally triggered conflict in producing actual advances toward liberalism and democracy has increased. Whereas the riptide of 1848 left behind many failures and frustrations, the third wave was mostly successful in producing actual transitions toward democracy in the two regions under investigation, Europe and Latin America. This increase in goal achievement is especially noteworthy because with the elimination of suffrage restrictions and other formal-institutional limitations of democracy, gradual advances, such as the sequence of British electoral reforms from 1832 to 1928, became infeasible; in the late twentieth century, regime change tended to entail a full transition from authoritarian rule to democracy. Yet although the task became more demanding, emulative regime contention during the third wave attained much more success in accomplishing this task. And while modernization theories argue that socioeconomic development produced a secular increase in the chances for democratic transition as well, these claims are hotly debated, especially with respect to Latin America (Mainwaring and

Pérez-Liñán forthcoming: ch. 4). For this study, which does not explain the objective advance of democracy, but the success of externally inspired efforts to advance toward democracy, the increase in oppositionists' rate of goal achievement is notable.

In sum, the negative correlation between the speed and success of contentious waves is clear and stark: In the nineteenth century, diffusion was rapid but not very successful; in the twentieth century, it became slower yet more effective in bringing steps toward democracy. The opposite direction of these two trends is remarkable and makes it particularly difficult to design a convincing explanation. In particular, can any theory establish an inner connection between these counteracting tendencies?

Extant approaches cannot come up with a persuasive account. The diminishing speed of diffusion contradicts widely held network, modernization, and globalization theories, which postulate shrinking distances among polities and an ever faster transmission of impulses. Conversely, the increasing success of imitative regime contention disproves arguments about nationalism, which postulate ever greater immunity and resistance to foreign precedents. World system theory and constructivism expect a speedup – not slowdown – of diffusion as regime contention moved with the secular advance of democracy from core countries to the periphery, which should be particularly susceptible to external influences. Finally, rational learning cannot explain the inverse relation between diffusion features; instead, increasing chances of success should induce rational calculators to emulate external precedents more quickly. From the perspective of cost/benefit analyses, the eagerness of people in the nineteenth century to join protests despite serious risks of repression is particularly puzzling. Indeed, investigations of the decision-making process demonstrate conclusively that common citizens and even political leaders did not apply comprehensive rationality.

Given the limitations of existing approaches, I develop a new account that invokes cognitive-psychological micro-foundations and highlights organizational macro-developments. To avoid the deficiencies of standard rational choice, this theory rests on mechanisms of bounded rationality. As psychologists have exhaustively demonstrated, people commonly deviate from the norms of comprehensive rationality and use inferential shortcuts to cope with uncertainty and overabundant information. Applying the availability heuristic, they pay disproportionate attention to dramatic, vivid events, such as the sudden overthrow of an important ruler in a neighboring country. And based on the representativeness heuristic, they infer from this single case of success that a similar challenge can succeed in their own polity. Due to these shortcuts, people jump to the conclusion that they can replicate the foreign precedent. Therefore, they throw rational prudence to the wind and embark on regime contention as well.

These rash inferences help explain the swift spread of political conflict during the nineteenth century. As Chapter 4 showed with a wealth of primary

evidence, discontented sectors "automatically" inferred from the downfall of
Louis Philippe in Paris that their own rulers were giants on feet of clay as well,
that the time had come to push for a regime change, and that the prospects
of success were high. But derived from cognitive shortcuts, these beliefs were
problematic, prompting emulative regime contention under conditions that
were actually not very propitious; Central and East European princes sat in
the saddle much more firmly than their French counterpart. As a result, autocrats sooner or later suppressed most protests and uprisings and reneged on
initial concessions and promises that they had made under duress. Rash and
ill-considered, the contentious wave of 1848 yielded a great deal of disappointment and failure. Bounded rationality thus provides the causal mechanisms
that underlie the negative correlation between diffusion's speed and success,
especially at the one pole exemplified by the tsunami of 1848.

Cognitive heuristics held particular sway when polities had low organizational density and the decision whether to join in regime contention rested
squarely with individuals or small informal networks. Ordinary people lacked
access to reliable information, the capacity to process it systematically, and the
political experience to put it in perspective. Given their weak base of knowledge, they relied heavily on cognitive shortcuts and were unable to cross-check
the resulting inferences. In the inchoate polities of the early to mid-nineteenth
century, citizens got carried away by stunning, dramatic external triggers and
jumped on the bandwagon of regime contention without carefully assessing
the political opportunity structure.

In the last third of the nineteenth century, however, mass organizations
emerged. Social democratic parties and trade unions encompassed an ever
larger share of the working class, and catchall parties later captured other sectors as well. As firm collective actors took the political stage and established
track records, the constellation of power became visible and political uncertainty diminished. Whereas the behavior of amorphous crowds had been
virtually unpredictable, it now became possible to ascertain the domestic opportunity structure. As a result, political attention came to focus predominantly on
the internal situation; external precedents, which had been the main observable events in the first half of the nineteenth century, lost in evidentiary value.
Therefore, these foreign triggers became less powerful in inspiring actors, who
instead based their decisions more on domestic developments and conjunctures.
Therefore, they did not rush into immediate emulation efforts, but defied their
governments only once a good opportunity seemed to have arrived.

Moreover, the rise of broad-based organization shifted the effective locus of
decision-making on whether to emulate foreign precedents from the individual
to the collective level. Due to their organizational encapsulation, most citizens
no longer made these crucial choices on their own, but now took cues and
guidance from their representative leaders. Due to their organizational position, these officials had better access to information, more experience in inter-
preting it, better capacities to process it, and a greater ability to weigh costs

and benefits thoroughly. While also influenced by cognitive shortcuts, leaders could counterbalance these simplistic inferences with firmer knowledge. Their bounds of rationality therefore were less tight than those of individual people.

Less distorted information-processing and decision-making prevailed, especially inside broad-based organizations such as social democratic parties and unions, which included a variety of political sectors and tendencies and thus encompassed diversity and pluralism. To maintain unity, these organizations instituted procedures for debate and criticism, negotiation and compromise. These mechanisms for discussion allowed for the cross-checking of inferences and opinions and made it more likely that unfounded beliefs derived from cognitive shortcuts were corrected or weeded out. By contrast, small organizations defined by ideology were intent upon guaranteeing uniformity and purity and therefore discouraged or purged internal dissent. Because they delegitimized internal debate, these radical groupings resembled sects and constituted a hotbed for groupthink, which reinforced and intensified the problematic inferences suggested by cognitive heuristics. Sectarian leaders, such as the Spartacus Group in Germany in 1917–19, therefore embarked on particularly ill-advised efforts to emulate what they regarded as successful external precedents. While these attempts universally failed, they created complications for the more prudent initiatives of representative leaders, partly by inducing these leaders to support disproportionately brutal repression, which – as Chapter 5 explained – betrayed their own reliance on cognitive shortcuts.

Though caught up in these side battles, the leaders of broad-based organizations acted less rashly than the unorganized crowds of 1848 in confronting incumbent autocrats. Drawing less heavily on cognitive shortcuts, they assessed the replicability of foreign instances of regime contention more carefully. Therefore, they were not immediately swept up by external impulses of diffusion. While affected by these stimuli, they waited to act until the circumstances were propitious for following the precedent. They did want to emulate a foreign success, but at the right moment. With the rise of representative leadership, waves of regime contention slowed down, yet achieved higher rates of success, as the in-depth analysis of the repercussions of the Russian revolutions in Chapter 5 shows.

In sum, the fundamental transformation of the processing of external stimuli produced by the rise of broad-based organizations and their representative leaders accounts for the significant change in diffusion features from the mid-nineteenth century to the early twentieth century. Thus, changes on the reception side of diffusion proved decisive until that point. Further organizational macro-developments then came to reshape the stimulus side of diffusion as well. The change in the main trigger of democratization waves reinforced the trends toward diminishing speed and increasing success that diffusion processes in the Western world have evinced.

As explained in Chapter 3, the proliferation of parties across the political spectrum ended up changing the precedents that could unleash waves of regime contention; in particular, it brought a shift from transgressive to contained modes. After more and more citizens were included in broad-based organizations, oppositionists backed away from escalating street protests and frontal assaults on autocrats – the only viable option in the inchoate, amorphous societies of the early to mid-nineteenth century. And as centrist and right-wing sectors also created broad-based organizations, democratic transitions via negotiation and compromise became feasible.

Due to their lower risks and greater prospects of success, pacted regime changes soon turned into the preferred mode of democratic contention. A successful instance induced representative leaders in other countries to seek replication. But negotiated transitions are unexciting and do not yield clearcut victories. Therefore, they do not spark massive enthusiasm inspired by the availability and representativeness heuristics. In the world of bounded rationality, contained contention does not constitute the kind of precedent that stimulates immediate emulation efforts. As pacted transitions come to prevail, diffusion waves therefore get under way slowly. But when representative leaders do conclude that an authoritarian regime is ready for negotiations, they press ahead and have a good chance of success.

The growing predominance of negotiated transitions was crucial to the further slowdown but increased payoff of contentious diffusion during the twentieth century, as Chapter 6 demonstrated through its analysis of the third wave of democratization in Latin America. Spain's pacted transition was the most important trigger for this wave of contention. Due to its positive payoffs, it elicited a great deal of interest from party leaders, who looked for opportunities to start negotiations with authoritarian rulers. But such chances arose slowly because dictators could not be forced to embark on political liberalization and on consultations with the democratic opposition. Yet when negotiations did get under way, they sooner or later opened the path toward democratization because they allowed challengers to push for more and more change while simultaneously reinsuring incumbents and their supporters that their core interests would be protected. The third wave therefore brought a large number of effective transitions in Latin America.

Democratic contention in the region was complicated and difficult, however; despite the advantages of negotiation and compromise, alternative strategies also held considerable attraction, especially for mass actors, ideologically driven groupings, and radical sects. In particular, mass protests were vivid and dramatic and therefore drew attention and support in line with the heuristics of availability and representativeness; and violent insurgency found backers among tight-knit cells among which groupthink was rife. Therefore, challengers of Latin American authoritarianism in the 1970s and 1980s faced a menu of options. Which strategy they preferred depended to a good extent on their ideological posture, which had crystallized as political organization spread across the left-right spectrum. The fact that different political groupings gravitated toward divergent external precedents and models is therefore particularly visible in a country like Chile with its programmatically defined multiparty system. Accordingly, centrist parties preferred Spanish-style negotiation, renovated socialists for a while pinned their hopes on protests à la Argentina, and Communists sought to replicate the Nicaraguan revolution.

This pursuit of conflicting strategies of contention hindered the initiation and advance of opposition challenges in the short run, as the analysis of the Chilean protests of 1983–84 in Chapter 7 documents. Disagreement limited the backing for any one strategy, and the simultaneous pursuit of several caused mutual blockage. In the medium run, however, the broader menu of options allowed for learning from political experience and led large sectors of the opposition eventually to settle on the most promising strategy, which – predictably – was Spanish-style negotiation. Thus, as the opposition had several irons in the fire, they managed to forge a weapon that enabled them to induce authoritarian rulers to give up power. The progress of emulative regime contention was slow, but achieved its goal. Therefore, the third wave displayed the opposite features as a diffusion process compared to the tsunami of 1848, namely, low speed and high success.

To explain these differences, my developmental approach explains fundamental historical change by adding macro-level factors, layer by layer, to a cognitive-psychological micro-foundation. Inferential heuristics shape political decision-making throughout the two centuries under examination, but they play out differently in the collective arena of political decision-making, depending on evolving macro-contexts. Their operation is most clear-cut and straightforward in inchoate societies in which potential challengers resembled an amorphous mass of individuals and small-scale, informal groupings.

As a new type of actor emerges, namely the representative leaders of broad-based organizations, cognitive shortcuts have less automatic sway: When organizational linkages tighten, the bounds of rationality loosen. This salutary effect arises from intra-institutional features, namely from the advantages of representative leaders in information access and political experience and from the scrutiny they face inside pluralistic parties and associations.

Then, as broad-based organization proliferates across the ideological spectrum, different political leaders embrace divergent external precedents and models. This diversity of positions brings forth a multiplicity of interorganizational discussions. These controversies tend to be more driven by political competition and less contained by common goals than intra-organizational debates, but they bring a wider range of perspectives to bear. As a result, they can further help to weed out distortions and biases and thus contribute to political learning. As more and more challengers converge on a promising mode of democratic contention, the prospects of success increase further. Thus, organizational development deepens and broadens the processing of information, including external stimuli, and diffusion therefore changes from rash efforts to imitate particularly striking foreign precedents to more considered efforts to learn from a variety of models – which takes time, but brings success.

COMPARATIVE PERSPECTIVES

This book has compared the three main waves of democratization in a longitudinal analysis that spans 150 years. Can the theory proposed in this volume explain additional diffusion processes as well? And can it account for regional variation inside wide-ranging waves, such as the third wave with its global scope? After all, the organizational density of politics varies across geographic areas; accordingly, my macro-structural argument predicts differences among regional diffusion processes.

The following examination concentrates by default on diffusion processes among relatively amorphous, if not inchoate polities. After all, no other region has approximated the organizational density that prevailed in Europe in the early twentieth century and in South America toward the end of the second millennium. In a global comparison, those regions reached particularly high levels of intraorganizational strength (Europe) and interorganizational diversity (Europe and Latin America). The countries at the center of empirical investigation in Chapters 5 and 7, Germany and Chile, scored especially high on these dimensions, respectively. They thus allowed for a clear illustration and plausibility probe of the different aspects of my theory that account for the slowdown and increased success of diffusion.

By contrast, the polities examined in this section rank much lower in organizational density; this was also the case for Europe in 1830. My theory therefore expects that diffusion processes unfold quickly yet achieve only limited success. These clusters of regime contention should approximate the one pole of the negative correlation between diffusion features that the tsunami of 1848 represents. The following analysis can therefore assess whether this side of my theory has broader validity. But since high levels of organizational density are rare, it is unclear whether the combination of low speed and increased success that my theory predicts in those settings also holds broader applicability; alternatively, it could be peculiar to Europe and South America. Due to limited variation – a common problem for theoretical inference in the social sciences – the comparative analysis conducted in the following section is therefore unavoidably truncated.

Given that the polities examined in the following subsections clustered toward the lower end of organizational density, my theory also makes some predictions about the prevailing type of democratic contention. In a nutshell, it expects the predominance of transgressive over contained contention. Due to the weakness of opposition parties and other societal organizations, my theory anticipates mainly mass mobilization and crowd protest, rather than negotiated, pacted transitions. It will be especially interesting to assess this prediction when analyzing the advance of the "third wave of democratization" in various regions: Did this diffusion process play out differently in Africa and Eastern Europe than it had in Latin America? Such cross-regional variation would provide especially strong corroboration for my theory.

Regional Variation in the Third Wave of Democratization

Democratization in Africa

To start the analysis with the third wave of democratization, the way in which it unfolded in different parts of the world indeed varied in line with the main causal factors highlighted by my theory. This diffusion process advanced slowly yet quite successfully in Latin America, where polities have a fairly high level of organizational density. By contrast, the third wave affected Africa more abruptly and swept across the continent faster during the early 1990s, after the dramatic collapse of communism in Eastern Europe (Anglin 1990).[1] Yet at the same time, this riptide had mixed outcomes and produced less effective progress toward democratization (comparative chart in Markoff 2009: 59; for the limited success in Africa, see Young 1996: 60–61, 67; Bratton and van de Walle 1997: 3–8, 116–22, 134–39, 217–18; Clark 1997: 28–33; Joseph 1997: 375–77; Bratton 2009: 340–43; more positive assessment in Lindberg 2006: ch. 3). Thus, the African manifestation of the third wave fits the negative correlation between speed and success found in the diffusion processes that this book has investigated in depth.

African dominoes began to shake as soon as socialism fell in Eastern Europe. Whereas the continent did not have anticommunist bureaucratic-authoritarian regimes and was therefore not affected by their demise in South America during the late 1970s and early 1980s, it did boast self-proclaimed Marxist states that had formerly been aligned with the Eastern Bloc. The implosion of communism in the USSR's European satellites gave these regimes, which already reeled under severe strain from mismanagement, corruption, and economic meltdown, the coup de grace (Anglin 1990; Bratton and van de Walle 1997: 105–6, 134; Gardinier 1997: 150–51; Takougang 1997: 166, 168). Accordingly, it was Marxist Bénin where the signal from Eastern Europe sparked a quick and totally unexpected transition to democracy in early 1990. This dramatic success in turn triggered the rapid diffusion of the mechanism applied for effecting this regime change, a "national conference" (discussed below), especially in Bénin's Francophone neighborhood.[2] Within weeks, protesters in other authoritarian regimes demanded such fora as well, and Gabon's president sought to preempt this pressure by convoking a government-controlled version. By 1991, seven African countries had some form of national conference, which sought to channel street contention into

[1] For an earlier wave of contentious diffusion in Africa during the 1960s, see Hill and Rothchild (1986).
[2] The tremendous appeal of the national conference for boundedly rational actors, which arose from the utterly unexpected, stunning success in Bénin (but which had long-standing roots in French and Francophone political thought: Robinson 1994: 577, 590, 593–96), immediately turned this mechanism into the preferred and predominant mode of democratic contention in West and Central Africa, drowning out alternatives. This subregion thus avoided the diversity of precedents and models that the unexciting nature of Spain's pacted transition allowed to emerge in Latin America.

negotiated transitions (overviews of this wave in Robinson 1994: 580–81, 588–93; Clark 1994). During the same timespan and inspired by the fall of communism as well (Baylies and Szeftel 1999: 88, 90; Southall 1999: 23; Szeftel 1999: 5), democratic challengers in other parts of Africa, especially central and eastern regions, pushed longstanding authoritarian rulers into allowing free and fair elections among multiple candidates (Bratton and van de Walle 1997: 175–77; Daniel, Southall, and Szeftel 1999). The outpouring of demands for freedom at the beginning of the 1990s was so amazing that an expert called it a "virtual miracle" (Joseph 1991: 11).

Just a few years later, however, the same specialist professed his disappointment when commenting on the short- and medium-term outcomes of this rapid wave of democratic contention: "What few analysts anticipated … was that the democratic wave in Africa would crest so quickly or that the countercurrents would surface so swiftly" (Joseph 1998: 3–4). In several countries, autocrats repressed or stifled democratic contention immediately. Elsewhere, for example in Zaire, they dragged their feet during negotiations in "national conferences" or undermined the implementation of their decisions. In other nations, including Zambia, initial transitions were soon reversed as newly elected leaders abolished effective competition and established their own undemocratic hegemony or open authoritarian rule. And in a further group of countries, new governments maintained the outer façade of democracy but surreptitiously hollowed it out and seriously skewed the electoral playing field, moving toward some form of competitive authoritarianism (Levitsky and Way 2010: ch. 6). In sum, the outcomes of Africa's amazing wave of democratic contention were rather mixed (see case studies in Villalón and VonDoepp 2005); the balance sheet was less favorable to freedom and competitiveness than in Latin America (Markoff 2009: 59).

The macro-structural argument of this book can account for these differences across regions: Compared to Latin America, where mass organizations began to arise in the 1930s, African polities have lower organizational density (Fatton 1995: 80, 91; Gyimah-Boadi 1996; Bratton and van de Walle 1997: 83–87). In particular, the imposition of single parties did not allow a pluralistic party system with representative leaders to emerge; and the erosion or implosion of these hegemonic organizations often gave way to a fragmented welter of fluid and fleeting electoral vehicles, many of them organized around "big men." Lower levels of economic development, large-scale informality, and frequent military coups also kept national-level interest associations weak. Oppositionists therefore were not represented by a limited number of authoritative voices, and there was political space for the spontaneous mobilization of amorphous crowds. As my theory predicts, African challengers therefore seem to have relied fairly heavily on the availability and representativeness heuristics. More rashly than their Latin American counterparts, they emulated foreign precedents, even under unpropitious conditions. Therefore, they achieved only mixed success.

Due to the weakly organized nature of African polities, the triggering precedents of this wave were not gradual, negotiated transitions, but more striking, transgressive forms of democratic contention. As Chapter 3 explained, more inchoate societies do not have a set of political leaders that could tame contentious mass energies and initiate and conduct transitions via elite-level bargaining. In Africa, therefore, pacts did not serve as the main mechanism for effecting regime change in nonconfrontational ways; bottom-up protests played a much more important role than in Latin America (Bratton and van de Walle 1997: 82–88, 177–79). This mass contention, in turn, served as a more powerful signal and set in motion faster waves of emulation efforts. In line with the argument of Chapter 3, the organizational weakness of African societies thus shaped the characteristics of the triggering precedents, which in turn help account for the relatively quick spread but mixed success of democratic diffusion.

Africa's organizational deficits became evident in the institutional innovation designed to compensate for them, namely the "national conferences" that proliferated in the early 1990s among Francophone countries. These fora intended to represent all the relevant political forces and thus induce oppositionists to switch from street protest and confrontation to negotiation and compromise.[3] Institutional engineering thus sought to enable polities of limited organizational density to cobble together pacted transitions. But the very underdevelopment and fragmentation of civil societies turned representation in these national conferences into a highly controversial issue (Joseph 1991: 18–19; Nzouankeu 1993: 48; Robinson 1994: 601–07; Gervais 1997: 93–94): Among the welter of weak, fluid organizations that existed in these rather inchoate polities, which deserved seats, and how many? The organizational weakness of the opposition, together with autocrats' active and passive resistance, helps account for the fact that "in the short run, it is apparent that the conferences were at best only modestly successful" (Robinson 1994: 608; Bratton and van de Walle 1997: 112, 196; see also the difference in outcomes emphasized by Heilbrunn 1993: 294–99).

In general, the mixed success of democratization efforts in Africa reflected lower organizational density, which entailed fairly tight bounds of political rationality. There were few representative leaders with a committed, disciplined mass following who commanded the information and experience to assess the domestic power constellation thoroughly and to wait for the right moment before acting on a foreign precedent. And where such leaders did wait, they could easily be outflanked by more spontaneous crowds, as well as by other organizations that did not want to cede the lead in regime contention to such crowds. African polities left considerable room for the contentious initiatives

[3] Bratton and van de Walle (1997: 173). As argued in Chapter 3 (note 11), the effort to make this switch reflects the preference of political elites for negotiation and compromise, which hold lower risks than street contention.

of common people who relied on cognitive shortcuts and were susceptible to the rash inferences such shortcuts yielded; and as soon as regime contention got under way, even organized forces were drawn into these street protests (Bratton and van de Walle 1997: 103, 106). Thus, inferential heuristics, as well as competitive calculations to follow their pull,[4] triggered confrontations with autocrats that were not based on thorough assessments of the political opportunity structure. Challengers confronted incumbents even where defiance had low prospects of success.

The mixed outcomes of the African wave are especially noteworthy because the continent was subject to stronger pro-democratic pressures than Latin America was. By the late 1980s, Western powers and the international financial institutions (IFIs) consistently pushed for political openness and accountable government; and the terrible economic problems plaguing Africa gave the IFIs enormous clout to press these goals via loan conditionality. If one takes this vertical influence into account, which weighed heavily on a region at the bottom of the global hierarchy, the limited success of democratic contention in Africa during the 1990s looks rather unimpressive. The checkered results of the African diffusion process show that external economic and political pressures do not exert a very strong effect; even vis-à-vis weak targets they do not have the overwhelming force that some lines of world system theory postulate.

In sum, the unfolding of the third wave of democratization in Africa confirms the negative correlation of speed and success found in the three diffusion processes analyzed in this book. Moreover, it seems that my theory, especially the macro-structural argument about the lack of organizational density, can account for these patterns.

The Collapse of Communism

Offering further corroboration for my central argument, the dramatic and amazingly rapid collapse of East European communism in 1989 also occurred in countries where autonomous political organization had been suppressed, in these cases by decades of totalitarianism and post-totalitarianism (Linz and Stepan 1996: ch. 17). The nations emulating the Polish precedent had "flattened" civil societies without representative leaders who could command organizational loyalty from broad segments of the citizenry (Howard 2003: 20–28, 82, 105–14, 122–36); this was true even in reform-communist Hungary (Bruszt and Stark 1992: 13–15, 20–21, 30, 42–44, 53). The masses of challengers lacked established overarching organizations and approximated agglomerations of individuals. Among these amorphous crowds, inferences about incumbents' weakness spread very quickly and set in motion cascading decisions to join in democratic contention, as Kuran (1995: ch. 16) and Lohmann (1994,

---

[4] As Chapter 7 explained, similar kinds of indirect competitive calculations led left-wing sectors of Chile's opposition to persist with its protest strategy from 1984 to 1986 despite ever greater awareness of its minimal prospects of success.

2000) elucidated with their formal models; in fact, Kuran's theory (1995: 74, 158–66, 180, 258) invokes some of the same cognitive shortcuts as the present study.

Moreover, as in Africa but different from Latin America, democratic transitions did not advance primarily via negotiation and pact-making, but mostly – and most successfully – via bottom-up contention and "revolutionary movements from below" (McFaul 2002: 222–23, 228–32). The widespread resort to transgressive contention in emulating countries is a particularly striking indication of prevailing organizational weakness because the initial precedent, the Polish roundtable negotiations, constituted an instance of pact-making. Yet while this instance of contained contention signaled incumbents' weakness and thus triggered a wave of challenges across the region, those inspired by the Polish opposition's success were unable to replicate its strategy of transformation; due to widespread organizational weakness, they could rely only on direct mass confrontation. These protests, of course, sent stronger signals to the countries still chafing under communist rule. Secondary diffusion thus added a good deal of fuel to the fire and helps account for the accelerating dynamic of socialism's downfall in all of Eastern Europe during the last few months of 1989.

While an exhaustive analysis of this explosive wave is beyond the scope of this study, the high and increasing speed of this diffusion process suggests the operation of cognitive shortcuts; as regime contention in late 1989 ended up crossing borders within days, there certainly was no time for a thorough, systematic assessment of its prospects and risks. In fact, emulators' reliance on more transgressive contention implied growing risks; defying the harsh Czechoslovak and East German regimes, for instance, required a great deal of boldness. Obviously, more and more citizens were willing and even eager to throw caution to the wind, deviate from rational prudence, and take to the streets despite serious threats of repression. As this striking courage suggests, East Europeans seem to have jumped to the conclusion that the time had finally come to shake off the yoke of communism, and of Russian domination – by whatever means that would take.

Interestingly, the tsunami of regime contention in 1989 brought many effective advances toward democracy. This unusual coincidence of diffusion's speed and success arose from the fact that this swift wave received its principal impulse from a vertical change, namely the withdrawal of Soviet protection for Communist satellite regimes (Brown 2000: 14–16, 19, 32; see also Hale 2013: 342). Whereas all of the other contentious waves examined in this book swept horizontally across autonomous polities, the countries behind the Iron Curtain had, effectively, been colonies of a powerful empire, which had imposed totalitarian rule in the first place, after World War II (Daniels 2000), and which had squashed several earlier challenges to communism with military force (Ekiert 1996). The essential precondition for the wave of 1989 to get under way was the renunciation of the Brezhnev Doctrine, which left Eastern Europe's communist regimes without strength and therefore allowed for effective challenges to externally imposed nondemocracy. Thus, the removal of the Soviet umbrella made these nondemocracies weak – whereas in other rapid diffusion processes, a striking precedent merely made autocrats *look* weak. Horizontal waves are driven by sheer inferences, whereas communism's downfall had an effective vertical trigger – a momentous change in the real world, namely the end of hegemonic imposition.

This abrupt "decolonization" (Daniels 2000) and sudden reestablishment of effective national independence accounts for the exceptional success rate of the quick diffusion process of 1989 in Eastern Europe. Soviet domination was the decisive obstacle that had for decades prevented political progress despite ongoing socioeconomic modernization. As soon as Mikhail Gorbachev removed this exogenous impediment, democracy was bound to emerge: Eastern Europe was more than ready for it. Some countries, especially Czechoslovakia, had already experienced political liberalism and – impressively resilient – democracy during the interwar years (Capoccia 2005: ch. 4). Since then, rising education and development levels had created an ever more propitious setting for democracy throughout the region. East Europeans were eager to attain freedom and had engaged in regime contention whenever an opportunity seemed to arise, as in 1953 in East Germany and 1956 in Hungary and Poland – products of the top-down relaxation of Stalinism (Owen 2010: 189–90) – or in 1968 in Czechoslovakia and in 1980–81 in Poland (Ekiert 1996). Only Soviet tanks had managed to forestall these advances toward democracy; and the traumatic experiences of these brutal interventions had deterred further challenges.[5] In 1989, the revocation of the Brezhnev Doctrine finally allowed citizens to reach their goal and establish the democracy they had patiently longed for (Brown 1991: 53–65; see also Brown 2000: 16, 19). Thus, the lifting of vertical imposition makes the East European wave unique and accounts for the exceptional coincidence of frequent success with dramatic speed.

In conclusion, the unfolding of the third wave of democratization in regions not examined in this book, namely Africa and Eastern Europe, largely corroborates my theory. Where diffusion progressed especially fast, its success rate tended to be lower (with the exception of East-Central Europe); this confirms the negative correlation between these two features. Moreover, greater velocity prevailed in polities that had inchoate or flattened civil and political societies. Organizational weakness in turn tended to go hand in hand with rash, indiscriminate emulation efforts and thus produced very limited success (except in East-Central Europe, where the withdrawal of the Soviet blockage suddenly created obvious opportunities for success). Furthermore, democratic contention in these regions took more transgressive forms than in Latin America; mass mobilization and crowd protests played a much more important role

---

[5] As Germany's current president Joachim Gauck (2011: 203), who had been a leading oppositionist in the communist East, writes in his memoirs: "We knew the defeats, everybody had internalized them," followed by a list of these tragic episodes.

than elite negotiations and pact-making (see recently Stoner et al. 2013: 15). Thus, the theory designed in this volume seems to hold as well, especially in its macro-organizational tenets.

Contentious Waves in Democratization History, 1830–2011

In addition to explaining regional variation inside the broad, heterogeneous third wave of democratization, can my theory also account for other diffusion processes? That is, does it apply beyond the three main waves highlighted in the conceptual discussion of Chapter 1? Given the global advance of political liberalism and democracy over the course of the last two centuries, these sequences of regime contention are distributed unevenly in space and time. There was one early horizontal wave in Europe, namely the revolutions of 1830, which also emanated from France. This riptide unfolded similarly to that in 1848, spreading quickly, yet with limited success; thus, the revolutions of 1830 show that the tsunami of 1848 was not a singular, unique process.

The other waves also advanced at the regional, not global level, yet they played out in recent years in developing areas, namely the color revolutions in the postcommunist world during the early 2000s and the Arab Spring that has stirred up the Middle East and North Africa (MENA) since January 2011. Because all of these clusters of contention occurred in polities of fairly low, inchoate or repressed organization, my theory predicts diffusion processes of high speed and low success.[6] What does the empirical record show, and can my argument make sense of it?

The Revolutions of 1830

Similar to the downfall of Louis Philippe in 1848, the overthrow of his predecessor, French king Charles X, in July 1830 also sent shock waves through Europe and proved quickly contagious.[7] Within one month, this dramatic event, immortalized by Eugène Delacroix's painting "Liberty Leading the People," triggered protests and uprisings in Belgium (Traugott 2010: 109–17), the Prussian Rhineland, Brunswick, and Southern England ("Swing rebellion" – see Rudé 2005: 150–54); then in Saxony, Hessen-Kassel, other German middle states, and Berlin in September; Switzerland in October; and Poland in November (Church 1983: 31–56; Schieder 1975; Holzapfel 1986; Hobsbawm 1996c: 104, 110–11, 117–19; Kermann 2006; Sheehan 1996: 263). Starting in September, the Parisian success also "increased general ferment and dissatisfaction" in

---

[6] These are "regime change cascades" à la Hale (2013), who stresses their dramatic sweep yet low success in "lead[ing] to actual regime change" (Hale 2013: 331).

[7] There was a more limited wave of democratic contention in 1820–21, when Spain's liberal revolution of January 1820 quickly set in motion emulation efforts in neighboring Portugal (1820), Naples and Sicily (1820), and Piedmont (1821); it also had an impact on the Greek war of independence, which started in 1821. Typically, except for the latter effort, all these challenges were suppressed (Pilbeam 1995: 134, 138–42; Altgeld 2002: 268–76; Isabella 2009: 21–41).

Central Italy, although it was "not enough to produce an immediate upheaval," which erupted only in February 1831 (Church 1983: 129–42). This wave thus advanced with similar speed as the riptide of 1848.

The rash of regime contention unleashed by the French Revolution of 1830 also achieved very mixed success (Botzenhart 1985: 105–20; Kossok and Loch 1985). On the one hand, Belgium managed to shake off the rigid rule of the Dutch king and pass a liberal constitution in 1831 (Lamberts 2006: 320–21), which served as a model for many other European countries in subsequent decades. Several Swiss cantons also achieved advances toward political liberalism and democracy (Church 1983: 64–69; Schaffner 1998: 192–203).[8] And in England, the desire to avoid revolutionary upheaval à la Paris contributed to the passing of the Reform Act of 1832, which constituted the first big step in the country's gradual move toward democratization (Ertman 2010: 1007–09).

But on the other hand, a number of uprisings were forcefully suppressed, leading to setbacks for the cause of political liberalism. This tragic outcome prevailed especially in Poland, where the brutal reimposition of tsarist rule forced the country's effective incorporation into the autocratic Russian Empire and eliminated the relative autonomy and constitutional rule that the Vienna Congress had instituted in 1815 (Church 1983: ch. 9; Davies 2005: 238–45). Poland's defeat also produced a stream of exiles, which depleted the country of advocates of political liberalism and national independence.[9] Similarly, Austrian troops squashed the protests, riots, and attempted revolutions that erupted in several Central Italian states (Church 1983: ch. 11), and in Southern England, the Swing rebellion was suppressed. Moreover, conspiracies and revolts in Spain that were inspired by the revolutionary wave sweeping across Europe quickly failed due to divisions among the rebels (Gil Novales 1985: 136–48; Church 1983: 38). Due to these setbacks, the net effect of the 1830 revolutions across European countries was very modest (see Table 1.4).

Inside the German Federation, outcomes were also mixed and overall disappointing. The greatest success was that citizens of the small Duchy of Brunswick managed to chase away their headstrong, arbitrary prince and force the adoption of a constitution. Moreover, Hessen-Kassel elaborated a particularly progressive charter, and Saxony and Hannover also promulgated constitutions (Holzapfel 1986: 108–16; Kermann 2006: 30–39). But these charters were soon suspended or hollowed out as the established dynasties tightened their reign again after the rapid fading of popular protest, especially after 1832 (Schieder 1975: 51–54; Hardtwig 1998: 21–22, 46–50). Many other German

---

[8] Schaffner (1998: 192) claims, however, that "contrary to the claims of later historiography, this [successful contention] was not the consequence of the July Revolution in Paris," but of internal developments in this very inward-looking country.

[9] This hemorrhage, together with the deterrent effect of the severe tsarist repression after 1831, explains why Poland was one of the few European polities that was not affected by the new wave of regime contention in 1848 (Davies 2005: 251–55).

middle states saw little if any progress, regardless of whether they already had constitutions or not. Most importantly, the two great powers, Austria and Prussia, did not cede one inch to the revolutionary wave stimulated by the Parisian precedent and the emulative success in Belgium. In Vienna, faint stirrings of contention were immediately suppressed (Bleiber 1974); in Prussia, riots that erupted in several cities, especially Aachen and Berlin, suffered the same fate (Hammer 1997: 63–68). In sum, diffusion's high speed was associated with meager results.

In line with my macro-structural argument, the inchoate nature of politics can account for this combination of diffusion features. During the 1820s, political mass organization was even more incipient than in 1848. Societal associations and political clubs were at very early stages of formation (Hammer 1997: 104, 132–33, 453, 476–80, 494–95; Hardtwig 1998: 117–24, 138–40). These small and incipient organizations encompassed at best some groups of better-educated citizens but left out the popular masses, the predominant social base of street contention, protest, and rebellion in 1830. Accordingly, ordinary people decided on their own whether to join the gathering wave of contention.

As the micro-foundation of my theory maintains, the decisions of common individuals who lacked representative leaders were shaped profoundly by cognitive shortcuts. While an in-depth analysis of the revolutions of 1830 is beyond the scope of this volume, statements of participants reported in the scholarly literature suggest that the heuristics of availability and representativeness held sway, just as in 1848. A particularly well-documented investigation of the protests in Saxony, for instance, cites impressions of contemporaries that "the 'thunder of the popular uprising in Paris' [appeared] like a 'bolt of electricity that shook up all of Europe.' … When … the first firm news of the happily completed great revolution in Paris arrived, one could see people standing everywhere … and communicate their joy that the net [of repression] covering Germany had been ripped apart" (Hammer 1997: 125). The common usage of the French *tricolore* and the frequent singing and playing of the *Marseillaise*, which in Dresden, "musicians were forced to repeat often six times in a row" (Hammer 1997: 149), demonstrate the inspiration in the French precedent and the hope to replicate this success right away. This immediate effervescence, a typical product of the cognitive shortcuts highlighted in this volume, spurred on demonstrations, protests, and uprisings in a wide variety of settings across Europe, ranging from major cities to small towns and rural areas. The precipitous and indiscriminate nature of these emulation efforts accounts for their very mixed results.

In sum, the July Revolution in Paris set in motion a dramatic wave of regime contention, which achieved only limited progress toward political liberalism – similar to 1848. This finding corroborates the negative correlation between diffusion's speed and its success that my book has highlighted. Moreover, it seems that the theory substantiated in this volume can explain this combination.

In the early nineteenth century, polities were organizationally inchoate, giving the inferential shortcuts of bounded rationality free rein.

The "Color Revolutions" in the Postcommunist World

Among recent diffusion processes, which have played out in developing areas, two regional waves of democratic contention have attracted particular interest from scholars and other observers, namely the color revolutions rippling across the southern and eastern fringe of the postcommunist world from the late 1990s to 2005; and the Arab Spring triggered by protests that erupted in Tunisia in December 2010. Can my theory elucidate these currents, which affected mostly countries with inchoate polities or suppressed civil societies?

In regard to the color revolutions, the main precedent event[10] and its imitation in other countries differed in nature from the street protests and mass assaults examined in this book and discussed in particular depth in Chapter 4. The latter uprisings sought to dismantle the institutional framework of fully authoritarian rule, and they arose mainly from proactive initiatives by the opposition; challengers therefore chose the timing of this transgressive contention. By contrast, the color revolutions combated incumbents' disrespect for the official institutions, especially serious electoral fraud (Kuntz and Thompson 2009). In these competitive-authoritarian regimes, the opposition played by the formal rules of the game, participated in the elections convoked by the non-democratic government, and sought to turn procedures established by autocrats against those rulers (McFaul 2006: 165–66, 190–91). It embarked on contention only when these autocrats violated their own official rules by trying to steal an election (Polese and Ó Beacháin 2011: 116–21).

By contrast to the anti-institutional and proactive revolutions of 1830, 1848, and 1917, the color revolutions were thus pro-institutional and reactive. It was not the opposition that first transgressed the official rules of the game, but the autocrat. Accordingly, the opposition had to respect the institutional calendar defined by the incumbent. Democratic forces could start a color revolution only after elections had been scheduled; and they moved to contention only if the current government engaged in heavy manipulation and tried to "erase" an impending or actual defeat with improper means (for a general model of this kind of contention, see Fearon 2011). Thus, the opposition had little control over the timing of this reparative contention; it could not start a color revolution at any moment it chose, but had to wait for the election called by the incumbent.

---

[10] The literature diverges on the original trigger that set in motion this diffusion process. Whereas the majority of authors highlight the Serbian protests of late 2000 against an election stolen by autocrat Slobodan Milošević (e.g., McFaul 2005: 5; Beissinger 2007; Polese and Ó Beacháin 2011: 112–13, 116–17), Bunce and Wolchik (2011) point to earlier cases in Slovakia in 1998 and Croatia in 2000, but acknowledge (pp. 112–14) that these precedents lacked the postelectoral protests that proved so crucial in Georgia 2003, Ukraine 2004, and Kyrgyzstan 2005. Therefore, I follow the predominant view that depicts Serbia 2000 as the precedent event.

The pro-institutional and reactive nature of the color revolutions imposed clear constraints on their sequential unfolding. Above all, it ruled out rapid diffusion in calendar time. Since challengers did not have the initiative over timing, but had to follow the incumbent's chronology, this mode of democratic contention could not give rise to a dramatic tsunami that was tightly clustered in real time.[11] Instead, the velocity of this diffusion process must be measured in terms of institutional intervals: Did efforts to emulate the precedent occur at the next election that autocrats had scheduled and that they tried to manipulate or steal? In terms of the institutional calendar, the color revolutions indeed proceeded quickly. After the toppling of Serbia's Slobodan Milošević in late 2000 set a dramatic precedent, emulation efforts happened at the next elections at which opposition forces were unfairly denied success, namely in Georgia in 2003, Ukraine in 2004,[12] and Kyrgyzstan in 2005, as well as in Armenia in 2003, 2004, and 2008, Azerbaijan in 2003, 2005, and 2008, and Belarus in 2006 and 2010; moreover, there was a local outburst in Uzbekistan in 2005 and some faint stirrings even in Kazakhstan in 2005 and 2007 (Isaacs 2010: 206–07).

Thus, in regard to institutional time, the color revolutions did spread quickly, broadly, and rather indiscriminately. Emulative contention erupted in a wide range of countries at the first institutionally defined moment at which it could possibly occur. Interestingly, the contention-triggering contests in Georgia and Kyrgyzstan were parliamentary – not presidential – elections (Bunce and Wolchik 2011: 149–50, 163, 166, 323–24), demonstrating the opposition's eagerness to emulate the Serbian precedent at the next possible opportunity. Rashly, oppositionists challenged election-manipulating incumbents not only in less repressive, relatively developed or Western-oriented nations such as Ukraine and Georgia, but also in harshly autocratic systems such as Belarus, booming oil rentier states such as Azerbaijan, and true backwaters without linkages to the West such as Uzbekistan. While scholars have often focused on the success cases only, the methodologically more appropriate expansion of the analysis to failed imitation attempts (Way 2008: 58–59; Ó Beacháin and Polese 2010; Bunce and Wolchik 2011) shows that the color revolutions constituted the kind of swift, precipitous, and unselective diffusion process that – according to my theory – typically occurs in polities of low organizational density.

The former Soviet republics that experienced these emulation efforts indeed had weak civil societies with inchoate party systems. Parties were held together precariously by personal charisma or patronage and corruption, rather than

---

[11] On the contrary, autocrats have every incentive to refuse calling a special election at a time when the precedent of a similar ruler's downfall inspires enthusiasm among challengers and thus facilitates their efforts at electoral mobilization.

[12] Despite serious incumbent manipulation, opposition forces achieved considerable success during Ukraine's parliamentary elections of 2002, which gave them hope for the upcoming presidential contest of 2004 and induced them not to initiate a contentious challenge in 2002.

program orientation and discipline. The opposition lacked firm, broad-based organizations that could have commanded reliable mass support; instead, it consisted of nuclei of activists, welters of nongovernmental organizations (NGOs), fluid movements, and spontaneous crowds. Certainly, the institution-ally conditioned delay in opportunities for emulation efforts allowed commit-ted oppositionists to use the lessons of earlier color revolutions to prepare for reactive contention in their own country. Supported by protagonists of success-ful precedents, such as the Serbian NGO Otpor, small networks in Georgia and especially Ukraine created mechanisms for election observation and laid the groundwork for mass protests.[13] Thus, the color revolutions differed from the unprepared, fully spontaneous diffusion that prevailed in 1848. Instead, emu-lative contention emerged from a kernel of organization, and among these net-works of activists, learning from precedents was quite thorough and systematic (Karatnycky 2006; Demes and Forbrig 2006; Bunce and Wolchik 2011: 132–36, 144, 160, 186, 190, 203, 236, 300–04; McFaul and Youngs 2013: 131–36). But these groupings lacked organizational connections to broader sectors of the citizenry and therefore could not command disciplined mass support for their challenges to fraudulent incumbents (Diuk 2006). In countries with weak civil societies, which includes even Ukraine (Howard 2003: 665–66, 75; Tudoroiu 2007: 316, 328–31), the participation of large numbers of people, which was decisive for making this defiance effectual and which was thus essential for the color revolutions, depended on spontaneous adherence and concurrence. The crucial role of spontaneity is evidenced by the fact that turnout at dem-onstrations and the escalation of contention (especially in Georgia) surprised the instigators themselves (Copsey 2010: 41; Bunce and Wolchik 2011: 138, 164–66, 174–75).

Given the weakness of mass organization and the rapid, broad spread of diffusion, my theory predicts a low rate of success. In fact, many attempts at color revolutions did not achieve their goals – they failed to bring signif-icant, nonfleeting advances toward democracy. While observers highlighted the cases in which incumbent autocrats were dislodged, that is, Georgia 2003, Ukraine 2004, and Kyrgyzstan 2005, there were more instances in which post-electoral protests did not manage to force change, namely Armenia in 2003, 2004, and 2008, Azerbaijan in 2003, 2005 (Alieva 2006), and 2008 (Hess 2010: 31–38), and Belarus in 2006 (Marples 2006) and 2010 (overviews in Bunce and Wolchik 2011: ch. 7 and Levitsky and Way 2010: 205–07, 211–13). Moreover, in two of the three cases of incumbents' overthrow, Georgia and

---

[13] Beissinger 2007; Bunce and Wolchik (2011: 123–25, 136–38, 160–65, 173–74). As Bunce and Wolchik examine a broader set of cases that includes East European countries with somewhat stronger civil societies such as Slovakia, Croatia, and Serbia, they stress organization and plan-ning (p. 303) more than the present analysis does, which follows the conventional delimitation of color revolutions as the attempted emulation of the Serbian precedent in a number of former Soviet republics with amorphous, inchoate civil societies.

Kyrgyzstan, new governments did not bring much democratic improvement over their predecessors, but quickly established their own hegemony, stifled political opposition and the media, and undermined free and fair competition (Hale 2006: 311–20; Tudoroiu 2007: 324–25, 334–35; Mitchell 2009: 172, 178–82; Lewis 2010: 45, 58; Huskey and Hill 2011). Even the political progress achieved in Ukraine remained limited and disappointing; infighting among the weakly organized and undisciplined former opposition soon allowed stalwarts of the authoritarian regime to recapture power – and to roll back the few advances toward democracy that had been accomplished (Tudoroiu 2007: 329–31; Kubicek 2009). For these reasons, a systematic scholarly investigation that measures the democratizing effect of color revolutions, considering the full set of cases, arrives at very sobering findings (Kalandadze and Orenstein 2009).

The disappointing outcomes of the color revolutions resulted in part from their pro-institutional and reactive nature. Because the opposition did not decide the timing of regime contention, but had to wait for an electoral contest scheduled by the incumbent, color revolutions did not spread in one sudden wave, but erupted sequentially in real time. Therefore, the authoritarian rulers of hitherto unaffected nations – just like the oppositionists – had opportunities to learn from earlier precedents, adjust their behavior, and prevent a replication of contention on their own turf. Indeed, whereas the domestic opposition had to await the next election, the incumbent could act right away and undermine the opposition's ability to mount any challenge. Therefore, precisely when the wave of color revolutions seemed to gather steam, a number of post-Soviet rulers, led by Russia's Vladimir Putin (Ambrosio 2010; Finkel and Brudny 2012b), came to harass and repress the opposition more thoroughly and systematically, isolate it from external supporters, rob it of opportunities to do well at the next election, and stifle its capacity for collective mobilization and postelectoral protests (Cheterian 2010; Markus 2010; Fumagalli and Tordjman 2010).

Thus, while successful precedents induced oppositionists to repeat the tactics that had worked so well in Serbia, Georgia, and Ukraine (Beissinger 2007; Bunce and Wolchik 2011), autocrats moved one step ahead and used all means to try to block this repetition. Through their control of the executive branch, incumbent rulers commanded an ample arsenal of instruments for constraining the opposition and preventing it from doing well at future polls. The opposition, by contrast, was rather defenseless because it could not mobilize mass support or strong foreign backing to fight against the constant but low-key harassment and suppression. For these reasons, autocrats soon won the upper hand. Cooperating in their counterrevolutionary efforts, they managed to extinguish this diffusion wave in 2005, just when it seemed to be gaining momentum (Hale 2006: 318–20, 322–25; Spector and Krickovic 2007; Polese and Ó Beacháin 2011: 121–29; Kubicek 2011; Finkel and Brudny 2012a).

In conclusion, the color revolutions exemplify the coincidence of high speed (in terms of the institutional calendar) with low success that this book has documented. As my theory would expect, this diffusion process unfolded in largely inchoate societies that lacked firm, broad-based organizations. While the unusual reactive nature of the color revolutions produced some differences from the usual pattern of spontaneous mass contention and allowed nuclei of more or less organized activists to play a triggering role, the central features of this diffusion wave are in line with the arguments advanced in this book.

The Arab Spring

In contrast to the pro-institutional and reactive approach of the color revolutionaries,[14] the protagonists of the ongoing wave of regime conflict in the Middle East and North Africa (MENA) undertook the kind of proactive anti-institutional challenges that have been much more common in the history of democratic contention.[15] Given that this Arab Spring began to blossom in inchoate polities and suppressed civil societies, my theory expects a diffusion process of high speed and uncertain, very limited success. Indeed, in its amazing sweep through a whole region and beyond, yet meager outcomes, which include severe repression or civil war in several nations, this riptide strongly resembles the tsunami of 1848, as I explain in depth elsewhere (Weyland 2012a).[16]

In both instances, stifling nondemocratic rule that for decades prevented oppositionists from appearing on the political stage with firm collective organizations faced spontaneous outbursts of leaderless challenges from amorphous, fluid crowds that swelled quickly and sought to overwhelm incumbents through frontal mass pressure. Within days of the triggering event, these rebellions spread extraordinarily fast to a wide range of divergent settings. But as this rash, indiscriminate diffusion suggests, contention often erupted under unpropitious circumstances, such as the totally closed, rigid, and brutal regimes of Bahrain, Iran, Libya, Saudi Arabia, and Syria, with faint stirrings even in China. In their overenthusiastic rush to emulation, which betrays the kind of world-embracing optimism prevailing during the "Springtime of the Peoples" in 1848,[17] oppositionists frequently ran into tremendous obstacles and problems. Despite some pro-democratic pressures from the developed West, the Arab Spring has therefore not yielded nearly the immediate success that its initiators expected; in many countries, sustainable advances toward political liberalism and democracy are unlikely. Thus, in its combination of extraordinary velocity

---

[14] For differences to the collapse of communism in 1989 (discussed above), see Way (2011).

[15] The difference is noteworthy. Strikingly, for instance, Egypt's rigged parliamentary elections of late 2010 (Lesch 2012: 23) did not trigger regime contention; but just a few weeks later, the Tunisian precedent had this effect.

[16] I am very grateful to Steven Brooks, Matthew Buehler, and Nivien Saleh for their excellent comments on this section, which draws heavily on Weyland (2012a).

[17] For the Arab wave, see the fascinating participant accounts in Rashed (2011), Ghonim (2012: ch. 5–6), Rashad (2012), and Al-Zubaidi et al. (2013).

and problematic outcomes, the recent wave is very similar to the European diffusion processes of the first half of the nineteenth century.

As the Tunisian revolt gathered steam in early January 2011 and especially as it managed to evict long-ruling autocrat Zine el Abidine Ben Ali on January 14, protests and demonstrations erupted in Jordan on January 14; in Mauritania, Oman, and Sudan on January 17; in Saudi Arabia on January 21; in Egypt on January 25; in Morocco on January 30; in Yemen on February 3; in Iraq on February 10; in Bahrain and Iran on February 14; in Libya on February 15; and so on.[18] Thus, this diffusion process literally progressed day by day,[19] exactly as in 1848. Inspired by the Tunisian precedent and then its quick replication in Egypt, where President Hosni Mubarak was forced out on February 11, emulators across these disparate settings often used the same slogans and symbols. Calls for revolutionary *journées* announced "days of rage," and protesters often intoned the chant coined in Tunisia, "The people want/ demand the overthrow of the regime." Even in faraway China, there were some sporadic calls for a "Jasmine Revolution," the label given to the Tunisian uprising – which provoked an immediate and strikingly disproportionate crackdown (Jacobs 2011).

The fact that the MENA uprisings spread with the same extraordinary speed as the tsunami of 1848 casts doubt on the frequent arguments about the impact of novel communications and networking technologies on democratic contention in the twenty-first century. These claims, inspired by the modernization approach discussed in Chapter 2, emphasize the importance of mass media such as Al Jazeera and of Internet-based social networks such as Facebook and Twitter, which facilitate the instant dissemination of news and the coordination of protest activities.[20] But while these modern technologies found heavy use among challengers in the Arab world, they did not make a significant causal difference;[21] diffusion patterns in 1848 were strikingly similar, long before the invention of these technologies. Participants at that time obtained information almost as quickly via telegraphs and newspapers, and they coordinated their actions and initiated mass demonstrations quite effectively through personal contacts and informal networks.

The only clear causal difference that novel means of communication made was to reduce the role of geographic contiguity.[22] Whereas the tsunami of 1848 had swept across Europe from neighbor to neighbor in concentric expansion,

[18] Useful, comprehensive overviews, charts, and maps in Blight and Pulham (2011); Nordhausen and Schmid (2011); Wikipedia (2011); and Lynch (2012: 80–124).
[19] For instance, Jubran (2013: 125) reports from Yemen: "Tunisia's president was toppled and fled and the next morning the students of Sanaa University took to the streets in celebration" – just like Carl Schurz and his fellow students had done 163 years before!
[20] Harb (2011); Howard and Hussain (2011). For thorough, balanced discussions, see Comninos (2011) and Joseph (2011).
[21] Protagonists of the Egyptian revolt stress this, as reported by Feiler (2011: 120).
[22] I owe this observation to Wendy Hunter.

contagion in 2011 did not advance like such a coherent wave but in an irregular pattern. For instance, the revolutionary impulse jumped from Tunisia directly to Egypt yet inflamed in-between Libya only later. Thus, Al Jazeera, Facebook, and Twitter loosened the geographic clustering of diffusion.

Despite its more fragmented spatial pattern, however, the spread of regime challenges in 2011 was as unselective and indiscriminate as the 1848 tsunami. Contention quickly swept through the whole MENA, not only to a few particular countries where emulation efforts seemed to have especially good prospects of success. Crowd protests challenged various kinds of authoritarian regimes that maintained different levels of repression and governed countries of diverse historical backgrounds, socioeconomic characteristics, and development levels. Imitative contention erupted in relatively open Morocco as well as totally closed Iran, Libya, and Syria; in Lebanon with its prior history of liberalism and democracy and in staunchly autocratic Saudi Arabia; in the neopatrimonial, sultanistic republics of Egypt and Yemen (Goldstone 2011) and the traditional monarchies of Bahrain and Morocco; in the rentier states of Algeria and Libya and in resource-poor Jordan and Yemen.

Typically, and precisely as in 1848, this precipitous spread of emulative challenges to many diverse settings quickly ran into a great deal of trouble and produced much more failure than success. The overoptimistic belief that "Yes, we can, too!" (Shahine 2011; Joseph 2011: 12) frequently turned out to be an illusion. After the wave's initiators in Tunisia and their early emulators in Egypt managed to topple their long-standing rulers, nowhere else did domestic crowds on their own accomplish this feat. In many nations, such as Algeria, Iran, Saudi Arabia, Sudan, and distant China, early stirrings of unrest suffered immediate suppression by overwhelming force. By deterring further challenges and destroying opponents' logistical and organizational capacity, these heavy-handed crackdowns have set back the cause of political liberalism and democracy. Reacting more flexibly, the kings of Jordan and Morocco managed to avoid escalation by granting preemptive reforms;[23] but effectively, these formal-constitutional changes did very little to open up the political system.[24]

Where crowd protests did get under way and escalated to serious threats to authoritarian regimes, rulers have put up a strong fight. The royal family of Bahrain squashed a spiraling mass uprising by brute force, with Saudi help. Bashar al-Assad in Syria keeps trying to accomplish the same feat by unleashing

---

[23] Some of these anticipatory moves were literally cosmetic, such as Jordan queen Rania's change in wardrobe, from glamorous gowns to Palestinian scarves (Buck 2011).

[24] For Morocco, see Chomiak and Entelis (2011: 11–13) and Maddy-Weitzman (2012: 90–92); for Jordan, see Yom (2013). MENA rulers are notorious for offering limited concessions under duress and then taking them back as soon as challenges fade. As King (2009: ch. 2, 4) explains, this was the main strategy with which authoritarianism in the region survived the third wave of democratization unscathed. Of course, this was also the strategy with which many European princes, most prominently Prussia's Friedrich Wilhelm IV, responded to the revolutions of 1848.

his security forces on whole towns and slaughtering hundreds of thousands of citizens, with Russian support. Similarly brutal efforts by Muammar el-Qaddafi in Libya to hunt down the opposition "house by house" like "cockroaches" (Fahim and Kirkpatrick 2011) backfired by triggering armed counterattacks and Western intervention,[25] which eventually managed to topple his erratic reign. But the price was full-scale civil war, which aggravated the profound regional and tribal tensions in this fragmented country – not a promising setting for democracy and the rule of law. And in Yemen, wily fox Ali Abdullah Saleh hung on for many months, using sporadic repression and exploiting the stark divisions plaguing his nation. While sustained pressure from the United States and its Arab allies finally eased him out of the presidency, he and his relatives and cronies have maintained considerable power (Büchs 2011). The country's political fragmentation has spawned an effort to negotiate constitutional agreements through a National Dialogue Conference (MacFarquhar 2013), an interesting equivalent to the national conferences proliferating in Francophone Africa during the early 1990s. But political paralysis, festering conflict, and stalled democratization look like the more likely outcome (Heinze 2013).

Even in Egypt, where the emulation of the Tunisian precedent achieved the greatest initial success, the effective institution of political liberalism and democracy is rather doubtful. The toppling of Hosni Mubarak did not automatically transform the power structure (Stacher 2012; Saleh 2012: 481); for more than a year, the military, the mainstay of authoritarian rule for decades, maintained a stranglehold over civilian politics to protect its own corporate interests (Barany 2011: 33; Kirkpatrick 2012; Lutterbeck 2013; see also Martini and Taylor 2011: 133–34).

Certainly, his election victory of June 2012 allowed President Mohammed Morsi, the Muslim Brotherhood's candidate, to push back against military tutelage. But the new chief executive quickly tried to establish his own political supremacy, raising serious concerns about suffocating the nascent democracy and ushering in another authoritarian regime (*Economist* 2012; Brownlee 2013). Besides Morsi's personal intentions, the Muslim Brotherhood's effective commitment to political pluralism, freedom, and competition remained unclear.[26] As the only firm, nationwide organization with long-standing roots among the popular sectors, this political force seemed to have good chances of cementing its hold on power. By contrast, the urban, modern, middle-class protesters who spearheaded the 2011 uprising lost out in the legislative and presidential contests. These liberal, democratic forces lack any solid, broad-based, and unified organization and do not have close connections to or affinities with the majority of citizens, who are poor, traditional, and often illiterate.

---

[25] As Ross (2011: 2) argues, without Western intervention, Qaddafi would have squashed the rebels.
[26] Trager (2011: 120–25); Wickham (2011); more sanguine Lübben (2013). For an optimistic assessment, see Hamid (2011); for a pessimistic analysis of sectarian conflict, see Tadros (2011).

Yet despite their electoral weakness, these modern, liberal sectors retained the capacity to instigate mass protests. In mid-2013, millions of Egyptians voiced their discontent over the president's exclusionary approach, which seemed to privilege the quest for power over broad-based efforts to address the ever more pressing problems facing the country, especially unemployment and crime. This outburst of crowd contention quickly induced the military, which had retained more power than the president thought (Kirkpatrick and El Sheikh 2013), to depose Morsi, finding support even among hard-core Islamists. Predictably, this coup triggered protests by the Muslim Brotherhood, which led to considerable bloodshed and left the country more divided than ever (*Economist* 2013). Modern, liberal sectors, in turn, are tainted by their push for a military coup against the first president to emerge from a democratic election (Knipp 2013). These paradoxes and self-contradictions, tensions and resentments create a very cloudy outlook for democracy. Whether the main contenders for power, especially the Muslim Brotherhood and the military (Albrecht 2012: 252, 264–70; Stepan and Linz 2013: 21–22), but also the electorally weak and therefore not-very-democratic liberals (Brownlee 2012), will submit to the whole system of democratic rules and procedures is questionable.

Due to all these problems, limitations, and setbacks, the short- and medium-term outcomes of the Arab Spring have been disappointing (Valenzuela 2012; Schlumberger, Kreitmeyr, and Matzke 2013: 51–52, 57) – just as in 1848. In fact, in its annual assessment of civil and political rights, Freedom House counted more cases of deterioration than improvement in the MENA during 2011 (Puddington 2012: 77–82). On balance, 2012 brought no turnaround either as instances of progress (especially in Egypt and Libya) were counterbalanced by further worsening elsewhere (Iraq, Jordan, Kuwait, Lebanon, Oman, Syria, and the United Arab Emirates; Puddington 2013: 46–55). The mid-2013 coup in Egypt and the subsequent trend toward a restoration of authoritarian rule sustained by the military has entailed a further setback.

As in the African wave of the early 1990s, the meager success of the Arab Spring and the limited prospects for substantial progress toward political liberalism and democracy are especially noteworthy because this diffusion of political regime conflict unfolded under the watchful eyes of the democratic West. While the United States had long supported its many autocratic friends in the region, its official commitment to human rights and popular sovereignty prompted in early 2011 a cautious shift of course in the face of widespread, predominantly peaceful protests. In particular, Western countries have tried to restrict the use of repression by challenged incumbents, leaning more or less heavily on the allied rulers of Bahrain, Egypt (Lynch 2011), and Yemen and sanctioning or attacking U.S. enemies, especially the dictators of Libya and Syria. Without these external restraints, which were not in operation in 1848, the fate of the Arab uprisings would have been even bleaker, especially in Libya and Yemen.

In sum, the Arab Spring shows the same coincidence of high speed and low success that this study has found in other diffusion processes and that anchors the negative correlation highlighted in Chapter 1. The parallels of this twenty-first century wave with the tsunami of 1848 are particularly striking: The precipitous, indiscriminate spread of regime contention yields frequent failure.

My explanation for the events of 1848 also seems to account for the recent MENA events (as demonstrated in depth in Weyland 2012a). In a nutshell, the absence or suppression of broad-based organizations and of representative leaders who could authoritatively guide the decision-making of citizens and the mobilization of contentious crowds has given cognitive shortcuts free rein. These heuristics have produced rash inferences about the replicability of the Tunisian model, which in turn have prompted many immediate, but ill-considered and imprudent emulation efforts. By challenging rulers under unpropitious circumstances, oppositionists have not managed to make much headway.

Since decades of authoritarian imposition have stifled organizational development in the MENA, broad-based associations and consolidated mass parties have been rare; Arab societies have lacked organizational density (Langohr 2004: 181–93; King 2009: 96, 104–06, 110, 125–30; Ottaway and Hamzawy 2009: 7–10; Beinin and Vairel 2011: 17; Vairel 2011: 33–38; Brownlee, Masoud, and Reynolds forthcoming, ch. 6: 20). Given the absence or suppression of collective actors that represented large segments of the citizenry, the distribution of political preferences and power was opaque and ordinary individuals did not have representative leaders who guided their political actions. Small nuclei of activists had for years tried to stir up regime contention, most prominently in Egypt, but because they lacked mass organization their sporadic protests elicited very limited support (Albrecht 2007: 66–74; Filiu 2011: 47–53; Ghonim 2012: 101–16). The sudden participation of tens and hundreds of thousands of discontented citizens in early 2011 was spontaneous, not guided by representative leaders and engineered by disciplined organizations (Shahid 2011).

Even the Muslim Brotherhood in Egypt, the exceptional case of a firm organization with broad societal roots, did not take the lead in the effort to replicate Tunisia's success (Wickham 2011: 212; Lübben 2013: 169; in general Schlumberger, Kreitmeyr, and Matzke 2013: 49).[27] Decades of repression had forced it to adopt a cautious, risk-averse posture, which induced its leadership to wait on the sidelines when protests erupted and quickly mushroomed in early 2011. In Egypt as in the remainder of the MENA, the uprising convoked and coordinated by loose networks of activists was spearheaded by fluid movements and spontaneous, leaderless crowds.[28] In fact, some of the

---

[27] Similarly, Egyptian trade unions joined the protests late, only during the last three days of the Mubarak regime (Bishara 2012: 93–99).

[28] Numerous "tweets from Tahrir" reproduced in Nunns and Idle (2011, 54, 56, 81, 84, 90–91, 96, 184) insisted on the spontaneous nature of this contention, the insignificant role of politicians who claimed leadership, and the noninvolvement of Egypt's principal political organization, the Muslim Brotherhood.

protagonists, such as Egypt's Wael Ghonim, creator of a crucial Facebook page, long remained invisible and anonymous to avoid repression (Ghonim 2012; Saleh 2012: 480). As in Europe during the mid-nineteenth century, mass contention lacked firm organization, well-oiled discipline, and authoritative leadership. Rulers in Cairo were at a loss when they undertook negotiation efforts in February 2011: Who could really speak for the rebellious masses? The absence of disciplined organizations is also evident in the fact that popular mobilization quickly receded and that the temporary unity of opposition forces fragmented immediately (Kasinof 2011; Masoud 2011; Valenzuela 2011).

Because regime contention in unorganized polities carried tremendous uncertainty and risk and because the lack of representative, organizational leadership placed the decision on whether to participate in the hands of ordinary citizens, cognitive shortcuts held unfettered sway, and political rationality has been tightly bounded. The availability heuristic drew enormous attention to the stunning precedents of Tunisia and then Egypt; and the representativeness heuristic suggested to large crowds that they could achieve a similar feat in their own country. All eyes were directed toward Tunis and then Cairo; events there sparked many people's imagination and raised their hopes. Consequently, challengers employed the symbols of these uprisings throughout the region and chanted the same slogans from Morocco in the west to Sudan in the south and Iran in the east.

The importance of the Tunisian and then Egyptian events as the essential catalysts is obvious. Discontent fueled by a host of serious problems had brewed for many years in the MENA. In some countries such as Egypt, fluid networks of activists had tried hard to spark contention on several earlier occasions.[29] But these efforts had never found much resonance. What changed in early 2011 and triggered mass demonstrations that in their breadth, intensity, and courage surprised even their initiators was the dramatic impact of the Tunisian precedent, which in line with the availability heuristic quickly captivated observers of all stripes.[30] Jumping to conclusions, discontented people in a wide range of countries immediately inferred via the representativeness heuristic that the time had come to defy their own rulers. Citizens across the MENA rashly believed that if Tunisians could topple their autocrat, they could probably replicate this feat. Due to this shortcircuit, the Tunisian example and the Egyptian events inspired the questionable belief that autocrats across the Arab world were vulnerable and that critical masses of people were ready

---

[29] As Cheterian (2011: 2) emphasizes, some of these efforts were inspired by the postcommunist color revolutions discussed in this chapter.

[30] For Libya, Mesrati (2013: 80) reports: "Mere hours before the start of the revolution in 2011, the very idea of such an uprising was still a joke to be bandied about on Facebook and Twitter. No one believed that Libyans would actually engage in a savage confrontation with Gaddafi." Yet right after Egyptians' success in evicting strongman Mubarak, "on the night of 15 February, Libya rose up" (ibid.: 81).

and able to force their dictators out. Participant accounts clearly reveal these rapidly congealing – but logically problematic – convictions.

The unfettered operation and powerful impact of the availability and representativeness heuristics is especially well-documented in the Egyptian case, where modern electronic media recorded participants' assessments and beliefs "in real time." Indeed, within minutes of receiving the news of Ben Ali's forced departure, an Egyptian activist, Tarek Shalaby, tweeted in response to the message, "Tunisians are the heroes of the Arab world:" "WE WILL FOLLOW!" (reproduced in Nunns and Idle 2011: 27). As mobilizational energy built up in Cairo over the following days, another cyber activist, Gigi Ibrahim, tweeted: "There is nothing that #Mubarak can do now to prevent the madness that will end his regime ... IT WILL HAPPEN THIS YEAR!! #DownWithMubarak 2011" (in Nunns and Idle 2011: 28). In the run-up to a large demonstration, Ibrahim announced with the certainty that is typical of the representativeness heuristic: "I am sure Egypt will rise up tomorrow on a Friday just like Tunisia did on a Friday also!" On the same day, with a bit more caution, Hossam el-Hamalawy remarked: "No one knows what tomorrow is gonna be like. But I'm very hopeful. I'm very optimistic Mubarak's reign is about to end" (both in Nunns and Idle 2011: 56). Finally, on February 11, right after Egypt's pharaoh had been evicted, Ibrahim wrote, "Thank you Tunisians 4m [sic] the bottom of my heart. Algeria, Yemen, Jordan, Palestine, Saudi, Syria & Libya: keep fighting, nothing is impossible" (in Nunns and Idle 2011: 220).

These raw, unvarnished expressions of participants' surprisingly optimistic beliefs, sent at the spur of the moment from the midst of mass demonstrations and street battles, best reflect the operation of cognitive shortcuts and their crucial contribution to propelling emulative contention. After detailing his earlier mobilizational efforts, which achieved little success and seemed headed into a cul-de-sac, Wael Ghonim (2012: 131) similarly wrote in his memoir: "But history kept intervening ... events outside Egypt suddenly gave us the spark we needed .... The victory of the people of Tunisia would send a strong message ... to our Facebook page members: we can effect change in Egypt." As Ghonim observed, "Analogies between Tunisia and Egypt were increasingly being drawn" (Ghonim 2012: 133); there was "mounting anger of many Egyptians who sought to replicate this situation with Mubarak" (Ghonim 2012: 136). Therefore, after some hesitation due to the obvious risks, Ghonim felt it "necessary to completely reposition [a limited protest] event" [that he had already called before Ben Ali's overthrow] and found himself "unable to resist the word *revolution*. Every time I attempted to steer away from it in my thoughts, it kept coming back" (Ghonim 2012: 136). The last statement reveals how the powerful inferences produced by the representativeness heuristic pushed aside the caution that – given obvious risks – a conventional rational assessment counseled. As a result, Ghonim (2012: 137) announced on his Facebook page: "After all that's happened in Tunisia, my position has changed. Hopes for real political change in Egypt are much higher now."

In more dramatic terms, film director Mohamed Diab recalls that after an ill-supported protest at the very beginning of 2011:

The chains of helplessness dangled menacingly .... Then a complete miracle appeared, almost out of nowhere. On the 14th of January, a mere week after the failed mourning/ protest, beautiful Tunisia brushed oppression off its shoulders and sent out the brightest beacon of hope to hit the Arab world in over fifty years .... On that glorious day, my Facebook status read: 'Our ordeal appears to be as good as over. It is now only a matter of time.' (Cited in Rashad 2012, 10)

Shaking off the frustration of several earlier failures, activist Mohamed Shawky also believed in the run-up to the initial protest of January 25: "I think it is all coming together because of Tunisia .... This one will be different. I can feel it in my bones .... This will not be like the meager gathering in 2005 [and other futile challenges]. *This* one ... we will have our revolution. It can really happen."[31]

In rational terms, the single precedent of Tunisia, potentially a product of accidental factors, should not have transformed people's assessments of opportunities and risks so thoroughly. Why jump to the conclusion that this foreign precedent can be replicated in a whole host of additional countries that have different domestic power constellations and experience variegated political conjunctures? The immediate tipping of citizens' beliefs,[32] the switch from long years of resignation and acquiescence to sudden contention, reveals the operation of the availability and representativeness heuristics. Only these shortcuts can account for the fulminant take-off of diffusion, which certainly did not reflect prudent cost-benefit assessments.[33]

In sum, the most recent and still ongoing wave of political regime contention has displayed precisely the features emphasized in this book, namely amazing speed combined with limited, questionable success. Participant testimony shows that rash inferences derived via cognitive shortcuts drove this tsunami. These heuristics prevailed because broad-based organizations were absent, weak, or repressed in the MENA and common people did not have

---

[31] Cited in Rashad (2012: 123). Cognitive shortcuts also affected people's thinking and decision-making in a wide range of other countries, such as Morocco (Abdelmoumni 2011; Najib 2011) and Libya (quoted in *El Mercurio* 2011).

[32] This tipping of beliefs, driven by cognitive inferences from a striking foreign precedent, also seems to have underlain the shift from "dispiriting" to "emboldening emotions" among emulators of Tunisia-style protests in other MENA countries, which Pearlman (2013) highlights as a complement to my bounded rationality explanation (Weyland 2012a). Whereas emotions such as anger and indignation fueled the original, domestically caused spread of protest inside Tunisia (Pearlman 2013: 394–96), the subsequent diffusion wave was triggered by the sudden belief derived from Ben Ali's downfall that challenges to seemingly powerful autocrats were feasible and promising.

[33] These causal mechanisms also can account for the observations of area specialists such as Eva Bellin (2012: 137, 141) and Marc Lynch (2012: 101, 103), who stress the euphoria and enthusiasm driving the protesters.

representative leaders to follow. Thus, my theory can explain the unfolding and preliminary outcomes of this wave as well.

Interestingly, a brand-new quantitative analysis of the Arab Spring confirms my bounded-rationality explanation. While statistical data cannot directly capture the micro-mechanisms that I hypothesize, especially the operation of cognitive shortcuts, they can test for their observable implications. Proceeding in this way, Bamert (2013) finds that the Tunisian and then the Egyptian success precipitated diffusion waves at lightning speed – probably without much careful, systematic deliberation. And this emulative contention spread across countries without any regard for their degree of similarity; contrary to conventionally rational expectations, even crucial differences in societal development level, specific regime type, and governmental repressiveness made no difference in oppositionists' eagerness to emulate the Tunisian and Egyptian precedents. Bamert (2013: 27) therefore concludes that "protest imitation followed the patterns suggested by bounded rational learning."

This brief analysis of several additional waves of regime contention corroborates the main findings of the present book. Above all, the negative correlation between diffusion's speed and its rate of success is clear and strong. The swift spread of protests usually fails to dislodge authoritarian regimes and bring significant progress toward democracy. Sparks that fly quickly and widely draw a great deal of attention and excitement but do not transform the political landscape. In fact, the enthusiasm and hope unleashed by dramatic precedents inspire an outburst of ill-considered challenges under unpromising conditions, many of which end up failing. This unrealistic optimism in turn results from the cognitive shortcuts introduced in Chapter 2, which hold special sway in polities of low organizational density. This macro-organizational factor thus shapes the operation of bounded rationality, the micro-foundation highlighted in this study.

Moreover, the comparison of the most recent contentious wave, the Arab Spring, with the oldest diffusion processes, the revolutions of 1830 and 1848, casts doubt on a potential alternative to my theory. Observers may wonder whether it was the global increase in the amount and quality of information that loosened the bounds of rationality, brought a more calculated, less precipitous response to external precedents, and boosted the success of emulative regime contention. Thus, the secular process of rationalization that modernization theory predicts, rather than the macro-organizational developments I emphasize, could drive the change in diffusion patterns examined in Chapters 4 through 7.

This world-historical argument founders on the experiences of the Arab Spring, however, which almost two centuries later, in a radically different informational and technological setting, is repeating the empirical patterns and causal mechanisms of the revolutions of 1830 and 1848. These striking similarities suggest that the quantity of information as such is not decisive for reshaping diffusion processes; what is crucial is the processing of information by experienced leaders of pluralistic organizations, as it happened in Europe beginning in the late nineteenth century. These representative leaders have better access to relevant information due to their institutional position, which leads to regular contacts with other groupings of potential contenders and even with the established, nondemocratic authorities. Furthermore, representative leaders rely on internal mechanisms of deliberation and debate to cross-check their inferences and consider their options, bringing to bear their prior experiences. Thus, what is important is not the raw amount of public information, but the inside information at the disposal of organizational leaders and the more thorough way in which they digest these multiple streams of information.

The protagonists of the Arab Spring certainly enjoyed easier access to a much wider range of information than the revolutionaries of 1830 and 1848. From a rational choice perspective, this improvement should have led to better calibrated, more successful political action. But the MENA protests spread precipitously and indiscriminately and have had meager outcomes, no better than in the mid-nineteenth century. In the real world of bounded rationality, more and more information is a distinctly mixed blessing, especially when – as in the Internet era – ease of information access tends to trump reliability and quality. The overabundance of information may induce more, and more unthinking, reliance on cognitive shortcuts: How else can we cope with the flood rushing toward us daily? Also, modern technology gives information overwhelming immediacy and vividness: Real-time video footage of the protests in Tahrir Square, for instance, served as a much stronger trigger of the availability heuristic than newspaper reports with their black-and-white etchings of barricade fighting in Paris. As the rash diffusion of contention in the MENA suggests, the expert discussions on the McNeil-Lehrer show did not manage to contain the resulting effervescence. There was indeed better information in 2011 than in the first half of the nineteenth century; but because for many regular mortals, "availability" beat relevance and quality, improvements in judgment proved limited. Even in the early twenty-first century, critical masses of unorganized people in a variety of countries responded to a dramatic precedent with rapid imitation efforts, as their European forebears had done almost 200 years earlier.

BROADER THEORETICAL IMPLICATIONS

My empirical findings and theoretical conclusions speak to several broader debates that focus on diffusion, both in the real world of politics and in the abstract universe of social science. First, my analysis of the cross-national spread of political impulses sheds light on the much-discussed topic of globalization. In particular, how strong are the pressures toward convergence that countries have faced in the modern era? Second, my explanation is itself a product of diffusion, namely the import of cognitive-psychological insights into political science. Yet it pushes this learning from another discipline one step forward by integrating these imported micro-foundations more closely with the macro-factors of our discipline than is commonly done. Specifically, my theory specifies not only how cognitive heuristics shape political decision-making, but also how organizational developments affect the bounds of political rationality, as the very last section discusses.

Diffusion is widely seen as a symptom and important contributor to the advance of globalization. The predominant view is that improved communication and transportation disseminate more and more innovations and precedents ever faster to an ever wider range of countries. This spread of similarity amid diversity produces a strong, almost irresistible move toward convergence. Globalization thus means growing uniformity and the erosion of differences among the nations of this globe. In metaphorical terms, globalization looks like a broad, strong stream that is fed by the confluence of many tributaries and that carries a great deal of flotsam to the same destiny.

The findings of the present book, by contrast, suggest a more differentiated picture. The observation that poses the puzzle for this book, namely the negative correlation between diffusion's speed and success, already casts doubt on the conventional view, which would expect parallel trends. Rather than a single stream, globalization resembles a welter of currents and cross-currents, eddies and whirlpools, and may well branch out into a delta (cf. Rosenau 2003: ch. 9). Indeed, the heterogeneity and fragmentation of this process seems to increase over time. Waves of democratization were more uniformly fast in the early nineteenth century, when most polities were organizationally inchoate, than in recent decades, given the fairly broad-based parties and interest associations that have formed in some regions. As the comparison of various regional manifestations of the "third wave" shows, diffusion in the late twentieth century played out differently in different areas of the globe and brought different levels of progress toward political liberalization and democracy.

The negative correlation between speed and success also means that diffusion does not entail an ever stronger sweep toward convergence. Swift riptides do not produce much effective change; slower waves are more successful because emulators take the domestic situation into account. Moreover, negotiated transitions, which have come to predominate in organizationally denser polities, involve adjustments and adaptations, rather than the simple repetition of an external precedent. Emulating countries do move toward the same broad regime type, but in different political-institutional variants; for instance, they vary in the powers assigned to the executive branch vis-à-vis the legislature; the authority and independence of the judiciary; and the effectiveness of civilian control over the armed forces.

The ideological differentiation of collective organizations and their gravitation toward diverse foreign models further deepened the heterogeneity of diffusion processes, as Chapter 7 exemplified. Whereas in 1830 and 1848, waves of contention emanated from a single source and spread concentrically, in the 1970s and 1980s there were several catalysts that spurred different currents, which in turn intersected in complicated ways. In the nineteenth century, diffusion had a radial pattern, sprouting spokes from one hub; during the twentieth century in Europe and Latin America, it became ever more fragmented and decentered because external precedents and organized groupings drawn to them multiplied. Diffusion waves lost their single message and clear voice and turned into polyphony or even cacophony.

This multiformity reduced the pressure toward convergence. The spread of one distinct message has a greater immediate impact than that of several incongruent messages. Whereas in 1848, actors of different persuasion were captivated by the same impulse and swept up in a potent tsunami, the surges, crosscurrents, and whirlpools of the third wave left more room for maneuver. Potential emulators had some liberty to pick and choose their own source of inspiration; and they could learn from one model's failure and embrace a more promising option. External impulses became less overwhelming; domestic agency turned more important. Accordingly, as Chapter 6 emphasized, the third wave constituted less of a clear-cut wave than the riptide of 1848.

In conclusion, this study helps correct simplistic images of globalization. It demonstrates the tremendous complexity of this multifaceted process, which does have powerful momentum, but also leaves domestic actors many options of response. In fact, my theory suggests ways to shape the process and outcomes of globalization itself, especially by improving the processing of external impulses. According to the macro-organizational argument substantiated in this book, mechanisms of political decision-making that are open to a plurality of voices and that allow for debate and criticism are decisive; homogeneous, close-knit teams that can breed "groupthink" need to be avoided. While this insight undergirds an obvious preference for democracy at the level of the political regime (cf. Lindblom 1965), and for "teams of rivals" at the level of the government, in the area of contentious politics it suggests the crucial importance of forming wide-ranging organizations that encompass various sectors and that give voice to diverse viewpoints. As the case studies in this volume have shown, the representative leaders of these organizations can more thoroughly assess the promise and value of external precedents and better keep the potentially distorted inferences provided by cognitive shortcuts in check. Essentially, individuals are overburdened by the complexity of the modern world; broad-based, pluralistic organizations are better able to cope.

With this fundamental point, my book also speaks to the controversial debate whether diffusion processes – and globalization in general – bring progress or lead emulators astray. On this issue, rational choice suggests an optimistic answer. Imitation decisions should bring improvements because they rest on careful information processing and systematic cost-benefit analyses. Some versions of constructivism yield the opposite prediction. If innovations spread because they turn into status symbols or even fads, then they may not work in new, different settings and even have deleterious consequences.

For instance, if backward countries eagerly import modern models that they cannot realistically sustain, they court failure, if not disaster.

The present book eschews these polar predictions and arrives at a differentiated answer, which emphasizes the features of different diffusion processes and the importance of recipient polities' organizational density. Ironically, dramatic and rapid waves of regime contention that evoke great excitement end up yielding disappointing results and can cause considerable human cost. As my discussion of the tsunami of 1848 and the Arab Spring suggests, wildfires do not contribute much to the construction of democracy. Instead, they turn out to be flashes in the pan, and they can even burn the cooks' fingers. By contrast, challenges that spread slowly because emulators wait for a promising political opportunity have much better prospects. These more controlled diffusion processes tend to bring a great deal of progress. In particular, they allow even countries that on their own may not have moved so far to take significant steps toward political liberalism and democracy.

My book argues that these differences in the processing of external stimuli and in the very catalysts and corresponding features of diffusion processes depend on organizational macro-structures, especially the emergence of broad-based parties and interest associations. This finding in turn suggests that there is some room for deliberate improvement. Political forces that create, strengthen, and broaden parties and unions help loosen the bounds of political rationality and thus boost the benefits and lower the risks of contentious waves. Although such upgrades in the organizational density of polities are difficult to engineer and can advance only at a glacial pace, the payoffs in the era of globalization promise to be substantial. Learning from foreign impulses and models is likely to improve in depth and quality, and it becomes easier to avoid international fads and fashions.

Besides examining and explaining the features of diffusion processes that play out in the political world, this study is an example of diffusion at the theoretical level. After all, it draws on insights from another discipline, namely cognitive psychology, and applies them in political science. This importation seeks to replace an earlier transplant, namely the rational-choice assumptions that political scientists borrowed from the field of economics. The premises of rational utility maximization and optimal information-processing provided the axiomatic micro-foundations on which rational-choice authors in their attack on macro-approaches such as culturalism, socioeconomic structuralism, and sociological institutionalism insisted.

But innumerable laboratory experiments and field studies have conclusively shown that rational micro-foundations lack realism and therefore cannot serve as productive building blocks for empirical analysis. Above all, cognitive psychologists have demonstrated that normal mortals deviate systematically from the postulates of rational choice, relying instead on bounded rationality (McFadden 1999; Kahneman and Tversky 2000; Thaler 2000; Camerer et al. 2004). By uncovering the normal patterns of human decision-making and documenting the inferential heuristics that people actually use, cognitive psychology offers alternative, empirically corroborated micro-foundations for political analysis. To start their research from a solid base, growing numbers of political scientists have drawn on these findings and used them productively for elucidating a variety of substantive issues (Levy 1997; McDermott 1998, 2004; Jones 2001; Weyland 2002, 2007, 2009; Jones and Baumgartner 2005).

Yet by applying psychological insights in political science, this literature imports the causal mechanism from a discipline that focuses primarily on individual-level decision-making. Many political phenomena, however, involve strategic interaction, collective action, and the institutional aggregation of individual choices and therefore require a higher level of analysis. For political science to properly digest this "foreign" import, it needs to extend bounded-rationality arguments to this macro-level and thus integrate them squarely into the study of politics.

This book takes an important step in this direction by embedding micro-foundations supplied by cognitive psychology in sociopolitical macro-factors. In this way, it makes bounded-rationality arguments more useful for understanding and explaining political decision-making and its outcomes. Specifically, my theory integrates cognitive-psychological micro-foundations with organizational developments. It shows how and why inferential short-cuts shape political decision-making, collective action, and conflict among various contenders, which in turn affect macro-phenomena such as political regime change. Yet it also shows how macro-structures, especially the emergence and type of political organizations, shape the operation of bounded rationality and cause differential deviations from the postulates of rational choice. Thus, organizational factors highlighted by political science affect the way in which cognitive-psychological micro-mechanisms play out in the sphere of political decision-making. My new theory does not simply layer macro-factors on top of micro-foundations, but stresses the thorough interaction between these two levels and integrates insights stressed by the two disciplines.

As argued in Chapter 2 and demonstrated especially in Chapter 5, broad-based organization that guarantees pluralism and internal debate loosens the bounds of rationality. As representative leaders submit their judgments and proposals to scrutiny and discussion, the perspectives of various actors are brought to bear and the rash inferences suggested by cognitive heuristics can be cross-checked and corrected. In inchoate societies, by contrast, political decision-making falls to ordinary individuals, who tend to lack solid information and political experience. Therefore, they rely heavily on inferential shortcuts and are fully exposed to the resulting distortions. And in small, close-knit groupings that seek ideological homogeneity and thus resemble sects, groupthink often prevails. In this hothouse atmosphere, problematic judgments derived from cognitive heuristics can fester and prompt excessively ambitious and particularly unpromising courses of action. In sum, organizational patterns examined by political science thoroughly shape the bounds of political rationality.

By substantiating these arguments, this book advances theorizing about bounded rationality in politics. Scholars who have imported cognitive-psychological findings to politics have treated bounded rationality as if it were uniform. But besides individual-level variations examined by psychologists, the aggregation mechanisms that are crucial to collective action and political decision-making profoundly affect the bounds of rationality and condition how tight they are. My comparisons of regime contention during different waves of diffusion demonstrate the importance of organizational factors. Further research needs to probe other political-institutional features and thus elaborate a bounded rationality approach that fully captures politics. Only then can scholars gain a comprehensive understanding of political decision-making in the real world and of its sometimes fascinating and sometimes disappointing outcomes.

Bibliography

Abbott, Andrew. 2001. *Time Matters: On Theory and Method*. Chicago: University of Chicago Press.

Abdelmoumni, Fouad. 2011. Nous sommes tous des Tunisiens! *Tel Quel* (January 22–28): 24–25.

Aberbach, Joel, Robert Putnam, and Bert Rockman. 1981. Paths to the Top. In Aberbach, Putnam, and Rockman, eds. *Bureaucrats and Politicians in Western Democracies*, 46–83. Cambridge, MA: Harvard University Press.

Abreu, Alzira Alves de. 2005. A Mídia na Transição Democrática Brasileira. *Sociologia, Problemas e Práticas* 48: 53–65.

Abugattas, Luis. 1987. Populism and After: The Peruvian Experience. In James Malloy and Mitchell Seligson, eds. *Authoritarians and Democrats: Regime Transition in Latin America*, 121–43. Pittsburgh: University of Pittsburgh Press.

Acevedo, Patricio. 1983. Jorge Lavandero: "Hay que leer entre líneas..." *Análisis* 6:57 (May): 23–25.

Ahlquist, John, and Margaret Levi. 2011. Leadership: What It Means, What It Does, and What We Want to Know About It. *Annual Review of Political Science* 14: 1–24.

Albert, Bill. 1988. The War and the Workers. In *South America and the First World War*, 233–305. Cambridge: Cambridge University Press.

Albrecht, Holger. 2012. Authoritarian Transformation or Transition from Authoritarianism? In Bahgat Korany and Rabab El-Mahdi, eds. *Arab Spring in Egypt: Revolution and Beyond*, 251–70. Cairo: American University in Cairo Press.

2007. Authoritarian Opposition and the Politics of Challenge in Egypt. In Oliver Schlumberger, ed. *Debating Arab Authoritarianism*, 59–74. Stanford: Stanford University Press.

Albuquerque, José Augusto Guilhon de, and Eunice Durham, eds. 1987. *Simpósio: A Transição Política – Necessidade e Limites da Negociação*. São Paulo: Reitoria da Universidade de São Paulo.

Alieva, Leila. 2006. Azerbaijan's Frustrating Election. *Journal of Democracy* 17:2 (April): 147–60.

Allamand, Andrés. 1999. *La Travesía del Desierto*. Santiago: Aguilar.

　1993. *La centro-derecha del futuro*. Santiago: Editorial Los Andes.

　1989. *Discursos, entrevistas y conferencias*. Santiago: Editorial Andante.

Almeyda, Clodomiro. 1984. Mirando a la Argentina. *Análisis* 7:88 (August 14), paid insert (*Solicitada*): 1–8.

Almond, Gabriel, and G. Bingham Powell. 1978. *Comparative Politics*. Boston: Little, Brown.

Altgeld, Wolfgang. 2002. Das Risorgimento (1815–1876). In Wolfgang Altgeld, ed. *Kleine italienische Geschichte*, 257–324. Stuttgart: Philipp Reclam jun.

Altman, David, with Sergio Toro and Rafael Piñeiro. 2013. Chile: Coordinating a Successful Democratic Transition. In Kathryn Stoner and Michael McFaul, eds. *Transitions to Democracy*, 192–218. Baltimore: Johns Hopkins University Press.

Alva Orlandini, Javier. 2009. Author interview with longstanding leader of Popular Action party. Lima, July 17.

Álvarez, Rolando. 2008. "Aun tenemos Patria, Ciudadanos:" El Partido Comunista de Chile y la Salida no pactada de la Dictadura (1980–1988). In Verónica Valdivia, Rolando Álvarez et al., eds. *Su Revolución contra nuestra Revolución*, vol. 2: *La Pugna marxista-gremialista en los ochenta*, 19–82. Santiago: LOM.

　2006. ¿La Noche del Exilio? Los Orígenes de la Rebelión Popular en el Partido Comunista de Chile. In Verónica Valdivia, Rolando Álvarez, and Julio Pinto, eds. *Su Revolución contra nuestra Revolución*, vol. 1: *Izquierdas y Derechas en el Chile de Pinochet (1973–1981)*, 101–52. Santiago: LOM.

Alves, Maria Helena Moreira. 1985. *State and Opposition in Military Brazil*. Austin: University of Texas Press.

Al-Zubaidi, Layla, Matthew Cassel, and Nemonie Craven Roderick, eds. 2013. *Writing Revolution: The Voices from Tunis to Damascus*. London: I. B. Tauris.

Ambrosio, Thomas. 2010. Russia. In Donnacha Ó Beacháin and Abel Polese, eds. *The Colour Revolutions in the Former Soviet Republics*, 136–55. London: Routledge.

Análisis (Santiago de Chile). 1987a. "Lucha frontal" contra Stroessner. *Análisis* 10:187 (August 10): 61.

　1987b. Otro dictador en dificultades. *Análisis* 10:182 (July 6): 61.

　1984. Después de Argentina, Chile y Uruguay. *Análisis* 7:75 (February 14): 31.

Anderson, Benedict. 1991. *Imagined Communities, revised ed.* London: Verso.

Angell, Alan. 2001. International Support for the Chilean Opposition, 1973–1989. In Laurence Whitehead, ed. *The International Dimensions of Democratization*, 175–200. Oxford: Oxford University Press.

Anglin, Douglas. 1990. Southern African Responses to Eastern European Developments. *Journal of Modern African Studies* 28:3 (September): 431–55.

Ansell, Christopher. 2011. *Pragmatist Democracy: Evolutionary Learning as Public Philosophy*. Oxford: Oxford University Press.

　2007. Network Institutionalism. In Rod Rhodes, Sarah Binder, and Bert Rockman, eds. *Oxford Handbook of Political Institutions*, 75–89. Oxford: Oxford University Press.

Arancibia, Patricia. 2006. *Cita con la Historia*. Santiago: Editorial Biblioteca Americana.

Arancibia, Patricia, Claudia Arancibia, and Isabel de la Maza. 2002. *Jarpa: Confesiones Políticas*. Santiago: La Tercera – Mondadori.

Arancibia, Patricia, and Isabel de la Maza. 2003. *Matthei: Mi Testimonio*. Santiago: La Tercera – Mondadori.

Arrate, Jorge. 2007. Author interview with Socialist Party leader. Santiago, July 16.

Arrate, Jorge, and Eduardo Rojas. 2003. *Memoria de la Izquierda Chilena*. vol. 2: *1970–2000*. Barcelona: Javier Vergara.

Arriagada, Genaro. 2007. Author interview with Christian Democratic politician and former Executive Secretary for the NO option in the 1988 plebiscite. Santiago, July 20.

2002. Política: Transición y Democracia. In Joaquín Almunia et al., eds. *Chile y España*, 87–97. Madrid: Santillana.

1998. *Por la Razón o la Fuerza: Chile bajo Pinochet*. Santiago: Editorial Sudamericana.

Avetikian, Tamara, ed. 1986. Acuerdo Nacional y Transición a la Democracia. *Estudios Públicos* 21 (Summer): 1–93.

Aylwin, Mariana. 2007. Author conversation with Christian Democratic politician and former education minister (2000–03). Santiago, July 10.

1980. *El Camino de España hacia la Democracia*. Santiago: Instituto Chileno de Estudios Humanísticos.

Aylwin, Patricio. 2007. Author interview with Christian Democratic Party leader and former president of Chile (1990–94). Santiago, July 10.

1998. *El Reencuentro de los Demócratas*. Santiago: Ediciones B.

1985. Exposición del Señor Patricio Aylwin Azócar. In Patricio Aylwin et al., eds. *Una Salida Político Constitucional para Chile*, 145–54. Santiago: Instituto Chileno de Estudios Humanísticos.

Baden, Prinz Max von. 1927. *Erinnerungen und Dokumente*. Stuttgart: Deutsche Verlags-Anstalt.

Bailey, Stephen. 1980. The Berlin Strike of January 1918. *Central European History* 13:2 (June): 158–74.

Bamert, Justus. 2013. *The Spread of Regime Contention during the Arab Spring*. Zürich: Center for Comparative and International Studies, Eidgenössische Technische Hochschule.

Barany, Zoltan. 2012. *The Soldier and the Changing State: Building Democratic Armies in Africa, Asia, Europe, and the Americas*. Princeton: Princeton University Press.

2011. Comparing the Arab Revolts: The Role of the Military. *Journal of Democracy* 22:4 (October): 24–35.

Barnechea, Alfredo. 1979. El ejemplo de Felipe González. *Caretas* 575 (October 30): 41–42.

1978. El punto fijo. *Caretas* 535 (February 13): 58–61.

1977. La Lección, algo Inglesa, de los Españoles. *Caretas* 514 (March 3): 27.

Barrón, Xavier. 2009. Author interview with former deputy of Constituent Assembly (1978–79) for Partido Popular Cristiano. Lima, July 13.

Barth, Emil. 1919. *Aus der Werkstatt der deutschen Revolution*. Berlin: A. Hoffmann's Verlag.

Bartolini, Stefano. 2000. *The Political Mobilization of the European Left*. Cambridge: Cambridge University Press.

Bassler, Gerhard. 1973. The Communist Movement in the German Revolution, 1918–1919. *Central European History* 6:3 (September): 233–77.

264 *Bibliography*

Bauer, Otto. 1923. *Die österreichische Revolution.* Vienna: Wiener Volksbuchhandlung.

Bayer, Hans, ed. 1948. *Das Jahr 48: Ein Buch der Erinnerung.* Gütersloh: Bertelsmann.

Baylies, Carolyn, and Morris Szeftel. 1999. Democratization and the 1991 Elections in Zambia. In John Daniel, Roger Southall, and Morris Szeftel, eds. *Voting for Democracy: Watershed Elections in Anglophone Africa,* 83–109. Aldershot: Ashgate.

Bayly, Christopher. 2004. *The Birth of the Modern World, 1780–1914.* Malden: Blackwell.

Becker, Ernst. 1999. *Zeit der Revolution! – Revolution der Zeit?* Göttingen: Vandenhoeck & Ruprecht.

Beinin, Joel, and Frédéric Vairel. 2011. The Middle East and North Africa. In Joel Beinin and Frédéric Vairel, eds. *Social Movements, Mobilization, and Contestation in the Middle East and North Africa,* 1–23. Stanford: Stanford University Press.

Beissinger, Mark. 2007. Structure and Example in Modular Political Phenomena: The Diffusion of Bulldozer/Rose/Orange/Tulip Revolutions. *Perspectives on Politics* 5:2 (June): 259–76.

2002. *Nationalist Mobilization and the Collapse of the Soviet State.* Cambridge: Cambridge University Press.

Bellin, Eva. 2012. Reconsidering the Robustness of Authoritarianism in the Middle East. *Comparative Politics* 44:2 (January): 127–49.

Bénabou, Roland. 2009. *Groupthink: Collective Delusions in Organizations and Markets.* Working Paper 14764. Cambridge, MA: National Bureau of Economic Research.

Bendor, Jonathan. 2010. *Bounded Rationality and Politics.* Berkeley: University of California Press.

Berg-Schlosser, Dirk. 2009. Long Waves and Conjunctures of Democratization. In Christian Haerpfer, Patrick Bernhagen et al., eds. *Democratization,* 41–55. Oxford: Oxford University Press.

Berliner März-Revolution. 1848. *Eine genaue und zusammenhängende Darstellung ... herausgegeben von Mitkämpfern und Augenzeugen.* Berlin: Verlag Gustav Hempel.

Berman, Sheri. 2006. *The Primacy of Politics.* Cambridge: Cambridge University Press.

Bermeo, Nancy. 1997. Myths of Moderation: Confrontation and Conflict during Democratic Transitions. *Comparative Politics* 29:3 (April): 305–22.

Bernales Ballesteros, Enrique. 1986. *El camino español de la democracia.* Madrid: Ediciones de Cultura Hispánica. Instituto de Cooperación Iberoamericana.

Bernstein, Eduard. (1921) 1998. *Die deutsche Revolution von 1918/19.* Heinrich August Winkler, ed. Bonn: Dietz.

(1899) 1991. *Die Voraussetzungen des Sozialismus und die Aufgaben der Sozialdemokratie.* Berlin: Dietz.

Bethell, Leslie, and Ian Roxborough, eds. 1992. *Latin America between the Second World War and the Cold War, 1944–1948.* Cambridge: Cambridge University Press.

Bhavnani, Ravi, and Michael Ross. 2003. Announcement, Credibility, and Turnout in Popular Rebellions. *Journal of Conflict Resolution* 47:3 (June): 340–66.

Bieber, Hans-Joachim. 1981. *Gewerkschaften in Krieg und Revolution,* vol. 1. Hamburg: Hans Christians Verlag.

Bishara, Dina. 2012. The Power of Workers in Egypt's 2011 Uprising. In Bahgat Korany and Rabab El-Mahdi, eds. *Arab Spring in Egypt: Revolution and Beyond*, 83–103. Cairo: American University in Cairo Press.

Bismarck, Otto von. 1898. Das Jahr 1848. In *Gedanken und Erinnerungen*, 20–53. Stuttgart: Cotta.

Bitar, Sergio. 1983a. La lección argentina. *Apsi* (December 13): 7.

1983b. Por qué ganó Alfonsín. *Análisis* 6:71 (December 20): 35–36.

Blackbourn, David, and Geoff Eley. 1984. *The Peculiarities of German History*. Oxford: Oxford University Press.

Blanco, Monica. 1983a. Más un foro democrático. *Hoy* 301 (April 27): 57–58.

1983b. Protesta "a la chilena." *Hoy* 319 (August 31): 58.

Blasier, Cole. 1985. *The Hovering Giant*. Pittsburgh: University of Pittsburgh Press.

Bleiber, Helmut. 1974. Die Unruhen in Wien im August 1830. *Zeitschrift für Geschichtswissenschaft* 22:7 (July): 722–29.

Blight, Garry, and Sheila Pulham. 2011. Arab Spring: An Interactive Timeline of Middle East Protests. *Guardian* (March 22).

Blom, J. C. Hans. 2006. The Netherlands since 1830. In J. C. Hans Blom and Emiel Lamberts, eds. *History of the Low Countries*, 393–469. New York: Berghahn.

Blum, Robert. 1981. *Briefe und Dokumente*. Leipzig: Philipp Reclam Verlag.

Boeker, Paul. 1990. *Lost Illusions: Latin America's Struggle for Democracy, as Recounted by its Leaders*. La Jolla & New York: Institute of the Americas & Markus Wiener Publishing.

Boeninger, Edgardo. 2007. Author interview with leader and strategist of *Concertación de Partidos por la Democracia*. Santiago: July 10.

1997. *Democracia en Chile*. Santiago: Andrés Bello.

Boerner, Paul. 1920. *Erinnerungen eines Revolutionärs*, vol. 1. Leipzig: Haberland.

Boix, Carles, and Susan Stokes. 2003. Endogenous Democratization. *World Politics* 55:4 (July): 517–49.

Booth, John. 1998. The Somoza Regime in Nicaragua. In Houchang Chehabi and Juan Linz, eds. *Sultanistic Regimes*, 132–52. Baltimore: Johns Hopkins University Press.

Botzenhart, Manfred. 1985. *Reform, Restauration, Krise: Deutschland 1789–1847*. Frankfurt am Main: Suhrkamp.

Boushey, Graeme. 2010. *Policy Diffusion Dynamics in America*. Cambridge: Cambridge University Press.

Bouvier, Beatrix. 2001. On the Tradition of 1848 in Socialism. In Dieter Dowe, Heinz-Gerhard Haupt, Dieter Langewiesche, and Jonathan Sperber, eds. *Europe in 1848*, 891–915. New York: Berghahn.

Bowman, Kirk, Fabrice Lehoucq, and James Mahoney. 2005. Measuring Political Democracy. *Comparative Political Studies* 38:8 (October): 939–70.

Boye, Gustavo. 1985. Nuevo Embajador de EE.UU. *Cauce* 3:49 (November 18): 4–6.

Braga, Roberto Saturnino. 2008. Author interview with national senator and former mayor of Rio de Janeiro. Rio: July 8.

Bramke, Werner, and Silvio Reisinger. 2009. *Leipzig in der Revolution von 1918/1919*. Leipzig: Leipziger Universitätsverlag.

Bratton, Michael. 2009. Sub-Saharan Africa. In Christian Haerpfer, Patrick Bernhagen et al., eds. *Democratization*, 339–55. Oxford: Oxford University Press.

Bratton, Michael, and Nicolas van de Walle. 1997. *Democratic Experiments in Africa.* Cambridge: Cambridge University Press.

Bravo Vargas, Viviana. 2010. *¡Con la Razón y la Fuerza, Venceremos! La Rebelión Popular y la Subjetividad Comunista en los '80.* Santiago: Ariadna.

Breuilly, John. 2000. The Revolutions of 1848. In David Parker, ed. *Revolutions and the Revolutionary Tradition in the West 1560 – 1991,* 109–31. London: Routledge.

Brinks, Daniel, and Abby Blass. 2009. The Role of Diffusion and Domestic Politics in Judicial Design. Paper presented at the 105th Annual Meeting, American Political Science Association, Toronto, Sept. 3–6.

Brinks, Daniel, and Michael Coppedge. 2006. Diffusion Is No Illusion. *Comparative Political Studies* 39:4 (May): 463–89.

Brodbeck, Felix, Rudolf Kerschreiter, Andreas Mojzisch, and Stefan Schulz-Hardt. 2007. Group Decision Making under Conditions of Distributed Knowledge. *Academy of Management Review* 32:2 (April): 459–79.

Broué, Pierre. 2006. *The German Revolution 1917–1923.* Chicago: Haymarket Books.

Brown, Archie. 2000. *Transnational Influences in the Transition from Communism.* Notre Dame, IN: Kellogg Institute. Working Paper 273.

Brown, James. 1991. *Surge to Freedom: The End of Communist Rule in Eastern Europe.* Durham: Duke University Press.

Brownlee, Jason. 2013. Morsi Was No Role Model for Islamic Democrats. Middle East Institute www.mei.edu/content/morsi-was-no-role-model-islamic-democrats, accessed July 18, 2013.

  2012. Liberalism vs. Democracy in Egypt. Middle East Research and Information Project www.merip.org/liberalism-vs-democracy-egypt, accessed July 8, 2013.

Brownlee, Jason, Tarek Masoud, and Andrew Reynolds. Forthcoming. *After the Awakening: Revolt, Reform, and Renewal in the Arab World.* Oxford: Oxford University Press.

Brubaker, Rogers. 1992. *Citizenship and Nationhood in France and Germany.* Cambridge, MA: Harvard University Press.

Bruneau, Thomas. 1992. Brazil's Political Transition. In John Higley and Richard Gunther, eds. *Elites and Democratic Consolidation in Latin America and Southern Europe,* 257–81. Cambridge: Cambridge University Press.

Bruszt, László, and David Stark. 1992. Remaking the Political Field in Hungary. In Ivo Banac, ed. *Eastern Europe in Revolution,* 13–55. Ithaca: Cornell University Press.

Büchs, Annette. 2011. Der Jemen am Scheideweg. *GIGA Focus. Nahost* 6: 1–7.

Buck, Tobias. 2011. Queen Rania Wins over Critics after Dressing-Down. *Financial Times* (July 2): 4.

Buenrostro, Lucia, Amrita Dhillon, and Myrna Wooders. 2007. Protests and Reputation. *International Journal of Game Theory* 35:3 (February): 353–77.

Bulnes, María. 1986. La Oposición se replantea su Estrategia de Lucha política. *ABC* (Madrid) (Oct. 1): 34.

Bunce, Valerie, and Sharon Wolchik. 2011. *Defeating Authoritarian Leaders in Postcommunist Countries.* Cambridge: Cambridge University Press.

Buse, Dieter. 1972. Ebert and the German Crisis, 1917–1920. *Central European History* 5:3 (September): 234–55.

Cáceres, Carlos. 2007. Author interview with former finance and interior minister under Pinochet regime. Santiago, July 18.

Camerer, Colin, George Loewenstein, and Matthew Rabin, eds. 2004. *Advances in Behavioral Economics*. Princeton: Princeton University Press.

Canning, Kathleen. 2010. Das Geschlecht der Revolution: Stimmrecht und Staatsbürgertum 1918/19. In Alexander Gallus, ed. *Die vergessene Revolution von 1918/19*, 84–116. Göttingen: Vandenhoeck & Ruprecht.

Capoccia, Giovanni. 2005. *Defending Democracy: Reactions to Extremism in Interwar Europe*. Baltimore: Johns Hopkins University Press.

Capoccia, Giovanni, and Daniel Kelemen. 2007. The Study of Critical Junctures. *World Politics* 59:3 (April): 341–69.

Capoccia, Giovanni, and Daniel Ziblatt. 2010. The Historical Turn in Democratization Studies. *Comparative Political Studies* 43: 8/9 (August-September): 931–68.

Cardemil, Alberto. 2007. Author interview with former sub-secretary of the interior (1984–88). Santiago, July 9.

Cárdenas, Juan Pablo. 1983. Gracias, Argentina. *Análisis* 6:68 (November 8): 3.

Cardoso, Fernando Henrique. 2006a. *The Accidental President of Brazil: A Memoir*. New York: PublicAffairs.

2006b. *A Arte da Política: A História que vivi*. Rio de Janeiro: Civilização Brasileira.

1983. Reencontrar a esperança: O quanto nos importa a democracia na Argentina. *Istoé* 364 (December 14): 64–65.

Cardoso, Fernando Henrique, and Roberto Pompeu de Toledo. 1998. *O Presidente segundo o Sociólogo: Entrevista*. São Paulo: Companhia das Letras.

Caretas. 1979. La lección de La Paz. *Caretas* 576 (November 5): 12–17.

Carnoy, Martin. 1984. *The State and Political Theory*. Princeton: Princeton University Press.

Carothers, Thomas. 2001. The Resurgence of United States Political Development Assistance to Latin America in the 1980s. In Laurence Whitehead, ed. *The International Dimensions of Democratization*, 125–45. Oxford: Oxford University Press.

Carr, Raymond, and Juan Fusi. 1981. *Spain: Dictatorship to Democracy*, 2nd ed. London: Unwin Hyman.

Carsten, Francis. 1988. *Revolution in Central Europe, 1918–1919*. Aldershot, UK: Wildwood House.

Carvallo, Mauricio. 1983. Gobierno-Oposición: Entre las cenizas del diálogo. *Hoy* 326 (October 19): 6–9.

1982. Proyecto contra la crisis. *Hoy* 280 (December 1): 7–9.

Castañeda, Jorge. 1993. *Utopia Unarmed: The Latin American Left after the Cold War*. New York: Alfred Knopf.

Castillo, Francisco. 1991. *La Fuerza del Diálogo*. Santiago: Centro de Estudios del Desarrollo.

Castro, Celso. 2008. Author interview with director of Centro de Pesquisa e Documentação de História Contemporânea do Brasil (CPDOC). Rio de Janeiro, July 16.

Cauce. 1983. Argentina en democracia: Lecciones y preocupaciones para Chile. *Cauce* 1:1 (November 18).

Cavallo, Ascanio. 1983. Argentina: Las elecciones en el horizonte. *Hoy* 304 (May 18): 63–64.

1982. El descalabro argentino. *Hoy* 257 (June 23): 45–47 & title.

Cavallo, Ascanio, Manuel Salazar, and Oscar Sepúlveda. 2008. *La Historia oculta del Régimen Militar*. Santiago: Uqbar.

Cavarozzi, Marcelo. 1986. Political Cycles in Argentina since 1955. In Guillermo O'Donnell, Philippe Schmitter, and Laurence Whitehead, eds. *Transitions from Authoritarian Rule: Latin America*, 19–48. Baltimore: Johns Hopkins University Press.

Cercas, Javier. 2010. *Anatomía de un instante*. Barcelona: Debolsillo.

Cheterian, Vicken. 2011. The Arab Revolt and the Colour Revolutions. N.p. Open Democracy www.opendemocracy.net/print/58461, accessed July 1, 2011.

   2010. Azerbaijan. In Donnacha Ó Beacháin and Abel Polese, eds. *The Colour Revolutions in the Former Soviet Republics*, 101–17. London: Routledge.

Chomiak, Laryssa, and John Entelis. 2011. The Making of North Africa's Intifadas. *Middle East Report* 41:2, Issue 259 (Summer): 8–15.

Christakis, Nicholas, and James Fowler. 2009. *Connected: The Surprising Power of Our Social Networks*. Boston: Little, Brown.

Church, Clive. 1983. *Europe in 1830*. London: George Allen & Unwin.

Clark, John. 1997. The Challenges of Political Reform in Sub-Saharan Africa. In John Clark and David Gardinier, eds. *Political Reform in Francophone Africa*, 23–39. Boulder: Westview.

   1994. The National Conference as an Instrument of Democratization in Francophone Africa. *Journal of Third World Studies* 11:1 (Spring): 304–35.

Collier, Ruth. 1999. *Paths toward Democracy*. Cambridge: Cambridge University Press.

Collier, Ruth and David. 1991. *Shaping the Political Arena*. Princeton: Princeton University Press.

Collier, Simon. 2003. *Chile: The Making of a Republic, 1830–65*. Cambridge: Cambridge University Press.

Colomer, Josep. 1998. *La Transición a la Democracia: El Modelo Español*. Barcelona: Editorial Anagrama.

Comninos, Alex. 2011. Twitter Revolutions and Cyber Crackdowns. N.p. Association for Progressive Communications.

Congleton, Roger. 2011. *Perfecting Parliament: Constitutional Reform, Liberalism, and the Rise of Western Democracy*. Cambridge: Cambridge University Press.

Coppedge, Michael. 2012. *Democratization and Research Methods*. Cambridge: Cambridge University Press.

Copsey, Nathaniel. 2010. Ukraine. In Donnacha Ó Beacháin and Abel Polese, eds. *The Colour Revolutions in the Former Soviet Republics*, 30–44. London: Routledge.

Corbo, Daniel. 2007. La Transición de la Dictadura a la Democracia en Uruguay. *Humanidades* 7:1 (December): 23–47.

Corrêa, Arsênio. 2005. A Frente Liberal e a Democracia no Brasil, 2nd ed. N.p.

Correa, Germán. 2007. Author interview with leader of Socialist Party of Chile. Santiago, July 5.

Correa, Germán, and José Sanfuentes. 1987. Al pueblo de Chile. *Análisis* 10:169 (April 7): 42.

Cortés Godoy, Juan. 1987. Cuando la fuerza que renuncia a matar puede más que las armas. In Francisco Geisse and Rafael Gumucio, eds. *Elecciones Libres y Plebiscito*, 338–42. Santiago: Ediciones Chile y América – CESOC.

Cronin, James. 1980. Labor Insurgency and Class Formation. *Social Science History* 4:1 (Winter): 125–52.

Dahl, Robert. 1971. *Polyarchy*. New Haven: Yale University Press.

Daniel, John, Roger Southall, and Morris Szeftel, eds. 1999. *Voting for Democracy: Watershed Elections in Anglophone Africa*. Aldershot, UK: Ashgate.

Daniels, Robert. 2000. The Anti-Communist Revolutions in the Soviet Union and Eastern Europe, 1989 to 1991. In David Parker, ed. *Revolutions and the Revolutionary Tradition in the West 1560 – 1991*, 202–24. London: Routledge.

D'Araujo, Maria Celina, and Celso Castro, eds. 1997. *Ernesto Geisel*. Rio de Janeiro: Editora Fundação Getúlio Vargas.

Davies, Norman. 2005. *God's Playground: A History of Poland*, vol. 2: *1795 to the Present*. New York: Columbia University Press.

Demes, Pavol, and Joerg Forbrig. 2006. Pora – "It's Time" for Democracy in Ukraine. In Anders Åslund and Michael McFaul, eds. *Revolution in Orange: The Origins of Ukraine's Democratic Breakthrough*, 85–101. Washington, DC: Brookings.

(La) Democracia. 1984. Suárez copó la convención. *La Democracia* 4:69 (August 24): 4.

———. 1983. Argentina: Esperando la carroza. *La Democracia* 2:28 (February 25): 16.

Denzau, Arthur, and Douglass North. 1994. Shared Mental Models: Ideologies and Institutions. *Kyklos* 47:1 (March): 3–31.

Dewan, Torun, and David Myatt. 2008. The Qualities of Leadership. *American Political Science Review* 102:3 (August): 351–68.

Díaz Cayeros, Alberto, and Beatriz Magaloni. 2013. Mexico: International Influences but "Made in Mexico." In Kathryn Stoner and Michael McFaul, eds. *Transitions to Democracy*, 244–65. Baltimore: Johns Hopkins University Press.

Dickson, Eric. Forthcoming. Leadership, Followership, and Beliefs about the World. *British Journal of Political Science*.

Dietz, Henry. 1992. Elites in an Unconsolidated Democracy: Peru in the 1980s. In John Higley and Richard Gunther, eds. *Elites and Democratic Consolidation in Latin America and Southern Europe*, 237–56. Cambridge: Cambridge University Press.

Diez Canseco, Javier. 2009. Author interview with former deputy of Constituent Assembly (1978–79) and longstanding leftist leader. Lima, July 10.

Dirceu, José. 2008. E-mail interview with former government minister and leader of Workers' Party (PT). September 5.

Dittmann, Wilhelm. 1995. *Erinnerungen*, vol. 2, ed. by Jürgen Rojahn. Frankfurt am Main: Campus.

Diuk, Nadia. 2006. The Triumph of Civil Society. In Anders Åslund and Michael McFaul, eds. *Revolution in Orange: The Origins of Ukraine's Democratic Breakthrough*, 69–83. Washington, DC: Brookings.

Dix, Robert. 1992. Democratization and Institutionalization of Latin American Political Parties. *Comparative Political Studies* 24:4 (January): 488–511.

Dobson, Sean. 2001. *Authority and Upheaval in Leipzig, 1910–1920*. New York: Columbia University Press.

Doorenspleet, Renske. 2004. The Structural Context of Recent Transitions to Democracy. *European Journal of Political Research* 43:3 (May): 309–35.

Dowe, Dieter, Heinz-Gerhard Haupt, Dieter Langewiesche, and Jonathan Sperber, eds. 2001. *Europe in 1848*. New York: Berghahn.

Drake, Paul. 2009. *Between Tyranny and Anarchy: A History of Democracy in Latin America, 1800–2006.* Stanford: Stanford University Press.

Duncan Baretta, Silvio, and John Markoff. 1987. Brazil's *Abertura:* A Transition from What to What? In James Malloy and Mitchell Seligson, eds. *Authoritarians and Democrats: Regime Transition in Latin America,* 43–65. Pittsburgh: University of Pittsburgh Press.

Ebert, Friedrich. 1926. *Schriften, Aufzeichnungen, Reden,* vol. 2. Dresden: Carl Reissner.

(The)Economist. 2013. Egypt's Coup: The Second Time Around. *The Economist* (July 6): 21–24.

     2012. Egypt: Dictatorship, Democracy, Dictatorship? *The Economist* (December 1): 52–53.

Ekiert, Grzegorz. 1996. *The State against Society.* Princeton: Princeton University Press.

Eley, Geoff. 2002. *Forging Democracy.* Oxford: Oxford University Press.

Elkins, Zachary. 2010. Diffusion and the Constitutionalization of Europe. *Comparative Political Studies* 43: 8/9 (August–September): 969–99.

Elkins, Zachary, and Beth Simmons. 2005. On Waves, Clusters, and Diffusion: A Conceptual Framework. *Annals of the American Academy of Political and Social Science* 598 (March): 33–51.

Ellis, Geoffrey. 2000. The Revolution of 1848–1849 in France. In Robert Evans and Hartmut Pogge von Strandmann, eds. *The Revolutions in Europe, 1848–1849,* 27–53. Oxford: Oxford University Press.

Emirbayer, Mustafa, and Jeff Goodwin. 1994. Network Analysis, Culture, and the Problem of Agency. *American Journal of Sociology* 99:6 (May): 1411–54.

Engels, Friedrich. 1895. Einleitung. In Karl Marx, *Die Klassenkämpfe in Frankreich, 1848 bis 1850,* 3–19. Berlin: Verlag des Vorwärts.

Ensalaco, Mark. 1994. In with the New, Out with the Old? The Democratizing Impact of Constitutional Reform in Chile. *Journal of Latin American Studies* 26:2 (May): 409–29.

Epstein, David, Robert Bates, Jack Goldstone, Ida Kristensen, and Sharyn O'Halloran. 2006. Democratic Transitions. *American Journal of Political Science* 50:3 (July): 551–69.

Errázuriz, Hernán Felipe. 2007. Author interview with former ambassador to United States (1984–88) and foreign minister (1988–90). Santiago, July 20.

Ertman, Thomas. 2010. The Great Reform Act of 1832 and British Democratization. *Comparative Political Studies* 43: 8/9 (August–September): 1000–22.

     1999. Liberalization and Democratization in Nineteenth and Twentieth Century Germany in Comparative Perspective. In Carl Lankowski, ed. *Germany's Difficult Passage to Modernity,* 34–50. New York: Berghahn.

Espinosa, Sergio. 2008. Las ofensivas del pinochetismo duro para modificar la transición. *El Mercurio* (December 28).

Esser, James. 1998. Alive and Well after 25 Years: A Review of Groupthink Research. *Organizational Behavior and Human Decision Processes* 73: 2/3 (February–March): 116–41.

Fahim, Kareem, and David Kirkpatrick. 2011. Qaddafi's Grip on the Capital Tightens as Revolt Grows. *New York Times* (February 22).

Falcoff, Mark. 1986. Chile: The Dilemma for U.S. Policy. *Foreign Affairs* 64:4 (Spring): 833–48.

Fatton, Robert. 1995. Africa in the Age of Democratization: The Civic Limitations of Civil Society. *African Studies Review* 38:2 (September): 67–99.

Fearon, James. 2011. Self-Enforcing Democracy. *Quarterly Journal of Economics* 126:4 (November): 1661–1708.

1999. Electoral Accountability and the Control of Politicians. In Adam Przeworski, Susan Stokes, and Bernard Manin, eds. *Democracy, Accountability, and Representation*, 55–97. Cambridge: Cambridge University Press.

1998. Deliberation as Discussion. In Jon Elster, ed. *Deliberative Democracy*, 44–68. Cambridge: Cambridge University Press.

Feiler, Bruce. 2011. *Generation Freedom: The Middle East Uprisings and the Remaking of the Modern World*. New York: Harper.

Feldman, Gerald. 1992. *Army, Industry, and Labor in Germany, 1914–1918*. Providence, RI: Berg Publishers.

Fenske, Hans, ed. 1996. *Quellen zur deutschen Revolution, 1848–1849*. Darmstadt: Wissenschaftliche Buchgesellschaft.

Fernández, Javier. 1982. Cuando la transición se llama Suárez. *Opinar* 2:85 (September 9): 17.

Fernández, Mariano. 1987. Elecciones Libres en Filipinas. In Francisco Geisse and Rafael Gumucio, eds. *Elecciones Libres y Plebiscito*, 305–17. Santiago: Ediciones Chile y América – CESOC.

Fernández, Sergio. 2007. Author interview with former interior minister (1987–88). Santiago, July 11.

1994. *Mi Lucha por la Democracia*. Santiago: Editorial Los Andes.

Fernández Abata, Joaquín, Álvaro Góngora Escobedo, and Patricia Arancibia Clavel. 2013. *Ricardo Núñez: Trayectoria de un Socialista de Nuestros Tiempos*. Santiago: Centro de Investigación y Documentación en Historia de Chile Contemporáneo (CIDOC), Universidad Finis Terrae.

Figueroa, Gabriel. 1985. España: El "ministro" para América Latina. *Hoy* 414 (June 24): 60–61.

Figueroa, Gonzalo. 1986. Uruguay habla a Chile. *Cauce* 3:70 (April 14): 14–18.

Filiu, Jean-Pierre. 2011. *The Arab Revolution: Ten Lessons from the Democratic Uprising*. London: Hurst.

Finkel, Evgeny, and Yitzhak Brudny. 2012a. No More Colour! Authoritarian Regimes and Colour Revolutions in Eurasia. *Democratization* 19:1 (February): 1–14.

2012b. Russia and the Colour Revolutions. *Democratization* 19:1 (February): 15–36.

Finnemore, Martha, and Kathryn Sikkink. 2001. The Constructivist Research Program. *Annual Review of Political Science* 4: 391–416.

Flisfisch, Angel. 1988. *La Política como Compromiso democrático*. Santiago de Chile: FLACSO.

1985. Enunciado General del Tema. In Angel Flisfisch, Germán Riesco, Juan Yrarrázaval et al., eds. *El Futuro Democrático de Chile: 4 Visiones Políticas*, 13–18. Santiago: Centro de Estudios del Desarrollo.

Flynn, Peter. 1979. *Brazil: A Political Analysis*. Boulder, CO: Westview.

Fontana, Andrés. 1987. *Political Decision Making by a Military Corporation: Argentina 1976–1983*. Ph.D. Dissertation, University of Texas at Austin.

Fontane, Theodor. 1920. *Die Berliner Märztage 1848*. Leipzig: Verlag von Dr. Werner Klinkhardt.

Forester, John. 1984. Bounded Rationality and the Politics of Muddling Through. *Public Administration Review* 44:1 (January-February): 23–31.

Franco, Wellington Moreira. 2008. Author interview with former leader of Partido Democrático Social and Partido do Movimento Democrático Brasileiro. Rio de Janeiro, July 18.

Frank, Rosa. 1983. Argentina: Desmilitarización, destape y democracia. *Mensaje* 319 (June): 243–46.

Frank-Döfering, Peter. 1988. *Die Donner der Revolution über Wien.* Vienna: Herold.

Freeman, John, and Duncan Snidal. 1982. Diffusion, Development and Democratization. *Canadian Journal of Political Science* 15:2 (June): 299–330.

Friedrich Ebert Stiftung. 2007. *Hacia la Democracia social: Cuatro Décadas de la Fundación Friedrich Ebert en Chile.* Santiago: Friedrich Ebert Stiftung.

Fuentes Quintana, Enrique, Guillermo de la Dehesa et al. 1989. *A Transição que deu Certo: O Exemplo da Democracia Espanhola.* São Paulo: Trajetória Cultural.

Fumagalli, Matteo, and Simon Tordjman. 2010. Uzbekistan. In Donnacha Ó Beacháin and Abel Polese, eds. *The Colour Revolutions in the Former Soviet Republics*, 156–76. London: Routledge.

Fundación Eduardo Frei. 1986. Video of December 1986 speech by and debate with Adolfo Suárez, former prime minister of Spain. Santiago.

Funk, Robert, ed. 2006. *El Gobierno de Ricardo Lagos.* Santiago: Universidad Diego Portales.

Gallus, Alexander. 2010. Die vergessene Revolution von 1918/19. In Alexander Gallus, ed. *Die vergessene Revolution von 1918/19*, 14–38. Göttingen: Vandenhoeck & Ruprecht.

Gamarekian, Barbara. 1988. How U.S. Political Pros Get Out the Vote in Chile. *New York Times* (November 18).

Garcés, Mario, and Gonzalo de la Maza. 1984. Der nationale Protest. *Lateinamerika: Analysen, Daten, Dokumentation* 2 (November): 29–36.

García Belaúnde, Domingo. 2009. Author interview with constitutional lawyer. Lima, July 7.

1996. *La Constitución en el Péndulo.* Arequipa: Editorial UNSA.

Gardinier, David. 1997. Gabon: Limited Reform and Regime Survival. In John Clark and David Gardinier, eds. *Political Reform in Francophone Africa*, 145–61. Boulder, CO: Westview.

Garrard, John. 2002. *Democratisation in Britain.* Houndmills, UK: Palgrave.

Garretón, Manuel Antonio. 2007. Author interview with Socialist Party intellectual. Santiago, July 6.

1991. The Political Opposition and the Party System under the Military Regime. In Paul Drake and Iván Jaksić, eds. *The Struggle for Democracy in Chile, 1982–90*, 211–50. Lincoln: University of Nebraska Press.

1989. *The Chilean Political Process.* Boston: Unwin Hyman.

Garretón, Manuel Antonio, and Malva Espinosa. 2000. Chile: Political Learning and the Reconstruction of Democracy. In Jennifer McCoy, ed. *Political Learning and Redemocratization in Latin America*, 37–71. Miami: North-South Center Press.

Gaspari, Elio. 2003. *A Ditadura Derrotada.* São Paulo: Companhia das Letras.

Gauck, Joachim. 2011. *Winter im Sommer – Frühling im Herbst: Erinnerungen.* Munich: Pantheon.

Geary, Dick. 2000. The Revolutionary Tradition in the Nineteenth and Early Twentieth Centuries. In David Parker, ed. *Revolutions and the Revolutionary Tradition in the West 1560 – 1991*, 132–50. London: Routledge.

Geis, Irene. 1983a. Argentina ya votó, Chile ¿por qué no? *Análisis* 6:68 (November 8): 4–6.

1983b. Democracia, única alternativa. *Análisis* 6:53 (January): 4–6.

1983c. En el filo de la navaja. *Análisis* 6:55 (March): 4–8.

1983d. Elecciones argentinas: "Se acabó y se acabó." *Análisis* 6:69 (November 22): 27–29.

Geisse, Francisco, and Rafael Gumucio, eds. 1987. *Elecciones Libres y Plebiscito.* Santiago: Ediciones Chile y América – CESOC.

Geisse, Francisco, and José Antonio Ramírez Arrayas. 1989. *La Reforma Constitucional.* Santiago: Ediciones Chile y América – CESOC.

George, Elizabeth, and Prithviraj Chattopadhyay. 2008. Group Composition and Decision Making. In Gerard Hodgkinson and William Starbuck, eds. *Oxford Handbook of Organizational Decision Making*, 361–79. Oxford: Oxford University Press.

Gervais, Myriam. 1997. Niger: Regime Change, Economic Crisis, and Perpetuation of Privilege. In John Clark and David Gardinier, eds. *Political Reform in Francophone Africa*, 86–108. Boulder, CO: Westview.

Geyer, Curt. 1976. *Die revolutionäre Illusion: Zur Geschichte des linken Flügels der USPD.* Wolfgang Benz and Hermann Graml, eds. Stuttgart: Deutsche Verlags-Anstalt.

Geyer, Michael. 2010. Zwischen Krieg und Nachkrieg: Die deutsche Revolution 1918/19 im Zeichen blockierter Transnationalität. In Alexander Gallus, ed. *Die vergessene Revolution von 1918/19*, 187–222. Göttingen: Vandenhoeck & Ruprecht.

2001. Insurrectionary Warfare: The German Debate about a Levée en Masse in October 1918. *Journal of Modern History* 73:3 (September): 459–527.

Ghonim, Wael. 2012. *Revolution 2.0: The Power of the People is Greater than the People in Power. A Memoir.* Boston: Houghton Mifflin Harcourt.

Gigerenzer, Gerd. 2006. Out of the Frying Pan into the Fire: Behavioral Reactions to Terrorist Attacks. *Risk Analysis* 26:2 (April): 347–51.

Gigerenzer, Gerd, and Reinhard Selten, eds. 2001. *Bounded Rationality: The Adaptive Toolbox.* Cambridge, MA: MIT Press.

Gil Novales, Alberto. 1985. Repercusiones españolas de la Revolución de 1830. In Manfred Kossok and Werner Loch, eds. *Die französische Julirevolution von 1830 und Europa*, 117–48. Berlin (Ost): Akademie-Verlag.

Gildea, Robert. 2008. *Children of the Revolution: The French, 1799–1914.* London: Allen Lane.

2001. 1848 in European Collective Memory. In Dieter Dowe, Heinz-Gerhard Haupt, Dieter Langewiesche, and Jonathan Sperber, eds. *Europe in 1848*, 916–37. New York: Berghahn.

Gillespie, Charles. 1991. *Negotiating Democracy: Politicians and Generals in Uruguay.* Cambridge: Cambridge University Press.

Gilovich, Thomas, Dale Griffin, and Daniel Kahneman, eds. 2002. *Heuristics and Biases.* Cambridge: Cambridge University Press.

Givan, Rebecca, Kenneth Roberts, and Sarah Soule. 2010. The Dimensions of Diffusion. In Givan, Roberts, and Soule, eds. *The Diffusion of Social Movements*, 1–15. Cambridge: Cambridge University Press.

Gleditsch, Kristian Skrede, and Michael Ward. 2006. Diffusion and the International Context of Democratization. *International Organization* 60:4 (Fall): 911–33.

Goldstone, Jack. 2011. Understanding the Revolutions of 2011. *Foreign Affairs* 90:3 (May-June): 8–16.

2003. Comparative Historical Analysis and Knowledge Accumulation in the Study of Revolutions. In James Mahoney and Dietrich Rueschemeyer, eds. *Comparative Historical Analysis in the Social Sciences*, 41–90. Cambridge: Cambridge University Press.

Goldstone, Jack, Ted Gurr, and Farrokh Moshiri, eds. 1991. *Revolutions of the Late Twentieth Century*. Boulder, CO: Westview.

Goodwin, Jeff. 2011. Why We Were Surprised (Again) by the Arab Spring. *Swiss Political Science Review* 17:4 (December): 452–56.

Goodwin, Jeff, James Jasper, and Francesca Polletta, eds. 2001. *Passionate Politics: Emotions and Social Movements*. Chicago: University of Chicago Press.

Gorman, Stephen. 1982. The Role of the Revolutionary Armed Forces. In Thomas Walker, ed. *Nicaragua in Revolution*, 115–32. New York: Praeger.

Gowda, Rajeev, and Jeffrey Fox, eds. 2002. *Judgments, Decisions, and Public Policy*. Cambridge: Cambridge University Press.

Grabendorff, Wolf. 2001. International Support for Democracy in Contemporary Latin America. In Laurence Whitehead, ed. *The International Dimensions of Democratization*, 201–26. Oxford: Oxford University Press.

Graham, Erin, Charles Shipan, and Craig Volden. 2013. The Diffusion of Policy Diffusion Research in Political Science. *British Journal of Political Science* 43:3 (July): 673–701.

Graham, Lawrence. 1992. Redefining the Portuguese Transition to Democracy. In John Higley and Richard Gunther, eds. *Elites and Democratic Consolidation in Latin America and Southern Europe*, 282–99. Cambridge: Cambridge University Press.

Granovetter, Mark. 1973. The Strength of Weak Ties. *American Journal of Sociology* 78:6 (December): 1360–80.

Guillier, Alejandro. 1986. Partidos politicos: Las cuentas de los presidentes. *Hoy* 491 (December 15): 8–9.

Gunitskiy, Vsevolod. 2010. *Hegemonic Transitions and Democratization in the Twentieth Century*. New York: Department of Political Science, Columbia University.

Gunitsky, Seva. 2013. Complexity and Theories of Change in International Politics. *International Theory* 5:1 (March): 35–63.

Gunther, Richard. 1992. Spain: The Very Model of the Modern Elite Settlement. In John Higley and Richard Gunther, eds. *Elites and Democratic Consolidation in Latin America and Southern Europe*, 38–80. Cambridge: Cambridge University Press.

Guntin, José. 1983. España ante América Latina: La transición como ejemplo. *Opinar* 3:113 (March 24): 14.

Guzmán, Jaime. 1991. El "Acuerdo Nacional" y la Transición a la Democracia. *Estudios Públicos* 42 (Fall): 511–19.

Gyimah-Boadi, Emmanuel. 1996. Civil Society in Africa. *Journal of Democracy* 7:2 (April): 118–32.

Haase, Ernst, ed. 1929. *Hugo Haase: Sein Leben und Wirken. Mit einer Auswahl von Briefen, Reden und Aufsätzen*. Berlin-Frohnau: Ottens-Verlag.

Hachtmann, Rüdiger. 1997. *Berlin 1848*. Bonn: Dietz.

Haenchen, Karl, ed. 1930. *Revolutionsbriefe 1848: Ungedrucktes aus dem Nachlaß König Friedrich Wilhelms IV. von Preußen.* Leipzig: K. F. Koehler.

Häusler, Wolfgang. 1979. *Von der Massenarmut zur Arbeiterbewegung.* Vienna: Jugend und Volk.

Hafner-Burton, Emilie, Alex Hughes, and David Victor. 2013. The Cognitive Revolution and the Political Psychology of Elite Decision Making. *Perspectives on Politics* 11:2 (June): 368–86.

Hagopian, Frances. 1990. "Democracy by Undemocratic Means?" Elites, Political Pacts, and Regime Transition in Brazil. *Comparative Political Studies* 23:2 (July): 147–70.

Hale, Henry. 2013. Regime Change Cascades: What We Have Learned from the 1848 Revolutions to the 2011 Arab Uprisings. *Annual Review of Political Science* 16: 331–53.

2006. Democracy or Autocracy on the March? The Colored Revolutions as Normal Dynamics of Patronal Presidentialism. *Communist and Post-Communist Studies* 39:3 (September): 305–29.

Hales, Jaime. 1986. Filipinas: Siete reflexiones y algo más. *Análisis* 9:134 (March 18): 28–29.

Hall, Peter. 2003. Aligning Ontology and Methodology in Comparative Research. In James Mahoney and Dietrich Rueschemeyer, eds. *Comparative Historical Analysis in the Social Sciences,* 373–404. Cambridge: Cambridge University Press.

Hamid, Shadi. 2011. The Rise of the Islamists. *Foreign Affairs* 90:3 (May-June): 40–47.

Hammer, Michael. 1997. *Volksbewegung und Obrigkeiten: Revolution in Sachsen 1830/31.* Weimar: Böhlau.

Harb, Zahera. 2011. Arab Revolutions and the Social Media Effect. *Media/Culture Journal* 14:2.

Hardtwig, Wolfgang. 1998. *Vormärz: Der monarchische Staat und das Bürgertum,* 4th ed. Munich: DTV.

Haro, Ricardo. 2005. Algunas reflexiones sobre la influencia de la Constitución española de 1978 en el constitucionalismo latinoamericano. *Anuario de Derecho Constitucional Latinoamericano* 11: 57–86.

Harrison, Casey. 2007. The Paris Commune of 1871, the Russian Revolution of 1905, and the Shifting of the Revolutionary Tradition. *History & Memory* 19:2 (Fall–Winter): 5–42.

Hartig, Franz de Paula. 1850. *Genesis der Revolution in Oesterreich im Jahre 1848,* 2nd ed. Leipzig: Friedrich Fleischer.

Hastie, Reid, and Robyn Dawes. 2010. *Rational Choice in an Uncertain World,* 2nd ed. Los Angeles: Sage.

Hautmann, Hans. 1971. *Die verlorene Räterepublik.* Vienna: Europa Verlag.

Hawkins, Darren. 2002. *International Human Rights and Authoritarian Rule in Chile.* Lincoln: University of Nebraska Press.

Heilbrunn, John. 1993. Social Origins of National Conferences in Benin and Togo. *Journal of Modern African Studies* 31:2 (June): 277–99.

Heimann, Larry. 1995. Different Paths to Success: A Theory of Organizational Decision Making and Administrative Reliability. *Journal of Public Administration Research and Theory* 5:1 (January): 45–71.

Heinze, Marie-Christine. 2013. Zeitenwende im Jemen? In Thorsten Schneiders, ed. *Der Arabische Frühling*, 253–67. Wiesbaden: Springer VS.

Heiss, Claudia, and Patricio Navia. 2007. You Win Some, You Lose Some: Constitutional Reforms in Chile's Transition to Democracy. *Latin American Politics and Society* 49:3 (Fall): 163–90.

Hess, Steve. 2010. Protests, Parties, and Presidential Succession. Competing Theories of Color Revolutions in Armenia and Kyrgyzstan. *Problems of Post-Communism* 57:1 (January-February): 28–39.

Higley, John, and Michael Burton. 2006. *Elite Foundations of Liberal Democracy*. Lanham, MD: Rowman & Littlefield.

Higley, John, and Richard Gunther, eds. 1992. *Elites and Democratic Consolidation in Latin America and Southern Europe*. Cambridge: Cambridge University Press.

Hill, Stuart, and Donald Rothchild. 1986. The Contagion of Political Conflict in Africa and the World. *Journal of Conflict Resolution* 30:4 (December): 716–35.

Hilson, Mary. 2007. Scandinavia. In Robert Gerwarth, ed. *Twisted Paths*, 8–32. Oxford: Oxford University Press.

Hirschman, Albert. 1982. *Shifting Involvements: Private Interest and Public Action*. Princeton: Princeton University Press.

   1970. *Exit, Voice, and Loyalty*. Cambridge, MA: Harvard University Press.

Hobsbawm, Eric. 1996a. *The Age of Capital, 1848–1875*. New York: Vintage.

   1996b. *The Age of Extremes: A History of the World, 1914–1991*. New York: Vintage.

   1996c. *The Age of Revolution, 1789–1848*. New York: Vintage.

Hodgkinson, Gerard, and William Starbuck. 2008a. Organizational Decision Making. In Hodgkinson and Starbuck, eds. *Oxford Handbook of Organizational Decision Making*, 1–29. Oxford: Oxford University Press.

   eds. 2008b. *Oxford Handbook of Organizational Decision Making*, 211–30. Oxford: Oxford University Press.

Hoegner, Wilhelm. (1958) 1979. *Die verratene Republik: Deutsche Geschichte 1919– 1933*. Munich: Nymphenburger Verlagshandlung.

Hofmeister, Wilhelm. 1999. *Los Demócrata-Cristianos Alemanes y su Relación con Chile*. Santiago: Konrad Adenauer Stiftung.

Hoffrogge, Ralf. 2008. *Richard Müller: Der Mann hinter der Novemberrevolution*. Berlin: Karl Dietz Verlag.

Hohenlohe-Ingelfingen, Prinz Kraft zu. 1897. *Aus meinem Leben*, vol. 1: *Vom Revolutionsjahr 1848 bis zum Ende des Kommandos in Wien 1856*. Berlin: Ernst Siegfried Mittler & Sohn.

Holzapfel, Kurt. 1986. Der Einfluß der Julirevolution von 1830/32 auf Deutschland. In Helmut Reinalter, ed. *Demokratische und soziale Protestbewegungen in Mitteleuropa, 1815–1848/49*, 105–40. Frankfurt am Main: Suhrkamp. Taschenbuch Wissenschaft 629.

Howard, Marc. 2003. *The Weakness of Civil Society in Post-Communist Europe*. Cambridge: Cambridge University Press.

Howard, Philip, and Muzammil Hussain. 2011. The Role of Digital Media. *Journal of Democracy* 22:3 (July): 35–48.

Howe, Daniel Walker. 2007. *What Hath God Wrought: The Transformation of America, 1815–1848*. Oxford: Oxford University Press.

Hoy. 1987. Las pistas de la carrera electoral. *Hoy* 498 (February 2): 8–10.

Hughes, Michael. 2009. "The Knife in the Hands of Children"? Debating the Political Mass Strike and Political Citizenship in Imperial Germany. *Labor History* 50:2 (May): 113–38.

Huneeus, Carlos. 2007. *The Pinochet Regime*. Boulder, CO: Lynne Rienner.

   1987. ¿Seguirá Chile el camino de Filipinas? *Mensaje* 36:361 (August): 313–17.

   1985. *La Unión de Centro Democrático y la Transición a la Democracia en España*. Madrid: Siglo Veintiuno de España.

Hunter, Wendy. 1997. *Eroding Military Influence in Brazil: Politicians against Soldiers*. Chapel Hill: University of North Carolina Press.

Huntington, Samuel. 1991. *The Third Wave*. Norman: University of Oklahoma Press.

   1982. American Ideals versus American Institutions. *Political Science Quarterly* 97:1 (Spring): 1–37.

   1968. *Political Order in Changing Societies*. New Haven, CT: Yale University Press.

Huskey, Eugene, and David Hill. 2011. The 2010 Referendum and Parliamentary Elections in Kyrgyzstan. *Electoral Studies* 30:4 (December): 876–79.

Hutton, Patrick. 1981. *The Cult of the Revolutionary Tradition: The Blanquists in French Politics, 1864–1893*. Berkeley: University of California Press.

Isaacs, Anita. 1993. *Military Rule and Transition in Ecuador, 1972–92*. Houndmills, UK: Macmillan.

Isaacs, Rico. 2010. Kazakhstan. In Donnacha Ó Beacháin and Abel Polese, eds. *The Colour Revolutions in the Former Soviet Republics*, 196–216. London: Routledge.

Isabella, Maurizio. 2009. *Risorgimento in Exile: Italian Émigrés and the Liberal International in the Post-Napoleonic Era*. Oxford: Oxford University Press.

Jacobs, Andrew. 2011. Chinese Security Officials Respond to Calls for Protests. *New York Times* (February 20).

Jarpa, Sergio Onofre. 2007. Author interview with former interior minister (1983–85) and leader of Renovación Nacional. Santiago, July 13.

Jaworski, Rudolf. 1998. Völkerfrühling 1848. In Dieter Langewiesche, ed. *Demokratiebewegung und Revolution 1847 bis 1849*, 36–51. Karlsruhe: Braun.

Jessen, Hans, ed. 1968. *Die Deutsche Revolution 1848/49 in Augenzeugenberichten*. Düsseldorf: Karl Rauch.

Jones, Bryan. 2001. *Politics and the Architecture of Choice: Bounded Rationality and Governance*. Chicago: University of Chicago Press.

Jones, Bryan, and Frank Baumgartner. 2005. *The Politics of Attention*. Chicago: University of Chicago Press.

Jørgensen, Claus Møller. 2012. Transurban Interconnectivities: An Essay on the Interpretation of the Revolutions of 1848. *European Review of History* 19:2 (April): 201–27.

Joseph, Richard. 1998. Africa, 1990–1997: From Abertura to Closure. *Journal of Democracy* 9:2 (April): 3–17.

   1997. Democratization in Africa after 1989. *Comparative Politics* 29:3 (April): 363–82.

   1991. Africa: The Rebirth of Political Freedom. *Journal of Democracy* 2:4 (Fall): 11–24.

Joseph, Sarah. 2011. *Social Media, Human Rights and Political Change*. Melbourne: Monash University.

Jost, John, Christopher Federico, and Jaime Napier. 2009. Political Ideology. *Annual Review of Psychology* 60: 307–37.

Jubran, Jamal. 2013. The Resistance: Armed with Words (Yemen). In Layla Al-Zubaidi, Matthew Cassel, and Nemonie Craven Roderick, eds. *Writing Revolution: The Voices from Tunis to Damascus*, 110–29. London: I. B. Tauris.

Kahler, Miles, ed. 2009. *Networked Politics*. Ithaca, NY: Cornell University Press.

Kahneman, Daniel. 2011. *Thinking, Fast and Slow*. New York: Farrar, Straus and Giroux.

Kahneman, Daniel, Paul Slovic, and Amos Tversky, eds. 1982. *Judgment under Uncertainty*. Cambridge: Cambridge University Press.

Kahneman, Daniel, and Amos Tversky, eds. 2000. *Choices, Values, and Frames*. Cambridge: Cambridge University Press.

Kaiser, Friedrich. 1948. *1848: Ein Wiener Volksdichter erlebt die Revolution. Die Memoiren Friedrich Kaisers*, ed. Franz Hadamowsky. Vienna: Bellaria.

Kalandadze, Katya, and Mitchell Orenstein. 2009. Electoral Protests and Democratizations Beyond the Color Revolutions. *Comparative Political Studies* 42:11 (November): 1403–25.

Karatnycky, Adrian. 2006. The Fall and Rise of Ukraine's Political Opposition. In Anders Åslund and Michael McFaul, eds. *Revolution in Orange: The Origins of Ukraine's Democratic Breakthrough*, 29–44. Washington, DC: Brookings.

Karl, Terry. 1990. Dilemmas of Democratization in Latin America. *Comparative Politics* 23:1 (October): 1–21.

Kasinof, Laura. 2011. Air Goes Out of Protests in a Leaderless Yemen. *New York Times* (July 7).

Kaufman, Robert. 1977. Corporatism, Clientelism, and Partisan Conflict. In James Malloy, ed. *Authoritarianism and Corporatism in Latin America*, 109–48. Pittsburgh: University of Pittsburgh Press.

Kautsky, Karl. 1918. Die Diktatur des Proletariats. Reprinted in Peter Lübbe, ed. 1981. *Kautsky gegen Lenin*, 28–77. Berlin (West): Verlag J.H.W. Dietz Nachfolger.

    1914. *Der politische Massenstreik: Ein Beitrag zur Geschichte der Massenstreikdiskussion innerhalb der deutschen Sozialdemokratie*. Berlin: Verlag Buchhandlung Vorwärts – Paul Singer.

Keane, John. 2009. *The Life and Death of Democracy*. New York: W. W. Norton.

Keck, Margaret. 1992. *The Workers' Party and Democratization in Brazil*. New Haven: Yale University Press.

Keil, Wilhelm. 1947. *Erlebnisse eines Sozialdemokraten*, 2 vols. Stuttgart: Deutsche Verlags-Anstalt.

Kermann, Joachim. 2006. Von den Nationalaufständen zur Solidarität der freien "Völker" Europas. In Joachim Kerman, Gerhard Nestler, and Dieter Schiffmann, eds. *Freiheit, Einheit und Europa*, 9–46. Ludwigshafen: proMessage.

Kessler, Richard. 1991. The Philippines: The Making of a "People Power" Revolution. In Jack Goldstone, Ted Gurr, and Farrokh Moshiri, eds. *Revolutions of the Late Twentieth Century*, 194–217. Boulder, CO: Westview.

King, Stephen. 2009. *The New Authoritarianism in the Middle East and North Africa*. Bloomington: Indiana University Press.

Kirchheimer, Otto. 1966. The Transformation of the Western European Party Systems. In Joseph LaPalombara and Myron Weiner, eds. *Political Parties and Political Development*, 177–200. Princeton: Princeton University Press.

Kirkpatrick, David. 2012. Judge Helped Egypt's Military to Cement Power. *New York Times* (July 4).

Kirkpatrick, David, and Mayy El Sheikh. 2013. Morsi Spurned Deals, Seeing Military as Tamed. *New York Times* (July 7): 1, 9.

Kluge, Ulrich. 1985. *Die deutsche Revolution 1918/1919*. Frankfurt am Main: Suhrkamp.

Knipp, Kersten. 2013. Egypt Opposition Bets on Risky Alliance with Military. *Deutsche Welle* (July 3).

Koh, Winston. 1992. Human Fallibility and Sequential Decision Making: Hierarchy versus Polyarchy. *Journal of Economic Behavior and Organization* 18:3 (August): 317–45.

Kolb, Eberhard. 1979. 1918/19: Die steckengebliebene Revolution. In Carola Stern and Heinrich August Winkler, eds. *Wendepunkte deutscher Geschichte, 1848–1945*, 87–109. Frankfurt am Main: Fischer Taschenbuch.

1968. Rätewirklichkeit und Räte-Ideologie in der deutschen Revolution von 1918/19. In Helmut Neubauer, ed. *Deutschland und die Russische Revolution*, 94–110. Stuttgart: Kohlhammer.

Kornbluh, Peter. 2003. *The Pinochet File*. New York: Free Press.

Korzeniewicz, Roberto. 2000. Democracy and Dictatorship in Continental Latin America during the Interwar Period. *Studies in Comparative International Development* 35:1 (March): 41–72.

Kossok, Manfred, and Werner Loch, eds. 1985. *Die französische Julirevolution von 1830 und Europa*. Berlin (Ost): Akademie-Verlag.

Kotscho, Ricardo. 1984. *Explode um novo Brasil: Diário da Campanha das Diretas*. São Paulo: Brasiliense.

Kramer, Lloyd. 1996. *Lafayette in Two Worlds: Public Cultures and Personal Identities in an Age of Revolutions*. Chapel Hill: University of North Carolina Press.

Kubicek, Paul. 2011. Are Central Asian Leaders Learning from Upheavals in Kyrgyzstan? *Journal of Eurasian Studies* 2:2 (July): 115–24.

2009. Problems of Post-Post-Communism: Ukraine after the Orange Revolution. *Democratization* 16:2 (April): 323–43.

Kuckuk, Peter. 2010. Revolution, Rätebewegung und Räterepublik in Bremen. In Peter Kuckuk, ed. *Die Revolution 1918/1919 in Bremen*, 61–86. Bremen: Edition Temmen.

Kuntz, Philip, and Mark Thompson. 2009. More than Just the Final Straw: Stolen Elections as Revolutionary Triggers. *Comparative Politics* 41:3 (April): 253–72.

Kuran, Timur. 1995. *Private Truths, Public Lies*. Cambridge, MA: Harvard University Press.

Kuran, Timur, and Cass Sunstein. 1999. Availability Cascades and Risk Regulation. *Stanford Law Review* 51:4 (April): 683–768.

Kurzman, Charles. 2008. *Democracy Denied, 1905–1915*. Cambridge, MA: Harvard University Press.

2004. Can Understanding Undermine Explanation? The Confused Experience of Revolution. *Philosophy of the Social Sciences* 34:3 (September): 328–51.

1998. Waves of Democratization. *Studies in Comparative International Development* 33:1 (Spring): 42–64.

Lafleur, Ingrun. 1976. The Bolshevik Revolution and Austrian Socialism. *Journal of the Great Lakes History Conference* 1: 82–96.

Lagos, Ricardo. 2012. *The Southern Tiger: Chile's Fight for a Democratic and Prosperous Future*. New York: Palgrave Macmillan.

2007. Author interview with leader of Socialist Party and former president of Chile (2000–06). Santiago, July 9.

1995. El Plebiscito de 1988: Una Jornada Inconclusa. In Matías Tagle, ed. *El Plebiscito del 5 de Octubre de 1988*, 45–54. Santiago: Corporación Justicia y Democracia.

1985. *Democracia para Chile*. Santiago: Pehuén.

1983. "Cabildos para una gran Asamblea Nacional." *Análisis* 6:70 (December 6): 27–29.

Lamberts, Emiel. 2006. Belgium since 1830. In J. Blom and Emiel Lamberts, eds. *History of the Low Countries*, 319–91. New York: Berghahn.

Lamounier, Bolivar. 1989. *Authoritarian Brazil* Revisited: The Impact of Elections on the *Abertura*. In Alfred Stepan, ed. *Democratizing Brazil*, 43–79. Oxford: Oxford University Press.

Landau, Martin. 1969. Redundancy, Rationality, and the Problem of Duplication and Overlap. *Public Administration Review* 29:4 (July–August): 346–58.

Landauer, Gustav. (1918–19) 2012. Letters from Bavaria. In Gabriel Kuhn, ed. *All Power to the Councils! A Documentary History of the German Revolution of 1918–1919*, 171–98. Oakland, CA: P M Press.

(1918) 2007. Bericht des "Provisorischen Zentralarbeiterrates." In Teo Panther, ed. *Alle Macht den Räten!* vol. 1: *Novemberrevolution 1918*, 190–99. Münster: Unrast.

Langewiesche, Dieter. 1998. Kommunikationsraum Europa: Revolution und Gegenrevolution. In Dieter Langewiesche, ed. *Demokratiebewegung und Revolution 1847 bis 1849*, 11–35. Karlsruhe: Braun.

1978. Die Anfänge der deutschen Parteien. *Geschichte und Gesellschaft* 4:3: 324–61.

Langohr, Vickie. 2004. Too Much Civil Society, Too Little Politics. *Comparative Politics* 36:2 (January): 181–204.

LAPR (Latin America Political Report). 1978. Latin America: Socialist Head-Hunters. *LAPR* 12:50 (December 22): 397–98.

1977. Bolivia: Another Red Plot. *LAPR* 11:7 (February 18): 50.

Lara, Francisco. 1983. Festejo en libertad. *La Democracia* 3:43 (December 16): 5.

Lara Curbelo, Alfredo. 1983. Adolfo Suárez con La Democracia. *La Democracia* 3:42 (December 9): 20.

Lavareda, Antônio. 1991. *A Democracia nas Urnas: O Processo Partidário Eleitoral Brasileiro*. Rio de Janeiro: Rio Fundo/IUPERJ.

LAWR (Latin America Weekly Report). 1984a. Fears of "Revanchismo." *LAWR* 84:3 (January 20): 4–5.

1984b. First Military Clash for Alfonsín as Nervous Neighbours Keep Watch. *LAWR* 84:3 (January 20): 1.

Leal, Claudio. 2008. General Leônidas: "Revanchismo tem que acabar." *Terra Magazine* (May 20).

Ledebour, Georg. 1954. *Georg Ledebour: Mensch und Kämpfer*. Minna Ledebour, ed. Zürich: Europa Verlag.

Lehoucq, Fabrice. 2012. *The Politics of Modern Central America*. Cambridge: Cambridge University Press.

2011. The Third and Fourth Waves of Democracy. In Jeffrey Haynes, ed. *Routledge Handbook of Democratization*, 273–86. London: Routledge.

Leonelli, Domingos, and Dante de Oliveira. 2004. *Diretas Já*. Rio de Janeiro: Editora Record.

Lerner, Jennifer, and Philip Tetlock. 1999. Accounting for the Effects of Accountability. *Psychological Bulletin* 125:2 (March): 255–75.

Lesch, Ann. 2012. Concentrated Power Breeds Corruption, Repression, and Resistance. In Bahgat Korany and Rabab El-Mahdi, eds. *Arab Spring in Egypt: Revolution and Beyond*, 17–42. Cairo: American University in Cairo Press.

Levi, Margaret. 2009. Reconsiderations of Rational Choice in Comparative and Historical Analysis. In Mark Lichbach and Alan Zuckerman, eds. *Comparative Politics: Rationality, Culture, and Structure*, 2nd ed., 117–33. Cambridge: Cambridge University Press.

Leviné-Meyer, Rosa. 1973. *Leviné: The Life of a Revolutionary*. Farnborough: Saxon House.

Levitsky, Steven, and Lucan Way. 2010. *Competitive Authoritarianism: Hybrid Regimes after the Cold War*. Cambridge: Cambridge University Press.

Levitt, Barbara, and James March. 1988. Organizational Learning. *Annual Review of Sociology* 14: 319–40.

Levy, Jack. 1997. Prospect Theory, Rational Choice, and International Relations. *International Studies Quarterly* 41:1 (March): 87–112.

1994. Learning and Foreign Policy: Sweeping a Conceptual Minefield. *International Organization* 48:2 (Spring): 279–312.

Lewald, Fanny. 1969. *Erinnerungen aus dem Jahre 1848*, Dietrich Schaefer, ed. Frankfurt am Main: Sammlung Insel.

Lewis, David. 2010. Kyrgyzstan. In Donnacha Ó Beacháin and Abel Polese, eds. *The Colour Revolutions in the Former Soviet Republics*, 45–61. London: Routledge.

Lichbach, Mark. 2003. *Is Rational Choice Theory All of Social Science?* Ann Arbor: University of Michigan Press.

Liebknecht, Karl. 1974. *Gesammelte Reden und Schriften*, vol. 9: *Mai 1916 bis 15. Januar 1919*. Berlin (Ost): Dietz.

Lill, Rudolf. 2002. Integrationspolitik oder Imperialismus? (1876–1918). In Wolfgang Altgeld, ed. *Kleine italienische Geschichte*, 325–69. Stuttgart: Philipp Reclam jun.

Lindberg, Staffan. 2006. *Democracy and Elections in Africa*. Baltimore: Johns Hopkins University Press.

Lindblom, Charles. 1965. *The Intelligence of Democracy*. New York: Free Press.

Linos, Katerina. 2013. *The Democratic Foundations of Policy Diffusion*. Oxford: Oxford University Press.

Linz, Juan, and Alfred Stepan. 1996. *Problems of Democratic Transition and Consolidation*. Baltimore: Johns Hopkins University Press.

Lohmann, Susanne. 2000. Collective Action Cascades. *Journal of Economic Surveys* 14:5 (December): 655–84.

1994. The Dynamics of Informational Cascades. *World Politics* 47:1 (October): 42–101.

Lorman, Thomas. 2006. *Counter-Revolutionary Hungary, 1920–1925*. Boulder, CO: East European Monographs.

Lübben, Ivesa. 2013. Auf dem Weg zum Gottesstaat? In Thorsten Schneiders, ed. *Der Arabische Frühling*, 163–80. Wiesbaden: Springer VS.

Lupia, Arthur, and Mathew McCubbins. 1998. *The Democratic Dilemma*. Cambridge: Cambridge University Press.

Lutterbeck, Derek. 2013. Arab Uprisings, Armed Forces, and Civil-Military Relations. *Armed Forces & Society* 39:1 (January): 28–52.

Luxemburg, Rosa. (1918) 2012. National Assembly or Council Government? In Gabriel Kuhn, ed. *All Power to the Councils! A Documentary History of the German Revolution of 1918–1919*, 113–15. Oakland, CA: P M Press.

   1970. *Schriften zur Theorie der Spontaneität*. Reinbek bei Hamburg: Rowohlt.

Lynch, Marc. 2012. *The Arab Uprising*. New York: Public Affairs.

   2011. America and Egypt after the Uprisings. *Survival* 53:2 (April–May): 31–42.

MacFarquhar, Neil. 2013. Yemen Making Strides in Transition to Democracy after Arab Spring. *New York Times* (May 26): A 12.

McAdam, Doug, Sidney Tarrow, and Charles Tilly. 2001. *Dynamics of Contention*. Cambridge: Cambridge University Press.

McDermott, Rose. 2004. *Political Psychology in International Relations*. Ann Arbor: University of Michigan Press.

   1998. *Risk-Taking in International Politics*. Ann Arbor: University of Michigan Press.

McFadden, Daniel. 1999. Rationality for Economists? *Journal of Risk and Uncertainty* 19:1–3: 73–105.

McFaul, Michael. 2006. The Orange Revolution in a Comparative Perspective. In Anders Åslund and Michael McFaul, eds. *Revolution in Orange: The Origins of Ukraine's Democratic Breakthrough*, 165–95. Washington, DC: Brookings.

   2005. Transitions from Postcommunism. *Journal of Democracy* 16:3 (July): 5–19.

   2002. The Fourth Wave of Democracy and Dictatorship. *World Politics* 54:2 (January): 212–44.

McFaul, Michael, and Richard Youngs. 2013. Ukraine: External Actors and the Orange Revolution. In Kathryn Stoner and Michael McFaul, eds. *Transitions to Democracy*, 120–43. Baltimore: Johns Hopkins University Press.

Mackie, Gerry. 1998. All Men Are Liars: Is Democracy Meanigless? In Jon Elster, ed. *Deliberative Democracy*, 69–96. Cambridge: Cambridge University Press.

Maddy-Weitzman, Bruce. 2012. Is Morocco Immune to Upheaval? *Middle-East Quarterly* 19:1 (Winter): 87–93.

Mainwaring, Scott, and Aníbal Pérez-Liñán. Forthcoming. *The Emergence and Fall of Democracies and Dictatorships: Latin America since 1900*. Cambridge: Cambridge University Press.

Maira, Luis. 1987. ¿Inscribirse o no inscribirse? *Análisis* 10:169 (April 7): 22.

   1984. *Chile: Autoritarismo, Democracia y Movimiento Popular*. Mexico City: CIDE.

Majumdar, Sumon, and Sharun Mukand. 2010. The Leader as Catalyst. Unpublished manuscript, Department of Economics, University of Warwick.

Makse, Todd, and Craig Volden. 2011. The Role of Policy Attributes in the Diffusion of Innovations. *Journal of Politics* 73:1 (January): 108–24.

Malia, Martin. 2006. *History's Locomotives: Revolutions and the Making of the Modern World*. New Haven, CT: Yale University Press.

Malloy, James, and Eduardo Gamarra. 1988. *Revolution and Reaction: Bolivia 1964–1985*. New Brunswick: Transaction.
Manrique, Victor. 1978. Entre la espalda y la pared. *Caretas* 540 (May 10): 10–14.
1977. Una Dama decidida. *Caretas* 520 (June 9): 15–17.
Mansel, Philip. 2001. *Paris between Empires: Monarchy and Revolution, 1814–1852*. New York: St. Martin's Press.
Mantzavinos, Chrysostomos. 2001. *Individuals, Institutions, and Markets*. Cambridge: Cambridge University Press.
Maravall, José María. 1995. *Los resultados de la democracia*. Madrid: Alianza Editorial.
Maravall, José María, and Julián Santamaría. 1986. Political Change in Spain and the Prospects for Democracy. In Guillermo O'Donnell, Philippe Schmitter, and Laurence Whitehead, eds. *Transitions from Authoritarian Rule: Southern Europe*, 71–108. Baltimore: Johns Hopkins University Press.
March, James. 1994. *A Primer on Decision Making*. New York: Free Press.
March, James, and Herbert Simon. 1993. *Organizations*, 2nd ed. Cambridge, MA: Blackwell.
Markoff, John (with Amy White). 2009. The Global Wave of Democratization. In Christian Haerpfer, Patrick Bernhagen et al., eds. *Democratization*, 55–73. Oxford: Oxford University Press.
1999. Where and When Was Democracy Invented? *Comparative Studies in Society and History* 41:4 (October): 660–90.
1996. *Waves of Democracy*. Thousand Oaks, CA: Pine Forge Press.
Markus, Ustina. 2010. Belarus. In Donnacha Ó Beacháin and Abel Polese, eds. *The Colour Revolutions in the Former Soviet Republics*, 118–35. London: Routledge.
Marples, David. 2006. Color Revolutions: The Belarus Case. *Communist and Post-Communist Studies* 39:3 (September): 351–64.
Martínez, Gutenberg. 2007. Author interview with Christian Democratic leader. Santiago, July 17.
Martínez Muñoz, Luis. 2004. *El Frente Patriótico Manuel Rodríguez, 1980–1987*. Tesis de Licenciado, Universidad de Santiago de Chile.
Martini, Jeff, and Julie Taylor. 2011. Commanding Democracy in Egypt. *Foreign Affairs* 90:5 (September-October): 127–37.
Martins, Luciano. 1986. The "Liberalization" of Authoritarian Rule in Brazil. In Guillermo O'Donnell, Philippe Schmitter, and Laurence Whitehead, eds. *Transitions from Authoritarian Rule: Latin America*, 72–94. Baltimore: Johns Hopkins University Press.
Marwell, Gerald, and Pamela Oliver. 1993. *The Critical Mass in Collective Action*. Cambridge: Cambridge University Press.
Marwick, Arthur. 1965. *The Deluge*. Boston: Little, Brown.
Marx, Anthony. 2003. *Faith in Nation. Exclusionary Origins of Nationalism*. Oxford: Oxford University Press.
Masoud, Tarek. 2011. Liberty, Democracy, and Discord in Egypt. *Washington Quarterly* 34:4 (Fall): 117–29.
Matthias, Erich. 1972. Der Rat der Volksbeauftragten. In Eberhard Kolb, ed. *Vom Kaiserreich zur Weimarer Republik*, 103–19. Köln: Kiepenheuer & Witsch.
Maxwell, Kenneth. 1986. Regime Overthrow and the Prospects for Democratic Transition in Portugal. In Guillermo O'Donnell, Philippe Schmitter, and Laurence

Whitehead, eds. *Transitions from Authoritarian Rule: Southern Europe*, 109–37. Baltimore: Johns Hopkins University Press.

Mensaje. 1983. El ejemplo argentino: Alfonsín 1983. *Mensaje* 325 (December): title page, 693–95.

Mercier, Hugo, and Dan Sperber. 2011. Why Do Humans Reason? *Behavioral and Brain Sciences* 34:2 (April): 57–74.

(El) Mercurio (Santiago de Chile). 2011. La ola de protestas alcanza Libia. (February 17).

Merz, Kai. 1995. *Das Schreckbild: Deutschland und der Bolschewismus 1917 bis 1921*. Berlin: Propyläen.

Meseguer, Covadonga. 2009. *Learning, Policy Making, and Market Reforms*. Cambridge: Cambridge University Press.

Mesrati, Mohamed. 2013. Bayou and Laila (Libya). In Layla Al-Zubaidi, Matthew Cassel, and Nemonie Craven Roderick, eds. *Writing Revolution: The Voices from Tunis to Damascus*, 66–91. London: I. B. Tauris.

Metternich, Clemens. 1883. *Aus Metternich's nachgelassenen Papieren*, vol. 7. Richard Metternich-Winneburg, ed. Vienna: Wilhelm Braumüller.

Meyer, John, John Boli, George Thomas, and Francisco Ramirez. 1997. World Society and the Nation-State. *American Journal of Sociology* 103:1 (July): 144–81.

Mezias, John, and William Starbuck. 2008. Decision Making with Inaccurate, Unreliable Data. In Gerard Hodgkinson and William Starbuck, eds. *Oxford Handbook of Organizational Decision Making*, 76–96. Oxford: Oxford University Press.

Michels, Robert. (1915) 1959. *Political Parties*. New York: Dover.

Miller, Susanne. 1978. *Die Bürde der Macht*. Düsseldorf: Droste Verlag.

Miller, Susanne, and Heinrich Potthoff. 1986. *A History of German Social Democracy from 1848 to the Present*. Leamington Spa: Berg.

Mintz, Alex. 2004. Foreign Policy Decision Making in Familiar and Unfamiliar Settings. *Journal of Conflict Resolution* 48:1 (February): 91–104.

Mir, Luis. 1983. Um acerto de contas. *Senhor* 136 (October 26): 16–22.

Mitchell, Lincoln. 2009. Compromising Democracy: State Building in Saakashvili's Georgia. *Central Asian Survey* 28:2 (June): 171–83.

Molina, Sergio. 2007. Author interviews with leader of Christian Democratic Party and protagonist of *Acuerdo Nacional*. Santiago, July 11, July 20.

Mommsen, Wolfgang. 1998. *1848: Die ungewollte Revolution*. Frankfurt am Main: Fischer.

Mönckeberg, Maria. 1986. Nerviosismo en el año del tigre. *Análisis* 9:133 (March 11): 4–6.

Moore Jr., Barrington. 1978. *Injustice: The Social Bases of Obedience and Revolt*. White Plains, NY: M. E. Sharpe.

Morales-Bermúdez, Francisco. 2009. Author interview with former military president of Peru (1975–80). Lima, July 16.

Morgan, David. 1982. Ernst Däumig and the German Revolution of 1918. *Central European History* 15:4 (December): 303–31.

Morlino, Leonardo. 2012. *Changes for Democracy*. Oxford: Oxford University Press.

Motta, Rodrigo Patto Sá. 2007. O MDB e as Esquerdas. In Jorge Ferreira and Daniel Aarão Reis, eds. *Revolução e Democracia: 1964... As Equerdas no Brasil*, vol. 3, 283–302. Rio de Janeiro: Civilização Brasileira.

Mühsam, Erich. (1920/29) 2007. Von Eisner bis Leviné: Die Entstehung und Niederlage der bayerischen Räterepublik [excerpt]. In Teo Panther, ed. *Alle Macht den Räten!*, vol. 1: *Novemberrevolution 1918*, 112–76. Münster: Unrast.

Müller, Richard. 1926. *Der Bürgerkrieg in Deutschland*. Vienna: Malik Verlag.

1925. *Die Novemberrevolution*. Vienna: Malik Verlag.

1924. *Vom Kaiserreich zur Republik*. Vienna: Malik Verlag.

Müller, Werner. 2010. Die KPD in ihrem ersten Jahr. In Alexander Gallus, ed. *Die vergessene Revolution von 1918/19*, 160–86. Göttingen: Vandenhoeck & Ruprecht.

Müller-Franken, Hermann. 1928. *Die November-Revolution*. Berlin: Bücherkreis.

Multipartidaria. 1982. *La propuesta de la Multipartidaria*. Buenos Aires: El Cid.

Mumford, Michael, Tamara Friedrich, Jay Caughron, and Christina Byrne. 2007. Leader Cognition in Real-World Settings. *Leadership Quarterly* 18:6 (December): 515–43.

Munck, Gerardo. 1998. *Authoritarianism and Democratization: Soldiers and Workers in Argentina, 1976–1983*. University Park: Pennsylvania State University Press.

Munck, Gerardo, and Carol Skalnik Leff. 1997. Modes of Transition and Democratization. *Comparative Politics* 29:3 (April): 343–62.

Munck, Gerardo, and Jay Verkuilen. 2002. Conceptualizing and Measuring Democracy. *Comparative Political Studies* 35:1 (February): 5–34.

Muñoz, Heraldo. 2008. *The Dictator's Shadow: Life under Augusto Pinochet*. New York: Basic Books.

Muñoz, Heraldo, and Carlos Portales. 1991. *Elusive Friendship: A Survey of U.S.-Chilean Relations*. Boulder: Lynne Rienner.

Muñoz, Reynaldo. 1980. Bolivia: Drama sin fin. *Caretas* 608 (July 21): 24.

Mutz, Diana. 2002. Cross-Cutting Social Networks. *American Political Science Review* 96:1 (March): 111–26.

Nader, Alceu. 1983. De volta às eleições. *Veja* 757 (March 9): 32–34.

Nader, Alceu, and José Meirelles Passos. 1983. Pra frente, Argentina. *Veja* 792 (November 9): 46–49.

Najib, Abdelhak. 2011. El Khlifi: "Nous Irons jusq'au Bout." *Maroc Hebdo International* 922 (March 4–10).

Namier, Lewis. 1992. *1848: The Revolution of the Intellectuals*. Oxford: Oxford University Press.

Narizny, Kevin. 2012. Anglo-American Primacy and the Global Spread of Democracy. *World Politics* 64:2 (April): 341–73.

NDI (National Democratic Institute). 1989. *Chile's Transition to Democracy: The 1988 Presidential Plebiscite*. Washington, DC: NDI.

Negreiros, Luis. 2009. Author interview with former deputy of Constituent Assembly (1978–79) and Congressional leader of American Popular Revolutionary Alliance (APRA). Lima, July 14.

Nettl, J. Peter. 1969. *Rosa Luxemburg*, abridged ed. New York: Schocken.

Neubauer, Helmut. 1958. *München und Moskau, 1918/1919*. München: Isar Verlag.

Nogueira, Paulo. 1983. Democracia faz bem. *Istoé* 365 (December 21): 64–66.

Nordhausen, Frank, and Thomas Schmid, eds. 2011. *Die arabische Revolution*. Berlin: Christoph Links Verlag.

Noske, Gustav. 1920. *Von Kiel bis Kapp: Zur Geschichte der deutschen Revolution*. Berlin: Verlag für Politik und Wirtschaft.

Novaro, Marcos, and Vicente Palermo. 2003. *La Dictadura Militar 1976/1983: Del Golpe de Estado a la Restauración Democrática.* Buenos Aires: Paidós.

NSA (National Security Archive). 2013. *Oscars: Declassified Documents Tell History behind Best Foreign Film Nomination, "No."* Washington, DC: National Security Archive. Electronic Briefing Book No. 412 (February 22).

Núñez, Ricardo. 2007. Author interview with leader of Socialist Party. Santiago, July 9.

    1991a. Carta abierta a los Dirigentes y Militantes de la Izquierda chilena. In Ricardo Núñez, ed. *Socialismo: 10 Años de Renovación*, vol. 1: 223–39. Santiago: Ediciones del Ornitorrinco.

    ed. 1991b. *Socialismo: 10 Años de Renovación*, 2 vols. Santiago: Ediciones del Ornitorrinco.

Nunns, Alex, and Nadia Idle, eds. 2011. *Tweets from Tahrir: Egypt's Revolution as It Unfolded, in the Words of the People who Made It.* New York: OR Books.

Nzouankeu, Jacques. 1993. The Role of the National Conference in the Transition to Democracy in Africa. *Issue: A Journal of Opinion* 21:1/2: 44–50.

Ó Beacháin, Donnacha, and Abel Polese, eds. 2010. *The Colour Revolutions in the Former Soviet Republics.* London: Routledge.

Oberländer, Erwin, ed. 2001. *Autoritäre Regime in Ostmittel- und Südosteuropa.* Paderborn: Schöningh.

Obermann, Karl. 1970. *Flugblätter der Revolution.* Berlin (Ost): Deutscher Verlag der Wissenschaften.

O'Donnell, Guillermo, and Philippe Schmitter. 1986. *Transitions from Authoritarian Rule: Tentative Conclusions about Uncertain Democracies.* Baltimore: Johns Hopkins University Press.

Oliver, Pamela, and Daniel Myers. 2003. Networks, Diffusion, and Cycles of Collective Action. In Mario Diani and Doug McAdam, eds. *Social Movements and Networks*, 173–203. Cambridge: Cambridge University Press.

Olson, Mancur. 1965. *The Logic of Collective Action.* Cambridge, MA: Harvard University Press.

Opinar. 1983a. Un formidable triunfo moral. *Opinar* 3:140 (November 3): 3.

    1983b. Una jornada con fuerte repercusión. *Opinar* 3:135 (September 1): 24.

    1983c. Uruguayos con Felipe y Craxi. *Opinar* 4:146 (December 15): 15.

    1982. Marcha cívica en Argentina: La posible caída de Bignone. *Opinar* 3:97 (December 2): 20.

Orenstein, Mitchell. 2003. Mapping the Diffusion of Pension Innovation. In Robert Holzmann, Mitchell Orenstein, and Michal Rutkowski, eds. *Pension Reform in Europe*, 171–93. Washington, DC: World Bank.

Ortega Frei, Eugenio. 1992. *Historia de una Alianza.* Santiago: Centro de Estudios del Desarrollo.

Ortega R., Eugenio, and Carolina Moreno, eds. 2002. *¿La Concertación desconcertada? Reflexiones sobre su Historia y su Futuro.* Santiago: LOM.

Ortiz, Eduardo. 1985. Socialismo, Democracia y Participación. In Angel Flisfisch, Germán Riesco, Juan Yrarrázaval et al., eds. *El Futuro Democrático de Chile: 4 Visiones Políticas*, 176–89. Santiago: Centro de Estudios del Desarrollo.

Ortiz de Zevallos, Javier. 1989. *Mi Palabra en la Constituyente.* Lima: Centro de Documentación Andina.

Osterhammel, Jürgen. 2009. *Die Verwandlung der Welt: Eine Geschichte des 19. Jahrhunderts.* München: C. H. Beck.

Ottaway, Marina, and Amr Hamzawy, eds. 2009. *Getting to Pluralism: Political Actors in the Arab World.* Washington, DC: Carnegie Endowment.

Owen, John. 2010. *The Clash of Ideas in World Politics. Transnational Networks, States, and Regime Change, 1510–2010.* Princeton: Princeton University Press.

Oxhorn, Philip. 1994. Where Did All the Protesters Go? *Latin American Perspectives* 21:3 (Summer): 49–68.

Page, Scott. 2007. *The Difference: How the Power of Diversity Creates Better Groups, Firms, Schools, and Societies.* Princeton: Princeton University Press.

Palmer, Robert. 1959. *The Age of the Democratic Revolution,* vol. 1: *The Challenge.* Princeton: Princeton University Press.

Pasquet Iribarne, Ope. 1984. Política y esperanza. *Opinar* 4:154 (February 9): 7.

Passarinho, Jarbas. 1989. A Construção da Democracia no Brasil. In CEDEC (Centro de Estudos de Cultura Contemporânea), ed. *Visões da Transição,* vol. 1, 114–89. São Paulo: CEDEC.

Paulsen, Fernando. 1986a. Los cinco rostros de la oposición. *Análisis* 128 (February 4): 4–6.

1986b. La definición impostergable. *Análisis* 9:131 (February 25): 4–6.

1986c. Haití probó que se puede. *Análisis* 9:129 (February 11): 4–6.

Pearlman, Wendy. 2013. Emotions and the Microfoundations of the Arab Uprisings. *Perspectives on Politics* 11:2 (June): 387–409.

Pease, Henry. 2009. Author interview with long-standing political leader and former presidential candidate (1990). Lima, July 14.

Peceny, Mark. 1999. *Democracy at the Point of Bayonets.* University Park: Pennsylvania State University Press.

Peicovich, Esteban. 1982. El Felipazo. *Somos* 320 (November 5): 20–22.

1981. Entre dos fuegos. *Somos* 245 (May 29): 22.

Peña, Juan. 2013. Los años clandestinos de Teillier. *La Tercera* (March 31) www.latercera.com/noticia/politica/2013/03/674-516439-9, accessed March 31, 2013.

Pérez, Cristián. 2013. Compañeros, a las armas: Combatientes chilenos en Centroamérica (1979–1989). *Estudios Públicos* 129 (Summer): 141–64.

2012. ¡A las armas, camaradas! Frente Patriótico Manuel Rodríguez (1983–1990). *Naveg@mérica: Revista electrónica de la Asociación Española de Americanistas* 9: 1–25.

Pérez, Juan. 1984. La Concertación en España. *La Democracia* 3:49 (March 23): 11.

Pérez Silva, Claudio. 2012. De la Guerra contra Somoza a la Guerra contra Pinochet. In Pablo Pozzi and Claudio Pérez, eds. *Historia Oral e Historia Política,* 213–44. Santiago: LOM Ediciones.

Pesendorfer, Alfred. 2012. *Die gescheiterte Revolution: Deutschland 1918/19.* Hamburg: Tredition.

Pieck, Wilhelm. 1959. *Gesammelte Reden und Schriften,* vol. 1: *August 1904 bis Januar 1919.* Berlin (Ost): Dietz Verlag.

Pilbeam, Pamela. 1995. Revolutionary Movements in Western Europe, 1814–30. In Pamela Pilbeam, ed. *Themes in Modern European History, 1780–1830,* 125–50. London: Routledge.

Pinochet, Augusto. 1998. *Camino Recorrido,* tome 3, vol. 1. Santiago: N.p.

Pinochet de la Barra, Oscar. 1983. Buena suerte, demócratas argentinos. *Análisis* 6:53 (January): 31.

Pinto, Julio, and Sebastián Leiva. 2008. Punto de Quiebre: El MIR en los ochenta. In Verónica Valdivia, Rolando Álvarez et al., eds. *Su Revolución contra nuestra Revolución,* vol. 2: *La Pugna marxista-gremialista en los ochenta,* 83–138. Santiago: LOM.

Pinto-Duschinsky, Michael. 1991. Foreign Political Aid: The German Political Foundations and their US Counterparts. *International Affairs* 67:1 (January): 33–63.

Pipes, Richard. 1990. *The Russian Revolution*. New York: Vintage Books.

Piven, Frances Fox, and Richard Cloward. 1979. *Poor People's Movements: Why They Succeed, How They Fail*. New York: Vintage.

Plättner, Karl. (1919) 2012. The Council Idea in Germany. In Gabriel Kuhn, ed. *All Power to the Councils! A Documentary History of the German Revolution of 1918–1919*, 164–66. Oakland, CA: P M Press.

Polese, Abel, and Donnacha Ó Beacháin. 2011. The Color Revolution Virus and Authoritarian Antidotes. *Demokratizatsiya: The Journal of Post-Soviet Democratization* 19:2 (Spring): 111–32.

Popkin, Samuel. 1991. *The Reasoning Voter*. Chicago: University of Chicago Press.

Posada-Carbó, Eduardo. 2002. New Granada and the European Revolutions of 1848. In Guy Thomson, ed. 2002. *The European Revolutions of 1848 and the Americas*, 217–40. London: University of London, Institute of Latin American Studies.

Prado, Matías. 1984. Como llegar y como seguir, versión española. *La Democracia* 3:64 (July 20): 21.

Prieto Celi, Federico. 1996. *Regreso a la democracia. Entrevista biográfica al General Francisco Morales Bermúdez Cerrutti, Presidente del Perú (1975–1980)*. Lima: Realidades.

Prittwitz, Karl von. 1985. *Berlin 1848*. Berlin: De Gruyter.

Przeworski, Adam. 2010. *Democracy and the Limits of Self-Government*. Cambridge: Cambridge University Press.

   2009. Conquered or Granted? A History of Suffrage Extensions. *British Journal of Political Science* 39:2 (April): 291–321.

   1991. *Democracy and the Market*. Cambridge: Cambridge University Press.

   1985. *Capitalism and Social Democracy*. Cambridge: Cambridge University Press.

Przeworski, Adam, Michael Alvarez, José Antonio Cheibub, and Fernando Limongi. 2000. *Democracy and Development*. Cambridge: Cambridge University Press.

Przeworski, Adam, and John Sprague. 1986. *Paper Stones: A History of Electoral Socialism*. Chicago: University of Chicago Press.

Puddington, Arch. 2013. The Freedom House Survey for 2012. *Journal of Democracy* 24:2 (April): 46–61.

   2012. Freedom House Survey for 2011. *Journal of Democracy* 23:2 (April): 74–88.

Purcell, Susan Kaufman. 1987. *Chile: The Limits of U.S. Leverage*. Santiago: Centro de Estudios del Desarrollo. Materiales para discusión No. 192.

Puryear, Jeffrey. 1994. *Thinking Politics: Intellectuals and Democracy in Chile, 1973–1988*. Baltimore: Johns Hopkins University Press.

Quintas, Amaro. 2004. *O Sentido Social da Revolução Praieira*. Rio de Janeiro: Atlântica Editora.

Quiroga, Hugo. 2004. *El Tiempo del "Proceso:" Conflictos y coincidencias entre políticos y militares 1976–1983*. Rosario: Homo Sapiens/Fundación Ross.

Quispe Correa, Sr., Alfredo. 2009. Author's telephone interview with constitutional lawyer and former minister of justice. Lima, July 9.

Rashad, Hoda. 2012. *Rising from Tahrir*. N.p.

Rashed, Mohammed. 2011. The Egyptian Revolution. *Anthropology Today* 27:2 (April): 22–27.

Rath, R. John. 1957. *The Viennese Revolution of 1848*. Austin: University of Texas Press.

Real, Willy. 1983. *Die Revolution in Baden 1848/49*. Stuttgart: Kohlhammer.

Realidad. 1983. Las condiciones de la apertura. *Realidad* 5:52 (September): 5–7.

Reichel, Peter. 2007. *Robert Blum: Ein deutscher Revolutionär 1807–1848*. Göttingen: Vandenhoeck & Ruprecht.

Reis, Daniel Aarão. 2007. O Partido dos Trabalhadores. In Jorge Ferreira and Daniel Aarão Reis, eds. *Revolução e Democracia: 1964… As Equerdas no Brasil*, vol. 3, 503–40. Rio de Janeiro: Civilização Brasileira.

Rellstab, Ludwig. 1849. *Zwei Gespräche mit Seiner Majestät dem Könige Friedrich Wilhelm dem Vierten*. Berlin: Verlag der Deckerschen Geheimen Ober-Hofbuchdruckerei.

Retzlaw, Karl. 1976. *Spartacus – Aufstieg und Niedergang: Erinnernugen eines Parteiarbeiters*. Frankfurt am Main: Verlag Neue Kritik.

Ricaldoni, Américo. 1983. Chile: Una nueva Jornada de Protesta. *Opinar* 3:124 (June 16): 14.

Ritter, Gerhard, and Susanne Miller, eds. 1975. *Die deutsche Revolution 1918–1919*. Hamburg: Hoffman und Campe.

Roberts, Kenneth. Forthcoming. *Changing Course: Party Systems in Latin America's Neoliberal Era*. Cambridge: Cambridge University Press.

1998. *Deepening Democracy? The Modern Left and Social Movements in Chile and Peru*. Stanford: Stanford University Press.

Robinson, Pearl. 1994. The National Conference Phenomenon in Francophone Africa. *Comparative Studies in Society and History* 36:3 (July): 575–610.

Rock, David, ed. 1994. *Latin America in the 1940s*. Berkeley: University of California Press.

Rock, David, and Mario dos Santos. 1971. Lucha Civil en la Argentina: La Semana Trágica de Enero de 1919. *Desarrollo Económico* 11:42/44 (July): 165–215.

Rodrigues, Alberto Tosi. 2003. *Diretas Já*. São Paulo: Editora Fundação Perseu Abramo.

Rodríguez, Ambrosio. 2007. Author interview with former *Procurador General* (1986–90) and legal counsel of President Augusto Pinochet. Santiago, July 12.

Rodríguez, Ignacio. 1983. Ludolfo Paramio, Socialista español: "Socialismo es democracia extendida a todas las formas de la vida." *Apsi* (December 27): 33–34.

Rogers, Everett. 2003. *Diffusion of Innovations*, 5th ed. New York: Free Press.

Rojas Núñez, Luis. 2011. *De la Rebelión Popular a la Sublevación Imaginada*. Santiago: LOM Ediciones.

Rosen, Michael, Eduardo Salas, Rebecca Lyons, and Stephen Fiore. 2008. Expertise and Naturalistic Decision Making in Organizations. In Gerard Hodgkinson and William Starbuck, eds. *Oxford Handbook of Organizational Decision Making*, 211–30. Oxford: Oxford University Press.

Rosenau, James. 2003. *Distant Proximities: Dynamics beyond Globalization*. Princeton, NJ: Princeton University Press.

Ross, Michael. 2011. Will Oil Drown the Arab Spring? *Foreign Affairs* 90:5 (September–October): 2–7.

Rossi, Franca. 1983. El amanecer ya no es una tentación. *Apsi* (November 15): 38–40.

Rouquié, Alain. 1986. Demilitarization and the Institutionalization of Military-Dominated Polities in Latin America. In Guillermo O'Donnell, Philippe Schmitter, and Laurence Whitehead, eds. *Transitions from Authoritarian Rule: Comparative Perspectives*, 108–36. Baltimore: Johns Hopkins University Press.

Rudé, George. (1964) 2005. *The Crowd in History*. London: Serif.

Rueschemeyer, Dietrich, Evelyne Huber Stephens, and John Stephens. 1992. *Capitalist Development and Democracy*. Chicago: University of Chicago Press.

Ruiz-Tagle, Jaime. 1983. Protesta nacional y alternativas políticas. *Mensaje* 320 (July): 312–14.

Runkel, Ferdinand. 1919. *Die Deutsche Revolution: Ein Beitrag zur Zeitgeschichte*. Berlin: N.p.

Ruttmann, Ulrike. 2001. *Wunschbild – Schreckbild – Trugbild: Rezeption und Instrumentalisierung Frankreichs in der Deutschen Revolution von 1848/49*. Stuttgart: Franz Steiner Verlag.

Ryfe, David. 2005. Does Deliberative Democracy Work? *Annual Review of Political Science* 8: 49–71.

Sah, Raaj. 1991. Fallibility in Human Organizations and Political Systems. *Journal of Economic Perspectives* 5:2 (Spring): 67–88.

Saleh, Nivien. 2012. Egypt's Digital Activism and the Dictator's Dilemma. *Telecommunications Policy* 36:6 (June): 476–83.

Samaniego, Augusto. 2002. "Lo Militar en la Política:" Lecturas sobre el Cambio Estratégico en el PC, Chile 1973–1983. *Revista Palimpsesto* 1: 1–19.

Sanchez, Peter. 1989. *Elite Settlements and Democracy in Latin America: The Dominican Republic and Peru*. Ph.D. Dissertation, University of Texas at Austin.

Sánchez-Cuenca, Ignacio, and Paloma Aguilar. 2009. Terrorist Violence and Popular Mobilization: The Case of the Spanish Transition to Democracy. *Politics & Society* 37:3 (September): 428–53.

Santibañez, Abraham. 1983a. Una lección desde Argentina. *Hoy* 328 (November 2): 5.
1983b. El único camino. *Hoy* 334 (December 14): 5.

São Paulo. Governo do Estado. 1987. *A Batalha pela Democracia no Governo Montoro*. São Paulo: Governo do Estado.

Sartori, Giovanni, ed. 1984. *Social Science Concepts*. Beverly Hills: Sage.

Schafer, Mark, and Scott Crichlow. 2010. *Groupthink versus High-Quality Decision Making in International Relations*. New York: Columbia University Press.

Schaffner, Martin. 1998. Direkte Demokratie: Alles für das Volk – alles durch das Volk. In Manfred Hettling et al., eds. *Kleine Geschichte der Schweiz*, 189–226. Frankfurt am Main: Suhrkamp.

Schattschneider, Elmer. 1975. *The Semisovereign People*. Hinsdale, IL: Dryden.

Schedler, Andreas, ed. 2006. *Electoral Authoritarianism*. Boulder, CO: Lynne Rienner.

Scheidemann, Philipp. 1929. *The Making of New Germany*, 2 vols. New York: Appleton.
1921. *Der Zusammenbruch*. Berlin: Verlag für Sozialwissenschaft.

Schieder, Theodor. 1975. Die Juli-Revolution und ihre Wirkungen auf Deutschland. In *Vom Deutschen Reich zum Deutschen Bund = Gebhardt: Handbuch der deutschen Geschichte*, vol. 15, 42–59. Munich: DTV.

Schieder, Wolfgang. 1979. 1848–49: Die ungewollte Revolution. In Carola Stern and Heinrich August Winkler, eds. *Wendepunkte deutscher Geschichte, 1848–1945*, 13–35. Frankfurt am Main: Fischer Taschenbuch.

Schiemann, John. 2007. Bizarre Beliefs and Rational Choices. *Journal of Politics* 69:2 (May): 511–24.

Schlumberger, Oliver, Nadine Kreitmeyr, and Torsten Matzke. 2013. Arabische Revolten und politische Herrschaft. In Thorsten Schneiders, ed. *Der Arabische Frühling*, 33–63. Wiesbaden: Springer VS.

Schmitt, Hans, ed. 1988. *Neutral Europe between War and Revolution 1917–1923*. Charlottesville: University Press of Virginia.

Schmolze, Gerhard, ed. 1978. *Revolution und Räterepublik in München 1918/19 in Augenzeugenberichten*. Munich: Deutscher Taschenbuch Verlag.

Schnake, Erich. 2004. *Un Socialista con Historia: Memorias*. Santiago de Chile: Aguilar.

Schneider, Cathy. 1995. *Shantytown Protest in Pinochet's Chile*. Philadelphia: Temple University Press.

Schneider, Erich, and Jürgen Keddigkeit, eds. 1999. *Die pfälzische Revolution von 1848/49*. Kaiserslautern: Kulturamt der Stadt Kaiserslautern.

Schock, Kurt. 2005. *Unarmed Insurrections: People Power Movements in Nondemocracies*. Minneapolis: University of Minnesota Press.

Schönhoven, Klaus, ed. 1985. *Die Gewerkschaften in Weltkrieg und Revolution, 1914–1919*. vol. 1 of series, *Quellen zur Geschichte der deutschen Gewerkschaftsbewegung im 20. Jahrhundert*. Cologne: Bund-Verlag.

Schorske, Carl. 1983. *German Social Democracy, 1905–1917: The Development of the Great Schism*. Cambridge, MA: Harvard University Press.

Schreiner, Albert, ed. 1957. *Revolutionäre Ereignisse und Probleme in Deutschland während der Periode der Großen Sozialistischen Oktoberrevolution 1917/1918*. Berlin (Ost): Akademie-Verlag.

Schulz, Gerhard. 1980. *Revolutionen und Friedensschlüsse 1917–1920*, 5th ed. Munich: Deutscher Taschenbuch Verlag.

Schulz-Hardt, Stefan, Dieter Frey, Carsten Lüthgens, and Serge Moscovici. 2000. Biased Information Search in Group Decision Making. *Journal of Personality and Social Psychology* 78:4 (April): 655–69.

Schumacher, Edward. 1984. Alfonsin's Moves Make for Nervous Neighbors. *New York Times* (January 22), section 4: 3.

Schurer, Heinz. 1961. The Russian Revolution of 1905 and the Origins of German Communism. *Slavonic and East European Review* 39:93 (June): 459–71.

Schurz, Carl. 1988. *Lebenserinnerungen*. Zürich: Manesse.

Schwartz, David. 1969. Toward a Theory of Political Recruitment. *Western Political Quarterly* 22:3 (September): 552–71.

Scott, Franklin. 1988. *Sweden: The Nation's History*, enlarged ed. Carbondale: Southern Illinois University Press.

Secchi, Davide. 2010. *Extendable Rationality: Understanding Decision Making in Organizations*. New York: Springer.

Seddon, J. H. 1984. The Petrashevtsy: A Reappraisal. *Slavic Review* 43: 3 (August): 434–52.

Serrano, Margarita. 2009. *La igual Libertad de Edgardo Boeninger*. Santiago: Uqbar.

Serrano, Margarita, and Ascanio Cavallo. 2006. *El Poder de la Paradoja: 14 Lecciones Políticas de la Vida de Patricio Aylwin*. Santiago: Norma.

Seton-Watson, Christopher. 1967. *Italy from Liberalism to Fascism*. London: Methuen.

Sewell, William. 2005. *Logics of History*. Chicago: University of Chicago Press.

Shahid, Anthony. 2011. In Crowd's Euphoria, No Clear Leadership Emerges. *New York Times* (January 31): A11.

Shahine, Selim. 2011. Youth and the Revolution in Egypt. *Anthropology Today* 27:2 (April): 1–3.

Share, Donald. 1987. Transitions to Democracy and Transition through Transaction. *Comparative Political Studies* 19:4 (January): 525–48.

   1986. *The Making of Spanish Democracy.* New York: Praeger.

Share, Donald, and Scott Mainwaring. 1986. Transitions through Transaction. In Wayne Selcher, ed. *Political Liberalization in Brazil,* 175–215. Boulder, CO: Westview.

Sheehan, James. 1996. The German States and the European Revolution. In Isser Woloch, ed. *Revolution and the Meanings of Freedom in the Nineteenth Century,* 246–79. Stanford: Stanford University Press.

   1995. *German Liberalism in the Nineteenth Century.* Atlantic Highlands, NJ: Humanities Press.

Shiller, Robert. 2005. *Irrational Exuberance,* 2nd ed. New York: Broadway Books.

Siemann, Wolfram. 1985. *Die deutsche Revolution von 1848/49.* Frankfurt am Main: Suhrkamp.

Sigmund, Paul. 1993. *The United States and Democracy in Chile.* Baltimore: Twentieth Century Fund.

Sikkink, Kathryn. 2011. *The Justice Cascade: How Human Rights Prosecutions Are Changing World Politics.* New York: W. W. Norton.

   2004. *Mixed Signals: U.S. Human Rights Policy and Latin America.* New York: Century Foundation/Cornell University Press.

Silva Cimma, Enrique. 2007. Author interview with leader of Radical Party. Santiago, July 20.

   2000. *Memorias Privadas de un Hombre Público.* Santiago: Andrés Bello.

Silva Ruete, Javier. 2009. Author interview with former minister of economy (1978–80). Lima, July 16.

   1982. "Yo asumí el activo y el pasivo de la Revolución." Lima: Centro de Documentación e Información Andina.

Silveira, Sérgio. 2001. *Oswaldo Lima Filho: Ação Política na Trincheira Nacionalista.* Recife: Assembléia Legislativa do Estado do Pernambuco.

Simmons, Beth, Frank Dobbin, and Geoffrey Garrett, eds. 2008. *The Global Diffusion of Markets and Democracy.* Cambridge: Cambridge University Press.

Simms, Brendan. 2013. *Europe: The Struggle for Supremacy, 1453 to the Present.* London: Allen Lane.

Simon, Herbert. 1976. *Administrative Behavior,* 3rd ed. New York: Free Press.

   1955. A Behavioral Model of Rational Choice. *Quarterly Journal of Economics* 69:1 (February): 99–118.

Sintomer, Yves, Carsten Herzberg, and Anja Röcke. 2008. Participatory Budgeting in Europe: Potentials and Challenges. *International Journal of Urban and Regional Research* 32:1 (March): 164–78.

Skidmore, Thomas. 1988. *The Politics of Military Rule in Brazil, 1964–85.* Oxford: Oxford University Press.

Skocpol, Theda. 1979. *States and Social Revolutions.* Cambridge: Cambridge University Press.

Skovmand, Roar. 1973. Die Geburt der Demokratie 1830–1870. In Roar Skovmand, Vagn Dybdahl, and Erik Rasmussen. *Geschichte Dänemarks 1830–1939,* 11–208. Neumünster: Karl Wachholtz Verlag.

Smith, Anthony. 1993. *National Identity*. Reno: University of Nevada Press.
Smith, Leonard. 1995. War and 'Politics:' The French Army Mutinies of 1917. *War in History* 2:1 (July): 180–201.
Smith, Peter. 2008. *Talons of the Eagle: Latin America, the United States, and the World*, 3rd ed. Oxford: Oxford University Press.
    2005. *Democracy in Latin America*. Oxford: Oxford University Press.
Smith, Tony. 1994. *America's Mission*. Princeton: Princeton University Press.
Soares, Gláucio Ary Dillon, Maria Celina D'Araujo, and Celso Castro, eds. 1995. *A Volta aos Quartéis: A Memória Militar sobre a Abertura*. Rio de Janeiro: Relume-Dumará.
Soifer, Hillel. 2012. The Causal Logic of Critical Junctures. *Comparative Political Studies* 45:12 (December): 1572–97.
Somin, Ilya. 2006. Knowledge about Ignorance: New Directions in the Study of Political Information. *Critical Review* 18:1–3: 255–78.
Southall, Roger. 1999. Electoral Systems and Democratization in Africa. In John Daniel, Roger Southall, and Morris Szeftel, eds. 1999. *Voting for Democracy: Watershed Elections in Anglophone Africa*, 19–36. Aldershot, UK: Ashgate.
Soza, Nelson. 1988. La 'sicopolítica' opositora. *Análisis* 11:211 (January 25): 6–8.
Spartakus. 1958. *Spartakusbriefe*, ed. Institut für Marxismus-Leninismus. Berlin (Ost): Dietz.
Spector, Regine, and Andrej Krickovic. 2007. The Anti-Revolutionary Toolkit. Paper for 103rd Annual Meeting, American Political Science Association, Chicago, IL, August 30–September 2.
Sperber, Jonathan. 2011. The Atlantic Revolutions in the German Lands, 1776–1849. In Helmut Walser Smith, ed. *Oxford Handbook of Modern German History*, 144–68. Oxford: Oxford University Press.
    1998. Germania mit Phrygiermütze. In Irmtraud Götz von Olenhusen, ed. *1848/49 in Europa und der Mythos der Französischen Revolution*, 63–80. Göttingen: Vandenhoeck & Ruprecht.
    1994. *The European Revolutions, 1848–1851*. Cambridge: Cambridge University Press.
    1991. *Rhineland Radicals: The Democratic Movement and the Revolution of 1848–1849*. Princeton: Princeton University Press.
Stacher, Joshua. 2012. *Adaptable Autocrats: Regime Power in Egypt and Syria*. Stanford: Stanford University Press.
Stepan, Alfred. 1988. *Rethinking Military Politics: Brazil and the Southern Cone*. Princeton, NJ: Princeton University Press.
Stepan, Alfred, and Juan Linz. 2013. Democratization Theory and the "Arab Spring." *Journal of Democracy* 24:2 (April): 15–30.
Stiles, William. 1852. *Austria in 1848–49*, vol. 1. London: Sampson Low.
Stinchcombe, Arthur. 1990. *Information and Organizations*. Berkeley: University of California Press.
Stoner, Kathryn, Larry Diamond, Desha Girod, and Michael McFaul. 2013. Transitional Successes and Failures. In Kathryn Stoner and Michael McFaul, eds. *Transitions to Democracy*, 3–24. Baltimore: Johns Hopkins University Press.
Streckfuss, Adolf. 1948. *Berliner März 1848*. Berlin (Ost): Das Neue Berlin.
Stumpf, Richard. 1967. *War, Mutiny and Revolution in the German Navy: World War I Diary*, Daniel Horn, ed. New Brunswick: Rutgers University Press.

Suárez, Adolfo, Oscar Alzaga, and Leopoldo Torres. 1986. Los mensajeros de la transición. *Hoy* 491 (December 15): 10–13.

Svolik, Milan. 2012. *The Politics of Authoritarian Rule.* Cambridge: Cambridge University Press.

Szeftel, Morris. 1999. Political Crisis and Democratic Renewal in Africa. In John Daniel, Roger Southall, and Morris Szeftel, eds. 1999. *Voting for Democracy: Watershed Elections in Anglophone Africa,* 1–18. Aldershot, UK: Ashgate.

Tadros, Mariz. 2011. Sectarianism and Its Discontents in Post-Mubarak Egypt. *Middle East Report* 41:2, Issue 259 (Summer): 26–31.

Tagle, Matías, ed. 1995. *El Acuerdo Nacional.* Santiago: Corporación Justicia y Democracia.

Takougang, Joseph. 1997: Cameroon: Biya and Incremental Reform. In John Clark and David Gardinier, eds. *Political Reform in Francophone Africa,* 162–81. Boulder: Westview.

Tarrow, Sidney. 2012. *Strangers at the Gates.* Cambridge: Cambridge University Press.
   2011. *Power in Movement,* 3rd ed. Cambridge: Cambridge University Press.
   2010. Dynamics of Diffusion. In Rebecca Kolins Givan, Sarah Soule, and Kenneth Roberts, eds. *The Diffusion of Social Movements,* 204–19. Cambridge: Cambridge University Press.

Temme, Jodocus. 1996. *Augenzeugenberichte der deutschen Revolution 1848/49.* Darmstadt: Wissenschaftliche Buchgesellschaft.

Teorell, Jan. 2010. *Determinants of Democratization.* Cambridge: Cambridge University Press.

Tetlock, Philip. 1985. Accountability: The Neglected Social Context of Judgment and Choice. *Research in Organizational Behavior* 7: 297–332.

Thaler, Richard. 2000. From Homo Economicus to Homo Sapiens. *Journal of Economic Perspectives* 14:1 (Winter): 133–41.

Thompson, Mark. 2004. *Democratic Revolutions: Asia and Eastern Europe.* London: Routledge.
   1998. The Marcos Regime in the Philippines. In Houchang Chehabi and Juan Linz, eds. *Sultanistic Regimes,* 206–29. Baltimore: Johns Hopkins University Press.

Thomson, Guy, ed. 2002. *The European Revolutions of 1848 and the Americas.* London: University of London, Institute of Latin American Studies.

Tilly, Charles. 2008. *Contentious Performances.* Cambridge: Cambridge University Press.
   2003. *Contention and Democracy in Europe, 1650–2000.* Cambridge: Cambridge University Press.
   1995. Contentious Repertoires in Great Britain, 1758–1834. In Mark Traugott, ed. *Repertoires and Cycles of Collective Action,* 15–42. Durham, NC: Duke University Press.
   1993. *European Revolutions, 1492–1992.* Oxford: Blackwell.

Tilly, Charles, and Sidney Tarrow. 2007. *Contentious Politics.* Boulder, CO: Paradigm.

Tilly, Charles, Louise Tilly, and Richard Tilly. 1975. *The Rebellious Century, 1830–1930.* Cambridge, MA: Harvard University Press.

Timmermann, Heiner, ed. 1989. *Die französische Revolution und Europa, 1789–1799.* Saarbrücken: Dadder.

Tironi, Eugenio. 2013. *Sin Miedo, sin Odio, sin Violencia: Una Historia Personal del NO.* Santiago: Ariel.

Tökés, Rudolf. 1967. *Béla Kun and the Hungarian Soviet Republic*. Stanford: Hoover Institution.

Toller, Ernst. (1933) 2009. *Eine Jugend in Deutschland*, 20th ed. Reinbek bei Hamburg: Rowohlt.

Torfason, Magnus, and Paul Ingram. 2010. The Global Rise of Democracy. *American Sociological Review* 75:3 (September): 355–77.

Tormin, Walter. 1968. Die deutschen Parteien und die Bolschewiki im Weltkrieg. In Helmut Neubauer, ed. *Deutschland und die Russische Revolution*, 54–68. Stuttgart: Kohlhammer.

Trager, Eric. 2011. The Unbreakable Muslim Brotherhood. *Foreign Affairs* 90:5 (September-October): 114–26.

Traugott, Mark. 2010. *The Insurgent Barricade*. Berkeley: University of California Press.

Tsebelis, George. 1990. *Nested Games*. Berkeley: University of California Press.

Tudoroiu, Theodor. 2007. Rose, Orange, and Tulip: The Failed Post-Soviet Revolutions. *Communist and Post-Communist Studies* 40:3 (September): 315–42.

Uggla, Fredrik. 2005. "For a Few Senators More"? Negotiating Constitutional Changes during Chile's Transition to Democracy. *Latin American Politics and Society* 47:2 (Summer): 51–75.

Ullrich, Volker. 1999. *Vom Augusterlebnis zur Novemberrevolution*. Bremen: Donat Verlag.

U.S. Director of Central Intelligence. 1975. *National Intelligence Estimate: The Outlook for Brazil. NIE 93–1–75*. N.p.: Director of Central Intelligence.

Vaccaro, Víctor. 1987. Andrés Zaldívar: "Con esta constitución no hay democracia." *Cauce* 4:120 (August 10): 10–13.

Vacs, Aldo. 1987. Authoritarian Breakdown and Redemocratization in Argentina. In James Malloy and Mitchell Seligson, eds. *Authoritarians and Democrats: Regime Transition in Latin America*, 15–42. Pittsburgh: University of Pittsburgh Press.

Vairel, Frédéric. 2011. Protesting in Authoritarian Situations. In Joel Beinin and Frédéric Vairel, eds. *Social Movements, Mobilization, and Contestation in the Middle East and North Africa*, 27–42. Stanford: Stanford University Press.

Valdés, Gabriel. 2009. *Sueños y Memorias*. Santiago: Aguilar–Taurus.

2002. Gabriel Valdés. In Eugenio Ortega R. and Carolina Moreno, eds. *¿La Concertación Desconcertada?* 42–50. Santiago: LOM.

Valenzuela, Javier. 2012. Desencanto árabe 2.0. *El País* (March 4).

2011. La Batalla del Nilo. *El País* (July 7).

Valenzuela, Raimundo. 2007. Author interview with legal counselor of Friedrich Ebert Stiftung. Santiago, July 4.

Valle-Riestra, Javier. 2009. Author interview with former deputy of Constituent Assembly (1978–79) and legislator for American Popular Revolutionary Alliance (APRA). Lima, July 15.

2009. *Javier Valle-Riestra: Parlamentario, litigante y defensor de los derechos humanos. Textos fundamentales*, Luis Ganoza Álvarez, ed. Lima: Fondo Editorial del Congreso del Perú.

Varnhagen von Ense, Karl. 1862. *Tagebücher*. Leipzig: Brockhaus.

Verdugo, Patricia. 1983a. Después del "Cacerolazo." *Hoy* 304 (May 18): 6–8.

1983b. Gobierno-Oposición: El primer encuentro. *Hoy* 319 (August 31): 6–10.

Veja. 1974. Grécia: Eclipse para os Coronéis. *Veja* 308 (July 31): 34–40.

Verney, Douglas. 1957. *Parliamentary Reform in Sweden.* Oxford: Clarendon.

Vicuña, Manuel. 2009. *Un Juez en los Infiernos: Benjamín Vicuña Mackenna.* Santiago de Chile: Ediciones Universidad Diego Portales.

Vicuña Mackenna, Benjamín. 2003. *The Girondins of Chile: Reminiscences of an Eyewitness,* Cristián Gazmuri, ed. Cambridge: Cambridge University Press.

Viera-Gallo, José Antonio. 1989. El Acuerdo Constitucional. In Francisco Geisse and José Antonio Ramírez Arrayas, eds. *La Reforma Constitucional.* Santiago: Ediciones Chile y América – CESOC.

Villalón, Leonardo, and Peter VonDoepp, eds. 2005. *The Fate of Africa's Democratic Experiments.* Bloomington: Indiana University Press.

Vitzthum von Eckstädt, Carl Friedrich Graf. 1886. *Berlin und Wien in den Jahren 1845–1852: Politische Privatbriefe.* Stuttgart: J. G. Cotta.

Vodanović, Hernán. 2007. Author interview with Socialist Party leader. Santiago, July 6.

1988. *Un Socialismo Renovado para Chile.* Santiago: Andante.

Vössing, Konstantin. 2011. Social Democratic Party Formation and National Variation in Labor Politics. *Comparative Politics* 43:2 (January): 167–86.

Walker, Ignacio. 1990. Un Nuevo Socialismo Chileno. In *Socialismo y Democracia: Chile y Europa en Perspectiva comparada,* 173–219. Santiago: CIEPLAN.

Way, Lucan. 2011. Comparing the Arab Revolts: The Lessons of 1989. *Journal of Democracy* 22:4 (October): 13–23.

2008. The Real Causes of the Color Revolutions. *Journal of Democracy* 19:3 (July): 55–69.

Weede, Erich, and Edward Muller. 1998. Rebellion, Violence and Revolution: A Rational Choice Perspective. *Journal of Peace Research* 35:1 (January): 43–59.

Weeks, Gregory. 2002. The "Lessons" of Dictatorship: Political Learning and the Military in Chile. *Bulletin of Latin American Research* 21:3 (July): 396–412.

Weffort, Francisco. 1984. *Por Que Democracia?* São Paulo: Brasiliense.

Wehler, Hans-Ulrich. 2010. *Deutsche Gesellschaftsgeschichte,* vol. 4: *Vom Beginn des Ersten Weltkriegs bis zur Gründung der beiden deutschen Staaten, 1914–1949.* Bonn: Bundeszentrale für politische Bildung.

1977. *Geschichte als historische Sozialwissenschaft.* 2nd ed. Frankfurt am Main: Suhrkamp.

Weitz, Eric. 1997. War and Revolution and the Genesis of German Communism. In *Creating German Communism, 1890–1990,* 62–99. Princeton: Princeton University Press.

1994. "Rosa Luxemburg Belongs to US!" German Communism and the Luxemburg Legacy. *Central European History* 27:1 (Spring): 27–64.

Wejnert, Barbara. 2005. Diffusion, Development, and Democracy, 1800–1999. *American Sociological Review* 70:1 (February): 53–81.

Werner, Eva. 2009. *Kleine Geschichte der deutschen Revolution von 1848/49.* Vienna: Böhlau – UTB.

Wette, Wolfram. 2010. *Gustav Noske und die Revolution in Kiel 1918.* Kiel: Boyens – Gesellschaft für Kieler Stadtgeschichate.

Weyland, Kurt. 2012a. The Arab Spring: Why the Surprising Similarities with the Revolutions of 1848? *Perspectives on Politics* 10:4 (December): 917–34.

2012b. Diffusion Waves in European Democratization: The Impact of Organizational Development. *Comparative Politics* 45:1 (October): 25–45.

2010. The Diffusion of Regime Contention in European Democratization, 1830–1940. *Comparative Political Studies* 43: 8/9 (August–September): 1148–76

2009. The Diffusion of Revolution: '1848' in Europe and Latin America. *International Organization* 63:3 (July): 391–423.

2007. *Bounded Rationality and Policy Diffusion.* Princeton: Princeton University Press.

2002. *The Politics of Market Reform in Fragile Democracies.* Princeton: Princeton University Press.

Whitehead, Laurence. 2001. Three International Dimensions of Democratization. In Whitehead, ed. *The International Dimensions of Democratization,* 3–25. Oxford: Oxford University Press.

1986a. Bolivia's Failed Democratization. In Guillermo O'Donnell, Philippe Schmitter, and Laurence Whitehead, eds. *Transitions from Authoritarian Rule: Latin America,* 49–71. Baltimore: Johns Hopkins University Press.

1986b. International Aspects of Democratization. In Guillermo O'Donnell, Philippe Schmitter, and Laurence Whitehead, eds. *Transitions from Authoritarian Rule: Comparative Perspectives,* 3–46. Baltimore: Johns Hopkins University Press.

Wiarda, Howard. 1989. The Dominican Republic: Mirror Legacies of Democracy and Authoritarianism. In Larry Diamond, Juan Linz, and Seymour Martin Lipset, eds. *Democracy in Developing Countries,* vol. 4: *Latin America,* 423–58. Boulder, CO: Lynne Rienner.

Wickham, Carrie. 2011. The Muslim Brotherhood and Democratic Transition in Egypt. *Middle East Law and Governance* 3(1–2): 204–23.

Wickham-Crowley, Timothy. 2012. Two Waves of Guerrilla-Movement Organizing in Latin America. Paper presented at 30th International Congress, Latin American Studies Association, San Francisco, May 23–25.

1992. *Guerrillas and Revolution in Latin America.* Princeton: Princeton University Press.

Wikipedia. 2011. Arab Spring. en.wikipedia.org/wiki/Arab_Spring, accessed July 6, 2011.

Wilson, James. 1995. *Political Organizations,* 2nd ed. Princeton: Princeton University Press.

Winik, Jay. 2007. *The Great Upheaval.* New York: HarperCollins.

Winkler, Heinrich August. 2000. *Der lange Weg nach Westen,* vol. 1: *Deutsche Geschichte vom Ende des Alten Reiches bis zum Untergang der Weimarer Republik.* Munich: C. H. Beck.

Wintrobe, Ronald. 2007. Dictatorship: Analytical Approaches. In Carles Boix and Susan Stokes, eds. *Oxford Handbook of Comparative Politics,* 363–94. Oxford: Oxford University Press.

Wirsching, Andreas. 2007. Antibolschewismus als Lernprozess. In Martin Aust and Daniel Schönpflug, eds. *Vom Gegner lernen,* 137–56. Frankfurt am Main: Campus.

Wohlgemuth, Heinz. 1975. *Karl Liebknecht: Eine Biographie.* Berlin (Ost): Dietz. Parteihochschule "Karl Marx" beim ZK der SED.

Wolff, Adolf. 1898. *Berliner Revolutionschronik.* Berlin: Dümmler.

Wood, Elizabeth. 2000. *Forging Democracy from Below: Insurgent Transitions in South Africa and El Salvador*. Cambridge: Cambridge University Press.

Wood, James. 2011. *The Society of Equality: Popular Republicanism and Democracy in Santiago de Chile, 1818–1851*. Albuquerque: University of New Mexico Press.

Yom, Sean. 2013. Jordan: The Ruse of Reform. *Journal of Democracy* 24:3 (July): 127–39.

Yopo, Mladen. 1983. Argentina: La Oposición en la ofensiva. *Análisis* 6:53 (January): 32–33.

Young, Crawford. 1996. Africa: An Interim Balance Sheet. *Journal of Democracy* 7:3 (July): 53–68.

Zabala de la Fuente, José. 2007. *Monseñor Fresno: "Quiero ser prudente, pero no seré cobarde."* Santiago: Quebecor World.

1995. Entretelones del Acuerdo Nacional. In Matías Tagle, ed. *El Acuerdo Nacional*, 79–134. Santiago: Corporación Justicia y Democracia.

Zaldívar, Andrés. 2007. Author interview with leader of Christian Democratic Party. Santiago, July 9.

Zapata, Francisco. 1985. Crisis económica y movilización social en Chile (1981–1984). *Foro Internacional* 26:2 (October-December): 214–28.

Zarusky, Jürgen. 1992. *Die deutschen Sozialdemokraten und das sowjetische Modell*. München: Oldenbourg.

Ziemann, Benjamin. 2011. Germany 1914–1918: Total War as a Catalyst for Change. In Helmut Walser Smith, ed. *Oxford Handbook of Modern German History*, 378–99. Oxford: Oxford University Press.

Name Index

Abbott, A., 63, 261
Abdelmoumni, F., 252, 261
Aberbach, J., 54, 261
Abreu, A. A. de, 160
Abugattas, L., 178
Acevedo, P., 199
Aguilar, P., 195n2, 290
Ahlquist, J., 53, 261
Albert, B., 132, 261
Albrecht, H., 248, 249, 261
Albuquerque, J. A. G. de, 165, 261
Alieva, L., 242, 261
Allamand, A., 194, 201, 203, 203n17, 206, 207, 207n22, 208, 215, 218, 220, 221n40, 262
Almeyda, C., 198, 198n5, 262
Almond, G., 54, 262
Altgeld, W., 237n7, 262
Altman, D., 212, 212n32, 262
Alva Orlandini, J., 23, 179n36, 262
Alvarez, M., 30, 31, 40, 288
Álvarez, R., 196, 202n14, 262
Alves, M. H. M., 19n11, 170, 262
Alzaga, O., 79, 164, 164n10, 165, 212, 212n32, 218, 294
Al-Zubaidi, L., 244n17, 262
Ambrosio, T., 243, 262
Anderson, B., 101n2, 262
Angell, A., 66n21, 262
Anglin, D., 231, 262
Ansell, C., 38, 54, 262
Arancibia, P., 178, 184n44, 193, 201, 203, 204, 205n17, 207, 208, 208n24, 209, 209n27, 213, 215, 218, 220, 262, 263, 271

Arrate, J., 196, 196n3, 197, 199, 200, 207n21, 263
Arriagada, G., 23, 161, 194, 200n8, 200n11, 203, 216n35, 217, 263
Avetiken, T., 206
Aylwin, M., 161, 164, 205, 263, 298
Aylwin, P., 23, 93, 161, 164, 172, 182, 193, 194, 199, 200, 204n18, 205, 206, 211n31, 216n37, 220n40, 263

Baden, M. von, 22, 84, 129, 144, 147, 150, 263
Bailey, S., 137, 263
Bamert, J., 253, 263
Barany, Z., ix, 173, 247, 263
Barnechea, A., 163n8, 263
Barrón, X., 165, 166, 169, 263
Barth, E., 22, 126, 132, 135, 136, 143, 144, 145, 149, 263
Bartolini, S., 53, 58, 84, 130, 263
Bassler, G., 133, 135, 151, 263
Bates, R., 30, 40, 270
Bauer, O., 22, 141, 264
Baumgartner, F., 11, 12, 47, 258, 277
Bayer, H., 41, 114
Baylies, C., 232, 264
Bayly, C., 18, 41n4, 264
Becker, E., 49, 264
Beinin, J., 249, 264
Beissinger, M., ix, 46n8, 240n10, 242n13, 243, 264
Bellin, E., 252, 264
Bénabou, R., 56, 264
Bendor, J., 13, 47, 53, 54, 56, 264
Berg-Schlosser, D., 1, 18n10, 264

Subject Index

Arab Spring and, 249–250; bounded rationality and, 8, 11, 12, 13, 52–59, 62, 77, 154, 258–259 (*see also* bounded rationality); Catholic parties and, 89; Central Europe, 84; cognitive heuristics, 8, 13, 35–77, 111–115, 126–127, 227; color revolutions and, 242; commoners and, 57; communism and, 127; conservatives and, 85; crowd protests and, 67, 113–114, 226 (*see also* mass demonstrations); democratization and, 90–91, 90n9; density and, 69–72; diffusion and, 9, 20, 35–77, 38f, 58f, 65f, 230, 255; diversity and, 55n15, 65, 256, 258; effects of, 69–72, 74; elites and, 56n18 (*see also* elites); emergence of, 10, 226; emulation efforts in, 194–196; Europe and, 64; external precedents and, 77; foreign models and, 10, 226, 255; globalization and, 71; groupthink and, 13, 56, 126, 139, 148, 227, 256, 258; homogeneity and, 55n15; ideology and, 227; inchoate polities and, 75; information-processing, 53, 54, 55, 70, 100 (*see also* information); interorganizational competition, 192–223; labor unions and, 137; Latin America and, 24, 64, 183; leaders, 53, 55, 57, 58f, 59, 67, 73, 74n27, 76, 84, 97, 111–115, 125–128, 139, 153, 226, 258 (*see also* representativeness heuristic); left and, 85; macro-structural development and, 20, 47–61, 126–127, 154–155, 225; MENA events and, 249 (*see also* Middle East and North Africa); military (*see* military); negotiation and, 67, 89–94, 184, 227 (*see also* negotiation); NGOs and, 242; pluralism and, 67; political attention and, 69–72; political parties and (*see* political parties); power relations and, 71; proliferation of, 89–91; reformism and, 63, 84; repression and, 183 (*see also specific countries*); revolution of 1830 239; revolutions of 1917–19 (*see also* revolutions of 1917–19); risk aversion and, 127; Russian revolutions and, 153; Social Democracy and (*see* Social Democracy); specialization and, 54; speed/success and, 38f, 71 (*see also* diffusion, speed/success). third wave and, 184, 192–223 (*see also specific countries*. third wave); twentieth century and, 37, 71; types

of, 53; uncertainty and, 71, 77; unions (*see* labor movements); violence and, 97; *See also specific countries, groups*

pacted transition. *See* negotiation
Paraguay, 2, 156, 169, 169n22
parliamentary reformism, 82–83
Peru: APRA and, 89, 172, 183; Argentina and, 176n31; cross-border diffusion, 169; foreign precedents and, 187n44; IMF and, 179; military and, 165n15; organizations and, 159n3; Spain and, 93, 165, 166; third wave and, 156; U.S. and, 178–179, 182
Philippines, 68, 214–219; Chile and, 216, 217, 218, 219; Marcos and, 69, 213n33, 215–219; U.S. and, 213n33
Poland, 104n3, 234, 236, 238
police, 45, 80, 81, 202, 203
political parties, 9, 54, 227–228; cognitive heuristics and, 125–126; effects of, 61; leadership and (*see* representativeness heuristic); negotiation and (*see* negotiation); organizations and, 9, 61, 139, 183 (*see also* organizations); revolutions of 1848 and, 112n8; Social Democracy (*see* Social Democracy); South America and, 183; structure of, 139; suppression and, 183; *See also specific groups, countries*
political science, 20–21. *See also specific theories, topics*
Polity IV dataset, 2n1, 3t, 4t
Portugal, 79; Brazil and, 160, 161, 162; coup of 1974, 92; emulation of, 162; Geisel and, 161, 162; Latin America and, 162–163; Lisbon explosion, 162; Pinochet regime and, 162n7; revolution in, 161–163; Spain and, 163n8; third wave and, 156
preference falsification, 14

rational choice theory, 13, 14n7, 45–46, 48, 74, 105; Bayesian theory and, 69; bottom-up mobilization, 90, 127n2; bounded rationality and, 11, 36, 45, 45n6, 48, 51, 54, 105, 257 (*see also* bounded rationality); cognitive heuristics and (*see* cognitive heuristics); cognitive psychology and, 256, 257; cognitive theory and, 12, 13, 256–257 (*see also* cognitive theory); cost/benefit analysis, 45, 87, 225, 256; decision-making and, 51, 104–105; diffusion and, 225, 256; external precedents and, 74n27; information

violence *(cont.)*
  negotiation and, 210; nonviolence and, 200n10; representativeness and, 158 *(see also* representativeness heuristic); repression and, 117, 120, 143, 195; strikes and, 199; *See also specific countries*

women, 2, 52, 136, 145
world system theory, 75; bounded rationality and, 48; diffusion and, 36, 42–44; tsunami of 1848 and, 102

World War I, 55n16, 82, 126n1, 146n33; democratization and, 9; Germany and, 88, 140, 141, 142, 154 *(see also* Germany); labor unions and, 141–142; representative leaders and, 146; revolutions of 1917–19 and *(see* revolutions of 1917–19); Social Democracy and, 128, 144, 145; strikes and, 140n18, 142, 143; Wilson and, 144

Yemen, 247